FAIL-SAFE BUSINESS
NEGOTIATING

Philip Sperber is president of REFAC International, Ltd., and vice president of REFAC Technology Development Corporation in New York City, a multinational manufacturer, exporter, and licensing conglomerate. The recipient of numerous awards for his outstanding contributions to industry and society in general, he has experience in negotiation that spans engineering, sales, legal, and general management positions. In addition, he is active internationally, working with the top brass in government and industry, and has written numerous articles and books on negotiation.

PHILIP SPERBER

FAIL-SAFE BUSINESS

NEGOTIATING

STRATEGIES AND TACTICS FOR SUCCESS

A SPECTRUM BOOK

PRENTICE-HALL, Inc., Englewood Cliffs, New Jersey 07632

Library of Congress Cataloging in Publication Data

Sperber, Philip.
   Fail-safe business negotiating.

  "A Spectrum Book."
  Bibliography: p.
  Includes index.
  1. Negotiation in business.   I. Title.
HD58.6.S65 1982   658.4   82-13271
ISBN 0-13-299586-7
ISBN 0-13-299578-6 (pbk.)

10 9 8 7 6 5 4 3 2 1

ISBN 0-13-299586-7

ISBN 0-13-299578-6 {PBK.}

Editorial/production supervision
and interior design by Eric Newman
Cover design by Jeannette Jacobs
Cover illustration by Jim Kinstrey
Manufacturing buyer: Barbara A. Frick

The material on pages 162–63 is from *The Human Side of Enterprise*
by Douglas McGregor. Copyright © 1960 by McGraw-Hill Book Company, Inc.
Used by permission of McGraw-Hill Book Company.

This book is available at a special discount when ordered in
large quantities. Contact Prentice-Hall, Inc., General
Publishing Division, Special Sales, Englewood Cliffs, N.J. 07632.

Prentice-Hall International, Inc., *London*
Prentice-Hall of Australia Pty. Limited, *Sydney*
Prentice-Hall Canada Inc., *Toronto*
Prentice-Hall of India Private Limited, *New Delhi*
Prentice-Hall of Japan, Inc., *Tokyo*
Prentice-Hall of Southeast Asia Pte. Ltd., *Singapore*
Whitehall Books Limited, *Wellington, New Zealand*
Editora Prentice-Hall do Brasil Ltda., *Rio de Janeiro*

To the company president
    the attorney
    the sales manager
    the purchasing officer
    the administrator
    the advertising executive
    the entrepreneur
    the public official
    the broker
    the labor union negotiator
    the controller
    the chief engineer
    the licensing executive
    the personnel manager
    the trade association director
    the military commander
    the investment banker
    the business partner
    the corporate planner
    the fund raiser
    the plant manager
    the management consultant

and every other executive
who wants to negotiate the best deal possible every time.

CONTENTS

PREFACE

You are about to read the first serious, comprehensive and in-depth treatment of business negotiation for executives, managers and professionals. This book is based primarily on the past two decades of scientific research and not merely the author's experience as a professional negotiator.

The theory and practical techniques of dealing with others are organized to help you develop your own master negotiating strategy and tactics. Key considerations are outlined and pictured in diagrammatic format so that, at a glance, you can review, analyze, and organize what you read. You will also find forms, charts, shortcuts, lists of facts and ideas and even questionnaires dispersed throughout the book. These are designed to save you time, trouble and expense. The questionnaires are especially important because people learn by doing. By answering the questions in the various tests in this book, you will be able to understand yourself better, identify your weaknesses and strengths and be consciously aware of what must be done to improve your attitude and performance long after you put the book down.

The topics in this book are very important. For instance, you will learn the secrets of systematic creativity in dealing with problems and people; how to ask for less and get more; how to be tough and likable at the same time; subconscious suggestion; PDC (personality dependent communication); psycho-decoration; how to use color as a negotiation tool; proxemics; voice communication without words; handwriting analysis; ego states; life scripts and communicating styles; how to manage your boss and strategies for job advancement; how to detect lies; how to package yourself; how to gesture; and even how to negotiate your way to the top if you are a woman.

Whether you are a seller or buyer, deal maker or deal breaker, job interviewer or job hunter, government official or company president, or supervisor or subordinate, this book will help you learn how to negotiate a better deal in every step and circumstance of a changing bargaining situation.

If you are willing to change your thinking, behavior and actions, your performance on the job should improve dramatically, and you can expect a significant increase in your lifetime's income, self-confidence, popularity and happiness. In short, if you study and adopt the advice given in this book, you can look forward to fail-safe business negotiation and career success as a management superstar.

What about others in your organization? Have you stopped to think about the hundreds and even thousands of negotiations that occur in your own company each day? They directly affect the flow of millions of dollars in profits each year.

If you could merely improve company-wide negotiating results by only 5 percent, or even 1 percent, the opportunity for massive dollar savings, increased productivity and enhanced efficiency is mind boggling. Just imagine that through better negotiating skills your purchasing agents reduce the cost of materials by an average of a few percent; your sales persons close a few percent more deals per week; your attorneys get better settlements and avoid expensive litigation in more cases; your advertising messages successfully appeal to a few percent more of the mass market; the margins given to distributors and dealers lessen by a few percent; the royalties you pay for a license are a few percent lower than normal; conflicts you have with your board of directors are now more easily resolved; employee turnover is a few percent less; productivity both in the factory and in the office is a few percent more; and on and on and on.

It all boils down to this: All of your officers, managers, department heads and professionals should develop and improve their negotiating skills. No organization can afford to have its people operating at less than full efficiency when it comes to dealing with themselves and others outside the firm.

It may be desirable to ask the executives reporting to you to read this book. They will become more productive, easier to understand and easier to work with. They will perform better for the company and will make you look better at the same time.

You may also wish to go beyond this book and have an in-house training program, which may be as short as one day or as long as five days. Negotiation training seminars, consulting assignments and related services are provided by The Negotiating Group, which can be contacted at 30 Normandy Heights Road, Convent Station, New Jersey 07961.

Aside from the royalties, I wrote this book out of a sincere desire to help you. It will give me great happiness to know I succeeded. Your comments, experiences in applying what you learned and criticism will be most welcomed and may be sent to the above address.

I have absolute confidence in the principles, approaches and techniques set forth in this volume. They have been tested both in the laboratory and in the real world. They work.

We may never meet in person, but in this book we have met. As you begin this book, I wish you a prosperous life and the start of a better future.

ACKNOWLEDGMENTS

A few persons greatly influenced my thinking regarding the negotiating process and wished me success in this endeavor. I would like to acknowledge the contributions and inspiration I received from Peter F. Drucker, the father of modern management practices and Clarke Professor of Social Sciences, Claremont College; Gerard I. Nierenberg, Esq., a pioneer in negotiation strategy and president of The Negotiation Institute; Elliot L. Richardson, the illustrious presidential advisor who served as Secretary of Defense, Secretary of Commerce, Secretary of HEW and as U.S. Attorney General; Dr. John Kenneth Galbraith, the most influential writer today on the economics of modern life, and Paul M. Warburg, Professor of Economics Emeritus, Harvard University; Julius Fast, best-selling author of *Body Language, Creative Coping* and many other books; Eugene M. Lang, founder of the international technology transfer industry and president of REFAC Technology Development Corporation; Arthur G. Linkletter, internationally acclaimed performer, best-selling author and chief executive officer of a multinational conglomerate, Linkletter Enterprises, Inc.; and Dr. Doreen F. Sperber, my wife, clinical psychologist in private practice and president of The Negotiating Group.

I also want to express my appreciation to the many other people who contributed to my ideas and information for this book. These persons include Joseph A. Califano, former Secretary of Health, Education, and Welfare; Dr. Alvin Toffler, best-selling author of *Future Shock* and *The Third Wave*; Dr. Henry Kissinger, former U.S. Secretary of State; Dr. Herman A. Estrin, professor, New Jersey Institute of Technology; Edward D. Collins, group vice-president, IPCO Corp.; Leonard B. Mackey, vice-president, International Telephone and Telegraph Corp.; Dr. H. Philip Hovnanian and John F. Casey, senior vice-presidents, Cavitron Corp.; Russell Banks, president, Grow Group, Inc.; Homer O. Blair, vice-president, Itek Corp.; Robert Goldscheider, chairman, The International Licensing Network; Norman A. Jacobs, president, Amicon Corp.; Sam Small, president, Pilot Industries, Inc.; William Poms, senior partner, Poms, Smith, Lande & Rose; Niels J. Reimers, manager, Technology Licensing, Stanford University; Tom Arnold, senior partner, Arnold, White & Durkee; Thomas J. Martin, president, Thomar Publications, Inc.; Thomas E. Costner, vice-president, Clark Boardman, Limited; Martin Sperber, vice-president, Chartwell Communications, Inc.; Arthur R. Albohn, New Jersey Representative; Martin Dale, senior vice-president, W.R. Grace & Co.; Allan Zelnick, senior partner, Zelnick & Bressler; Herbert W. Leonard, president, Scriptomatic, Inc.; Maurice Feigenbaum, director, management services, Columbia University; John E. Hunger, editor, Prentice-Hall; Dr. Harold I. Zeliger, president, ZZ Industries, Inc.; Philip Gotthelf, chairman of the board, Equidex, Inc.; Jerome H. Lemelson, president, Licensing Management Corporation; Frederick R. Adler, senior partner, Reavis & McGrath; Henry B. Rothblatt, senior partner, Rothblatt Rothblatt Seijas &

Peskin; William E. Riley, director of marketing, Battelle Development Corporation; Eric P. Schellin, chairman of the board, National Small Business Association; Zachery S. Flax, managing editor, Bureau of National Affairs, Inc.; Herb Brown, director of research, Textron, Inc.; Robert Milano, chairman, Grow Ventures Corp.; Richard F. Katis, manager, personnel relations, Westinghouse Electric Corp.; William G. Friggens, chairman, Pratt Engineering Corp.; Gerald V. Petac, supervisor, purchasing, TRW, Inc.; Donald W. Banner, director, Graduate School of Intellectual Property, John Marshall Law School; Roger W. Robbins, manager of government regulatory affairs, DuKane Corporation; James E. Smallwood, manager–industrial sales, The Bendix Corporation; Joel Green, president, Cymaticolor Corp.; Ervin Steinberg, secretary, Smith Kline Instruments; Dr. Edward J. Murry, vice-president, Fibra-Sonics, Inc.; Edward G. Fronko, manager—technology marketing operation, General Electric Co.; Alfonse W. Scerbo, director, Board of Chosen Freeholders, Morris County, New Jersey; Glenn L. Sisco, mayor, Kinnelon, New Jersey; Dr. James Dana, president, Composite Technology, Inc.; Dean Robert J. Hall, Worcester Polytechnic Institute; David B. Ruff, executive director, The Better Business Bureau; Bernard Haldane, chairman of the board, Bernard Haldane Associates, Inc.; Pat Windham, sales manager, Coca-Cola Bottling Co.; Joseph Molines, President, Lasermation, Inc.; Joel Berger, president, Meridian Associates, Inc.; Alan McMillan and William Freeman, vice-presidents, Cooper Laboratories, Inc.; Richard E. Lutz, contracts director, NCR Corporation; Dr. Martin Welt, president, Radiation Technology, Inc.; Howard Spear, senior partner, Spear Lipkin Tabor & Huston; Jerry C. Schusterman, vice-president, Health Extension Services, Inc.; Martin Fass, president, Fass, Kaplan & Co.; and Joseph J. Raymond, chairman, Raycomm Industries, Inc.

Not to be forgotten are those people who, in one way or another over the years, contributed to my knowledge base for writing this book. They are Jeffrey P. Morris, Dr. Juanita Kreps, Hugh Scott, Jimmy Breslin, Matthew Bender III, Stanley H. Lieberstein, Dudley B. Smith, Francis C. Hand, Bruce M. Eisen, Michael S. Jarosz, Richard T. Laughlin, Robert L. Baechtold, Stephen A. Zelnick, Lloyd Frank, Daniel H. Bobis, Lawrence I. Lerner, Kenneth J. Stempler, Herb Steinberg, Richard I. Samuel, James H. Wallace, Gerald D. Sharkin, Daniel F. O'Keefe, Jr., Dr. Sanford S. Epstein, Albert L. Earley, John P. Sinnott, Samuel G. Layton, Birgit E. Morris, Edwin A. Shalloway, Kenneth E. Payne, Eugene L. Bernard, Philip Mitches, Corwin R. Horton, James M. Wetzel, Joseph R. Conley, Stanley J. Ross, Dee Kampman, Michael N. Meller, Richard G. Moser, John L. Sniado, Robert E. Bayes, Jon S. Saxe, John E. Bartolini, Clive Allen, Robert I. Pearlman, Edwin D. Hamby, William Burggraf, Peter F. Casella, Carl Ray, Edward Reynolds, Aaron N. Wise, David T. Nikaido, Cyrus S. Nownejad, William S. Campbell, Stanley P. Fisher, Edwin J. Bassler, Winfried J. Fremuth, Dr. Mark Bealor, Gerald G. Birdsall, Ruth Miles, Alan Matisoff, Roger G. Ditzel, Gerard J. Weiser, Edward J. Brenner, Larry W. Evans, Myron Cohen, Arthur S. Tenser, Martin A. Levitin, Joseph Weingarten, Harry G. Weissenberger, Rosemary Whiteside, Joseph K. Andonian, Bill

Quick, Robert J. Radway, Paul M. Enlow, Walter Parnes, Zachary Bernard, Richard B. Robertson, Robert Murphy, Dr. Donald M. Coyne, Jack Stuart Ott, Dr. Donald H. Polk, Roland Plottel, Jack Matalon, Leo F. Costello, Ronald Lupkin, Stanley Bernstein, Milton Fein, Mindi Cohen, Sharon Edelman, Mary C. Werner, Robert E. Navin, Nathan H. Gates, Roderick B. Anderson, Jr., Albert L. Gazzola, Frederick W. Padden, Bertram Bradley, William F. Pinsak, John R. Pegan, Glen P. Winton, William M. Lee, Edmund G. Astolfi and Robert H. Johnson.

Chapter 1
THE BASIC APPROACH

REASONS FOR NEGOTIATING SUCCESS

The successful negotiator is acutely aware of the five fundamental considerations for concluding a favorable deal: *One*, satisfy the psychological needs of the other person. *Two*, solve his or her problem or assist in attaining his or her goal so that the resultant change, in the form of concessions to you, is more desirable than the status quo. *Three*, if the other person's objective or solution to a problem is unreasonable, convince him or her that it has been reached, even though this is not the case, so that desirable concessions will be made to you. *Four*, create a problem for the person in order to encourage concessions to you in return for your help in preserving or improving upon the status quo. *Five*, keep in mind that a bargain is struck only when a final concession is made by one party who feels that the other will make no further concession. The key to a successful closing is making the other person believe that you will not make any further concessions.

In general, only three of these considerations are prerequisites for successfully concluding the negotiation: *one*, *five* and *two* or *three* or *four*. The first consideration is important because a person's ego must be put in the proper state before he or she will agree to your requests and demands. Unless "ego need" is met, the other person's likely to look upon your proposals with a negative attitude—regardless of personal gain or loss. The fifth consideration is a prerequisite because without it you may have to make the final concession before the deal can be closed, thereby decreasing the success of your efforts. In general, either the second, third or fourth consideration will fill the final prerequisite by leading the other person to believe that the deal will supply something he or she desires. It should be mentioned, however, that in complex negotiations all five considerations may become prerequisites at different times before an agreement can be successfully consummated.

1

The two key elements in satisfying psychological needs and in offering an attractive alternative to the status quo are cooperation and logic. Your logic must appear as fault free as possible regarding the truth of facts, assumptions, inferences, analysis and conclusions. Simultaneously, your cooperative attitude should emanate friendship, trust and respect and should fulfill a person's ego needs, hence making him or her receptive to your logic and to the equity of making the last concession to close the deal.

The successful negotiator has an excellent command of planning, strategy, procedure and the many tactics and techniques used to communicate persuasive logic and sincere cooperation. Use is made of all three communications channels: verbal communication; nonverbal communication; subconscious communication, which employs color, symbols, the physical site and arrangements, gestures, dress, smell, voice, proxemics, design, packaging and other forms of sensation transference. For a summary of the fundamentals of successful negotiation, see Figure 1.1.

Even without formal training in the science of negotiation, a person may be quite successful because of the right personality and outlook. For instance, the ideal, or "born," negotiator possesses the cooperative traits of

Figure 1.1. Fundamentals of successful negotiation.

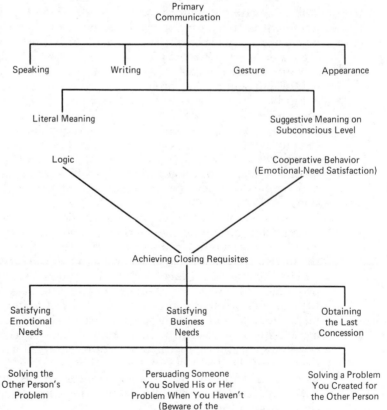

understanding human nature and need satisfaction, courage, confidence (high self-esteem and self-acceptance), flexibility, great patience, humility and charm (being likable), as well as the logical traits of high tolerance for ambiguity, high cognitive complexity (abstract thinking), high intelligence and realistic decision-making ability.

Of the two (logic and cooperation), a Purdue University survey suggests that the cooperative traits are much more important to negotiating success. Five years after its engineering students graduated, Purdue found only a $200 difference in income between its best students and its poorest students. However, the difference was ten times this between the students who had demonstrated a marked ability to deal with others in social situations and those with low personality ratings. Experiments conducted by the Carnegie Institute of Technology also show that personality has more to do with business success than superior or specialized knowledge. Perhaps this is why John D. Rockefeller said, "I will pay more for the ability to deal with people than for any other ability under the sun."

Yet, I find that close to half of all executives who attend my seminars claim that logic is more important than cooperative behavior. The following thought is thrown out for their consideration and comment: What good is the logic of your argument if the other party does not trust or like you? You could be offering something at a fraction of its true value, but the other person may think you are giving it away because of some ulterior motive or concealed defect. On the other hand, if the other person feels you are sincere and are trying to be fair, he or she may illogically go for a deal that is more favorable for you merely because you represent less risk and uncertainty.

ARE YOU AN EFFECTIVE NEGOTIATOR?

The successful negotiator recognizes how little he or she does know about negotiation, that it is a very complex process, and that many, many factors affect its outcome. (Just turn to the index of this book to glance at the pages and pages of factors.) The successful negotiator has a clear overview of most of the important factors, how they work, when to use them and how to utilize them to influence, persuade and motivate others to accomplish the negotiator's personal and business objectives. Because he or she has the big picture, as well as the tools, to negotiate successfully, this person is frequently seen as having a knack for cutting to the core of the problem and clarifying and resolving complex issues effortlessly.

Let's take a look at your own negotiating skills. Take a sheet of paper and respond to each of the following statements by writing a number from zero to five, with zero being no and five being yes. Put down your true feelings, not what you think the response should be. There are no correct answers. The purpose of this "test" is to learn more about yourself, and you should assume that no one else will be seeing your answers. An interpretation of your responses follows.

1. The object of negotiation is to win.
2. Methodical personal preparation in advance of a negotiation is unnecessary for success.
3. You are uncomfortable and do not enjoy the situation when you are facing direct conflict.
4. People you negotiate with are generally honest.
5. It is important to you to be liked.
6. You do not know why you negotiated a successful deal in the instances when you did.
7. You never attended a negotiating seminar or read a book on negotiating.
8. You rarely know anything about the other negotiator until you meet him or her for the first time.
9. "Low-balling" has no place in business negotiation.
10. People do not negotiate on a subconscious level.
11. Logic is more important than emotional needs in negotiation.
12. There are only two ways to break a deadlock.
13. It can always be assumed that the other party has the authority necessary to negotiate with you.
14. You do not have to know the other person's ego state in order to successfully negotiate with him or her.
15. The discipline of negotiation leaves little room for creativity.
16. Monetary compensation is more important in creating a climate that will motivate workers than is participation in management and responsibility for meeting goals.
17. When you are 100 percent correct, you must do your best to convince the other party of that fact.
18. A negotiator should not listen in silence as the other party is making an explanation based on faulty logic.
19. Little courtesy should be shown to a party who is rude or hostile to you.
20. You normally do not look at a person's hand when negotiating with him.
21. Once you establish your company's goals and demands, you lay them out on the table with convincing arguments that they are reasonable and should be accepted.
22. When the other party states that something is nonnegotiable, you only try to get compromises on other points to offset the lack of compromise on that item.
23. In a negotiation, you do not want to get too friendly with the other side.
24. There is no cause for alarm if the other negotiator is wearing tinted glasses.
25. The executive who is not involved with buying, selling, labor contracts and the like does not need to be an expert at negotiating.
26. Satisfying a negotiator's esteem needs is not of major importance.
27. Fait accompli belongs in the history books.
28. The best place for a negotiation is at a neutral site.
29. You usually know all the issues before the negotiation starts.
30. Once you begin a negotiation, you do not ask to be replaced by your boss or a peer.
31. If you appear strong and competitive, you will negotiate a better deal and probably negotiate it quicker.

32. You never negotiate price with a department store sales person.
33. You are nervous when going into a negotiation.
34. You are uncomfortable with ambiguous situations where you do not have many of the facts.
35. You do not like to speak before large groups of people.
36. You do not figure out what the other party's goals are until you hear him or her out at the first meeting.
37. You would rather deal with the general manager than the president.
38. You would not display irrational behavior in a negotiation unless provoked.
39. You would slow up the negotiation if a coalition tactic was being used against you.
40. You could not rattle off at least a half-dozen techniques of closing just about any deal.
41. It is unethical to use bland withdrawal.
42. You have never used the tactic of reversal.
43. You are too impatient to use the technique of forbearance.
44. You do not lie to other executives in your own company.
45. You do not lie to people you do business with outside the company.
46. You understand the tactic of mirage.
47. You rarely implement the technique of feinting.
48. The tactic of bracketing is too arduous to be effective.
49. A low-pitched voice is not as effective as a higher pitch when dealing with others.
50. How the other negotiator signs a letter or note has no significance to you.
51. Negotiators do not communicate by smell in the Western world.
52. Where you sit has no bearing on what you are thinking.
53. There is nothing wrong with covering your mouth with your hand during a negotiation.
54. Rigidly crossing your arms in a negotiation means that you are listening attentively to what is being said.
55. There are few top executives who act like children.
56. It shows weakness to express your true emotional feelings when you are hurt by another person.
57. You do not know the four basic communicating styles that people have.
58. You do not ask probing questions if they might prove personally embarrassing.
59. You telegraph your feelings rather easily.
60. The good guy–bad guy team ploy belongs in police stations, not the real world of business.
61. The problem with the deadline tactic is that it creates too much pressure on the parties.
62. If you have bad news for the other side, delay giving it until the last possible moment.
63. You do not dress in accordance with the principles of sensation transference.
64. Competence, not image, is what gets you promoted to top management.
65. You are more careful than most executives when taking risks that affect your career.

66. You feel somewhat uncomfortable with people of higher status.
67. Your negotiating experience is limited.
68. You have difficulty thinking fast when under pressure.
69. You have a short fuse when the back-and-forth arguments get heated.
70. You would be fairly embarrassed if you had to say "I do not understand that" three times after three good explanations.
71. To resolve conflicts of opinion, confrontation is more effective than compromise.
72. You do not adjust your own personality just to try communicating better with the other negotiator.
73. Body language is not as important as most people think.
74. You are not one of those people who are extremely sensitive to the feelings of others.
75. You do not believe in setting targets that are very hard to reach in negotiation because you know that they are unrealistic.
76. Making sure that the other negotiator commits no blunders and enters into a bad deal is not your business.
77. You would feel bad making a ridiculously low offer for buying something you know is worth much more.
78. You normally try to move the negotiation along at a good pace by making the compromises necessary to get to the point.
79. It is prejudice or ignorance not to trust a person merely because that person does not look at you.
80. A workaholic makes a better negotiator than most.
81. You normally try to stick to your prepared game plan in negotiations.
82. It does not hurt to subtly insult the other party every now and then when appropriate.
83. You normally give tit for tat in order to reach a happy bargaining conclusion.
84. You have no particular attire that you use especially for negotiation.
85. If bullying the other side will get you what you want, then you do it.
86. When they make the final offer and you cannot accept it, you will usually walk out at that point.
87. You would not immediately know what to do if, after making your demands, you are met with frozen silence.
88. You usually do not listen as well when someone expresses ideas you dislike.
89. You would avoid negotiating a 10 percent raise if the average department increase was only 5 percent.
90. In meetings and groups you participate in, others usually emerge as recognized leaders.
91. You are more frank than you are tactful or discreet.
92. You are rather closed minded about your important opinions.
93. You usually keep you feelings to yourself in a negotiation.
94. You dominate the people reporting to you because they are your subordinates.
95. It would not surprise you if you discovered that your employees respect you out of fear.
96. You worry too much about becoming sick or ill.

97. A negotiator who plans well does not need a quick mind.
98. You become irritated when it is obvious the other side is in no hurry to negotiate.
99. You work so hard that sometimes you wonder if you will have a nervous breakdown one day.
100. You have your share of enemies at work.

INTERPRETATION OF YOUR NEGOTIATING SKILL RATINGS

To obtain your overall rating, add your responses. You are a negotiator par excellence if the sum of your ratings is five or less. The appropriate response to each the above situations is zero. If it is less than fifteen, you are probably an extremely effective negotiator. In both instances, your expertise and skills probably need little improvement, and you would only want to read this book as a refresher and to find out about new ideas.

If you have less than twenty-five, you are a good negotiator. If you have less than thirty-five, you are an average negotiator. In both instances, you can significantly improve your negotiating batting average by reading and studying this book.

If your rating exceeds forty-five, it is more than likely that you are missing out on good opportunities, you are winding up with less than you should in deals, and you are hindering your own career. You definitely need to learn and apply both the negotiating fundamentals and the sophisticated techniques explained in this book.

You may be wondering why ratings other than zero are not appropriate for the particular negotiating situation listed. As you go through the book, the reasons will become apparent, and this chapter's thumbnail sketch of what it takes to be a successful negotiator will take on meaning. The following chapters will open up a new world of dealing with others more successfully than you ever imagined.

HOW COOPERATION LEADS TO SUCCESS

If the strategy of cooperation is so important, then why are so many bargaining situations adverse and combative? Apparently, the scientific research on the effects of cooperative and competitive behavior in negotiation has not filtered down into the business literature. In the business world, there are two sides to every negotiation, "yours" and "theirs," and the emphasis is on getting the other side to yield to your position. This is the essence of game theory, which has acceptance in both the military and industry. Game theory is nothing more than mathematical equations stating the possible courses of action available to the negotiators and the outcome, based on probability, of any combination of such actions. The foundation of this form of mathematical theory is the zero-sum game, in which the sum of the gains and losses to the negotiators must always be zero.

For example, if a manufacturer and a distributor have to negotiate how the income from the sale of a product is to be shared, this involves a zero-sum situation. If they split the net income equitably, both parties win. However, if one party obtains a disproportionately larger share of the profits, then the other party will get a smaller share of the profits. This is the win–lose situation, where the gains of the winner must equal the losses of the loser.

Scientific research and actual case statistics show that, if the manufacturer and distributor conduct a win–win negotiation by cooperating through problem-solving behavior, the money to be shared will be divided equitably in accordance with the expenses and risks of the parties, whether it be fifty–fifty or sixty-five–thirty-five.

The negotiation will be concluded quicker, and the bargain will endure longer than would have been the case had the negotiation been a competitive win–lose situation (where the manufacturer might stick to its demands of 80 percent of the income, leaving only the slightest profit margin for the distributor).

The general conclusion reached by experimental researchers is that early initiation of cooperative behavior tends to promote the development of trust and a mutually beneficial relationship, whereas early competitive behavior tends to induce mutual suspicion and competition. Thus, without a party's confidence, the harder the concentration on conflicting issues, the harder it is to achieve your goals. An atmosphere of trust is necessary to prevent hypercritical evaluation of your products, proposals, persuasive arguments and bottom-line goals.

To get someone to take favorable actions, you must make that person believe that the actions are necessary; this is achieved through problem-solving behavior on your part. You must find out what the other person wants, show sincere concern for his or her personal interests as well as those of the company, and talk in terms of those interests. Why? It is because research has shown that if you are seen as being really interested in individuals' aspirations and goals, they will behave similarly with respect to your goals.

This approach to negotiation is called the *reflection theory*. In research conducted by the U.S. Navy and Kenyon College, it was proven that when a person is shouted at that person simply cannot help but shout back, even without being able to see the speaker. It has been shown that the actions and beliefs of one person will cause counterreactions by the other person that are of the same nature. Your behavior, therefore, encourages the behavior and attitude you want on the part of the party with whom you are negotiating. Problem-solving behavior on your part reduces the other party's defense mechanisms to the point of willingness to experiment with preconceived attitudes, ideas and goals. He or she is then willing to genuinely explore and consider new information in a shared quest to resolve the conflict in a mutually satisfactory manner.

Most people have an excellent sixth sense for knowing when a party is sincerely interested in them. Hostility, disrespect, deceit and indifference are difficult to mask. Avoid thinking of the other person in a negotiation as your opponent. In fact, one of the many ways this book differs from others is the total absence of these two labels used to describe the other negotiator. Develop the habit of viewing the other party as a partner, and your cooperative behavior will shine through.

Even in the situation where your cooperative behavior results in the opportunity to "make a killing" at the expense of the other party, the tempting win–lose closing is as inadvisable as starting off the bargaining with that strategy. Scoring too big in a negotiation can be bad. If you get a lopsided, unreasonable victory, you may very well be confronted in the future with an unhappy contractual partner who feels economically justified in breaching obligations, risking litigation, or simply terminating the contract. If the goals the other party thought were achieved during the negotiation do not materialize, you may find yourself losing a lot more money, time and prestige later, when the negotiation outcome is translated into business reality—much more than you would have lost had you made adequate concessions to assure there was enough in the deal for both. The adage that you get what you pay for applies here. If you are too successful in negotiating a good price for goods ordered, you are liable to wind up with a shoddy product or no product at all (at a point when it is too late to switch to an alternate source). Gordon Cooper, one of our first astronauts, hit the nail on the head when asked, after returning from a space shot, if he had been worried. He replied, "Only once. While concentrating on the panel, I suddenly looked at all the dials and gadgets and it occurred to me that every one of those parts was supplied by the lowest bidder."

To sum up, the key to successful negotiation is that both sides should win. The win–lose concept stressed by many people in top management and those who counsel them can often do more harm than good. Any strategy for obtaining an agreement in principle and executing a binding document should be reasonable and fair to both sides. If both parties view the final agreement as profitable in that it will achieve their personal goals, this happy environment will assure no conflict or litigation in the future. Cooperative problem-solving behavior will generally result in an equitable bargain that will be reached quicker and last longer than the competitive win–lose strategy. In fact, most organizations today practice the cooperative approach internally because it has been recognized as a valuable and effective business technique. Witness "team building," MBO (management by objectives) and MBP (management by participation), which emphasize problem-solving behavior through cooperation.

The major exception to the win–win approach is when you are negotiating a one-shot deal. This situation occurs when you will never see the customer again, the goods are defective or special in some other aspect or you are getting out of the business. Even in this situation, tread with caution because you can get a bad reputation in general and you risk litigation if the other person has lost enough money to make a lawsuit worthwhile.

Chapter 2
PRENEGOTIATION PLANNING FOR THE BUSINESS PRO

UNDERSTANDING THE HIDDEN
BUSINESS REASONS FOR NEGOTIATION

The reasons for negotiating must be carefully analyzed before you can even begin to establish your maximum concessions and minimum requirements. This advice is so basic that most people tend to gloss over it. Too often, even in simple bargaining situations, only the initial motive for entering into the negotiation is emphasized. Other primary and secondary reasons are thought of haphazardly or not at all. One study showed that 46 percent of corporate managers did not really know what they wanted.

Let's take the situation where a chemical company develops a new compound useful as an insecticide. Although the chemical does not kill insects any better than what is on the market at present, it appears to be significantly safer as far as human exposure is concerned. The hitch is that the company has never been in insecticides and feels that it would be too costly and too risky to try to grab a significant share of the market away from the companies entrenched in the area.

Assume the chemical company president is your boss and tells you that the new compound does not fit in with the company's long-range product–market plans. You are assigned the task of "spinning off" this R & D (research and development) by-product as profitably as possible.

You promptly research the insecticide market, as well as those companies that appear to be potential entrants. With the aid of technical personnel, you prepare a prospectus on the benefits and potential of your company's new compound. You then contact your prospects and offer the product development to the highest bidder.

Unfortunately, the firms with the large market shares have a lot of money invested in their existing insecticides and are not too enthusiastic about another insecticide that does not have a dramatic improvement in killing power. The potential entrants to the insecticide market show interest in the product but are worried about the risk of competing with the well-known brands. As a result, you sell the rights to the product for only $20,000, notwithstanding the fact that the research and development costs were $200,000. After all, you did the best you could under the circumstances.

Nothing of the sort! Before implementing any negotiation strategy, the business reasons for entering into negotiation must be viewed as a set of problems to be solved. The facts and assumptions pertinent to the situation should be assimilated. The problem or problems should be defined. All alternative solutions, no matter how unlikely they appear on the surface, should be listed. The benefits and disadvantages of each should then be analyzed. Finally, the best solution to the problem should be selected, at which time the appropriate negotiating strategy will become apparent. Other attractive solutions should be kept in mind as negotiation proceeds. They may have to be implemented should the ideal solution become impractical or be opposed.

In the preceding example, the most attractive solution was to recoup the company's R & D expense and make a profit. When it became apparent that this goal was not feasible, another desirable alternative to sale should have been considered.

The candidates for product purchase were, for one reason or another, not willing to put up a great deal of front money. In the end, it was one of the entrenched firms with a large market share that finally bought the product development for $20,000. The alternative of licensing one of the potential entrants should have been considered. Unlike the entrenched firm that already had an insecticide on the market, the potential entrant would have the incentive to introduce the new product and compete with the entrenched firms. If this firm were successful, the royalties generated by sales from the new insecticide would greatly exceed the $200,000 investment made by the chemical company.

As a matter of fact, your president wanted to spin off the product because of the cost and risk of commercialization, not because the product was incompatible with company operations. In view of this, analysis of the business reasons would have indicated that it might be possible to strike a bargain for both royalties and the future right to commercialize the product. Although the product is of little interest now, the licensee might be successful in capturing a healthy share of the market by creating demand for a product that is safer. The insecticide venture might eventually represent a profitable low-risk option your president would like to exercise.

It is vital that you understand and analyze the reasoning for initiating a negotiation. If you evaluate the various negotiating alternatives and their consequences for meeting business objectives, you can enter the negotiation with flexibility and foresight and change emphasis on issues and concessions under the pressure of the firing line. You then can be confident of shooting for the best deal during each different bargaining situation. To further illustrate the benefits of proper business preparation, let us assume you persuade a company to pay you a healthy royalty on sales of the insecticide to be commercialized. The only issue is whether the product patent and trade secret rights are sold outright or are merely licensed. You are assured that the firm will agree to a diligence clause requiring them to spend at least a minimum effort in terms of facilities, personnel and money in a good faith attempt to successfully commercialize the insecticide. Therefore, there is no reason for you to keep title to the product rights. Secretly, you feel there is great value in keeping open the option of entering the market at some future point in time. You therefore tell the company that a written guarantee will not suffice. You are only willing to grant a license for exclusive manufacture and sale of the insecticide, with the reservation of rights in your company to also make and sell the insecticide if you feel that the licensee is not being diligent or aggressive enough in the marketplace. The other firm reacts negatively to the threat of future competition from you and refuses to agree to this without a reduction in royalties. You assent, provided they agree to a final concession of granting you a nonexclusive license to make and use any improvements they develop in the insecticide area.

The agreement in principle has been reached, and you shake hands and agree to have your attorneys work out the details for execution. The other party leaves happy with the knowledge that front money is not required and resources can be used solely for the investment necessary to commercialize the product. The royalty rate decrease is also a matter of personal satisfaction for the other negotiator. You leave happy because your company will be receiving much more money than the nominal lump-sum purchase price that was offered if the licensee is successful. You are also happy because you have the right to jump on the bandwagon after the other company does the spade work in obtaining market acceptance. And finally, you are happy because you will also have access to their insecticide improvements so that your company will not be at a disadvantage if it later decides to compete with the superior insecticide they develop.

TECHNIQUES OF RESEARCHING
THE NEGOTIATOR AND THE COMPANY

There are five main considerations in researching the negotiator and his or her company. First, the company with which you are about to negotiate a deal and the specific individuals you meet at the bargaining table should be thoroughly investigated. In order to plan the negotiation, you must have a good understanding of their business and psychological needs, how they think and react and their negotiation procedure, tactics and strategy. With these data, you will be prepared and will have an edge in the bargaining process.

Second, the simplest method of learning about the other firm, its past history and its present policies, and learning about its individual negotiators is to research the published literature. A good picture of the business can be obtained by studying annual reports, press releases, institutional advertising, reports of security analysts, government agency records, stock market guides, clipping services, credit information and litigation reports. Information about the individuals with whom you will be negotiating can be obtained from biographies in *Moody's, Standard & Poor's* and *Dun & Bradstreet*, speeches and articles and *Who's Who* directories.

Third, more sophisticated sources of information can include interviewing other parties involved in litigation or settlements of disputes with the company with which you are about to deal—especially parties who have unsuccessfully negotiated with the company and those who presently have some type of business relationship with it. To obtain unpublished personal information about the individual with whom you will be negotiating, it will be necessary to speak to former classmates, acquaintances, friends, co-workers in previous employment and fellow members of clubs, professional societies and trade associations.

In some sensitive situations, it may even be necessary to use a private investigator. The information that can be obtained in this manner is invaluable in determining the negotiator's status socially and within the company, authority to make commitments, integrity, prior tactics, strengths and weaknesses, emotional needs and even religion, race and IQ, all of which play a role in how he or she will approach the negotiation. Sometimes, even mannerisms, voice modulation or other personal characteristics, if known prior to confrontation at the bargaining table, will tip you off about the negotiator's thinking and reactions enough to give you an edge.

Unfortunately, there are many executives who use an investigator for tasks that are unethical and even illegal. One expert estimates that $800 million is annually spent on industrial spying. Using an insider, a wiretap or a bug to find out what the party's real bottom line is, the sincerity of its assurances and its actual reasons for entering into the deal is an invasion of privacy.

Fourth, if the deal is of major importance to your company's business in the future, then the prenegotiation research can be taken even one step further by going through one or more dry runs with the second- or third-choice candidates. This will give you a better feel for the kind of deal that can be reached. You will have a better understanding of what concessions the first-choice candidate will expect. You will also have the flexibility of falling back on the second or third choice, should your first choice be unreasonable.

Fifth, when you are about to negotiate a deal with your first-choice candidate, you should consider making further use of all the research data you have gathered and analyzed. This can be accomplished using the technique of role playing, a combination of business gaming and brainstorming. Your negotiating team is split so that one or more persons represent the other party, and the team acts out the entire negotiation.

Role playing will introduce the members of your negotiating team to the facts and issues with dramatic impact. It transforms the intellectual and logical exercise of forecasting and formulating strategy into an emotional experience that your negotiating team will both feel and hear.

After the role playing, your negotiating team can have an in-depth discussion as to what took place, the difficulties that arose, the mistakes that were made, the behavior to be changed, and new issues and points of view that were not anticipated. Probably the greatest benefit of role playing is bringing human behavior into the laboratory where you can put yourself into the other party's shoes in order to experience the different emotions. Role playing even has the advantage of giving the junior members of your negotiating team the chance to play devil's advocate in the role of the other party, allowing them to say how they actually feel about your strategy and tactics instead of what they think you want to hear.

To sum up, role playing is a valuable research tool that enables you to discover problem areas you have overlooked or ignored and correct and polish your presentation and strategy. Based on responses I have received from thousands of seminar attendees, there is less than a 10 percent chance that you have participated in role playing in preparation for a negotiation. You will be making a valuable contribution to your company by introducing role playing for major deals.

SECRETS OF THE CREATIVE NEGOTIATOR

A creative idea, plan or solution to a problem almost always involves using a principle or relationship that everyone knows but everyone also didn't remember and relate. Creative negotiators aren't more intelligent. They simply have a way of using their memory and cognitive and perceptual abilities far more effectively than others. These individuals put their subconscious to work in addition to applying abstract thought and analytical skills, and their insight comes after relaxing and stepping away from the problem. There are six basic steps to the personality trait of creative thinking, and you can adopt them:

1. Formulate the problem to be solved and possible alternative solutions.
2. Gather all the data considered relevant to defining the problem and clarifying conflicting approaches to solving it.
3. Organize, study, and digest these data in the context of the problem to be solved.
4. Put the problem aside consciously, and wait for the subconscious mind to act upon it and "report back."
5. Act on the feedback from the subconscious, which will come in the form of a sudden idea or hunch.
6. Rigorously test the solution chosen.

In Step 1, before you can gather information and facts relevant to the matter being considered, you must define the problem and possible alternative solutions. Alfred P. Sloan, former chairman of General Motors, often would postpone making a decision until there was sufficient disagreement among the executives considering the problem. Only then would he look at the facts to see which of the approaches and opinions were practical and desirable. He would not tolerate starting out with a conclusion and then looking for facts to support it.

Write down the aspects and characteristics of the problem from the first moment it has become of interest. And keep writing, writing, writing as you go along. Putting information, ideas and other people's opinions down in written form is an essential part of abstract thinking, recognized by virtually all problem solvers. Never be without paper, pencil or pen. Ideas strike at any hour and under any circumstance, and those that aren't immediately translated into an appropriate notation almost always vanish back into the subconscious. Memory behaves in the same fashion.

Once you honestly start the writing process, you'll find that it leads into a sharp focus on the task undertaken, reduces wasted motion—both intellectual and physical—brings practical guidelines into existence as if by magic. Even if you are not a strong abstract thinker (test yourself in the following section), you will greatly improve your creativity by disciplining yourself to use the approach outlined in this chapter.

Step 2 should continue until you have much more data than can possibly apply to the problem. Even then, you'll probably realize you stopped too soon and will need to gather more data before finishing Step 3.

For the mass of data to be useful, it must be arranged pursuant to Step 3 in some scheme that is appropriate. One of the best approaches is to key the various notes, reports, books, transcripts and so on into an outline, a chart or some similar schematic or graphic representation of your objective (or the problem).

It is important to rearrange and regroup the data, trying different combinations, trade-offs and basic changes in the model and considering all alternative approaches suggested by the data until you are convinced you have exhausted all the realistic possibilities. Then, and only then, when you honestly believe there are no other new realignments worth considering, should you move to the next phase of this problem-solving technique.

Forget it all in Step 4. With the first three steps properly completed, you are ready to turn the problem over to the subconscious—where the full intellectual resources can be applied. Drawing upon memory, which has recorded every scrap of information, every concept, every impression ever heard, seen, thought or otherwise received, your subconscious can tremendously augment the available data in the areas you have been deliberately "stirring up" while sorting the information gathered consciously. In a process that can only be called synthesis, cross-linkages are established, often between products and principles that have seemed totally unrelated. New frames of reference form, and unsuspected causal relationships are activated. All this goes on while the conscious mind is otherwise occupied—a condition that one must establish and maintain.

This is the incubation period or gestation phase of the creative cycle. Generally speaking, its length cannot be predicted. Its outcome, however, is completely predictable. There will be a "report" to the conscious mind, and that report will most likely be the solution to the problem.

In the interim between conscious commitment to the subconscious domain and the flash of revelation, it is imperative that you "forget" the problem completely.

The subconscious flash will come. It may be in a whisper, a hesitant thought that hardly seems worth noting or as increasingly happens with those who are "veterans" in the technique, a stunning hunch that literally wipes the mind clean and makes the hands tremble. It will come in many instances at the least expected or welcome time: You may be driving off the first tee, staring out the window of a bus or plane, or waiting for a court to play tennis.

At any time, in any situation, you may suddenly think again of the problem deliberately put aside. If you ignore the thought, you may have "blown" the solution. It is most unlikely that the subconscious will ring again on the particular matter. Step 5 opens with an invitation—strong or subdued—but its characteristics are unmistakable: All of a sudden, you will be seeing the problem from a new perspective and with new ideas.

When the invitation comes, it must be accepted immediately for Step 5. Record every idea received. Be noncritical. Judgment must be withheld until you are sure no more ideas or hunches are forthcoming. There may be times when you experience an "avalanche effect." Ideas come in a flood, perhaps including the clear-cut solution of a difficult problem.

There is a tendency for people, especially conformists, to dismiss wild ideas. (Test your degree of open-mindedness and creativity in the following section.) Record them all. Remember that information is blind to the use to which it may be put by its possessor. Ideas that are totally unrelated may emerge. There's no way of predicting the subconscious linkages that will be established during mental synthesis. Failure to record them all could cost you the solution to the problem in the near or distant future. Put down everything that comes into your mind at this time.

Now the first five steps of the creative process have done the work. Chances are, you'll have the solution to the immediate problem before you. Step 6 is to prove it workable in practice and undertake whatever further experimentation, discussion, consultation or other follow-up is required.

Now is the time to apply judgment—rigorously—to the ideas and hunches that have come to you. Rate them as well as you can according to difficulty of implementation, costs, conformance with organizational policies and time required to find out whether the approach will be satisfactory. This done, work should be resumed, perhaps by a team of investigators if there are enough approaches.

Just as important as presenting your creative plan or solution are the form and substance of your answers and explanations in response to questions stemming from your proposal. If you present a new idea or solution to a problem without adequate evaluation, thorough examination of all the negative consequences that could result and a full and organized comprehension of all the supporting arguments and reasons, a few pointed questions could place you in a defensive position. You must be able to communicate your position so that it will withstand close scrutiny from people who are looking for every little way in which your proposal can damage them or be misconstrued to their detriment. In fact, questions give you an extra opportunity to make your ideas even more attractive, logical and personal.

In addition to the dry runs and role playing already discussed, you must analyze expected areas of resistance and counter arguments. You must go even further and be ready to counter rebuttals to your explanations by addressing counter arguments. You will appear confident, intelligent and strong even if your proposal is shot down. This rigorous exercise of being one step ahead of the other party also facilitates catching your own mistakes before you make them.

You must closely examine all of the effects each of the best solutions and approaches will have on the parties and individuals involved. Will their financial, personal and other goals be promoted or retarded? Who will be misled or confused? How will each person and party be motivated, and what reaction can be expected? Who can you expect an objection from, and what will that objection be? How will your plan affect the future? Will additional financing be needed? Will improvements or modifications be required? Will additional personnel be needed? Will the other party be happy with your solution over the long run?

ARE YOU A STRONG ABSTRACT AND CREATIVE THINKER?

Abstract thinking and creative thinking are two important skills for the successful negotiator. To see how strong your skills are in these areas, rate yourself by responding to the following two lists of statements.

First, to evaluate your abstract thinking skills, rate yourself from 0 to 5 for each of the following statements, with 0 being *no* and 5 being *yes*. Put down your true feelings, not what you think the ratings should be, because there are no correct answers. See the end of this section for an interpretation of your responses.

1. I do not play by the book.
2. I frequently seek comfort and protection.
3. The overall effect art has on my emotions is important to me.
4. I am not a doer.
5. I find new solutions to problems.
6. I do not take care of others.
7. Detail and realism in art are not important to me.
8. I am a misty-eyed romantic.
9. I like dreaming and planning.
10. I do not control my emotions effectively.

Now, to see how creative you are, rate yourself from 0 to 5, for the following statements, with 0 being *no* and 5 being *yes*. Again, put down your true feelings, not what you think the ratings should be, because there are no correct answers.

1. Nonfiction books can be a waste of time. If you want to read, read novels.
2. You have to admit that some criminals are very smart.
3. There are more important things to do than trying to be a fastidious dresser.

4. I do not have very strong convictions. What's right is not always right; what's wrong is not always wrong.
5. It doesn't bother me when my boss gives vague instructions.
6. Business before pleasure is not a hard-and-fast rule in my life.
7. Taking a different route to work can be fun, even if it takes longer.
8. Most rules and regulations can be broken under the right circumstances.
9. Playing with a new idea is fun, even if it doesn't come to anything.
10. When people are nice to me, I don't care why.
11. I do not try to avoid unusual words and word combinations when writing.
12. Detective work sounds like a fun job.
13. Crazy people can have good ideas.
14. I write letters to friends even though there are so many clever greeting cards available.
15. Pleasing myself means more to me than pleasing others.
16. You will not find the true answer to many questions no matter how long you dig.
17. A logical, step-by-step method is not best for solving problems.
18. It's not a waste of time to ask questions if I have no hope of obtaining answers.
19. I am often uncertain that I'm following the correct procedures for solving a specific problem.
20. I concentrate harder on what interests me than do most people.
21. When trying to solve a problem, I spend a great deal of time analyzing it.
22. I occasionally voice opinions that seem to turn people off.
23. I waste little time thinking about what others think of me.
24. Complex situations interest me because they are challenging.
25. It is more important to do what is right than to win acceptance of others.
26. People who seem unsure and uncertain about things have my respect.
27. More than others, I want things to be interesting and exciting.
28. On occasion, I get overly enthusiastic on the job.
29. I often get my best ideas when doing nothing in particular.
30. I rely on hunches or a "gut" feeling that I am right when moving toward solving a problem.
31. I sometimes enjoy doing things I'm not supposed to do.
32. I dislike hobbies that involve collecting things.
33. I have capacities that have not been tapped yet.
34. Daydreaming helps me on the way to many important projects.
35. I dislike people who are objective and rational.
36. I am more enthusiastic and energetic than most people.
37. I get along more easily with people in the same social and business class as myself.
38. I have a high degree of aesthetic sensitivity.
39. I have a good capacity for self-instruction.
40. I dislike people who are very sure of their conclusions.
41. Inspiration is important for solving problems.
42. In an argument, I feel that it would be great for the person who disagrees with me to become a friend, but not at the price of sacrificing my point of view.

43. I do not avoid situations in which I might feel inferior.
44. The source of information is more important to me than the content.
45. I get a certain enjoyment from things being uncertain and unpredictable.
46. My self-respect is more important than the respect of others.
47. People who strive for perfection are wise.
48. I prefer to work solo rather than in a team effort.
49. Creativity can be utilized in any field of endeavor.
50. It is unimportant to have a place for everything and everything in order.
51. I never think other people can read my thoughts.
52. The trouble with people is that they often take things too lightly.
53. I am a self-starter.
54. I am curious and playful.
55. My motivation and enthusiasm for my projects stay even in the fact of obstacles or opposition.
56. People who are willing to entertain "crackpot" ideas are practical.
57. What could be, rather than what is, is the important question.
58. After I've made up my mind, I often can change it.
59. I think the statement "Ideas are a dime a dozen" is a misconception.
60. I don't mind asking questions that show ignorance.
61. Sometimes ideas come to me as if from some external source.
62. There are times when I have an "avalanche" of ideas.
63. I look for ways of converting necessities into advantages.
64. It is a good idea not to expect too much of others.
65. I cannot change my interests to pursue a job or career as easily as I can change a job to pursue my interests.
66. Many breakthroughs are due to chance.
67. People who are theoretically oriented are no less important than those who are practical.
68. It is important to understand the motives of people you deal with.
69. I see things in terms of their potential.
70. When brainstorming, I come up with more ideas and come up with them faster than most others in the group.
71. I am not ashamed to express interest in the opposite sex if so inclined.
72. I tend to rely more on my first impressions and feelings when making judgments than on a thorough analysis.
73. I frequently anticipate solutions to my problems.
74. I rarely laugh at myself for my quirks and peculiarities.
75. Clever thinkers resort to metaphors and analogies.
76. When someone gets ahead of me in line, I usually point it out to him or her.
77. Problems that do not have clear answers interest me.
78. I usually work things out for myself rather than get someone to show me.
79. I let my feelings guide me through experiences.
80. I frequently begin work on a problem that I remotely sense and cannot yet express.
81. I frequently tend to forget names of people, streets and towns.
82. I tolerate frustration more than the average person.

83. During adolescence I liked to be alone to pursue my own interests and thoughts.
84. I feel that the adage "Do unto others . . ." is less important than "To thine own self be true."
85. Things obvious to others are not so obvious to me.
86. I feel I will make important contributions to society.
87. I have more problems than I can handle and more work than there is time for.

Your abstract thinking and planning abilities are strong if the sum of your ratings in the first list of statements exceeds 25 and get stronger as you approach 40.

You are probably exceptionally creative if the sum of your ratings in the second list exceeds 375, very creative if it is above 300, above average in creativity if it is above 225, average if it is above 175, below average if it is above 125 and noncreative if it is below 125.

BOTTOM-LINE STRATEGY

Even the most complex business negotiation boils down to one of two situations: *One,* you are trying to sell a product or service to somebody, or vice versa. *Two,* you have been wronged in some manner and are looking for reparation, or vice versa.

How the other side views its position in these two broad negotiating situations may always be analyzed in dollars and cents. If a competitor is making false statements about your project in its advertising, your ability to persuade the competitor to cease and desist is dependent primarily upon the economics of the situation. The money the competitor has spent on the inventory of promotional literature containing the false statements, the money lost from cancelling advertising at the last minute and the expense of printing new advertising will be weighed against the persuasiveness of your demand. If you threaten to sue, then your competitor will also have to weigh the cost of the defense against the cost of complying with your demands. If your competitor is getting a lot of mileage and is capturing a substantial share of the market by using the false statements, it may feel that its success is worth the cost of defending a lawsuit. If you counteract the false advertising with your own ads and successfully repulse the inroads being made by your competitor, this may be more economically costly for the competitor than a lawsuit and might result in a stand-off where it makes sense to cease the false advertising. As we see, although many of the issues involve intangibles and actions, everything can be viewed in terms of dollars and cents in analyzing your competitor's needs.

Prior to each negotiation, you should conduct an objective economic analysis of what the other party would like to realize from the negotiation, what the party would be willing to settle for and what the party's bottom line is. Thus, if you wish to construct chemical process facilities for a potential customer, you must determine their current per-unit-volume profit, their return-on-investment and payback period expectations and their desire to modernize existing facilities. Based on the answers to these questions and your own knowledge of the profit per unit volume that can be anticipated after planned start-up, you will have a fairly good feel for your customer's bottom-line settlement figure for the construction price as well as the low figure at which the customer will aim.

Once you go through the economic analysis of perceiving the other side's business needs, you will have a relatively good idea of what that side's reasonable goals should be. Based on this information, you will be able to determine whether the goals you would like to achieve, the goals for which you would settle and the bottom-line goals you must have overlap with those of the other party. If the reasonable goals each of you would settle for more or less coincide, then you should continue bargaining until you reach that point, at which time the negotiation can be closed. However, if your bottom-line goals (the least for which each of you would settle) are far apart, you probably will not conclude an agreement that is mutually acceptable unless unexpected circumstances that alter the assumptions of your goal analysis are found during the negotiation. By establishing a three-tier level of goal analysis, as described above (and shown in Figure 2.1), you will know how unreasonable others' initial demands are and whether they are being sincere in setting forth their reasons.

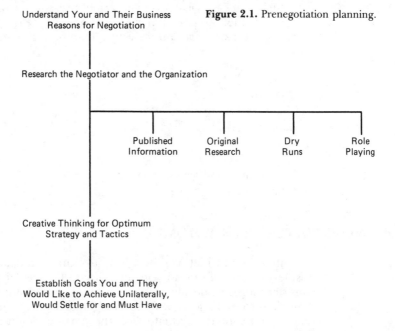

Figure 2.1. Prenegotiation planning.

Chapter 3
PRENEGOTIATION MANEUVERS

There are certain maneuvers you can employ to give yourself greater bargaining power or put a party in a worse bargaining position even prior to the first meeting. For instance, there are actions you can take to make someone want to deal with you: You can create a problem for the other party that you can solve; you can apply pressure at the right time or with the right influential party; or you can shrewdly select, control and arrange the negotiating environment. Some common prenegotiation maneuvers are

1. weakest link,
2. principal,
3. audience,
4. coalition,
5. timing leverage,
6. site selection,
7. site control and arrangement, and
8. fait accompli.

WHO NEGOTIATES WITH WHOM?

In a situation in which you may have to transact a deal with more than one business entity, whom do you select first? Figure 3.1 illustrates the major considerations. Generally, when it is more important to establish a precedent than to make a show of force against a party with strong bargaining power, you should negotiate with the party deemed most likely to accept the deal you have in mind; for instance, when you wish to make the first sale of a new half-million dollar computer system that your company has just developed.

On the other hand, where a precedent with a weak opponent will not

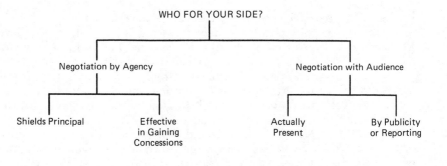

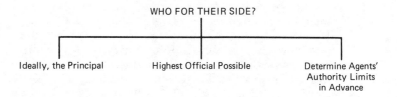

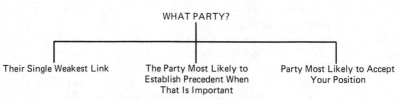

Figure 3.1. Who negotiates?

materially influence the negotiation of subsequent deals, it is generally best to select the party with the greatest bargaining power first. If negotiation is successful, this may obviate the necessity of subsequent negotiation with other parties. For example, if you conclude a successful negotiation with the strongest infringer of your patent or the infringer having the greatest financial interest, this may serve as a powerful deterrent to others from starting or continuing their infringing activities. For example, consider a company that must deal with several labor unions whose contracts end in the same year. Commencing negotiation with the strongest union may be advisable, regardless of how undesirable the outcome, because striking a favorable bargain with one of the weaker unions would not serve as a precedent in other union negotiations. A favorable contract with the strongest union, however, would bring the other unions in line.

Once you have selected the business entity or group that you intend to negotiate with, you will want to bring pressure against the single weakest link or part. Thus, in negotiating with a labor union that represents your workers in a number of plants, you should seriously consider dealing with the union in the plant where it is in its weakest bargaining position. A favorable settlement there will serve as a reasonable reference point for bargaining in the other plants.

As further illustration, assume that in the case mentioned earlier you select the infringing product that is doing the most competitive harm to your company. You have a choice of initiating negotiation with the manufacturer, the distributor or one or more vendors. By carefully determining the weakest link in the infringing supplying–manufacturing–marketing chain, you can get the negotiating edge by approaching the company most receptive to your demand that it cease and desist its infringing activities. Let's say you are confronted with a large, aggressive national distributor, a small manufacturer who sells the product to the distributor and a vendor of a critical subassembly that comprises the heart of the infringed product. It would not make sense to approach the national distributor with your demand. The distributor probably would not settle even if a lawsuit was filed. Likewise, although the manufacturer is small and more vulnerable to litigation, it would probably dispute your facts for alleging patent infringement. Negotiations would certainly be drawn out, with the probability of having to file suit prior to a favorable settlement. The best bet is to make initial contact with the vendor. The subassembly it is making for the manufacturer probably represents only a small portion of the vendor's business, and the vendor probably will not be willing to assume the risk of defense against a patent infringement suit. Also, the vendor probably will not be content with an assurance from the manufacturer that the vendor will be held harmless regarding damages and the cost of litigation because of the manufacturer's limited financial resources. It is very likely that the vendor will terminate its relationship with the manufacturer out of fear of a messy legal dispute, which outweighs the profits from its supply contract with the manufacturer. The same reasoning for selecting the right link in the chain also applies when the distributor is small and would weigh the same considerations as the vendor in bowing out of the business arrangement with the manufacturer. In addition, some distributors might pull out merely on ethical considerations if it appears that there might be infringement of a patent or if they feel that adverse publicity of threatened litigation could ruin their other marketing operations.

When arranging for the first negotiating session, you should insist on dealing only with the principal or, at the very least, someone who is designated to conduct the negotiations and has final decision-making authority. (See Figure 3.2.) A party will sometimes employ the tactic of "agency," where the agent of the principal negotiates with you. This enables the agent to feel out your strengths, weaknesses and intentions, while making commitments that can be overruled by the principal. Even if the party is not intentionally using the "agency" ploy, it is a scientifically proven fact that an agent tends to make smaller concessions and greater demands than the principal because of the pressures of accountability.

Unfortunately, based on a number of surveys of my classes, I find that about half of all business executives would rather deal with a department manager than the general manager. They are more comfortable dealing

Figure 3.2. Site strategy.

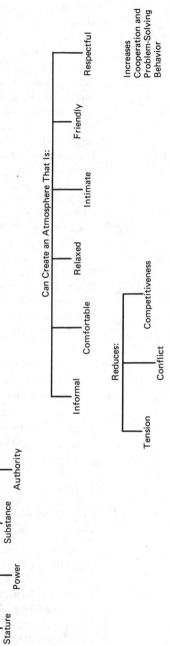

25

with their counterpart, who is intimately familiar with the subject of discussion and issues involved. This reluctance or fear of talking to the most senior employee possible must be overcome for the benefits of negotiating with the principal.

Study an organization in advance. Have the courage to ask the negotiator to describe his or her authority. Do not accept a partial or evasive answer. If necessary, get the negotiator's boss to indicate what authority limits exist and what the prerequisites are for final approval.

Insufficient thought is usually given to the question of who should negotiate for you. For the reasons discussed above, it is desirable that your negotiator not have final authority. One ploy is for your vice-president or your attorney to do the negotiating and state the constraints imposed by the president. This makes the other party more psychologically restrained than he or she would be in negotiating with another principal. Also, "chiefs" do not usually have as much knowledge of the specifics of the subject being covered, whereas "Indians" (agents) do and are generally better prepared because they have more time than their bosses to spend on such matters.

Unfortunately, in most companies, the Peter Principle (whereby executives rise in the corporate hierarchy relative to their level of incompetency) still dictates who the senior negotiator will be. Although the executive may have risen to a high position because of a brilliant business mind, he or she may have actually risen to a level of incompetence with respect to negotiating capabilities. The ideal person to head up your negotiating team or assume responsibility for your negotiating efforts should:

1. be thoughtful and sensitive to the feelings of others;
2. understand human nature;
3. be adaptive in order to satisfy the psychological needs of others;
4. not have a strong compulsion to be liked by peers;
5. be able to listen creatively and patiently;
6. be respected by the other members of the negotiating team as well as the other party;
7. be goal oriented; and
8. be highly logical, with good probability estimating and decision-making abilities in order to exercise the best business judgment possible during the heat of negotiation.

Sometimes showing respect for the other party becomes more important than the benefits of negotiating through your agent, even if he or she is more skilled, knowledgeable and shrewd than you. When the Libyan revolutionary leader Moammar Qadhafi announced foreign oil company nationalization, Dr. Armand Hammer, chairman of the board of Occidental Petroleum Corp., flew all night to get to Libya. Qadhafi greeted him with open arms and said, "Of all the companies with investments here, you are the only chief executive to visit me in person." Needless to say, Occidental worked out a mutually agreeable deal and avoided nationalization.

STRATEGICALLY TIMING THE NEGOTIATION

It is desirable that you initiate negotiation either when the other party is in its weakest bargaining position or you are in your strongest. For example, when a company is about to merge or be acquired, is about to consummate a large business deal or is about to make a public offering, this is the moment when it is most vulnerable to adverse publicity. If you have a business dispute to air with this company, this is the best time to do so because the company will be most agreeable to a quiet settlement under the implicit threat of a lawsuit.

As a matter of fact, extremely favorable settlement terms can generally be extracted in any situation where the importance of the other party's business plans completely overshadows the magnitude of concessions you are demanding to settle your dispute. Why do you suppose teacher's and sanitation workers' contracts expire in September and June, respectively? Those times are when the public officials are most concerned with education for the children and the stink of garbage under the hot summer sun. On the other hand, many companies insist that union contracts be on a calendar year basis so that a negotiating deadlock will throw picketers out into the cold and snow.

An overriding factor in delaying or expediting the commencement of negotiation is whether business benefits can be obtained by continuing the status quo or business detriments can be avoided by changing it. For instance, suppose you are a small company with a unique product for which there is only incipient market demand. A large competitor hires away your chief engineer, learns of your trade secrets for making the product and begins to make and sell your product. Rather than requesting your competitor to stop its wrongful activity, you may wish to delay negotiation and possible litigation until after your competitor has helped educate the customer and developed market acceptance and demand for your product. Once your competitor has laid the groundwork (at its own expense) for large volume sales of your product, you should move rapidly in demanding that it cease to exploit your trade secrets.

The drawback to this type of dilatory tactic is that your competitor will be entrenched, having made a substantial investment and commitment to the business line, and will be reluctant to terminate its venture short of litigation. However, the advantages of delay can still be significant. If your competitor should fail in its venture to obtain widespread market acceptance for your products, you will have the benefit of its mistakes and will be in a position to terminate your own venture before incurring serious losses. If your competitor is successful, you will be able to ride the crest of its wave, provided you are in a good bargaining position (that is, you can prove improper appropriation of your trade secret and put the competitor on notice to avoid reliance on your silence or acquiescence in their activities as a defense).

Once you have decided the most opportune time to begin negotiation, you should select the most favorable day of the week and time of the day.

In general, people are most alert and receptive Tuesday through Thursday. People have not gotten back to the full swing of things on Monday. (In fact, Monday has the highest rate of suicides and fatal heart attacks, according to the statistics.) And they are looking forward on Friday to the weekend's social activities.

Since businesspeople become more strained, tense, and mentally fatigued as the day wears on, it becomes more difficult to persuade someone at an afternoon meeting. In general, our memory peaks in the morning and our mental skills peak in the early afternoon.

Although some negotiators feel it is advantageous to catch people when they are not in their most effective mental state, it is generally beneficial to have a person relaxed and able to readily grasp your ideas and suggestions. When someone is confused or thinking of other things while you talk, he or she will often take the easy way out by responding negatively instead of intelligently considering what you say or requesting that you repeat yourself.

A breakfast meeting to explore ideas and discuss issues in general can be beneficial. Although a little tired from commuting, a person usually feels fresh in the morning and is in a good frame of mind when he or she starts off the day in the quiet, relaxed atmosphere of a good dining room instead of an office. Breakfast should not be used for hard bargaining or deal closing. Neither should lunch or dinner, which can, however, be used to generate friendly understanding of specific points of view, concerns and controversial issues. People cannot enjoy their meals if things get too tense. Nothing eliminates resistance and mistrust quicker than breaking bread with someone and getting to know the person behind the title and the company behind the name.

Of course, the overriding factors in selecting the day and the time are your own body metabolism, habits, and traits. You should choose the time of negotiation so that it is most suitable to your own make-up to assure you will be at your best. If you are a late riser (an owl) and do not get moving until after lunch, be sure to set up afternoon meetings, when your circadian body temperature (daily cycle) is at its peak. If you should develop a headache or other discomfort that will impair your ability to fully concentrate at the negotiating session, you would be wise to call off a meeting, especially if it involves the consideration of complex issues. To sum up, you should not let anything tip the scale in the other party's favor when it is time for you to actually negotiate.

Chronobiologists have scientifically proven that people, from the moment of birth, are influenced by three separate rhythms in their lives: a twenty-three-day physical cycle or rhythm, a twenty-eight-day emotional rhythm, and a thirty-three-day intellectual rhythm. The physical rhythm affects energy, endurance and strength; the emotional rhythm affects feelings, sensitivity and creativity; and the intellectual rhythm affects mental alertness, reasoning power, creative abilities and logic. The positive cycle of each rhythm is when a person is at his best, and the negative cycle is when efficiency is reduced.

When any one of the three rhythms changes from plus to minus or vice versa, it is a "critical" day, and the individual is more vulnerable to problems. You will tire more quickly, be less resistant to infection and disease and feel less energetic on a physical-rhythm critical day. You will even be more sensitive to pain and should avoid things like dentist appointments on critical days. You will be irritable, perhaps depressed or given to emotional outburst, and may lack good judgment during an emotional-rhythm critical day. You may not be using common sense, or your logic may be faulty; and you will probably be forgetful on an intellectual-rhythm critical day.

The negative cycle day before or after a critical day is a "caution" day. The peak and valley of each cycle is a "minicaution" day. Some difficulty with physical, emotional and/or intellectual states may be experienced on "caution" and "minicaution" days. When any combination of critical, caution or minicaution days for two or three rhythms coincide, the probability of error or accident is increased.

Although the topic is still controversial in the United States, findings on biorhythms are being applied by over 5,000 American companies and have been used for years on a widespread basis in other countries. In Switzerland and Japan, for instance, tens of thousands of companies use biorhythm controls for their employees. Even clerical workers benefit from biorhythm controls. The keypunch operators of one company were taken off their machines and put to work in less sensitive functions on critical days of their biorhythms. Mistakes were reduced by 35 percent within six months. According to the Tokyo Metropolitan Police, 82 percent of all reported accidents in one year occurred on the driver's critical day. Recent research indicates that most sports injuries occur on critical, caution and minicaution days. Swiss Air prohibits its pilots and co-pilots from flying together if both are experiencing critical days at the same time.

What all this means is that you should not ignore the biological ups and downs that affect your performance as a negotiator. Get a biorhythm chart or electronic biorhythm calculator; schedule important negotiations when two and preferably all three rhythms are in the plus phase simultaneously; and avoid important meetings that fall on a critical day. Even the most skillful negotiator welcomes luck. "Bio-luck" does really exist when the emotional and intellectual cycles are both in the positive cycle.

In short, time the negotiation to obtain the maximum business benefits and to be in the strongest bargaining position. Consider the following points in deciding *when* to negotiate:

1. the day of the week;
2. the time of day;
3. whether to meet over a meal; and
4. your optimal biorhythm time.

THE BEST PLACE TO NEGOTIATE

Scientific research indicates that you will do best in a negotiation when you are at your home office and the other party is in unfamiliar territory. The reason appears to be that a bargainer on home ground is more assertive and confident. In contrast, a bargainer who is a guest may feel a subordinate status and may be induced to behave less aggressively with a host than in home territory.

The general rule that you do better at home is not surprising. Statistics show that athletic teams win more frequently in their home town. The explanation is that suffering a defeat at home is a blow to a negotiator's self-image—hence, the increased level of aggressiveness by the host. Also, the host negotiator enjoys the legitimate right to manipulate the home environment by confident assertions in familiar surroundings, whereas the visitor is constrained from assertiveness by a need for caution in unfamiliar surroundings and by the inherent expectation that he or she be courteous and not offensive in the role of a guest.

An additional advantage for you in being the host is that your mind, filled with facts, law, strategy and tactics, will not be distracted with the need to adapt to new surroundings. Your memory will serve you better because of the many associations with different aspects of your surroundings that were formed during your preparation. Furthermore, your train of thought and calmness under pressure will be optimal because of your prior experience under similar situations in your own office surroundings.

In light of this, it is a good idea to hold a "getting acquainted" or "polishing up" session at the other party's facilities. If at all possible, be sure to bring the other party to your headquarters to negotiate the agreement in principle and other critical matters that subsequently arise. If you do, you increase the probability of a favorable outcome. If bargaining at your home base is not feasible or is firmly resisted by your opponent, then the next best thing is to meet on neutral grounds where no one will have the psychological edge.

If you are as shrewd as one-third of the executives that attend my seminars, you will turn the neutral meeting place into your home base without the other side even realizing it until it is too late. How do you do this? If the neutral place is a restaurant or hotel, make arrangements in advance to be responsible for the tab. Arrange for the maitre d' and the waiters to repeatedly and respectfully cater to your every wish and call you by your last name. Make sure that only you will have control over when cocktails, the meal and every other event takes place. Arrange for phone service at your table. Bring your secretary along to take notes.

The last thing you want to do is what the majority of my seminar attendees do, namely, share the expenses of the neutral meeting place. As soon as you do that, you lose the home court advantage. Furthermore, you lose the opportunity to be gracious and fulfill the other side's friendship and esteem needs. Taking care of the expenses and arrangements show that you respect the other side, you think the other party is important enough for you to take care of the mundane details yourself, and you really do care.

FUNDAMENTALS OF ARRANGING THE PHYSICAL ENVIRONMENT

Almost all physical characteristics of the meeting room (as shown in Figure 3.2) have either a beneficial or adverse effect on the negotiation. If you are the host, you should take great pains to arrange the physical environment to assure an informal, comfortable and relaxed atmosphere to reduce tension, conflict intensity and competitive instinct.

In fact, if the meeting room is your own private office, your image to strangers will reflect the image projected by your office. According to the science of psycho-decoration, your office layout, decor and furniture illustrate your personality.

In contrast to the harsh fluorescent lighting and highly reflective white walls of some offices and conference rooms, an intimate and friendly atmosphere can be best established by a combination of natural sunlight from the window and the warmth of yellow tinted light from standing and table lamps. Furthermore, such lamps—and other objects, such as flower vases, abstract sculptures and paintings—can be selected to facilitate informality and affiliative behavior. Apparently this is because they invite commentary and thus a psychological climate of social interaction.

With respect to the color of walls and carpeting, blue will not only prove relaxing for your guests, but will also convey the image of power and authority. Yellow is thought to be too frivolous and weak; beige and tan are fairly neutral; dark brown and gray are depressing; and red, although a warm color in small amounts, tends to excite and even frighten some people. Since white gives a sense of space and freedom, a good combination of colors for an office would be white and dark blue, with moderate accents of red. Tile and linoleum floors create a negative impression, and bare wood gives a cold feeling.

A handmade Oriental rug, an original painting, framed certificates and awards, an unusual and obviously expensive clock, multibuttoned call-director phone units and other phones throughout your office, seven-foot plants, a Harvard or Yale graduation class photo, a color TV set and video recorder and other grand possessions transfer to you an image of importance, authority and power. You are not a person whose time can be wasted. You are a negotiator to be respected. You will not tolerate negotiating games and ploys. Similarly, having your office in a prestigious building in the exclusive downtown section will also add to this image. Likewise, a receptionist and secretaries who dress and act professionally will supplement your image of professionalism and power. Other symbols of authority and power are a padlocked filing cabinet in your office from which you can remove material, during negotiations, that will be viewed as being of great importance and confidentiality, a private bathroom adjoining your office with a telephone next to the toilet, a private front office for your secretary that serves as a buffer between you and a receptionist, and a long distance between your office door and your desk through which your visitor must dodge coffee tables, chairs, sofas and indoor trees in order to make his or her way to you. A clock radio, bar, small refrigerator, exercise equipment, light dimmer and even a convertible sofa bed will suggest that you often stay late into the night—possibly sleep over because of the pressure of business—and may even be powerful in the sexual arena. The Chicago Playboy Headquarters is a typical example of a company that utilizes power and authority symbols to the fullest. Even the junior editors have plush, cork-paneled hideaways, many equipped with soft chairs, stereo sets and stunning secretaries.

You should have the largest and most expensive wooden desk possible to show that you are someone of substance and power. It will create a negative impression if it crowds the office or is made of metal. You should acquire a large executive chair with a head rest (but not if you are short, because it will make you look even smaller). The ultimate image maker is the electronic executive desk, first offered for sale in 1980 by New York's Hammacher Schlemmer. It has a built-in voice stress analyzer for detecting the lies of your guests, paper shredder for destroying evidence, cassette tape recorder for storing the lies, digital clock, AM/FM radio-alarm clock, telephone system that stores and dials numbers, electronic calculator, digital thermometer, color TV, and electric cigarette lighter. At the other end of the spectrum is the ordinary metal filing cabinet, which detracts from your authority.

One technique for immediately increasing your stature is the visual impact created by framing yourself behind your desk in a thronelike setting. This can be accomplished by having a picture window or a wall of glass directly behind you with a beautiful view, by centering a magnificent painting behind you or by having a suit of armor standing behind you if your office is furnished in antiques.

Articles such as books and magazines tend to create a formal atmosphere with a fair amount of tension. You should make sure that the room is very neat and that books and papers are shelved or stacked away inconspicuously. A tidy appearance also suggests that you're efficient and well-organized. Bulletin boards, wall charts and plans should be in unobtrusive places and never on the wall behind your desk. A clean, neat and uncluttered desk in a spacious room enhances your prestige and power.

It cannot be overemphasized that you should go all out for the comfort and convenience of your guests. They will be in a good frame of mind for receiving your proposal not only because of the intimate and relaxing setting but also because of your obvious thoughtfulness in taking the trouble of creating a pleasing meeting room atmosphere that implies respect for your guests and the importance you attach to their physical and mental needs. In this vein, you should assure privacy and no interruptions. It is impolite to take telephone calls while your guest is waiting. The bargaining room should be quiet. Not only will noise interfere with your concentration, but it will also make it difficult to hear and will invariably result in a high level of tension. There should be adequate air conditioning and ventilation. Your guest will also appreciate the availability of an adjoining conference room for caucusing. Having refreshments of various types brought in at appropriate times during the negotiation does wonders in establishing a friendly and cooperative atmosphere.

Scientific evidence indicates that seating arrangements influence the nature of informal social interaction. Scientists have found that cooperative behavior is optimal when the negotiators are between two and a half and four feet away from each other. Also, it has been found that sitting at right angles to the other negotiators or side by side is conducive to casual conversation and cooperative relationships. In contrast, opposite seating at spaces above four feet (face to face) tends to encourage competitive behavior. It has been suggested by researchers that round-shaped tables increase informality and feelings of closeness in contrast to square or rectangular tables. Arrange a group of comfortable, roomy chairs (to permit shifting of the body, which prevents fatigue and slouching and permits full breathing) around a circular coffee table in the midst of potted plants and trees and some unusual pieces of sculpture. This arrangement could go a long way toward making your guest receptive and cooperative.

Finally, you can gain a psychological edge over your guest by sitting in a higher chair. Nothing can dampen optimism more than having to look up at your host during the negotiation. Although the technique may be a carry-over from the days when kings sat high on their thrones, it still works and is utilized by judges, police desk sergeants, priests and others who tell us what to do from several feet above our heads. By looking down at your guest as you are presenting your proposal or pressing a point on a particular issue, you are able to convey an air of respectable superiority and omnipotence, which induces submissiveness on the part of the guest looking up at you.

To avoid too much intimidation and tension on the part of your guests, your chair does not have to be irregularly high. Your guest can be asked to sit down on a low, soft chair or sofa that he or she will comfortably sink into just a few inches above the floor.

Probably the ideal office is one that gives you the option to intimidate your guests if the negotiating circumstances call for such action, yet also allows you to sit with a guest away from your desk. Some examples in the intimidation arena are Harry Cohn, the tyrannical president of Columbia Pictures, who had a raised desk at the far end of a huge, elongated room, and Nelson Rockefeller, who had a trick desk with large pull-out steps that enabled him to walk right to the top of his desk during discussions with guests. Another common ploy is to have your desk arranged with a window in the rear so that the glare all but blinds your guest. Again, blinds can be adjusted at any time the host desires, thereby permitting him or her to intimidate the guest if the situation calls for it.

THE TACTIC OF INVITING AN AUDIENCE

A number of investigations show conclusively that audiences, especially those dependent upon the negotiation outcome, generate pressures toward loyalty, commitment and advocacy of their preferred positions. In light of this principle, it may sometimes serve a useful purpose to send some of your nonnegotiating executives along with your sole negotiator. This will assure that your negotiator will be psychologically constrained against making concessions too prematurely. Some labor unions do just this by conducting negotiations before an assembly of members. Under these conditions, a union negotiator would be hard pressed to make even a minor concession if it would mean losing status and respect in the eyes of the union members. Thus, you should seriously consider resisting the other party's attempts to have an observing audience present. With certain exceptions, it will generally work to your detriment.

If someone prevents you from having your audience at the bargaining table, you can circumvent the problem by having your negotiator appear before a press conference after the negotiation session or before a company manager's meeting to report on the session outcome. This tactic of accountability on the part of your negotiator will serve the same basic purpose as an audience present at the actual negotiation. The negotiator will be careful in strongly advocating the principal's positions and making minimal concessions, knowing that this will be reported to the news media or the company's management.

Another twist to strategic use of audiences is applying pressure through social influence. If an organization is highly visible to the public and is making unreasonable demands, you may be able to bring it back in line by publicizing its conduct. The threat of a loss of self-esteem and respect from the public at large and interested groups is a powerful weapon that can be wielded to your advantage. The master at this was Mohandes K. Gandhi, who strengthened India's independence movement by mobilizing public opinion against the policies of the British government. Another example is former Secretary of Defense Melvin Laird. A reliable source reports that Laird was a master of the inspired leak during the Nixon Administration: When he complained about a newspaper story, he was its probable source.

COALITION

Coalition may be defined as the unification of the power of two or more parties to increase their chances of obtaining a favorable outcome in negotiating with a common party. When you are in a weak position or you feel that your image is weak, find an ally or two. It has been scientifically shown that coalition increases bargaining difficulty for the other side, increases the time needed to reach an agreement and extracts a more favorable outcome than would have been obtained through individual negotiation.

Examples of coalition are the European Common Market, class action lawsuits on behalf of many plaintiffs, tenants' strikes, OPEC, joint ventures, the Uniformed Civil Service Workers and the National Association of Manufacturers. Apparently, coalition succeeds not merely because of the greater influence wielded by parties joining forces, but also because it creates a more complex situation and, in some instances, almost a desperate need by the other side to settle the matter before the dispute gets out of hand, especially when there is a possibility of further alliances.

In fact, coalition is so effective that it is illegal under many circumstances. Price fixing, reciprocal dealing, boycotting and exclusive dealing, for instance, violate the antitrust laws.

It should also be mentioned that coalition parties need not have totally common interests. In a patent infringement situation, the infringer's vendor can be turned into an ally by threatening suit and forcing it to pressure the infringer for assurances that the vendor will be held harmless in any litigation, or for a license from the patent holder. Another common example is when a department head and an assistant, both Machiavellians, plot to discredit and knock off an extremely competent executive who the supervisor sees as a threat to his job, whereas the assistant also wants to push his boss up or out. A more unique example is when the United States normalized relations with the People's Republic of China. The bargaining positions between the Soviet Union and the United States immediately changed, notwithstanding the fact that U.S. and Chinese goals do not coincide in many areas.

FAIT ACCOMPLI

Fait accompli is a French phrase meaning "an accomplished fact." This maneuver puts someone in a position of weakness as a result of action that has changed circumstances (see Figure 3.3). If you wish to acquire a company and negotiations get bogged down, buy a minority stock interest for voting influence and you can project the threat of further stock purchases to gain control. By making your determination and increased bargaining strength an accomplished fact, you are encouraging the acquisition candidate to be more reasonable in its buy-out terms.

A more subtle example of fait accompli occurs when you receive a contract proposal in the mail containing disagreeable provisions. Rather than set up a meeting to argue about the points of conflict, merely cross out the portions you do not want, sign the contract and send it back. The other party will be confronted with a fait accompli that puts him or her in the position of having to reject the deal and open up negotiations. There is a psychological tendency for the party sending the original proposal to accept the signed contract as an accomplished fact, rather than get into the problem of negotiation on changed items that are not terribly critical and that have the appearance of being nonnegotiable by you.

If you are the buyer, you can execute a fait accompli in numerous ways, including the following:

1. If there is a dispute over a bill, give the seller a "paid-in-full" check for an amount less than what is being asked.
2. Let the seller begin preliminary work or at least conduct extensive research and evaluation on the basis of an anticipated order. Then back off.
3. Serve the seller with a summons and complaint. Then talk.
4. Have a machine installed or at least delivered. Then reject it and bargain for better terms if the other party wants to avoid taking it back.
5. Tell the seller that the material delivered is already assembled or cut up. It can't be returned, and you can't pay.
6. Tell the seller you are insolvent or bankrupt. Ask if he or she will settle for twenty cents on the dollar.

Examples of fait accompli that can be implemented by the seller are the following:

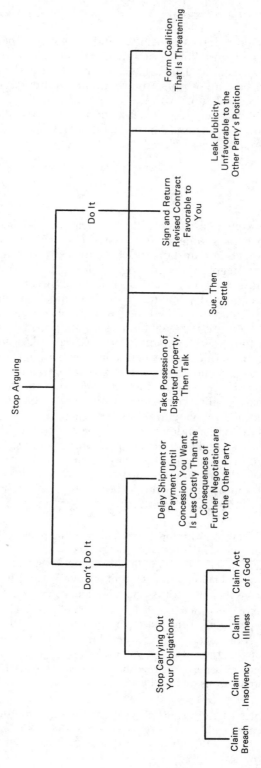

Figure 3.3. Initial considerations for fait accompli.

1. Pick up and repair the equipment you are servicing prior to agreement on price. Keep it if the buyer does not go along with the price you give.
2. Make a change in quality, quantity, price, delivery or some other key term when it is too late for the buyer to go elsewhere for his or her needs. Then negotiate.
3. Stop work. Then negotiate a new price based on unforeseen circumstances.
4. If the buyer phones to cancel the order, say it is already on the freight car or it was already modified to meet the buyer's specifications.
5. Tell the buyer you need a little more money to finish the job. Say that if there is no money there is no completion.
6. Remove the equipment from the buyer's premises without his or her authority in order to repair it at your own facilities. The buyer complains. You say, "I did it because I had to. It doesn't make any sense now to bring it back before the work is done."

Illustrations of how you can effectively maneuver your bargaining position through the use of fait accompli can go on and on. For instance, if a patent holder demands royalties or files suit because you are infringing, you can redesign your project so that infringement is eliminated or at least not as clear. Then you can bargain from a much better position. Another example is a partner who disagrees with you on a venture. Make a deal. If the partner still doesn't like the terms you negotiated, then say, "You tell him it's off." Another example is where your partner or colleague says, "I got caught. We'll have to cover up." (Without asking your consent first, your partner did something unethical [fait accompli] that was discovered.)

An up-to-date example of an attempted fait accompli is the September 1980 war between Iraq and Iran. For centuries the two countries have disputed their common boundary line along the Shatt al-Arab shipping lane, a body of water formed by the confluence of the Tigris and Euphrates Rivers, the area where civilization probably began. This one-hundred-mile channel is Iraq's sole outlet to the sea for its oil exports. Iraq's President Hussein asked Iran's Khomeini regime to relinquish complete control of the channel so that it could be shared equally. Khomeini spurned Hussein's demands for a border revision that would give Iraq more territory. When it became clear that Khomeini would not be releasing his fifty-two American hostages and hence would not have access to U.S. military supply and support, Iraq sent its forces into Iran. At the time this book was written, Iraqi forces already controlled a ten-mile strip of Iranian territory and much of the disputed waterway (the fait accompli).

Although Iraq at this point might be willing to negotiate from its new position of strength, its attempt at fait accompli may fail for two reasons. First, Iran's U.S. trained and supplied army has put up a much better fight than expected. Second, the Khomeini regime declared that Iran is waging a holy war against Iraq and will never accept mediation, reconciliation or discussion. In effect, Iran is not recognizing Iraq's newly won bargaining leverage and is giving notice that it plans to take such leverage away.

Iran's response to the attempted fait accompli illustrates one of the best countermeasures available against this tactic. Take your own aggressive action to offset the leverage the other party achieved with his or her initiative. Then trade off and negotiate. In the commercial world, your own aggressive action means starting a new lawsuit or filing a counter claim that is worrisome for the other side.

Chapter 4
THE THREE STRATEGIC POSITIONS IN EVERY NEGOTIATION

Most business negotiations fall into one of two broad categories. The first is a situation in which someone else needs you. For instance, your product or service is in demand. The second occurs when you are attempting to persuade someone to deal with you. For instance, you are trying to sell an innovative product or when you are seeking compensation from a company that has breached its contract with you.

Although the basic approach, as mentioned in Chapter 1, is cooperative behavior, there are actually three distinct approaches dependent on the two negotiation situations mentioned above (see Figure 4.1). In the first instance above, the key approach is a high aspiration level. In the second instance, the key approaches are enticement and threat. Cooperative behavior, as will become apparent in this chapter, is important for all three strategic positions.

THE STRATEGY AND TECHNIQUE OF ASKING FOR AND GETTING MORE THAN YOU DESERVE

Aspiration Level
Aspiration level affects the outcome of a negotiation. In the first instance, when you are being sought after, your best strategy is to take an extreme position with high or many demands. It is a psychologically and statistically proven fact that a negotiator who initially asks for more and offers to give less usually winds up obtaining more and giving less. The research offers a number of explanations for this phenomenon.

First, the bargainer making extreme initial demands obtains more time to assemble information about the other person's preferences and intentions. Second, the bargainer communicates expectations of proper treatment and no exploitation. Third, high demands demonstrate a firm conviction. Fourth, the extreme position has a tendency to lower the other

39

Figure 4.1. Initial negotiation strategy and tactics.

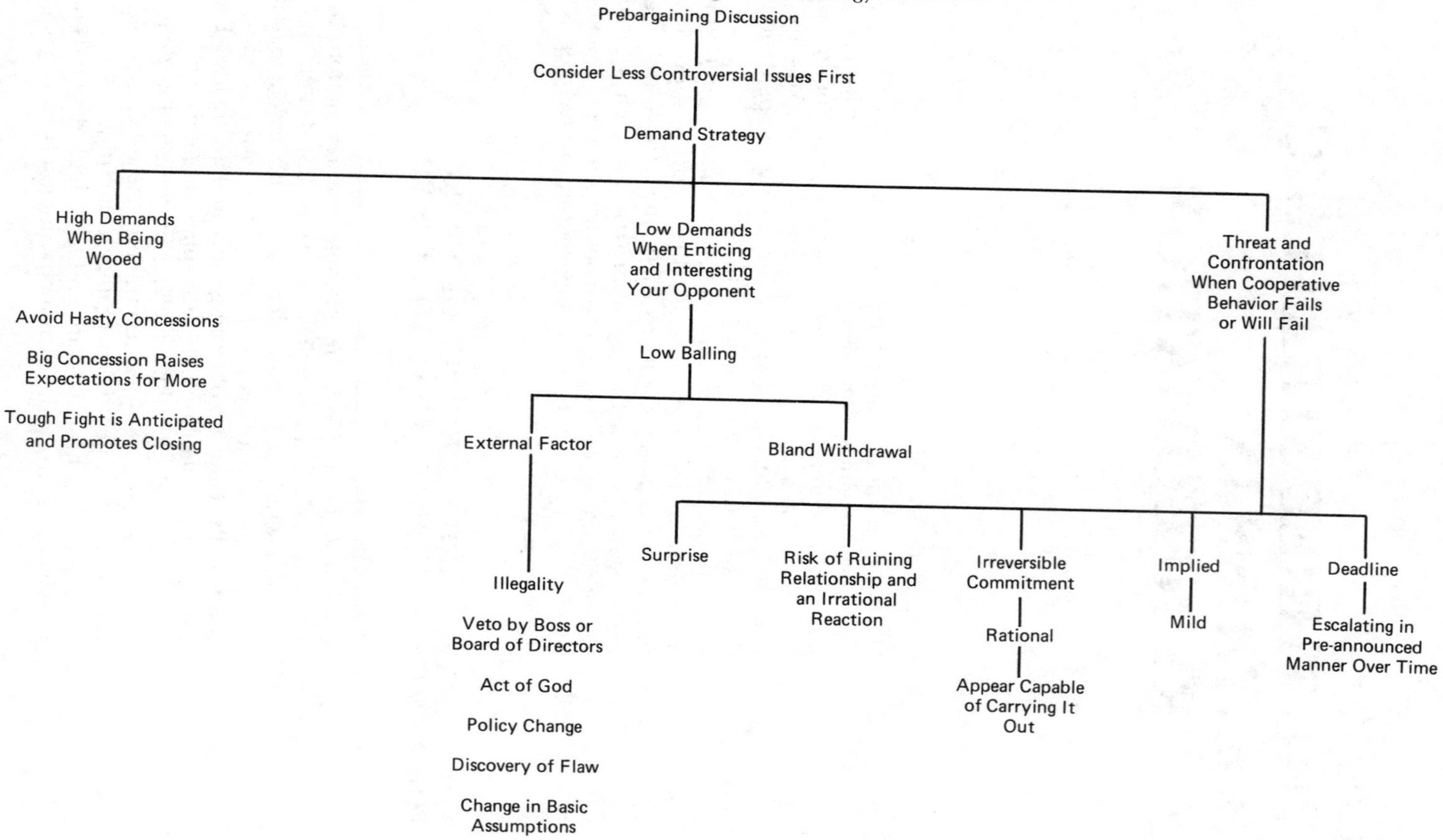

Prebargaining Discussion

Consider Less Controversial Issues First

Demand Strategy

High Demands When Being Wooed

Avoid Hasty Concessions

Big Concession Raises Expectations for More

Tough Fight is Anticipated and Promotes Closing

Low Demands When Enticing and Interesting Your Opponent

Low Balling

External Factor

Illegality

Veto by Boss or Board of Directors

Act of God

Policy Change

Discovery of Flaw

Change in Basic Assumptions

Bland Withdrawal

Surprise

Risk of Ruining Relationship and an Irrational Reaction

Irreversible Commitment

Rational

Appear Capable of Carrying It Out

Threat and Confrontation When Cooperative Behavior Fails or Will Fail

Implied

Mild

Deadline

Escalating in Pre-announced Manner Over Time

side's expectations. Fifth, high demands enable you to make concessions to satisfy the other party's need for accomplishment and control over his or her own destiny. In many instances, incredible as it may seem, after tough bargaining and many concessions received, a negotiator will appreciate the tough fight he or she had to put up and will be more satisfied buying something at $50,000 that was originally offered at $70,000 than he or she would have been if the seller had initially offered a price of $40,000 and had refused to make any concessions at all.

When using this strategy of taking an extreme position, you must be careful to skillfully communicate and establish the facts supporting the reasonableness of your maximum desires and minimum concessions so that there is minimal risk of turning the other party off due to a seemingly hard-nosed, rigid and unreasonable attitude on your part. Sometimes, the extremist approach backfires because the other party views the unreasonable demands as a threat to self-preservation.

There is an impressive body of evidence showing that factors that threaten a negotiator's honor, self-esteem, status or appearance of strength are likely to create intangible issues that may become more difficult to resolve or repair than the tangible issues for which the negotiation is being held in the first place. It has been shown that when a negotiator takes a position on an issue that is unreasonably demanding, resistant or punishing, intangible issues develop because of the negative implications of submitting to the adversary with a loss of face, public image and self-esteem. When intangible issues are raised because of high demands or unyielding behavior, the negotiator feels unjustly victimized and injured and is under considerable pressure to restore the balance or redress the insult with whatever threats and resistance may be necessary.

Serious consideration should be given to any demands before you call them nonnegotiable. You eventually want to convey the possibility of change on your part in order to keep the negotiation alive. Thus, make an offer that does not offend but must be refused. You will quickly find out what other party's thoughts, reasoning and acceptable terms are, especially when the party is talking candidly because no deal seems possible. In short, make others work for what they get.

Do not be in a big hurry to make major or even moderate promises and concessions. People don't appreciate easy victories, so don't be easy to get. Make them work hard for your important chips while making minor concessions, which show that you are a reasonable person and which make them feel that they may be overreaching in asking for more. Even the words "I'll consider it," constitute a minor concession. A big concession raises the other person's expectations for even more.

In fact, unless you know in advance that someone has a high aspiration level, encourage the other party to lay his or her demands on the table first. Sometimes, you will be offered more than you would have asked for. No matter how good the proposal sounds, do not accept it. The other party is probably still willing to make some concessions. Furthermore, he or she may feel foolish for giving away too much if you immediately accept. If the demands are very high, do not honor them with a counteroffer. Insist that they be reduced to something more reasonable. When the other party makes an important concession, be matter of fact about the logic of the decision. If you make a big deal about thanking the other party or the wisdom of the decision, he or she may have second thoughts about his or her blunder and renegotiate. If he or she refuses to concede on a major issue, do not assume that an impasse will result in a deadlock for the entire negotiation. Simply go on to the next issue.

FEAR OF FAILURE

Unfortunately, many negotiators lack the necessary self-confidence, courage and risk-taking attitude to take advantage of high aspiration strategy. Some people have an intense fear of failure. This type of individual is afraid to ask for too much in negotiation because of an undue worry of rejection or being the target of anger and scorn. According to Henry Kissinger, President Nixon dreaded meeting people in a position to rebuff or contradict him. This is why White House assistants such as Bob Haldeman played a dominant role as intermediaries.

Many negotiators go through their career never even realizing that they have a mediocre or low aspiration level. Following is a test that you can take to determine where your own aspiration level is and whether you need to change you attitude and negotiating strategy. You will probably want to rate yourself in the section that immediately follows the test before reading on here, because the following text will bias your current aspiration level feelings. Rate yourself from 0 to 5 for each statement, with 0 being *no* and 5 being *yes*. Put down your true feelings, not what you think the ratings should be, because there are no correct answers. An interpretation of your responses follows.

1. I have difficulty completing tasks successfully.
2. I feel uncomfortable about the formal education I had.
3. I recheck things even though I really know they were done right.
4. I enjoy the company of others much more than being alone.
5. I wish I could act more spontaneously more of the time.
6. I have qualms about meeting new people of either sex.
7. Sometimes it seems that no one ever wants my opinion.
8. The one word that best describes me in my childhood is *inadequate*.
9. I sometimes get so depressed about myself that I am unable to take productive steps to remedy the situation.
10. My sexual habits and fantasies are a source of guilt to me.
11. I regret not living up to my parents' expectations.
12. I do not get enough feedback at work to know that I am performing satisfactorily.
13. I often think self-condemning thoughts.
14. I don't have the right to criticize anyone because I have my own failings.
15. I would have difficulty looking into the mirror and saying, "I love you," truthfully.

16. I have doubted my parents' love for me.
17. I feel a sense of accomplishment from my work infrequently.
18. I accept and respect myself for who I am only when I am feeling great.
19. I have never been satisfied with my physical appearance.
20. I often worry what others are thinking about me.
21. I play down my achievements so as not to irritate others.
22. I would feel ashamed of staring with envy at another person's spouse or house.
23. I am conscious of being too materialistic.
24. I resent those who treasure their possessions.
25. I fear a highly visible position of leadership or achievement.
26. I believe that "A rolling stone gathers no moss."
27. When there are contradictory opinions, it is wise to refrain from tentative conclusions to test their validity.
28. I am prouder of my ability to solve difficult problems than my ability to unearth them.
29. It upsets me that I might be less capable than others think I am.
30. I fail to recall even one time when I wished another person dead.

You have a winning attitude if the sum of your ratings is below 15, and you could use some improvement in your self-confidence and esteem if you are between 15 and 30. Above 30, you are uncomfortable with greed, taking risks and the consequences of failure. In short, you have a passive and possibly a losing attitude, depending on how high your ratings added up.

If you happen to be shy, have low self esteem, be insecure, be constantly concerned about rocking the boat, or fear it is wrong to be greedy, these are all signs of low self confidence. It is not uncommon. One survey shows that four out of five college and high school students feel they were disturbingly shy for a large part of their lives. Almost half considered their shyness a current problem that needed to be overcome. A survey of corporate managers showed 59% had difficulty saying what they mean and 35% avoided people in general. The author's own survey of executives attending his courses indicates that the majority are uncomfortable asking for a lot more than is actually fair. Many of these executives were plain scared of being turned down or angering someone. Another study showed that 59% of corporate managers give in too easily to others. The first step towards increasing your self confidence and aspiration level in negotiation is to acquire an understanding of why you currently feel the way you do.

As you will find out in Chapter 6, people adopt one of four basic life scripts that influence their behavior from childhood until the day they die. The most common life script is the Not-OK person. This person feels inferior, not good about him- or herself, discouraged about things, and afraid of failure and rejection. Research shows that close to one-half of corporate management falls into this category.

Two major groupings of Not-OK people are based on the accommodation-oriented script and the conformity-oriented script.

Accommodation people learn to get positive strokes (recognition and good feelings) while still children by stroking other people first—or to at least stay out of their way if they do not stroke back. The Accommodators are nice to people, avoid pressure, controversy and other unpleasant matters, and often are found living in their Adaptive Child and Nurturing Parent ego states (see Chapter 5 for definitions).

Accommodators often are found running the personnel department, sales promotion department, house organs and other nonpressure positions. By nature, these people have a low aspiration level because of the importance attached to being liked by others, not offending others, not hurting others and being good to others.

The conformity-oriented person is even more concerned with good strokes. This person does not make waves, sticks to the tried and true, stays out of the limelight, avoids controversy and takes no action that has even a taint of risk.

Conformity people stick to the status quo and end up in banks, insurance companies and other businesses where changes come very slowly. Comformity people have almost no aspiration level at all because they are afraid to take a chance on anything of significance.

In general, the Not-OK person fears failure and rejection to the extent that he or she lacks the courage, ambition and self-confidence needed for a higher aspiration level in negotiation.

DEVELOPING SELF-CONFIDENCE

How do you change to an OK outlook and overcome inadequacies and poor attitudes? Following is a fifteen-step plan for dealing with self-doubt and developing a new feeling of power and confidence:

1. A simple technique called *programmed visualization* can be practiced ten minutes a day to develop a better self image. You picture yourself as a success, never thinking of yourself as failing and never doubting the reality of your mental image. Ideally, you should close your eyes, relax and force yourself to see yourself as superior to others, perhaps as a company president or in some other role that you hold in awe.

The mind always tries to complete what it pictures, and after a couple of weeks, you will find that some of your attitudes and actions are beginning to change. You may be more decisive, less aloof, less fearful of error, more aware that you are as competent as others and more willing to take chances because the intuitive side of your brain has gently led you to the success you visualize and want.

The president of a major corporation was once asked what he felt was the difference between him and those who didn't make it to the top. His answer was, "I have a better opinion of myself. Fifteen years ago I already saw myself sitting in this chair. There was no doubt in my mind that I would make it. When I started visualizing myself as the company president, I began to dress and act in a manner that was consistent with being company president. I had self-confidence. I knew I could do it."

Athletes likewise find that the most difficult part of their training is to hold onto the conviction that they can do what their competitors can't or what has not been done before. Once Roger Bannister accomplished this feat in his mind, he freed himself physically and broke the four-minute mile barrier. Once he eliminated this psychological block, other runners duplicated his feat. If you are a golfer, you can dramatically improve your chances of sinking the putt by confidently visualizing that this is going to happen prior to taking the swing.

2. Like the company president mentioned above, if you see yourself wearing expensive three-piece suits, walking around with an impressive briefcase and preparing reports with a portable dictating machine, then treat yourself to these symbols today. Your outward appearance lets other people know that you are successful and have a high aspiration level. They will treat you with respect, and you will make yourself feel at home with success.

3. Do not build up obstacles in your imagination. Cancel negative thoughts with positive thinking. Fear of failure, fear of rejection, fear of competition, fear of ridicule, fear of success and the like must be deflated by realistically studying the difficulty involved. These problems must be seen for only what they are and eliminated, not inflated by fearful thoughts.

4. When thinking about yourself as a success, you can make the mental picture very real and attainable by thinking backwards to the various stages you have gone through on your way up. Visualizing the lesser goals that you have passed will make you feel comfortable and at home with the idea of success.

5. Resist your inclination to hold others in awe and copy them. Nobody can be you as well as you can. Regardless of their confident appearance and demeanor, people are often as scared as you are and have the same self-doubts.

6. Make a true estimate of your abilities, and then raise that estimate by 10 percent. Force yourself to be optimistic about yourself, proud of yourself and self-respectful.

7. If you are a religious person, your faith in God can be most helpful. Whenever you become discouraged, consciously reflect on the following:

> With God for us, who can be against us? I can do all things through God who strengthens me. I am in God's hands. In short, put yourself in God's hands and believe that you will receive all the power you need. Affirm to yourself that "the Kingdom of God is within me" and that nothing can defeat you. "All things are possible to him that believeth." "If Ye have faith . . . nothing shall be impossible unto you." (Mark 9:23; Mathew 17:21).

8. If you still find yourself having problems with self-confidence, do not hesitate to seek guidance from a qualified psychotherapist. You will learn the origin of your inferiority complex and feelings of self-doubt. Through consultation and self-knowledge, your Not-OK attitude may eventually be eliminated.

9. You must force yourself to expect the best instead of the worst. This frees you from self-doubt so that you can pour your whole self into your endeavor and nothing will stand in your way. People are defeated in life not because of inability but because they do not wholeheartedly expect to succeed. Their heart isn't in it, and they haven't given all they've got.

For the next two days, intentionally speak optimistically about everything, including your job, your health, your spouse and your future. You will discover that you've been deluding yourself by saying you were "realistic" regarding your feelings and thoughts. You were simply being negative.

10. Choose an acquaintance, friend or family member who is the most positive thinker you know and get closer to that person. Absorb this person's spirit of optimism. When others express negative attitudes, make an active will to counter with optimistic opinion.

11. Consciously think about the cost of worrying in terms of time, money and health. You must decide just how much anxiety something is worth and draw the line about any further worry. If you diligently make sure that you learn from your mistakes, there is no need to worry about what has happened in the past. It is a proven fact in the medical profession that worry causes stress, which in turn causes sickness and even serious illness and death. Many people worry simply because of the uncertainty that may happen. If you make a conscious effort to analyze the situation and determine the worst that can possibly happen, quite often you will be relieved because you can accept the worst and maybe even prevent it. Finally, quite often there is no need to worry about criticism, even when it is given unfairly. Unjust criticism is often a disguised compliment.

12. If you perceive an opportunity, do not assume that someone else probably already thought of it. Pursue it. Quite often you will surprise yourself that you were indeed first. For instance, the University of Wyoming received the actor David Niven's papers simply because they were the first to ask.

13. You must force yourself to think about yourself and look out for yourself regardless of how friendly and fair the other person seems to be. Always remember that there are four types of people you will be dealing with. The first type lets you know from the outset, either through words or actions, that he or she is out to get all of your chips, and this individual will attempt to do just that. The second type says he or she is not interested in getting all your chips. This person wants a win–win negotiation, with you getting everything "that's coming to you." He or she then attempts to grab all of your chips anyway, just like the first type. The third type tells you that he or she wants a fair deal and is not interested in getting all your chips— and sincerely means it. However, through bungling or because of warped personal standards for rationalizing what is right and wrong, this individual, like the first two types, still ends up trying to grab all your chips. The fourth type tells you he or she does not want your chips, really means it and makes no attempt to get them because this is the one who actually has a low aspiration level. Unfortunately, even professional negotiators have a difficult time weeding out the fourth type from the other three until well into the bargaining sessions. Thus, always assume the other guy is out to get all your chips. If it turns out you are wrong, you will always have time at the end, before closing the deal, to return some of the chips you have grabbed so that it is not a lopsided win–lose victory.

14. Ease your discomfort and reluctance to act in unpleasant situations by using an agent, as already illustrated in connection with President Nixon's use of intermediaries. In general, you can increase your aspiration level when you do not have to face the person you are disagreeing with or hurting.

15. Realize in advance that you will lose or fail a certain percentage of the time. Do not take it personally. These statistics apply to the best negotiators. In fact, the person who always manages to close the deal is probably a failure because he or she doesn't demand enough.

THE STRATEGY AND TACTICS OF ASKING FOR LESS AND GETTING MORE

In the second instance, where the other party has to be persuaded that it is advantageous to deal with you, a different approach to position strategy is called for. Here, you want to entice and interest the other person in what you have to offer before stating the ultimate price wanted and the specifics of other critical terms. By using omission and face-saving negotiating techniques, more profitable deals can be consummated than can be obtained from putting all your cards on the table regarding your demands and critical terms before whetting the other's appetite for what you are offering. The ethical dilemmas posed by the following tactics will be discussed at a later point.

A common technique used in this situation is "low-balling." The vendor makes a sales pitch to the purchasing agent, stressing all the benefits and profits to be obtained by replacing old machinery. The vendor suggests or even clearly states a "low-ball" price, which is unreasonably favorable to the purchasing agent, to entice him or her to evaluate the new machinery and continue with further negotiation toward purchase.

Once the agent is convinced that it makes sense to replace the old machinery because the vendor is offering a good buy, the vendor puts the next stage of the gambit into operation. This involves either the ploy of the "external factor" or "bland withdrawal."

The "external factor" is a tactic that makes use of a fictitious or actual change in circumstance that is beyond the control of the negotiator and that changes the previous position, commitment or concession. This is illustrated when the purchasing agent fills out a purchase order for new machinery, only to be told that the price has just been raised and there is nothing that the vendor's sales person can do about a price increase that came from above. The theory behind low-balling is that if the increased price is still reasonable for the new machinery, the purchasing agent will still go through with the buy because a lot of time and money has been spent in evaluation and negotiation and there is still a chance for a fair deal.

Another external ploy that may be used is the factor of illegality. Upon receiving the purchasing agent's purchase order, the vendor's marketing manager (the sales person's boss) apologetically replies to the purchasing agent, expressing surprise at the prices that were quoted. The marketing manager then explains that the price quoted is below that which is charged to other customers for the machinery. It would be price discrimination and a violation of the Robinson-Patman Act. This good guy–bad guy team technique establishes credibility and a logical reason for raising the price of the machinery. The purchasing agent will undoubtedly go along if the deal is still fair. Other circumstances that can be used as an external factor are:

1. You let the prospective purchaser of your business, product or technology wait in the reception room at the same time competitors are there. This justifies and makes believable your request for more money or better terms than already verbally agreed upon.
2. Your engineering department discovers a defect or tolerance inaccuracy that makes the agreed-upon price too high if substitute components that meet your incoming quality control inspection cannot be supplied in time.
3. You tell the seller that management has decided to make the equipment in house, and then you proceed to buy it at a lower price than originally agreed upon that is attractive in comparison with the cost of building the machine yourself.
4. You notify the seller that management has decided to drop the product line you have been buying components for because of heavy losses, and then you proceed to negotiate a more favorable purchase price.
5. You tell the buyer that the purchase order will have to be rejected because it looks like there will be a strike and existing inventory is being diverted to long-term customers. After you tell the buyer that these preferred customers are paying a premium, the buyer equals or betters the increased purchase price, and you reluctantly give in due to the buyer's pleas for equal treatment.

The ploy of "bland withdrawal" involves innocently backing away from a previously stated position or commitment. It may be used in place of the "external factor" in a situation where the vendor initially implied or indicated a low-ball price proposal in a vague or ambiguous manner. After the purchasing agent accepts the machinery at the price mentioned, the vendor informs the purchasing agent that there must have been some misunderstanding. The vendor explains that such a low price could not have been mentioned and simultaneously whips out the price sheet showing the higher price of the machinery. This adds credibility to the fact that there really was a misunderstanding and the vendor never offered the price the purchasing agent heard.

WHEN AND HOW YOU ACHIEVE GOALS THROUGH THREATS

There is a third business situation in the situation where the other party has to be persuaded to deal with you that arises from time to time and calls for a totally different approach to position strategy. It involves a situation in which a competitor or other party takes action or refrains from taking action that can cause irreparable damage to your business. In this situation, a threat of force or undesirable action on your part if the injurious conduct is not immediately stopped makes sense.

Scientific research shows that threats tend to increase the likelihood of immediate compliance and concession. A threat is most effective if it is combined with a deadline for compliance plus communication or conduct showing a renunciation of alternatives, or a statement to the effect that you will not back out of the threatened action.

An illustration of the strategy of confrontation, last discussed, will now show the use of "surprise," "irreversible commitment" and "deadline." You place a phone call to the president of your sole supplier of a profitable product that you distribute. You just learned that this manufacturer is supplying the same product to another distributor in violation of your exclusive distribution agreement. You announce to the president that, after disassembly and a thorough study of the product being shipped to the other distributor, you conclude it is substantially the same and therefore in violation of the agreement. You then announce that suit will be brought within fifteen days if the president does not terminate the new distributorship. This surprise phone call will have a shock effect, and the ultimatum and deadline will pressure the president and staff into frantic reevaluation of the situation to determine if this is a bluff or the beginning of an expensive lawsuit.

Studies conducted by investigators show that the use of promises tends to elicit a general liking for the communicator, while the use of threats tends to elicit hostility and is a short-term tactic that can ruin an important relationship. Thus, confrontation should only be used when you know that cooperative behavior will fail. Such hard-line tactics should not be used in dealing with others in your own company. A threat is not only less effective than a promise, but also less effective than no communication at all. The carrot is better than the stick, but even better than the stick is no stick at all. One of the common but little appreciated drawbacks of a threat that seemingly produces the desired results is subtle sabotage and abuse by the party that feels pushed around—for instance, the small supplier that reduces component quality and service for the bullying corporation in ways that are not realized or cannot be detected or the employee who misplaces files.

Research shows that the drawbacks of a threat may be reduced if the threat is implied rather than spoken, mild rather than massive, and rational rather than emotional. The greater your appearance of having the means to carry out a threat, the less forceful you have to be and the more cooperative you can still seem. In fact, a vague threat is more worrisome to the other side than spelling out specific consequences because uncertainty and the unknown can conjure up fearful scenarios.

A threat involving a series of actions increasing in seriousness and potential harm against a party is probably the most credible and effective threat technique. When the first few actions are executed, the likelihood that everything else will be done also becomes very real. This is the approach President John F. Kennedy successfully used against the Soviet Union during the Cuban missile crisis, wherein the blockade was one of seven steps that ultimately would have led to major military conflict.

The least effective threat is the emotional outburst that is out of proportion to the problem—for instance, General LeMay's threat of a nuclear attack on North Vietnam, your boss's threat to axe you if you miss one more Saturday meeting and the vendor's threat to cut off shipments if your payments are even one day late. These threats show a lack of cooperative behavior.

Chapter 5
THE PSYCHOLOGY
OF PRESENTING
YOUR POSITION

Regardless of whether a negotiator is cognizant of the fact, negotiations are almost always conducted on three basic levels of communication: the subconscious level, the emotional level and the level of reason and logic. Consistently high achievement in negotiating can be obtained by mastering all three levels of negotiation so that, whether a complex negotiating proposal or a single point is involved, the negotiator's position can be communicated in a manner that is simple, attractive, suggestive, enthusiastic, truthful, fair, logical and personal. Thoughts communicated in this manner will:

1. attract and hold a person's attention;
2. create interest;
3. extinguish suspicion and build up credibility so that the other party will trust you;
4. appeal to the other person's feeling of individuality and identity by showing that he or she is not being treated as an anonymous representative of a firm or as just one invisible negotiator in a sea of many;
5. fan the other party's desire to pursue the deal;
6. result in his high memory retention; and
7. ultimately motivate a decision to make the deal after investigating its benefits and risks and determining that alternative deals or courses of action are not as beneficial.

Communicating your position on the subconscious, emotional and logical levels involves the following:

1. Keep it simple. Convey major points only; use common language and unambiguous words; be specific; avoid burdensome information requests; avoid discussing the other person's motives; and employ repetition of key points.

2. Be attractive, fair, enthusiastic and truthful. Start with reason for communication; stress similarities; give pros and cons; deliver the side that is desirable first; make liberal use of adjectives and examples; avoid argument; understate, discuss issues that are easy to resolve first; avoid criticism; emphasize rewards; entertain; cooperate; give choices; minimize monetary liability; and open with prebargaining discussion.

3. Use suggestive techniques. Exploit sensation transference and subconscious motivation through illustrations, charts, stationery, handwriting, organization, product mock-ups, slides, movies, packaging, symbols, designs, coloring, your appearance, dress, voice, furniture, smell, seating, spacing, eye contact, smile, and other props and body language.

4. Be logical. Facts, assumptions, hypotheticals, analogies, deduction and inductive reasoning must be fault free.

5. Be personal. Satisfy emotional needs for: physiological comfort and relaxation; safety and security in terms of economic, social and career position; friendship and belonging (affiliation); esteem in terms of respect, praise and recognition; aesthetics in terms of fairness, balance, order and harmony; knowledge and understanding through cooperative information giving; and self-actualization through problem solving and participation.

6. Apply PDC (personality dependent communication). Strategy and communication determined by ego state (adult, critical parent, nurturing parent, natural child, manipulating child, adaptive child), life script (confident/OK–OK, superior/OK–Not OK, inferior/Not OK–OK, hopeless/Not OK–Not OK), communicating style (thinker, feeler, intuitor, sensor-introvert, extrovert), and behavior attitude (comformist, accommodator, compromiser, performer).

MAKE IT SIMPLE AND PRECISE
FOR IMPACT AND RETENTION

The most logical and sound reasoning will be of little value if it is not communicated in simple and precise terms. You should set forth only the points needed to encourage the action you desire. You should be informative with regard to supporting details only to the extent necessary to make your offer clear. Not only should you avoid giving a complex presentation, but you should also guard against asking for substantial information. Not only will such a data request present a bothersome burden, but it may also create the feeling that you are not being sincere in your desire for a deal. If a person feels that you are simply trying to "go to school" and get some confidential or competitive information under the shield of negotiation, he or she may break off the negotiation. This is a fairly common concern of acquisition candidates in merger discussions, so make sure that the information you request is relevant to the negotiation at hand.

In short, ask yourself if your presentation clarifies the situation or complicates it. Have you eliminated all points that do not objectively describe or set forth the problems or benefits you are about to discuss? Have you shortened a long list of issues into something more manageable for yourself and not overwhelming for the other person? Will you consciously avoid all statements and implications describing the other person's attitude, motive and intention (which would distract him or her from being receptive to your presentation no matter how simply put)?

Simple language should always be the rule regardless of whether or not the negotiation is on a high level of sophistication and importance. The more complex and difficult the issues, the more basic your language should be. The five hundred most commonly used words in the English language have 14,000 different meanings. Words and expressions also mean different things to different people. So remember, the simplest and most unambiguous words and phrases that can achieve your objectives should be used. Winston Churchill said, "Old words are best; short words are better!"

Some of the most common and serious errors committed by negotiators involve their use of words and terms having broad or ambiguous meanings. If you mean 70 percent, then do not say "substantial." If you mean $55,000, then do not say "in the fifties." The other side will automatically assume that you are agreeing to the lowest value or element in the range you suggest. In short, be precise and use specific terms. Do not say something is large if you can give exact measurements. Help the other person gain a better mental image of what you are trying to convey.

Sentences should also be simple, with the subject first, the verb next, and the object last. A sentence should be five to thirty words long, averaging about fifteen words, so that one is not forced to backtrack to search out meanings and relationships. Where commas would appear in written text, you should pause in order to give the other person more time to understand what you are saying. Keep your modifiers close to the words they modify. ("He searched the records in May, where he discovered the flaw." This should be replaced by "In May, he searched the records, where he discovered the flaw.") Use the active voice instead of the passive for conciseness and impact. ("He signed the purchase order before the amendment," instead of "He had signed the purchase order prior to the amendment.") Avoid splitting compound verb forms. ("He bottled up the bill in committee," instead of "He bottled the bill up in committee.") Do not use different words just to keep from using the same words twice in a sentence or paragraph.

Simplicity is more important than variety at the risk of confusing, and repetition serves to emphasize what you are saying and promote good memory retention. Dr. Martin Luther King, Jr., repeated phrases frequently for emphasis. (For example, in his last major speech in 1963, delivered at the Lincoln Memorial in Washington, D.C., he said, "I have a dream" numerous times with great effect.) Highlights of your claims and conclusions should be repeated at the end of your position statement in an exuberant manner. This is important in view of scientific evidence showing that repetition of a message leads to learning and acceptance, and people remember best what they hear last.

Even when you use simple words and simple sentences, the possibility for confusion is great because you may be saying one thing and think you are saying something else, while your listener may think you are saying another thing. This form of confusion is illustrated by a common quote used in the legal profession: "I know you believe you understand what you think I said, but I am not sure you realize that what you heard is not what I meant." Voltaire put it very nicely when he said, "Men use thought only to justify their wrong doings and speech only to conceal their thoughts."

TACTICS THAT MAKE A TOUGH POSITION ATTRACTIVE

Your presentation should be executed in an attractive manner that is pleasing, not offensive; that appears to be fair and consider the pros and cons, not suspicious; that is cooperative and friendly, not argumentative or hostile; that emphasizes the positive, not the negative; that stresses the familiar, not the unknown; that is democratic, not dictatorial; that is understatement, not exaggeration; that promotes progress by starting with easy issues, not the frustration and stalemate promoted by hard issues; that is complimentary and encourages agreement, not offensive or demeaning, discouraging cooperation; that reveals reward consequences, not punishment or a threatening outcome; and that entertains and is enthusiastic, keeping the other person glued to your thoughts, not that is dull.

Friendship and Respect

Two of the most common strategic mistakes made by negotiators are quickly getting down to the business of negotiation at the first session and stating one's position and demands in a competitive manner.

The first meeting, or at least much of it, should involve prebargaining communication for a frank discussion and mutual understanding of each party's needs without any position taking. Scientific evidence indicates that discussing issues, rather than taking positions, will resolve them more quickly and effectively because of cooperative behavior and absence of aggressiveness and competition.

Scientific investigators found that bargainers who are deprived of an opportunity for prebargaining contact took longer to reach agreement, remained further apart on the issues involved and were less yielding than those given the opportunity for prebargaining discussion. Some scientists explain that in the absence of prebargaining communication a competitive atmosphere tends to develop, and negotiators have a tendency to view communications as coming from opponents and as unreliable, misleading and intimidating. It was found that under such conditions negotiators do not trust each other and communicate more lies, threats and ultimata than in a situation where there is prebargaining discussion.

To sum up, the clinical and empirical research conducted shows that early initiation of cooperative behavior by means of prebargaining communication tends to promote the development of trust and a mutually beneficial, cooperative relationship. Early competitive behavior, on the other hand, in the form of position statements, tends to induce mutual suspicion and competition. Thus, if you are trying to interest a distributor in taking on your new product for nationwide sales and the initial meeting is at your offices, make sure the meeting room will provide an informal, comfortable and relaxed environment. Assist the distributor's negotiator with travel plans and book reservations at the local hotel to establish a cooperative climate before the meeting even starts. Show your product to the distributor. Talk about its great selling features. Field the distributor's questions about the product. Steer away from raising issues and stating positions on such critical terms as price, termination and minimums and other matters to be negotiated later. These should be discussed after a cooperative relationship based on trust has been established.

You will succeed more by emphasizing the rewarding consequences of an approach that you favor than by dwelling on penalties and undesirable contingencies. The story is told that Charles Schwab, the first chief operating officer of a company to receive an annual salary exceeding a million dollars, came across some employees in one of his steel mills who were smoking below a sign that said "No Smoking." Schwab gave each one a cigar and said, "I'll appreciate it, boys, if you smoke these on the outside." Instead of criticizing them or pointing out their mistake, which they well knew, and instead of threatening them if he saw it happen again, he rewarded them for complying and doing it his way. Reward is a powerful tool that satisfies a person's esteem, friendship and aesthetic needs.

Common, everyday statements can be turned around to emphasize positive consequences. ("If you will give me your undivided attention in going through this analysis, I think we will both get home for dinner tonight.") The reward does not have to be something tangible that the other person gets. Your message will encourage positive action, even when the reward and consequences are for your benefit, if the other person feels that the outcome is fair. In other words, the reward is his or her satisfaction in doing the right thing. Instead of saying, "You didn't do . . . ," say, "I need . . . so that I can accomplish . . . and my boss will be happy with me." Not only does a message that conveys rewarding consequences encourage the desired behavior because a need is aroused, but such a message also is remembered best.

If you sound final in your statement, it is as if you are talking down to the other negotiator. "This is the only way it can be done," puts him on the defensive, promotes argument and gives the impression that you are more knowledgeable or a better person. It is better even to put your conclusions on a tentative basis and imply that you are still looking for a better approach if there is one. If you give your conclusion as an understatement rather than as a forceful declaration of your opinion, it will be given more serious consideration and will be more readily accepted. One way of avoiding opinion that takes too much for granted and offends is to ask appropriate questions. "Do you think it would work if we tried this?" "Do you have any approaches in mind that will work?" "Is there another way to handle this so that . . . ?" In short, understatement and talking up to the person convey a candor and elicit confidence.

If you have to call attention to a person's mistake and cannot do so with the question technique, then you should still attempt to correct him or her indirectly to avoid resentment. One indirect approach is to make the correct statement as if you are paraphrasing what was said in order to give the other person credit for it and take for granted that that is what was meant. You allow the other person to save face and fulfill his or her esteem need at the same time.

When presenting your information, assumptions and ideas, you must show that you are giving equal consideration to all the pertinent facts and issues, good and bad. If it is perceived that you are doing this in a frank and friendly manner, it is logical to believe that you have a commitment to negotiating a fair deal and that you can be trusted. If you are not sure of the facts or the proper inferences to draw, let the other person know that your remarks are based on uncertain thoughts and leave the door open for discussion.

Be *for* a point of view, not against. "Why can't we put in this clause?" fails in motivating the desired behavior because it is expressed negatively and assumes rejection. "Let's put this clause in," is expressed positively as a cooperative activity.

Almost any message will be more attractive if you begin with praise and honest appreciation. Compliment the other person; make him or her feel important; explain why you picked him or her to talk to; emphasize your feeling that he or she will be able to grasp your explanation without any difficulty at all. A person who has your respect and an inflated ego will not easily become argumentative and will remain alert and receptive to your presentation.

People tend to ignore anything that conflicts with their beliefs, practices and customs. Any proposal that appears too aggressive or threatening to the status quo will probably meet with rejection.

Procedure

Thus, your message should place stress on similarities of position in contrast to differences. When more than one message is to be delivered, the most desirable for the party should come first. When you give the pros and cons of the matter, the viewpoint you favor should be brought out last for impact and memory retention.

In light of the research conducted, it is best to take up the less controversial issues first to evoke an initial "Yes" response, which will promote a forward-moving open attitude of acceptance. If a major issue is taken up first, it could easily spawn intangible issues resulting from hard-nosed positions and defensive behavior. Agreement on initial issues in a friendly, problem-solving climate satisfies the needs of the negotiators for accomplishment, control, power and fairness with each other and should result in subsequent cooperative behavior when the critical issues are taken up.

The research shows that a bargainer who makes even minor concessions early in the game is more likely to elicit cooperation later on. Thus, if there are issues on which you can proceed without much detriment, by all means do so. You will be in a better position psychologically when considering other issues of more importance to you. By making concessions, you are telling others that they are strong, worthy and tough, thereby increasing the likelihood of positive concessions in return on the issues of real importance.

If you start off with easy-to-settle issues, even controversial issues can be resolved quicker and more in your favor if they are tied to issues on which agreement has been or can be easily reached. Associate each new point with something pleasing related to the bargainer's position or a point on which prior agreement has been reached.

Proper description and use of adjectives and examples will bring a matter alive and help form a mental picture for impact and memory retention, in contrast to a general statement in the abstract. We read in the papers that millions are starving in Cambodia and Vietnam and forget ten minutes later. If we pick up a magazine and see just one color photo of a starving child with all his bones sticking out, crying and holding onto his mother's leg with skeletal fingers, it makes a permanent impression in our minds. Nothing is truer than the Chinese proverb "One picture is worth ten thousand words." When we want to know if someone understands us, we ask, "Do you see?" not "Do you hear?" and he or she says, "I see what you are talking about." In short, "seeing" is "understanding," and painting a picture with words is the next best thing to having one, especially when we remember that the average American has an eighth-grade language comprehension level.

Too many people fail to make a persuasive case because they give a choice between something and nothing. As famous sales expert Elmer Wheeler said, "Don't ask if—ask which." Give someone a choice between something and something, not a choice between accepting and rejecting your proposal.

When discussing money, do whatever you can to minimize the actual liability involved while maximizing the value to be received. Speak in terms that are attractive. Examples of making proposals seem more attractive are pennies a day instead of $200 for the year, a half-percent more instead of $5,000 more, funny money such as amusement ride tickets and casino chips instead of hard cash, and a few minutes more per day instead of several thousand hours more for the entire labor force per year. Casually say "a million" instead of emphasizing the amount when you say "one million dollars" or write $1,000,000. Your wording and voice tone can indicate your feelings about whether the amount is a lot or little for the agreed-upon consideration.

If the party is looking at your deal as a long-term investment, concentrate on the future value in order to raise your front money demands. "Just think, Mr. Bradley, you will probably get $50,000 in six or seven years for an investment that is only one eighth of that." If the party is mainly interested in immediate satisfaction, you should concentrate on extracting your pound of flesh in the future. This, of course, is the cornerstone of the loan-sharking business, but loan sharks do not have a monopoly on the idea. For instance, the largest savings & loan association in the country had a mortgage clause that required the payment of six months' interest on the original loan if the house was sold before the mortgage was paid off. Home buyers, in their excitement of getting present satisfaction, did not worry much about the burdensome penalty in the future.

A common mistake is to start talking to the other person before telling him or her what it's all about. Always try to specify the purpose of your communication. Leave as little as possible to the imagination. People fear uncertainty and quite often expect the worst, especially when approached by a supervisor or other person that can injure them. They will be more receptive when they know at the outset why you are talking to them.

Enthusiasm

It is important that your reasoning be delivered in an enthusiastic manner. This reinforces your sincerity and also attracts and holds attention.

When you speak, you determine the attitude of your hearers toward what you say. If you are complacent, they will be complacent. If you are enthusiastic, they will catch the flavor and spirit of your delivery.

How do you convey enthusiasm? Start off your presentation quickly, with confidence, looking straight at the listeners. Start off with a powerful lead. State what you will accomplish and make the other party take notice. Use emphatic gestures, revealing your attitude in addition to merely giving facts. Speak naturally and spontaneously as if you were speaking to a single friend instead of a group of strangers and as if you expected that friend to immediately respond and talk back to you; vary the pitch of your voice and the rate of speaking, spending more time on words you wish to make stand out, and pausing before and after important ideas. The story is told that a country minister asked Henry Ward Beecher what to do when an audience went to sleep on a hot Sunday afternoon. Beecher replied, "Have an usher get a sharp stick and prod the preacher." It is enthusiasm that makes the listener receptive and attentive.

There is nothing that dampens enthusiasm and credibility more than the person who reads a presentation from notes. Prepare an outline beforehand. Memorize key words from the outline that will serve as your cues for going from one topic to the next and knowing what you want to say. Also, do not attempt to memorize your presentation the day before the meeting. Most people can only work effectively at memorization for a short period of fifteen minutes or so. After that, your attention and concentration wane while your frustration increases. Memorization will take place almost effortlessly if you work on it a couple of short time periods a day for several days before the meeting.

The Open and Close

The most important parts of your presentation are the opening and closing statements, especially if you are talking to a group of people and do not have the closeness and attention of a one-to-one exchange. The beginning is important because your listeners are fresh and easy to impress. The end is important because people remember best what they hear last. It is therefore advisable to give much thought to your introduction and finish. They should not be left to chance, as is so often the case. For example, how many times have you heard the speaker end with, "Thank you," or "That's all."

There are a number of approaches you can use to attract immediate attention. You can arouse curiosity by asking a question related to your talk. ("Would you like to hear how one person made $100,000.00 for two hours' work?") You can say something humorous. You can start off with an interesting news item. ("You may have read in yesterday's paper about the appointment of Gloria Streisand as president of General Electronics. She received her MBA only eight years ago and started off as. . . .") You can begin with a specific illustration or case, which tends to lend an air of seriousness and reality to your talk. ("The Techno Control Corporation has just developed a computerized wall timer that can control a number of electric circuits while the homeowner is away. The home marketing company is interested in distributing this device to construction and contractor firms. A meeting has been set for. . . .") You can show an exhibit, which can be either a chart, picture or item related to your talk. You can open with the impact of a profound quotation (see Chapter 6). You can open with a simple explanation of how your topic affects the common interest of the listeners. ("Almost every U.S. company that has introduced products abroad has had its share of flops because of improper or misunderstood market research. You can increase your batting average by. . . .") You can start off with a shocking statement. ("From 1966 to 1976, the confidence of the American public in people heading up major companies dropped from 55 percent to 16 percent, and specifically for advertising agencies, from 21 percent to 7 percent.") You can casually comment on something that has just happened or been said at the meeting if it ties into your presentation.

Your closing statement can be the same as one with which you would end a memorandum, summarizing and briefly outlining the main points you covered. You can appeal for action. You can pay the listeners a sincere compliment by making reference to their organization, state or other aspect of common interest. Do not throw out the standard compliment that sounds shallow and insincere, such as, "You've been a great audience." You can also leave them laughing or with a biblical quotation when appropriate.

SUGGESTION ON A SUBCONSCIOUS LEVEL

Suggestion on a subconscious level is one of the most effective methods of communication because it bypasses people's inhibitions and defense mechanisms. The average person transfers the sensation or image received from outward appearance to the subject being viewed, whether it be judging people by their looks or clothing or a product by its shape or package. Also, marks, symbols, signs, shapes, designs and colors are more effective than the written word in motivating feelings and actions favorable to your position.

Thus, it becomes important to supplement your presentation with illustrations, charts, product mock-ups, slides, movies and other visual props. They will make your position statement more interesting, vivid and dramatic. Also, people tend to place more credibility on what they see than on what they hear. These little extras will help suggest favorable characteristics for whatever product, service or idea you are trying to promote.

For instance, if you are trying to persuade a distributor to take on a new product you are in the process of developing, your presentation should include illustrations, slides on product features and market potential, a prototype with packaging and an impressive-looking prospectus covering the production, sales and financial aspects of the business venture in colored bar-graph format. Such a presentation will enhance the acceptability and marketability of the product because it suggests a finished product that has already been market tested and that is ready for commercialization, even if this is not actually so.

Just as the package covering the product acts as a nonverbal signal of the product characteristics and features, your dress and your appearance convey impressions that can affect behavior toward you. For instance, if you look as though you know what you are talking about, you will project that image, and you will be carefully listened to. On the other hand, a wrinkled collar, a loose necktie or rolled up shirtsleeves may project a tired, weak image, regardless of whether you are inwardly full of enthusiasm for holding a discussion. Another way to turn someone off is to extend greetings to new visitors in the executive suite without your jacket and tie on, if you are a man. Nobody likes to be taken for granted.

Just as important as your clothes is your physical condition. A trim person makes a better first impression than an obese or slovenly one. Likewise, a person with acne, scars, warts or other unsightly physical features projects an initial image of someone who cannot even take care of him- or herself if it is apparent that the physical problem is curable, correctable or capable of being hidden or camouflaged. On the other hand, it commonly happens that the physical remedy is worse than nothing at all. A bald man will have a better image than the man who wears a poorly made hairpiece.

Subconscious suggestion for a winning image has much greater application than just a good appearance for you and your product. Many successful restaurants always seem to have a Rolls-Royce, Mercedes, Cadillac or Lincoln Continental conspicuously parked in front. This is not because the owners of the automobiles give big tips for quick getaways. The real reason is that these restaurants want the public to know that they cater to discriminating people and that their food has to be excellently prepared, even for the owners of jalopies. Another technique of image building through sensation transference is to have the most prestigious law and accounting firms represent you. A further symbol of power and authority is to have your name printed on company stationery. If you are entertaining more than a half-dozen colleagues and their wives at home, engage a professional bartender to serve drinks and add class to your image. Likewise, always pick up the tab at lunch. This indicates that the investment is cheap next to the time being consumed, you are confident the other party will enter into the deal with you, and you are projecting friendliness and respect for him or her as a person, and an important person. An even more effective image builder is to pick the other party up by limousine for the luncheon or meeting. Another suggestion is to take him or her to the most exclusive restaurant in the city and tip the waiter to say, "Good afternoon, _____. Shall I bring your usual?" You can also arrange to be called and to have a phone brought to your table in the dining room. After lunch, if it is feasible and the deal is important, whisk your guest to your countryside retreat by helicopter.

As with vision, the sense of hearing can be used for subconscious suggestion. Certain words make the heart beat faster, whereas others cause the breathing rhythm to change and even alter perspiration. "Fear" words cause the blood vessels to contract, which is the reason a person turns pale when frightened. Words suggesting flight, escape and running actually affect one's feet, as does music. Likewise, certain words can be employed to relax a person and reduce and eliminate anxieties. Still other words can create a subconcious compulsion to become excited. People throughout history have been known for their careful choice of words to create frenzy and mass hysteria.

These same suggestive words, when rapidly flashed or mixed in with bland music, create a powerful subliminal communication. At the present time, dozens of department stores in North America use sound mixers in their music systems to repeat as much as 9,000 times an hour at a very low volume the words "I am honest. I will not steal." These words are barely audible to shoppers, yet the chain stores claim that theft has been cut by more than one third. This kind of subconcious communication is being used by psychologists to help people lose weight, stop smoking and overcome phobias like the fear of flying. One real estate office used subliminal communication to motivate its sales personnel with such subconscious messages as "I love real estate, and I will prospect for new listings for clients each and every day."

The negotiator's arsenal of subconscious motivation does not end with sight and sound. Smell is probably the most basic of the five senses. It greatly affects how you feel about yourself and everything around you. It can convey far more emotionally potent messages than what you see and hear.

Companies have synthesized aromas ranging from baking ham to fresh pizza. These odors are packaged in aerosol cans along with time release devices that periodically fire a burst of scent. Certain odors or perfumes are so powerful that they can actually bring about the release of sex hormones from the pituitary gland and affect ovulation and conception. One of the components of such odors is musk, which is chemically related to the male sex hormone, testosterone. Studies have already shown that men wearing a steroid musk scent are found more attractive by women.

With pollution all around us today, the science of biometeorology shows how even proper ventilation, temperature, humidity, air pressure and ions can be used for subconscious motivation because of their impact on the hypothalamus, pituitary, nervous system, thyroid and other body parts. The ion generator is particularly of interest these days because it emits negatively charged particles or ions into the air. People who breathe

the ionized air are said to feel more alert, energetic and comfortable. The restaurant chain Trader Vic's has installed Israeli-made ion generators, and the employees do not go home tired any more; they go home refreshed and say that the customers are more pleasant. Studies indicate that negative ions remove pollution, bacteria and viruses from the air, whereas positive ions cause serotonim to be released in our bodies, causing irritability, headaches, tension and nausea.

Even persons' names are suggestive of an initial image. Donald E. Morgan III conveys stature, importance and power. Donald E. Duck, named in the early 1930s before the Disney character became famous, produces amusement, surprise, curiosity why the name hasn't been changed and a certain degree of disrespect. Almost as bad, and sometimes worse, are many names involving no coincidence, such as Donald Will Fail, Teddy Baer, Jack Ash, names that create confusion as to sex, such as Cyril, Kermit, Jackie, Pat, Percy, Mavis, Carroll and Allister, and names that tarnish a person's image because of occupation, such as Jonathan Blood, D.D.S., Jess A. Shark, Esq. and C.U. Dead, M.D. Even common names such as Arthur, Hubert, Maurice, Otis, Stanley, Hildegarde, Isabel, Norma and Zelda have unfavorable connotations.

Foods have hidden meanings and can be used to your advantage when you are serving refreshments to your guests. Soft, creamy foods like yogurt, pudding and ice cream are enjoyed by many adults because of the subconscious feeling they are being loved, protected and comforted as they were when babies. Soft foods also relax people and give them a full, satisfying feeling—especially ice cream, which is associated with reward for good behavior, stemming from childhood years. Crispy foods like potato chips, corn chips, cookies, crackers and peanuts allow people to act out aggressive and active feelings, especially when they are in a passive situation, whether it be listening to someone or watching TV. Avoid giving your guests crumbly foods like certain cakes that fall apart because they are difficult to handle and will make your guests feel they are out of control and at a disadvantage in the environment you are providing. Firmness is an important food characteristic to most people. At the other extreme, you will see spongy cakes and other feminine foods at ladies' tea parties. This is not what you want to offer in your office or conference room.

PDC (PERSONALITY DEPENDENT COMMUNICATION)

Delivering logic in a personal manner takes into account the other person's needs for physiological survival and comfort, security and safety, friendship and belonging, esteem, self-actualization, knowledge and understanding and aesthetics. Although these emotional needs have been listed in descending order of importance, when the more basic needs can be fulfilled without much difficulty, the satisfaction of the other needs takes on more importance.

A person's psychological needs may sometimes overshadow the rational factors of price, value, quality and other basic contractual terms with respect to negotiating progress. The more basic the need you can use to advantage, the greater is the probability that you will achieve your goals.

By recognizing and analyzing a person's ego state, life script, behavior attitude, and communicating style, you can identify the type of person you are dealing with and his or her specific psychological needs. Whether someone is in the Adult, Critical Parent, Nurturing Parent, Natural Child, Manipulating Child or Adoptive Child ego state; whether he or she is a Thinker, Feeler, Intuitor or Sensor; whether he or she is a Conformist, an Accommodator, a Compromiser or a Performer; whether he or she has a confident, superior, inferior or hopeless attitude; whether he or she is in the role of a rescuer, persecutor or victim; and whether he or she is an introvert or an extrovert are all factors that shape his or her personality. People's personalities, which define their emotional needs, determine the best way of presenting your position and dealing with them. This is what PDC (personality dependent communication) is all about.

Once you pinpoint a person's ego state, life script, behavior attitude, communicating style and primary needs, you can adjust your own personality in order to use PDC on the level in which he or she is transacting feelings. A primary use for PDC is in dealing with others in your own organization because of the daily or weekly opportunity you have to understand what makes them tick. However, after reading Chapter 7 of this book, you will know how to detect various personalities so that the benefits of PDC can be obtained at the very first meeting with another negotiator.

Chapter 6
SCORING
HIDDEN VICTORIES

This chapter deals with the strategy and techniques of communicating messages on a subconscious level. Stress is also placed on identifying and controlling suggestive messages you are presently unaware of conveying.

COLOR AS A NEGOTIATING TOOL

Although a person's defense mechanism may react to a trademark or theme that suggests favorable product characteristics, he or she is not conscious of the further effect that color has. The individual's concerns that the message being received is not accurate, is deceiving or does not fulfill his or her needs are overcome through the proper use of color to suggest favorable characteristics associated with the product or deal being presented.

The proper color will produce the warmth, stimulation, closeness, intimacy, visibility, attraction and attention, memory retention, legibility, coolness, relaxation, distance, spaciousness, preference (according to consumer type), symbolism or psychological effect desired. The characteristics of each color discussed below can be seen at a glance in Figure 6.1.

What Colors Do
The color red produces the greatest association with or feeling of warmth, stimulation, closeness, intimacy, aggressiveness, sensuality, youthfulness, good health, positiveness, restlessness, rage, desire, excitement, courage and sex. Red particularly appeals to and attracts women and has a high preference rating in general in our society. Red has a strong appetite appeal, which is the reason why so many restaurant interiors are red. Red strongly suggests vibrance, beauty and good health, which is the reason for its use in cosmetics. Red is so stimulating that entering a red room will actually increase a person's blood pressure and pulse. Such exposure can cause overstimulation and irritation because of the brilliance of red or the

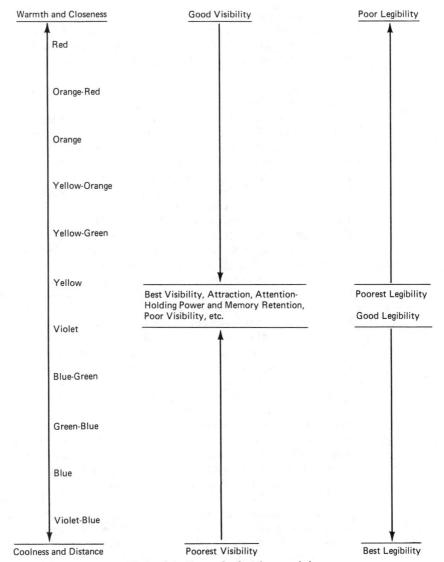

Figure 6.1. Chart of color characteristics.

primary hue of magenta red. In symbolism and psychology, red and magenta red are associated with all strong emotions, whether love and hatred, patriotism and revolution, a red-hot deal, a company in the red, a red stop light, a red-blooded American or a red complexion.

Red and magenta red colors also have good visibility from a distance, attraction and attention-holding power, and memory retention characteristics. These colors have low legibility as a printer's type color or for handwriting.

Pink, a tint of red or magenta red, has many of the favorable attri-

65

butes of the more brilliant red colors. However, because it is more subdued than red when mixed with white, it has less power, stimulation, aggressiveness, visibility and legibility. Pink is generally associated with food, warmth, good health, festivity, sweetness, tenderness and poetry, as well as cosmetics and femininity.

Orange-red produces the warmth, stimulation, closeness and other qualities of red to a slightly lesser degree than red; however, it has greater visibility, attraction and attention-holding power and memory retention characteristics than red and magenta red, but lower legibility. Orange-red, particularly a tint of orange-red, such as peach, is associated with food, warmth and good health. Peach especially has a favorable sensation transference for cosmetics and is one of the most preferred colors in our society. On the other hand, deep tones of orange-red may lend a luxury or deluxe sensation to consumer appliances because of the association of these colors with bronze and fine wood grains and finishes, such as black walnut. Otherwise, orange-red is a low preference color in our society.

Orange and yellow-orange produce almost as much warmth, stimulation and closeness as the orange-red and red colors and have greater visibility, attraction and attention-holding power and memory retention characteristics, but less legibility. Although not as potent, orange and yellow-orange have favorable connotations for food, good health and cosmetics.

Although yellow-green gives less feeling of warmth, stimulation and closeness than the colors already discussed, it has greater visibility, attraction, attention-holding power and memory retention characteristics, but lower legibility. Although yellow-green is otherwise a low preference color in our society, it rates high in association with warmth, nature, food and health and is appropriate for products in these areas.

Yellow produces a feeling of warmth, stimulation, closeness and intimacy, but not to the extent produced by the colors mentioned above. However, yellow has the greatest visibility, attraction and attention-holding power and memory retention characteristics and lowest legibility of all colors. The primary hue of yellow is so brilliant that it can produce eye strain if there is too much of it to look at.

Bright yellows are associated with energy, vitality, well-being, cheerfulness, intellectual appeal, sunshine, nature and food. Dark shades of yellow are associated with sickness, disease, indecency, cowardness, jealousy, envy, conceit and treachery and are the least popular of colors.

Because yellow conveys an image of cheapness, a number of discount retail outlets and generic food packagers are painting their stores and their products yellow and are having a great deal of success as a result. Many firms are coloring their "Save" and "Sale" signs yellow with similar success.

Violet-blue, which we know as the color purple, produces the greatest feeling of coolness and relaxation, distance and spaciousness, and tranquility and serenity. It has the greatest legibility of any color and is less visible, has less attraction and attention-holding power and results in less memory retention than the warm yellow, orange, and red colors discussed above.

Possessing the exact opposite qualities of the warm, positive hues, violet-blue has a cold, negative effect that can actually physiologically depress a person exposed to too much, with accompanying sluggishness due to a drop in blood pressure and pulse. As expected, violet-blue is a low preference color in our society. However, the violet-blue color symbolizes dignity, exclusiveness (associated with royalty) and distinctiveness (for example, in the Purple Heart). It is generally effective in marketing to persons who have achieved maturity, wisdom and satisfaction. If people were to associate the color purple with descriptive words, it would bring to mind the following: *stately, rich, pompous, impressive, courageous, virile, spiritual, noble, enigmatic, dramatic, aristocratic* and *dignified*. As with all the blue and violet colors, purple has a negative effect on one's appetite, exactly opposite to the effect produced by the warm colors.

The color blue produces almost as much coolness and relaxation and distance and spaciousness as purple, has almost as poor visibility, attraction and attention-holding power and memory retention and has almost as much legibility.

Blue has a high preference rating in our society. Deep blue, which we call navy blue, has a high preference among men. Blue is associated with distinction (for example, the first-prize designated by the blue ribbon), nature, pureness, cleanliness, the sky, dreaminess, the sea, depression (having the "blues"), isolation and passiveness. Blue shades and tones are used effectively for hardware items, steels and other materials that must be of high quality, strength and reliability, as well as for instrument cabinets and front panels.

Blue-green and green-blue (turquoise) colors also produce coolness and relaxation and distance and spaciousness, but to a lesser extent than the blue and purple colors already discussed. They also have slightly better visibility, attraction and attention-holding power and memory retention, but poorer legibility. They are high preference colors in our society; however, green-blue has a low preference for men, yet is preferred by women over navy blue. Blue-green is not popular in connection with food products, and green-blue is a first-class color for jewelers to use because of its association with precious things.

Violet produces less coolness and relaxation and distance and spaciousness than the other cool colors discussed above, but it is more visible, has greater attraction and attention-holding power and produces greater memory retention but less legibility. Violet is a low preference color in our society and is associated with introspection, meditation, mystery, melancholy, affliction, resignation, the occult, the exotic, sweetness, coolness and being retiring.

The color green produces no noticeable warm or cool effect because it is a product of equal parts of the primary hues of green-blue and yellow. Although neutral, green is unconsciously associated with food, nature, forest, growth, freshness, callow youth, immaturity and safety (arising from our traffic light system).

The color brown can be earthy, solid, firm and warm, as well as somber and sad. A brown tint or beige is associated with food and good health and produces favorable sensation transference for cosmetics. Brown colors can also convey the impression of quality wood and finishes.

The color black optically reflects little or no light and is even more of a depressant and has even more negative connotations than purple and blue (such as in blackballing, blackmail, black-listing and black magic). Black brings to mind sorrow, death, secrecy, terror, formality, darkness and an atmosphere that is subdued, depressing, solemn or profound. As expected, black has a very low preference rating in our society.

Black tints and gray are noncommittal and sedate. These shades are associated with old age, passive resignation, humility and restrained excitement.

The color white reflects nearly all light and produces an irritating glare, yet it symbolizes purity, virginity, cleanliness, peace, innocence, truth and delicateness. Otherwise, white is a very low preference color in our society.

Needless to say, gold and silver colors give the image of quality and reliability as well as distinctiveness (as with medals), exclusiveness and luxury.

Using Color

A shade (the addition of black to a color) or a tone (the addition of white and black to a color) reduces the color's visibility at a distance, increases its legibility and gives a greater impression of security and a sense of heaviness. A tone or a tint (an addition of white to a color) reduces the color's warmth and increases its distance and spaciousness. Tinting a color makes it seem more delicate and light in weight. Indeed, when looking at the balanced blocks of Figure 6.2, we automatically expect the right block to go up and the left block to go down.

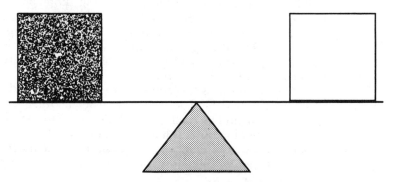

Figure 6.2. Which block will drop?

Color impressions and preferences will vary with different classes, groups and cultures. For instance, deep shades rate much higher in preference with men. Women prefer delicate tints and tones. Persons with many emotional outlets or with the ability to purchase emotional satisfaction prefer light tones and tints, whereas others, such as low-income consumers or those who lack education or those who have limited emotional outlets, prefer the purer vibrant hues of high visibility and warmth. This is particularly true in cities where the underprivileged are starved for stimulating colors to liven up their environment, especially green, which compensates for the lack of grass, plants and trees. Children in primitive cultures normally prefer the purer, stimulating hues, such as red and green, but not yellow, notwithstanding its great visibility. Cool colors, tones, shades and tints of colors do not appeal to children in underdeveloped civilizations because their attraction is basically symbolic and identified with psychological feelings having meaning to adults in civilized society. The classical example of variation in meaning is the color white, symbol of purity in the western world and symbol of death and mourning in the Asian culture.

Each primary pigment reflects exactly two-thirds of white light and absorbs the other third, which is a primary of light and the complementary color to the primary pigment. The primary pigment and the primary color light are complementary because they reflect the full gamut of colors, which is white, and they are physically, optically and psychologically balanced and do not conflict, clash or disharmonize. Pairs of complementary hues are yellow (primary color) and violet-blue (equal amounts of magenta red and green-blue), orange (two parts yellow to one part red) and blue (one part magenta red to two parts green-blue), orange-red (equal amounts of yellow and magenta red) and green-blue (primary color), red (one part yellow to two parts magenta red) and blue-green (two parts green-blue to one part yellow), magenta red (primary color) and green (equal amount of green-blue and yellow), and violet (two parts magenta red to one part green-blue) and yellow-green (one part green-blue to two parts yellow). Each of these hues consists of a primary color of pigment and a primary color of light (which is a secondary color of pigment).

Two pure complementary colors should not be adjacent each other since their brilliance is hard on the eyes. However, if one complementary color is deeper than the other, then the other complementary color will have greater visibility and attraction power than it normally would have alone, against a neutral background or a background consisting of some other noncomplementary color. Thus, the suggestive powers of one color can be accentuated by using its complement. For example, a tint or light tone of orange, which is a beige, on part of an instrument housing will emphasize the cool accuracy and reliability of the blue equipment.

The complementary colors discussed above provide the strongest contrast and are shown at a glance as opposite colors of the twelve-pointed star in Figure 6.3. Two alternate or "harmonious" colors, such as blue and violet-blue, however, need additional contrast, which is provided by the color on the star opposite the middle of the two—in this case, yellow-green.

Adjacent colors, such as blue and violet, greatly lack contrast and are visually difficult to separate. On the other hand, triads of color formed by a triangle on the color wheel—orange, blue-green, and violet-blue, for example—are so rich in contrast that they must be used with caution to maintain unity. Tetrads of opposing colors, formed by a cross—red, blue-green, yellow-green, and violet, for example—are gaudy.

No color ever stands alone. It must be viewed in relation to the surrounding color or colors. Stronger results are obtained from a light color on a dark or black background than from the reverse. A light color on dark

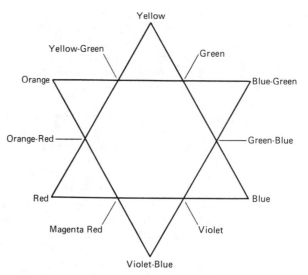

Figure 6.3. Complementary color star.

appears larger than it really is; it seems to radiate in a glowing blur. The hue tends to wash out and become weak and whitish. A white background, on the other hand, will strengthen the color or a light hue.

White or light-colored printing on a black background illustrates the illuminating effect of light on dark. The radiant effect will call immediate attention to the type, but it will also make it more difficult to read.

The reverse of this situation is also true. A spot of dark color appears almost black on a light or white background. On black, however, its hue will be more noticeable and more brilliant.

Everything else being equal, red dominates all other colors. Red is striking on either a light or dark background, it it is a poor background color for anything except black and white.

Yellow, on the other hand, is a satisfactory background for all other colors, except white. Blue, while better than red, is a less usable ground than yellow.

Because of the physical way by which blue is focused in the eye, it appears to recede, particularly in regard to red, whose focal-length characteristics make it appear to advance, almost seeming to move up from a surface. A blue dot on a red background looks like a hole in the red, but a red dot on a blue background seems to sway over it.

In addition to the effect of colors and combinations of colors, the texture and type of surface that the colors will appear on must be considered for total impression on the viewer. A color's message will convey different images depending on such variables as gloss, roughness, lighting, material used and the item being colored. For instance, for a deep red on a plastic component, you will convey cheapness and unreliability if you print with black lettering, and the component has a dull finish. On the other

70

hand, a glossy finish with white print will make the plastic component appear rich and of high quality.

Although black has a very low preference as a color, it can play the important role of making adjacent colors more vibrant and beautiful while at the same time producing a narrowing effect. Thus, a black gown will make a woman's complexion look richer and her figure appear more slender. White, which also has a low preference when used by itself in relatively large areas, can make adjacent colors more appealing, not by contrast, but by illumination because of its great reflecting power.

A color will be highly preferable for people who are subjected to an excessive amount of the color's complements. Thus, farmers almost always paint their barns red because of the unconscious desire to counteract the excessive green to which they are exposed in order to add balance to their lives.

Sometimes noncomplementary colors adjacent to one another can also produce a favorable psychological effect because of tradition, conscious symbolism or other social significance of the colors. For example, red, white and blue suggest a real American product.

PACKAGING YOURSELF: THE EXECUTIVE'S WARDROBE

How you look and what you wear have immediate impact and can make a lasting impression on people who meet you. A three-piece suit stereotypes you as an executive with authority, credibility and likeableness. The tie itself is a symbol of respectability and responsibility.

In general, the darker your suit, the more authority it conveys. However, a black suit is too powerful and has negative connotations and even funereal overtones. A dark blue suit will give you high credibility and a strong authority image. The solid dark gray suit conveys credibility and authority with people of the upper middle class, but it has negative impact with the lower middle class. The medium blue suit is positive with both classes, but the medium gray suit again is only positive with the upper middle class. The light blue and light gray suits are positive with both classes and, although all right for television, they have a negative effect on public audiences. Dark brown suits are negative with the upper middle class, neutral with the lower middle class and negative before the public on television. On the other hand, beige suits are proper for the businessperson.

The best suit patterns, in descending order of authority conveyed, are the pinstripe, the solid, the chalk stripe and the plaid. The dark blue and gray pinstripe suits with narrow vertical white stripes give excellent credibility and authority with people of the upper middle class, but are negative with the lower middle class. They are excellent suits for addressing the public, but not for television because the stripes jump all over the place if there is reception trouble at home, reducing concentration and attention on the part of the viewer. Medium gray and medium blue pinstripes convey the same image, except that they are neutral before the public.

The best suit materials, in descending order, are wool, polyester and wool blend, texturized polyester and polyester and cotton blend. Wool does not snag, fits well, retains its shape, is resilient and is more durable than any other fabric. Knit suits snag, bag, stretch, shrink, heat you up and generally look lousy. Cotton and linen suits are comfortable in warm weather, but wrinkle within hours. Corduroy and denim suits are the least conservative and belong in the fashion fields. Also avoid suits with other materials, such as nylon, rayon, mohair and silk.

Your suit pants should be positioned slightly above the navel, exactly horizontal to the ground. Studies show that lower-middle-class men tend to let their pants droop, hang from the hips, and drop lower in front than in back. This sloppy image certainly detracts from your authority.

Likewise, you hurt your stature if your jacket and sleeve lengths are too long or short. With your arms straight down along your sides, you should curl your fingers under the bottom of the jacket and feel the jacket bottom just fitting into the curl. The end of the jacket sleeves should be about five inches from the tip of your thumb. Your suit jacket should be plain, with no fancy or extra buttons, unusual stitching, flaps on the breast pocket, patches on the sleeves or belts along the back.

Studies show that you are not taken seriously when wearing short-sleeved shirts, which are symbols of lower-middle-class workers. Long-sleeved white shirts and blue pinstriped shirts create the highest credibility and authority for dealing with top management. Pink, pale lavender, red, bright yellow and other colors that are gaudy or are considered feminine should be avoided. In general, the shiny, dark, harsh and bright shirts are associated with the lower middle class, whereas the white, pale and subtle shades give the upper-middle-class image. You should also make sure your shirt is lighter than your suit to avoid that "gangster" look.

In general, the closer the stripes, the more acceptable is the pinstriped shirt. Stripes more than one-quarter inch apart and wide stripes should be avoided. The darker the stripe, the more acceptable it is. Multicolored stripes may make a shirt more of a sports shirt than a business shirt.

The best materials for shirts are the polyester and cotton blends, which wrinkle very little. Although the look of a good quality, well-tailored cotton shirt can't be beat, it wrinkles too quickly. Also avoid knit, silk and shiny shirts, especially the "see-throughs."

If your shirt is pulling at the buttons when you are sitting, it is fitted too tight, and you will look like a slob of little substance. Likewise, make sure your shirt has enough buttons down the front to avoid the shirt riding up and the last button slipping out above your pants, with your shirt spreading out, exposing your undershirt or your belly.

If your collar is too tight, a common phenomenon among executives who have gained weight, it will wrinkle and look bad over your tie. Senior managers, who are beginning to lose weight, tend to wear their collars too loose. Also, a short collar on a neck that has developed wrinkles or on a long neck emphasizes the neck. The same applies to a man with a short neck who buys high collar shirts and gives himself the image of a turtle.

The end of your shirt sleeve should be just slightly below your wrist bone and about one-half inch past your suit jacket sleeve. The executive whose shirt sleeve sticks far beyond the end of the jacket or remains completely hidden within the jacket detracts from his professional stature and image of power.

Your shirt should be devoid of pockets, decorative pleats, different-colored thread and colored or fancy buttons.

The bottom of your tie should stop at your belt buckle. The tie lining and material must provide sufficient substance and body to avoid easy wrinkling and slippage of the knot. Silk and inexpensive polyester ties can slip quite readily, and you will find yourself continuously tightening your knot as the day progresses. You must also make sure that your tie knot is not too small or too large and bulging from the space provided by your shirt collar spread. Since tie pins and clasps are passé, you should choose a tie with a tab on the back of the large end into which the smaller end may be slipped so that it does not stick out sloppily.

The best materials for ties are silk, polyester, polyester and silk blends, wool and cotton, in descending order of desirability. Linen, acetate and rayon ties should be avoided because of wrinkling, durability and other problems. At present, ties at the widest end should be in the three-and-one-half to four-and-one-half inch range.

The solid tie is the most versatile because it will go with so many different suit and shirt patterns. The polka-dot tie or other tie with an evenly spaced repeating pattern is the most elegant tie you can wear. The background color of the tie should match or contrast with the suit color, and the dots or other pattern should pick up the color of the shirt. Generally, the smaller the dot or other pattern, the more sophisticated the tie. The traditional polka-dot tie is dark blue with white dots. The repeating diamond pattern, as with polka-dot ties, is also sophisticated and is probably the best tie for a man in an authority position because it conveys a conservative upper-class image without turning off the lower-middle-class person. The next best acceptable tie pattern is the "rep," which is a diagonally striped tie. The paisley is the sports tie of the upper middle class and should not be worn to serious business meetings. You should avoid anything gaudy and faddish, including ties with large symbols or big pictures. You should avoid black ties, purple ties, and bow ties. A person is not taken seriously when wearing a bow tie; some people will not trust him, and many will think that he is not responsible or not important.

Your shoes should be black or brown, not untraditional colors and not patent leather and other artificial surfaces that belong in the fashion industries. The wingtip and other plain lace shoes are the traditional footwear you should choose from. You should avoid shoes with shiny metal accessories, tassels, high heels and other decorations that detract from your professional image. Because people tend to look at your shoes when they are not looking at your face, the image that your shoes convey will stick in their minds. Your socks should be dark and not droop below the calf so that your skin is exposed when you cross your legs.

Coordination of the various components of the business wardrobe is as important as selecting the proper individual components. The basic rule in the well-coordinated business suit is that a pattern that travels in one direction is not put next to a pattern that travels in another direction because the lines will clash. The conservative dresser will normally have only one pattern in a suit, whether it be the tie, shirt or jacket and pants. Thus, with a pinstripe suit, which has a vertical pattern, one would wear a solid shirt and tie. If one is wearing a "rep" pattern tie, one will wear a solid suit and solid shirt. If you are going to have more than one pattern, make sure it is separated by a solid color even if the patterns do not clash. Thus, if you may wish to wear a pinstripe suit with a polka-dot tie, you would detract from your authority image by wearing a chalk stripe shirt instead of a shirt with a solid color matching the color of the polka dots.

ACCESSORIES AND PSYCHOLOGY

Too much or the wrong type of jewelry will give you a negative or even effeminate image. Avoid heavy or ornate belt buckles. Gold or silver pens and pencils in your vest pocket definitely add to your stature, as do a gold vest watch and chain. If you prefer to wear a wristwatch, a plain gold watch with a gold or expensive leather band is acceptable. The more intricate the watch, the thicker the watch, the bigger the numbers and hands, and the more sophisticated the watch's functions, the lower is your image of power and authority.

The large pocket secretary wallet that can only be carried in your suit pocket is an upper-middle-class symbol. Your importance is also enhanced if the wallet is made of expensive, dark, rich brown leather and is not bulging full of junk.

Likewise, a dark, rich, brown leather attache case that is plain with no conspicuous decorations is acceptable. The bulkier the case, the less importance you carry, with the lowest power status being a large boxlike piece of luggage such as that carried by a salesperson to demonstrate samples. You will convey even greater authority if you carry merely a thin leather portfolio. Even better, carry nothing at all. The most important people are at a business meeting because of what they think, not because of reports, contracts and other file information that a messenger can carry. If you can come into a negotiation empty handed together with an assistant who carries perhaps a thin brief and a secretary lugging a briefcase, you will immediately have the image of a $100,000 plus executive. As a last parting comment, if you must have an attache case, avoid the color black because it lowers your status.

In the winter, you should wear rich brown leather gloves that are thinly lined to avoid a bulky look.

Camel hair and dressy blue cashmere overcoats give a soft, rich appearance. Beige and blue are the most acceptable colors for topcoats. Beige is the color of the upper-middle-class raincoat; blue is acceptable, and black will endow you with an air of unimportance. It would be best to avoid fur collars, suede and leather in your outerwear.

Sloppy hair, light hair, ears that stick out, a thin face or a round face are all characteristics that reduce your image of importance. Each of these features can be camouflaged with some thought or guidance from a barber or professional makeup person. For instance, if you have blonde or red hair, do not pick up these colors in your clothing. If you have funny ears, mask them as necessary with your hair. In general, long sideburns are for the rock set and fashion industry, not the business world. If your hair is easily disheveled by the wind outdoors, consider wearing a hat. In fact, a hat is a symbol of authority and power and can enhance your image as a high-level executive. As with your suits, your hats should be conservative looking, dark blue or gray, felt, and obviously expensive looking.

If you are a small man, if you have a high-pitched voice, or if you are skinny, you need to package yourself for greater authority and credibility. You should wear clothing associated with high authority, such as pinstripe suits, pinstripe shirts, vests, polka-dot and diamond patterned ties, and heavy shoes, such as wingtips. Your shirts should be white; your suits and ties should be dark; and your hair should be dyed dark to pick up the darkness of your attire for a more powerful image. You can consider wearing a beard or moustache for a more masculine image even though facial hair generally leaves a negative impression when worn by men of average or large build. Any moustache you grow should be moderate. Handlebars are out; goatees will lower your credibility; and heavy or long beards are not power symbols. Just look at the chief executive officers of Fortune 500 companies and count how many of these executives have heavy beards—or any facial hair, for that matter. You should have heavy frames if you wear glasses in order to add substance to your face.

Make sure that your outerwear extends below your knees to avoid a dumpy look. Also consider not carrying an umbrella because of the Wally Cox pipsqueak image you may project. Depend on raincoats and hats.

You should also use attention-getting props on your person to amplify your presence and stature. A handkerchief extending from your suit jacket breast pocket, a diamond stick pin, diamond cuff links, a conspicuously expensive gold watch and other like accessories will elevate you into a strong figure. You will also literally increase your presence by wearing lifts for your shoes.

In studies of the most appropriate business suits for short and thin men, it was found that the dark blue pinstripe suit conveyed the best image for short men. Thin men would do best with the solid medium gray suit and the solid light blue suit; these tend to project a fuller figure than the dark solids and pinstripes, which tend to emphasize a thin frame.

If you are a large person, if you are tall, if you have a great sense of presence or if you have a gruff or highly masculine facial appearance, you want to package yourself to reduce your domineering, aggressive and even frightening image.

This can be accomplished by wearing lighter business suits, such as solid dark gray, solid medium blue, and solid medium gray suits. You should consider foregoing high authority clothing such as pinstripes, vests and polka-dot ties. You should also avoid strong color contrasts, heavy, dark shoes, and coats that end above the knees and make you look like you're so tall that you are growing right out of your outerwear.

Do not be too concerned that all this nonauthoritative clothing will reduce your powerful image and important stature. Large men inherently have greater credibility and convey a greater sense of importance and power than those of average height or below-average height. Your strategy is to retain this advantage while doing away with the pitfall of scaring people because of your size.

Heavyset men and men who are overweight should heed the following guidance. If you have a big behind, buy suits with side vents in the jackets, not center vents. Stay away from double-breasted suits. Stick to solid navy, solid dark gray, dark blue pinstripe, and dark gray pinstripe suits. If you wear glasses, choose heavy frames.

If you are a young executive with responsibilities far beyond your age and experience, you will want to heed the advice given to the small man, who gives a boyish, ineffective appearance in our society. You should also consider graying your sideburns for a more distinguished look. Heavy plastic or horn rims are more traditional and powerful and will give you an older look. You will increase your authority by picking up your hair color in the color of your frames.

Regardless of your physical characteristics, there are certain clothes that will make you more likable. Solid suits are more friendly than pinstripe suits. You will be perceived as being more cooperative and credible by the upper middle class if you wear gray suits and by the lower middle class if you wear blue suits. The best combinations tested for likableness are gray suits with pale blue shirts and maroon solid and rep ties, beige suits with blue shirts, and dark blue suits with pale yellow shirts. Clothes that have too much contrast or that are gaudy tend to create an unfriendly image. If you wear a clothing style that reminds someone of his or her youth, it will generally create a pleasing effect, hence making you more likable.

In a negotiation you may not want all members of your team to look friendly or to look authoritative. If your colleague is going to assume a tough bargaining position and you are the backup or senior member of the team who will be ready to jump in and prevent the deal from falling through should your colleague's trial balloon or low-ball gambit fail, you do not want to be wearing similar outfits. You will want to wear friendly attire. Your colleague should wear a dark pinstripe suit to lend importance and seriousness to his proposal. Visually fitting the roles you play in a negotiation subconsciously lends greater credibility to your verbal communication and body language.

A recent survey shows that the average businessperson earning $30,000 a year spend $1,200 annually for clothes. Start putting that money to work effectively by thinking of yourself as a product to be packaged each time you walk into a shop. Reinforce your new outlook on clothes by going through your wardrobe closet and eliminating or putting aside everything that makes you look or feel like a loser.

PROXEMICS

The science of proxemics is the study of space and the movement of people within it. There are four basic distances in U.S. culture: intimate, personal, social and public. Spacing between people who choose one of these four distances is determined by sex, body position, vision, touch or contact, voice, thermal radiation from the body, smell and codes of conduct.

The close range of intimate distance is from skin to six inches. In addition to touching any part of the other person's body, you can sense heat radiating from that person; you can smell that person's washed skin and hair, shaving lotion or perfume, breath, sexual odors, smelly feet and other bad odors; your view of the person is blurred and distorted, and you even have the sensation of being cross-eyed; and you can hear breathing, sighs, grunts and groans. This close contact is normally reserved for private encounters in our society, such as lovemaking, comforting, protection and medical procedures. Our social code also permits intimate contact this close by the public in such exceptions as a crowded elevator, bus or subway, contact sports such as wrestling, or in shows and other forms of public entertainment.

In the outer range of intimate distance, from twelve to eighteen inches away from the other person, you still hardly have any elbow room, and the major differences are that you can now clearly see enlarged details of the person's iris, eyeball, face pores, fine hairs, eyes, nostrils, mouth and lips clearly and you can hear whispering, but no longer breathing. This spacing is still considered improper in business situations; however, there are exceptions, such as when two people are simultaneously looking closely at fine print or a detailed diagram on the desk in front of them or when someone, in response to a question, looks over the shoulder of a secretary at the letter being typed.

The close range of personal distance is eighteen inches to two and one-half feet. Here, people just barely have elbow room; body heat can no longer be detected; and whispering must be increased to a soft voice to be easily heard. This spacing is normally used for comfortable interaction with close friends and family; however, this spacing is proper in the business context for private and confidential discussions between colleagues and business associates who are within earshot of strangers or members of the other negotiating team. This spacing is also proper for businesspeople standing around conversing with several others at a cocktail party.

The outside range of personal distance, two and one-half to four feet, is the limit of physical domination through touching, is the limit of detecting most odors, except for smelly feet, permits details of the face to be seen at normal size, requires a voice of casual or moderate volume to be clearly heard, and is normally used for discussing subjects of personal interest and involvement.

The close range of social distance is four to seven feet. Here, people can only touch each other by reaching out, and the smallest blood vessels in the eye can no longer be seen; yet wear on clothing can still be detected. This spacing is primarily used for impersonal business, whether by people who work together or at a casual social gathering.

In general, when you like people, things, ideas and yourself, you open up, remove barriers and move toward them. When you don't like others or yourself, you are inclined to withdraw, build defenses and move away. In fact, studies conclusively show that people stand or sit closer to someone they like than someone they don't, friends get closer to each other than acquaintances and acquaintances get closer to each other than strangers.

The distance between two people is also determined by status and rank. When you enter an executive's office, you tend to hesitate near the doorway if he or she is your boss's boss until you are motioned closer. This may be in the outside range of social distance, from seven to twelve feet, which is usually reserved for formal business and social discourse in the office or home when the occupants are uninvolved. Upon receiving the executive's nod or other gesture, you approach the desk but still remain in the close range of social distance out of respect for his or her superior position, as well as your concern about not invading this individual's personal space and demonstrating that you know your place. On the other hand, if you walk into your subordinate's office, you have no hesitation about invading personal space and even joining him or her behind the desk to discuss the subordinate's latest memorandum. Here you are silently asserting your superior status even before you open your mouth.

As already hinted above, the relative postioning of persons engaged in bargaining is an indication of the type of relationship they have. Persons who view each other in a cooperative relationship will normally sit next to each other on either side of a table corner, with their spacing somewhere in the outside range of personal distance. If they are both concentrating on the same document on the table, they will sit side by side instead of at a right angle. If they do not trust each other or perceive each other in a competitive relationship, they are inclined to take seats at opposite sides of the table. This puts them out into the close range of social distance and enables them to see each other and their gestures clearly while reducing intimidating, dominating and overly revealing eye contact.

Armed with this knowledge, you will have a feel for a person's attitude and sincerity if you are already sitting at the bargaining table when he or she comes in to join you. Likewise, you will want to position yourself in close proximity to the other person should you be the one walking into the meeting room in order to lend credibility to your willingness to cooperate in solving this person's problems as well as yours. If your negotiating team is on one side of the table and the others are on the other side, sitting on their side will be a dramatic gesture of good will and cooperation.

If you happen to be the host, it is also favorable for you to sit at the head of the table in the "father" seat, where you will have the attention and respect of all assembled. Symbolically, the person sitting at the head dominates and has the psychological edge in persuasiveness for reasons similar to the negotiator who sits elevated above others. Studies show, for instance, that the average jury picks a foreman from one of the two individuals who occupy end chairs at the rectangular table they sit at.

In fact, studies show that in any gathering around a conference table, even when there is no identifiable host, the people at the ends of the table are likely to be viewed as the leaders or persons having superior status. These people will have more comments addressed to them, will participate more in the discussion and are more likely to make the most significant contributions to the meeting. In general, whether at a conference table, factory floor, field site or other location, people who take center stage will encompass and mold the interaction.

The next best thing to sitting in the head seat is to sit close to the dominant member of the group. You create a powerful image of yourself in the eyes of others who see you next to an influential person and conclude that such seating is either by invitation or subtle consent. If the meeting table is round, you will want to sit to the left of the most important person because the order of power generally descends around the table clockwise from the most powerful individual.

The outside range of social distance is usually the space between a person sitting behind a desk and the guest across the desk, who must be far enough from the desk to allow for knee room. People normally feel more comfortable and secure behind a large, heavy, wooden desk, and they are more competitive because they find themselves in an adversary relationship by being directly opposite you on the other side of the desk; they are also more inclined to say no and be argumentative regarding your proposals. Yet, my own research with thousands of seminar attendees indicates that the majority of us will take that seat directly opposite our host. At the very least, you should adjust the chair on an angle while moving it closer to the rear of the desk to show your desire to be closer and friendly with your host. If there is a chair on the side of the desk, you should politely ask if you can sit there; this brings you closer for a more personal discussion and enables you to move within the close range of social distance while sitting at a right angle to your host for a more cooperative discussion.

Ideally, you want to suggest that your host come out from behind the desk and sit on a chair next to you or on the sofa next to his or her coffee table. You will have put yourself into the outside range of personal distance, and you will have created a better psychological climate for agreement on the part of the other person. In fact, when you want to put your subordinate or other guest at ease, you may wish to voluntarily go around your desk and sit with him or her as you discuss matters.

The close range of public distance is twelve to twenty-five feet. This spacing dissolves sharp facial features, prevents detection of eye color and reduces the ability to view eye expressions. It is used for formal speech, presentations to small audiences and brief, impersonal messages, such as requests to get something.

The outside range of public distance is more than twenty-five feet. Here, nonverbal gestures become more important and speech amplification should be used to avoid shouting.

If you are speaking to a group, you might consider getting off the raised platform. By doing this, you put the table and chairs behind you; you are now on the same level as your audience; and you are able to make your talk more intimate, informal and conversational because you have reduced space to at least the short range of public distance for a large portion of the audience and you are within a social distance of a number of listeners.

WHAT PEOPLE SEE IN YOUR FACE

Many times you have heard another person agreeing with you but for some reason felt that he or she really did not mean it. You pride yourself in being a good judge of people and having intuition regarding their true feelings. The truth is that you are unconsciously sensitive to body language. In fact, studies show that people communicate more information through bodily gestures than by the spoken word.

This section is primarily devoted to messages that are sent by the eyes and mouth. You will learn that these are your most revealing nonverbal signals. You will also discover that some of your habits are bad and some are good regarding the attitude and image your facial gestures convey to others.

Proceed with caution if you decide to change any of your gestures after reading this book. Each individual gesture is like a word and only has complete meaning when viewed in connection with preceding, simultaneous and subsequent gestures and the spoken word. Interpreting an isolated gesture or attempting to convey such a gesture to another person is analogous to taking a word or a sentence completely out of context with other words in the sentence or other sentences in the paragraph.

Furthermore, people are generally quick to sense artificiality in movement and mannerisms. Any gesture that is too prevalent is probably contrived and deliberately planned for effect. In fact, studies indicate that an exaggerated gesture usually means that the opposite feeling is being masked. Before attempting to improve your body language remember that your natural mannerisms cannot be easily replaced to improve your total power of persuasion. As Samuel Johnson said, "Almost all absurdity of conduct arises from the imitation of those whom we cannot resemble." If you are not a smiler, showing a row of shiny teeth will not project warmth and friendship if it is not framed by what you say, how you say it and the whole "you." In President Gerald Ford's 1975 State of the Union Address, he conspicuously gestured with his hands and body with great forcefulness to demonstrate energy and reflect the image of an effective head of state. Subsequently, a cartoon appeared in a major paper stating that the poll taken found 38 percent approved of the President's speech, 29 percent disapproved and 33 percent were too busy watching his hands to hear what he said. Nonverbal gestures must be natural and harmonized with the verbal message and the rest of the person's body in order to carry influence with the audience, whether it be one person or ten million.

The Eyes

Eye contact is so important to us that we will even avoid the eyes of a blind beggar when we do not want to give anything. Subordinates being chewed out will normally avoid eye contact with a superior by keeping their gaze directed stiffly in front of them. Staring in America is generally considered an invasion of someone's privacy, and it's embarrassing when you are caught at it. Just think about the last time you were in a confined space such as an elevator with just one other person. Most encounters begin with eye contact. This is why people will not look at beggars, blind or not, and why waiters and waitresses will not allow their eyes to be caught by you when they are too busy to come over to your table.

Studies show that an individual tends to make eye contact with others more when they approve of him or her than when they disapprove. In general, during conversation people look at each other between 30 and 60 percent of the time. If their eye contact is more than 60 percent, they are probably more interested in each other than in what is being said—for instance, if they are lovers or arguers.

In our society, it is proper and even flattering to look at length into the eyes of someone talking to you. You are indicating agreement or at least attention and respect for what is being said to you. The speaker will also feel that the more-than-average eye contact and glances you give are a sign of friendship and that you actually like the speaker as a person. In fact, people generally do more looking at the eyes of someone they like.

Do not overdo eye contact because it can easily become a stare, which signals hostility, disrespect, a threat or an insult. Have you ever had a boss, teacher or other person of high rank look at you for as long as they pleased? An extra long glance makes someone feel like a nonperson, which arouses anxiety and resentment. This may be the reason we tell our children that it is not nice to stare. Staring reaches the extreme when you are angry or shouting at someone. Both of you may glare at each other in an "eyeball-to-eyeball" confrontation wherein the first individual to lose eye contact by looking away signals defeat or fear. Even average eye contact can be overbearing if done at the wrong time. Most business executives find it uncomfortable and unusual to be gazed at by the person doing the talking.

A person who looks away a lot while listening to you is indicating dissatisfaction with either you or what you are saying. Also, short glances are usually a sign of dislike. Although a person looking at you too much while he or she is talking can make you uncomfortable, it is even more significant when someone looks at you too little while talking to you. Studies do show that turning or bowing your head, peripherally moving or shifting your eye away from the other person's, or an evasive glance at a critical moment as you are stating your position could easily leave the other party with the impression that you do not believe what you are saying.

A person avoiding eye contact while listening or talking does not necessarily dislike you or tell lies. Depressed people avoid eye contact even with friends. People who are embarrassed or upset or are discussing personal matters usually try to avoid eye contact. Some people are just plain shy. Every time they fail to look at the other person, these honest, sincere and dedicated individuals are unintentionally signaling that they are not confident with respect to their statements or, worse yet, are lying.

The science of pupillometry has given researchers much information about the pupils of your eyes. It is a biological fact that the pupil expands when we look, taste, touch or hear something we like. If you notice someone speaking to you who has large pupils, it indicates interest and suggests that this person likes you. Studies show that we find people more attractive when their pupils are dilated. Because your pupils will contract in response to something unpleasant, such as telling a lie, some people prefer to wear tinted glasses since eye response cannot be controlled when telling a lie. It was reported that this is a primary reason why Yasir Arafat, the PLO leader, is never found dealing with others without his sunglasses on.

Since the mid-1970s, researchers have been taking a close look at the relationship between the color of our eyes and the way we behave. Studies show that the darker your eyes, the tougher your personality and the more explosive your reactions in times of crisis or danger. For instance, the dark-brown-eyed boss tends to be impulsive and ready to rebuke a subordinate for minor problems but also takes command in a crisis and usually makes snap decisions that turn out to be right.

The perfect boss would probably have green or light gray eyes. People with green/hazel eyes are happy, stable, imaginative and determined, yet aware of their limitations. People with gray eyes show obstinancy and courage but also show a weakness for sticking to tedious routine work.

Blue-eyed people have great stamina, but tend to be sentimental, bogged down in routine work, or moody and inclined to bear grudges. Light-brown-eyed people are individualists, tend to be shy and somewhat antisocial or dependent on personal routine, find it hard to take orders, and seem to be happiest when they are self-employed.

Although we think blinking is just for keeping our eyes moist and removing dust particles, studies show that we blink more when we are angry, excited, fearful or guiltridden. Normal blinking is hardly noticeable, but a higher frequency of blinking is conspicuous if we are looking for it and may indicate that something is being hidden or lies are being told.

Investigators have isolated four distinctive forms of eyebrow behavior: lifted-brow, lowered-brow, knit-brow and single-brow movement. Eyebrows are normally raised as an expression of curiosity, as an expression of surprise, as an expression of indignation, as an expression of arrogance and when a question is being asked or someone is voicing rejection or disapproval. Eyebrow flashing (i.e., raising) accompanies situations involving greeting, flirting, approval, seeking confirmation, thanking, emphasizing and friendly surprise.

Ralph Waldo Emerson summed up the importance of your eyes as follows: "An eye can threaten like a leveled and loaded gun or can insult like hissing and kicking; or in its altered mood, by beams of kindness, it can make the heart dance with joy."

The Mouth

Next to your eyes, your mouth provides your most important nonverbal signal. When you greet someone, you should do so with a warm, genuine smile. You are silently saying how pleased you are to see this person and that you are willing to cooperate, even if the topic to be discussed may be distasteful.

What is a warm, genuine smile? Researchers call it the *upper smile* because the upper incisors are exposed as the lips part. This is contrasted with the *simple smile*, where your teeth are hidden. It is also contrasted with the "broad smile," which displays both upper and lower teeth and occurs during play, excitement and laughter.

The above information on why and how to smile can be dangerous if used improperly. For instance, there are low-smile areas in the United States, such as New England and western New York State, where you may be asked what's so funny. On the other hand, in Georgia you may be asked whether something is wrong if you don't smile much. Just watching Jimmy Carter for a couple of minutes confirms that Georgia is a high-smile area. People unaware of this wonder why he smiles so much, especially when saying things that are serious.

You also want to be careful about whom you are smiling at. Researchers have found that a person who holds a lower status position tends to do more smiling than the person he or she is talking to. Thus, if you overdo your smiling, you may unintentionally convey the image that you are subordinate to the other person and not an equal. This is not all bad because you are fulfilling the other person's esteem needs for respect and recognition. On the other hand, you do not want to be considered unworthy as a negotiator to deal with this person. A final precaution is to make sure that your upper smile does not become a lip-in smile, which occurs when your upper teeth are sunk lightly into or resting on the lower lip. People use the lip-in smile when meeting someone they feel subordinate to.

Dry lips suggest fear and tension. Wet your lips when necessary. If the skin is cracked or raw, use lip balm to hide the condition.

Think twice before you cough, even if your throat is sore or does have a tickle. Coughing has many implications. It can suggest nervousness, lack of confidence, covering up a lie or doubt or surprise on the part of the listener when someone talks with too much conceit or confidence.

What you have in your mouth and how you use it can be quite revealing. Studies show, for instance, that you will throw out, remove or put down the toothpick, gum, cigarette, cigar or pipe from your mouth when you consider yourself subordinate to someone who walks into your office.

When cigarette smokers are under extreme stress in a meeting, they will normally put out the cigarette are retrieve it from the ashtray only after their tension has subsided. On the other hand, cigar smokers tend to blow smoke and puff rapidly when the going gets rough.

So far, the research finds that cigarette smokers tend to be fact oriented and quick decision makers. Pipe smokers are more patient, conservative and abstract in their thinking. Cigar smokers, consciously or not, generally associate themselves with wealth, confidence and the "macho" image, which actually applies in some of the Latin American countries. If a man blows his cigar smoke upward with slow, uniformly spaced puffs, he probably feels smug and self-assured.

Other Gestures of the Head

The cocking of your head is a sign of interest and of being open and flexible to the opinions of others. However, if you hold your head at a slant all the time, the gesture will lose its meaningful effect.

The seven categories of facial emotion are happiness, sadness, anger, fear, surprise, disgust and nothing. These emotions are represented by thirty-two different facial expressions isolated by investigators. The key gestures and their various meanings are shown as follows:

1. Right side of face: emotions are controlled.
2. Left side of face: true emotions show.
3. Dilated pupils show:
   a. pleasure,
   b. friendliness,
   c. interest.
4. Contracted pupils show:
   a. displeasure,
   b. anger,
   c. lying,
   d. embarrassment,
   e. fear.
5. Eye contact shows:
   a. friendship,
   b. respect,
   c. sincerity.
6. Staring shows:
   a. hostility,
   b. threat,
   c. disrespect.
7. Short glances show:
   a. deceit,
   b. dislike,
   c. fear,
   d. intimidation,
   e. embarrassment,
   f. depression,
   g. uncertainty.
8. Evasive glances or a momentary bowing of the head shows:
   a. deceit,
   b. embarrassment,
   c. uncertainty.
9. An open mouth shows:
   a. surprise,
   b. shock,
   c. disbelief.
10. A shut mouth shows
    a. pursed lips,
    b. anger,
    c. displeasure.

11. Coughing shows:
    a. a sore throat,
    b. uncertainty,
    c. deceit,
    d. doubt,
    e. surprise,
    f. nervousness.

12. Thrusting out the chin shows:
    a. anger,
    b. displeasure,
    c. frowning.

13. Dropping the chin shows:
    a. surprise,
    b. shock,
    c. disbelief.

14. Dry lips show:
    a. tension,
    b. nervousness,
    c. deceit,
    d. fear,
    e. embarrassment.

15. Pursed lips show:
    a. anger,
    b. displeasure,
    c. frowning,
    d. sadness.

16. A smile shows:
    a. warmth,
    b. friendship,
    c. cooperation.

17. Over-smiling or lip-in smiling shows:
    a. a demeaning attitude,
    b. artificiality.

18. A smile lacking laugh lines around the eyes shows:
    a. coldness,
    b. artificiality,
    c. hostility,
    d. disgust.

19. A poker face shows:
    a. hidden emotion,
    b. deceit,
    c. fear,
    d. frozen silence.

20. Excessive blinking shows:
    a. lying,
    b. anger,
    c. fear,
    d. embarrassment.

21. Lowered eyebrows show:
    a. anger,
    b. intimidation,
    c. threat,
    d. displeasure,
    e. frowning.
22. Raised eyebrows show:
    a. curiosity,
    b. surprise,
    c. indignation,
    d. rejection.

We discussed some of the major expressions above, but now we will get into the more complex expressions that involve combinations of gestures. First of all, the seventh category of emotion can be called negative emotion. The "poker face" or blank look lacks expression. This assumed mask, however, conspicuously tells us that people do not want to show their true feelings.

Disgust, or even anger, may be signaled while you are smiling. A smile that does not bring out the laugh lines around the eyes usually seems forced. Without the warmth at the outer corners of the eyes, even a broad smile may seem cold. However, even a cold, defensive smile serves as a link between people and as a buffer against aggression. There are war stories about how a soldier who suddenly comes upon one of the enemy is momentarily disarmed if the other soldier smiles or holds out a morsel of food.

Anger, displeasure or antagonism may be shown by a frown, wherein the eyebrows are usually lowered, the jaw muscles tighten, the eyes squint, the chin thrusts out and the lips tighten in a pursing gesture. The pursing action is a defensive expression that permits the person to reveal or react as little as possible. Hence, the expression "tight lipped."

Shock, surprise, disbelief and even envy may be conveyed when a person's mouth opens and chin drops (due to relaxation of the jaw muscles) and the eyebrows are raised.

Recent research finds that people are able to portray positive, confident and pleasant emotions through expressions appearing on the right side of the face; however, the true negative feelings of a person register on the left side of the face no matter how hard he or she tries to control him- or herself. The research also shows that people in general emphasize the right side of the face they are looking at and assume that the whole face is like it. The reason is that it is the right eye that studies the left side of the face (which registers negative emotions more heavily) and the right eye is controlled by the left hemisphere of the brain, which is not as developed at reading images as the right hemisphere. What all this means is that you should concentrate on studying the left side of a person's face (which is on your right when you are facing each other) in order to detect true feelings as conveyed by the left eyebrow, eye, mouth, lips and jaw.

Now that you have learned some good things and some bad things about your own facial gestures, what should you do? As already mentioned, you should avoid changing anything that will look unnatural when making favorable gestures. If you don't feel like smiling, for example, but you want to convey a friendly smile, a good way you can show a natural smile is to act or feel happy because this tends to make you happy. Before your meeting, whistle or hum your favorite tune, think of pleasurable thoughts, think about how well you have done in life, think about how great your kids are or think about how bad things could be if you never went to college and didn't have a profession.

WHAT THE REST OF YOUR BODY SAYS

Your entire body, including your head, arms, hands, fingers, legs and even your posture can be utilized to convey messages on a subliminal level. Many people have trouble projecting the emotions they feel through proper body language. Yet, little more than 40 percent of communication between two people is accomplished by the spoken word. This startling consensus of the researchers may mean that your body language is more important than the words you say. Furthermore, because facial gestures that most people look for can be more easily controlled than other parts of the body, the true meaning of your messages are indicated to knowledgeable negotiators by other body movements; to them, these movements convey a more accurate assessment of your emotional state (unless they are skilled at analyzing the left side of the face).

The Hands
Aside from facial gestures, what you do with your hands is the next most significant form of body language. Of all hand signals, the handshake is the most revealing and can give important clues to what someone really thinks of you. The following list outlines the various shakes. You may find it useful to refer to the list to review them from time to time.

1. A firm handshake indicates:
   a. confidence,
   b. a relaxed attitude,
   c. friendliness.
2. An intimate handshake indicates:
   a. warmth,
   b. friendship,
   c. fondness,
   d. falseness if the people are not close.
3. A "bone-crusher" handshake indicates:
   a. insecurity,
   b. friendliness.
4. A "pump-handle" handshake indicates:
   a. insecurity,
   b. friendliness.
5. A handshake with the fingers only indicates:
   a. unfriendliness,
   b. a competitive attitude,
   c. disinterest.

6. A "wet-clam" handshake indicates nervousness.
7. A limp, weak handshake indicates:
   a. nervousness,
   b. coldness.
8. A "going-steady" (overly long) handshake indicates:
   a. warmth,
   b. falseness if the people are not close.

A firm handshake gives the impression of quiet confidence and says that this person is glad to meet you. It also says that the individual is a no-nonsense person, confident and at ease. The firm handshake is executed by extending the hand easily, fitting it warmly against the palm of the other person's hand, gripping his or her hand snugly but respectfully, giving one brief squeeze, giving one slight pump from the elbow only and then letting go.

In an intimate situation or in circumstances where it is proper to show excessive warmth, such as when a politician is campaigning, you may warmly grasp the other person's arm or shoulder with your other hand for a brief moment, simultaneous with the handshake. An alternative is to cup the person's hand with your other hand as you are shaking. Under normal circumstances, the other person may see this as false and an attempt at ingratiation. You may also make this person uncomfortable if you are not good friends.

If a man uses a bone-crushing grip that finds you standing on your toes, do not try to outsqueeze him, but rather let your hand go limp so that it will slip from his bear trap. This is the "macho" man who is proving that he has the power to cause pain if he wants to and is unintentionally telling you that he has a basic insecurity, a need to prove himself with every meeting. A variation of the bone-crusher is the pump handle, which is a vigorous up-and-down stroke that has a tendency to dislocate your shoulder.

There are several other careless handshakes that can give a bad first impression. If the other person offers you only the fingers of his or her hand, chances are this person does not like you too much or does not want to become too involved. Of course, this does not apply if you shoot your hand out as if in a gunfight in the Old West and latch onto the person's fingers before the person thrusts his or her own hand out. The wet-clam handshake is sweaty and cold and suggests nervousness. This can be avoided by keeping your hand in your pocket or having a glove on if you are outside in the cold just prior to your meeting. Carry a handkerchief to dry any noticeable perspiration before your greeting. The weak handshake has no energy at all and suggests a certain lack of confidence and warmth. The going-steady handshake lasts for minutes—or at least it seems so. If you were the recipient of such a handshake, you might try to pull back your hand, but you would find that it is being held firmly enough to make your retreat look embarrassing. You wonder if there is something wrong with this person or if the individual is trying insincerely to show friendship that is really not there.

When a negotiator is sitting at a desk or conference table with his or her hands touching each other at the fingertips in a raised position from the elbows or arms that rest on the desk, table, knees or abdomen, this person is "steepling." See the illustration in Figure 6.4. It is a gesture of confidence. The more important the negotiator feels or the stronger his or her position is, the greater is this person's tendency to hold the hands higher while steepling. A great deal of superiority and dominance is conveyed when someone is steepling at eye level, staring at you through his or her hands.

Figure 6.4. Steepling.

Be careful when using your finger to make a point. If you are wagging your finger back and forth as you talk, you are signaling to others that they are wrong, and you are antagonizing them. In a heated discussion, a pointed finger may be construed as a threat and will put the other person on the defensive even more. The threatening action becomes even more acute when the person points with a pencil, cigarette, cigar or eyeglasses because this seems to intrude farther into the other party's personal zone of privacy than just the bare finger.

When a man is holding a cigar high in an upward tilt, he probably feels that he is in a strong, dominant position. When a negotiator's hands are both on the table and the negotiator is leaning forward, he or she is probably feeling confident and ready to get down to business. Likewise, someone is probably feeling confident and even tough if his or her hands are on the hips. If someone is counting off things on his or her fingers, starting with the thumb (the symbolic seat of power), this person is expressing logic and confidence in a forceful presentation. If someone vigorously rubs the hands together or rubs a part of the body with one hand, this person probably is anxious to get on with the discussion and feels confident of its outcome. A person who raises a hand and makes a circle with the thumb and index finger is happy and confident with the way things are going. In short, this person has unconsciously given the American OK gesture. If someone has been taking notes as you do the talking and suddenly stops writing, this person probably has come to a decision and is confident about his or her response. If someone is holding both hands together behind his or her back, this person probably feels in command of the situation. If someone is leaning back with hands laced behind the head, this person probably feels that he or she is in the driver's seat and is pleased with the progress being made.

If a person touches your arm, shoulder or back with a hand, this displays confidence, superiority and/or friendship, depending on the specific circumstances. In general, the right to touch someone else in our society is determined by status, with people who are richer, older, at a higher rank and male having a social right to touch those who are poorer, younger, subordinate and female. You can particularly expect to be touched when: the other person is giving you information, advice or an order; the other person is asking a favor or trying to persuade you to do something; you are worried; the other person is excited; both of you are in deep conversation; or you are at a party or other informal gathering. Experiments show that a person who is touched in a friendly, cooperative atmosphere will have a warmer and more positive feeling toward the toucher and the toucher's organization. During the Camp David talks for peace between Israel and Egypt, President Anwar Sadat frequently put his hand on President Carter's knee as a warm gesture of friendship.

Many hand-to-head gestures signal a lack of confidence, indecision and defensiveness. Touching the nose or slowly rubbing it usually expresses someone's doubt in what he or she is saying and may even indicate that this person is lying. Putting a hand over the mouth when there is no reason to be surprised, astonished or apologetic about something indicates an unconscious desire to shut up because of self-doubt or bald lies. Stroking or touching the chin, beard or upper lip is a sign that the other party is probably giving serious thought to your proposal and will remain indecisive until the hand is taken away. The same is true of bringing the thumb and index finger to the bridge of the nose, possibly accompanied briefly by the closing of one's eyes and the lowering of one's head. If someone touches his or her face with the palm of the hand faced outward toward you, this person probably feels threatened. Placing a palm on the back of the neck, possibly combined with a hair grooming movement, generally shows that a person is feeling very defensive and may have just made a mistake.

There are a number of hand gestures that indicate need for reassurance. Clenched hands, possibly accompanied by the thumbs rubbing each other, suggest anxiety and a certain lack of confidence; this detracts from someone's ability to persuade others. The same applies to wringing hands, picking at cuticles, pinching a hand, sticking a pen, pencil or paper clip in the mouth to chew or suck, biting nails, hiding the hands in the comforting enclosure of the pockets or clutching a part of the body because of the unconscious feeling of being vulnerable.

When a person throws a pen or glasses down onto the table, he or she is signaling dissatisfaction or disappointment. This person will probably continue to resist your ideas until you can get him or her to pick it back up by changing your approach and probing to determine the cause of concern.

Clenching a hand into a fist generally shows tension or anger and means that someone is ready to take hostile action out of desperation or fierce determination. A repetitive gesture, such as finger or pencil tapping, shows that someone is probably impatient or nervous. Unlike the person who tilts his or her head into the palm of the hand, resting on an elbow and leaning forward, someone who draws his or her body back from you is probably viewing you in a critical, negative manner. If the other person has crossed arms with the hands tightly gripping them, this person is probably defensive and resisting what you have to say. This also applies if someone is clutching onto the armrests of the seat to the degree that the knuckles become slightly white. If a person is taking notes and appears to be underlining things heavily or numbering points, this individual may be about to say no and rebuff your suggestions. If, on the other hand, the pencil is moving erratically, he is probably doodling and is bored or indifferent to what you have to say and is not being persuaded at all.

Following is a summary of hand-to-face gestures:

1. Holding the thumb or index finger to the bridge of the nose shows:
   a. interest,
   b. uncertainty.
2. Hands laced behind the head show:
   a. confidence,
   b. pleasure.
3. Placing the palm on the back of the neck, possibly combined with hair grooming, shows:
   a. defensiveness,
   b. alarm.
4. Shielding the face with the hand, palm facing outward, shows a sense of threat.
5. Stroking or touching the chin, beard or lip shows:
   a. interest,
   b. uncertainty.
6. Biting or sucking on a pen, clip or nail shows:
   a. nervousness,
   b. uncertainty.
7. Placing a hand over the mouth in the absence of surprise shows:
   a. embarrassment,
   b. uncertainty,
   c. lying,
   d. that something is being hidden.
8. Touching or rubbing the nose shows:
   a. uncertainty,
   b. lying.
9. Holding the hands at eye level shows:
   a. superiority,
   b. dominance,
   c. power.

The Legs, Sitting and Standing
The way a person sits is generally the way he or she feels. A person whose legs are crossed and who, perhaps, is leaning away from you probably views you in a competitive manner. Studies show that most negotiations are not successfully completed until both negotiators have uncrossed their legs and moved closer toward each other. If crossed legs are also coupled with crossed arms, you have a difficult adversary. If the top crossed leg is moving up and down in a rhythmic motion, the other person is probably also bored with your ideas. Normally, a person who dislikes you or feels threatened by you will lean far back in the chair or may instead sit up very straight and tensely. In contrast, someone who likes you or your discussion will lean forward slightly in a relaxed manner with the back a little curved. Of course, no gesture should be taken out of the entire body context. A person sitting back in the chair may simply be lounging while thinking about your proposal in a relaxed manner.

A person sitting with a leg over the arm of a chair probably will not be terribly cooperative, even if this person seems relaxed. This position expresses indifference about what you think of the person, and it shows hostility toward you. This individual may also be showing superiority and dominance in the same manner that bosses might by putting their feet up on a subordinate's desk, nonverbally announcing that the subordinate's office is within their territorial rights. Furthermore, a person willing to expose the soles of his shoes generally feels secure and superior. So does a person who has both feet planted on the floor out in front, with the toes pointing outward on each side at a 45-degree angle.

On the other hand, a person whose toes are turned toward each other or even tucked under the chair out of sight is probably timid or fearful. A person who taps a foot is probably impatient or nervous if this motion is not accompanied by music or relaxed or cheerful humming. A person who places one hand on each knee or both hands clasped in front of the stomach, possibly accompanied by a slight bending forward, is being respectful. If a person is sitting on the edge of the chair with the elbows resting on the thighs and the hands hanging loose, this individual is interested in what you are saying and probably is getting ready to respond or take some action, especially if the head is slightly tilted, indicating intent listening. On the other hand, if the head becomes erect, the back periodically straightens up and then slouches, the person glances at the ceiling or his or her watch and the body is positioned so that it is pointing more toward the exit, you have lost this individual's attention, interest and motivation to deal with you.

Each person has a distinctive walk, and the manner in which a person walks is a good barometer of personality and immediate feelings. People who walk rapidly and swing the arms freely tend to be goal oriented and readily pursue their objectives. People who walk with their hands in their pockets, even in warm weather, tend to be critical and secretive and may play the role of devil's advocate because they like to put other people down. If in addition to having the hands in his or her pockets, someone does not look up or notice where he or she is heading, this person is probably depressed. If a person who is walking slowly with his or her head down has both hands clasped behind the back or the thumbs tucked into his or her belt, this individual is probably preoccupied with a problem that is receiving deep thought as he or she walks. If a person is walking with chin raised, arms swinging in an exaggerated fashion and legs pacing in a stiff, deliberate manner, he or she is probably somewhat pompous and needs to impress people with this strut.

We have discussed many body gestures that signal anxiety, tension and a lack of confidence. How do you get rid of this detrimental body language? The best way to relax and feel good about yourself is to force yourself to believe you are superior. Make believe the other person or the group of people you are talking to is indebted to you. Imagine the group has assembled to beg you for an extension of credit. You will find that you actually feel more confident, and pretense will change to reality because a person becomes fearless when practicing fearlessness. If you feel your hands making nervous movements, put them behind your back or in your pockets. In short, by forcing your mind to be confident, you will simultaneously display an attitude of external calm and deliberation and convey the impression of authority, knowledge, courtesy and cooperation. Frequently review the hand-to-face gestures outlined previously and the other body language, which is summarized in the following list:

1. Rigid posture, with the body turned away, shows disinterest.
2. Leaning forward at a table shows:
   a. confidence,
   b. readiness for action.
3. Leaning away from someone shows:
   a. a threatened feeling,
   b. competition,
   c. anger,
   d. indifference.
4. Steepling shows:
   a. confidence,
   b. authority,
   c. power.
5. Pointing shows:
   a. antagonism,
   b. threat.
6. Placing the hands on the table shows:
   a. confidence,
   b. readiness for action.
7. Placing the hands on the hips shows:
   a. confidence,
   b. authority,
   c. power.
8. Rubbing the hands together or rubbing other parts of the body shows:
   a. confidence,
   b. readiness for action.
9. Stopping taking notes before someone finishes talking shows confidence in one's reply.

10. Touching someone shows:
    a. confidence,
    b. warmth,
    c. friendship.
11. Placing the hands on the knees or clasping them on the stomach shows respect.
12. Clenching or wringing the hands shows:
    a. nervousness,
    b. uncertainty.
13. Placing hands in pockets shows:
    a. nervousness,
    b. uncertainty.
14. Clenching part of the body shows:
    a. nervousness,
    b. uncertainty.
15. Throwing a pen or glasses on the table shows:
    a. displeasure,
    b. anger.
16. Placing one's watch on the desk and facing the visitor shows impatience.
17. Clenching a fist shows:
    a. nervousness,
    b. anger.
18. Tightly clenching the armrests shows:
    a. nervousness,
    b. anger.
19, Placing one's feet on someone else's desk shows:
    a. superiority,
    b. dominance.
20. Foot tapping shows:
    a. impatience,
    b. nervousness.
21. Tucking feet under the chair shows:
    a. timidness,
    b. fear.
22. Crossing the legs shows that someone is dissatisfied and is not ready to close the deal.
23. Placing a leg over an arm of the chair shows:
    a. indifference,
    b. disgust,
    c. hostility.
24. Crossing the arms tightly shows:
    a. defensiveness,
    b. anger,
    c. feeling threatened.
25. Counting the fingers, starting with the thumb, shows:
    a. logic,
    b. confidence,
    c. authority,
    d. power.

26. Making a circle with the thumb and index finger shows:
    a. confidence,
    b. pleasure.
27. Picking at the hand or cuticle shows:
    a. nervousness,
    b. uncertainty.
28. Tapping with fingers or pencil shows:
    a. nervousness,
    b. impatience.
29. Taking notes and underlining points heavily while someone else is talking shows:
    a. disagreement,
    b. disgust.
30. Doodling shows:
    a. disinterest,
    b. disgust.

VERBAL MESSAGES WITHOUT WORDS

Each of us speaks an average of about 30,000 words per day, about the amount in a small book. This "Book of the Day" is our best or worst advertisement to those who hear us. Our speaking voice is one of the first impressions people have of us, and that impression is often dominated by our voice quality.

A person may be characterized as friendly if his or her voice sounds warm and well modulated. Someone may be thought of as dull and uninteresting if the voice sounds flat and monotonous. Someone who is too loud may appear bombastic. Someone who is too soft may be tagged as timid. Speaking too fast may convey impatience or anger. Speaking too slow may cause someone to be viewed as hesitant or fearful. A nasal voice may suggest stupidity. A thin, wispy voice conveys weakness, whereas a lisp suggests immaturity. In short, our little "Book of the Day" may say we are educated, illiterate, intolerant, egotistical, ambitious, incapable, slovenly, neat, cultured, coarse or reliable. Because listeners unconsciously judge us by how we talk, you will want to make your "Book of the Day" a best seller.

It has been concluded that 90 percent of all friction caused in day-to-day living is due to voice tone. When you speak, your words convey your thoughts, and the tone conveys your mood. In fact, researchers found that less than 10 percent of face-to-face communication is done by words. Voice tone, pitch, volume, speed and inflection account for almost 40% of communication, with facial and body gestures accounting for the balance.

Speaking in a monotone is monotonous, fatigues the listener, repels the listener's initial attraction and hurts memory retention. Most people speak in too high a pitch, especially when they get excited. A high, shrill voice is irritating and unconvincing.

Measurements of superior speakers indicate that the ideal pitch for men is close to C below middle C, whereas for women it is close to G sharp below middle C. By saying a sustained "Ohhhh" and finding the matching key on the piano, you will locate your own average pitch and will be able to compare it with the ideal pitch. If you are four or more tones lower or higher than the ideal pitch, either you are not speaking in your natural tone because of cultural or psychological reasons or your pitch simply is not within normal limits. Quite often, people will use a different pitch depending on the business and social circumstances they are in. You can find your natural pitch by listening to your voice alone or when you are relaxed with a friend with whom you do not have to put on any airs. This is the pitch that you want to use for all circumstances. However, if it is four or more tones from the ideal pitch, you may wish to consider training from a voice teacher.

There are three basic pitch variations, called inflections: these are rising, falling and complex. The same word or sentence with each different inflection can express totally different emotions and actually change the message communicated. President Franklin Roosevelt had an excellent speaking voice that varied all the way up and down the scale. This made him easy to listen to, was reassuring and pleasant to the ear and created a feeling of poise and charm.

Your talking rhythm—that is, your speech speed and pauses—will depend on how complicated your message is and how clearly you articulate your words. The human ear can absorb words at a rate of 400 words per minute. Most people will absorb about 150 words per minute leisurely and easily. A rate of 120 words per minute is a slower pace that irks many of us; 180 words per minute is fast talking; and 200 words per minute will begin to lose our attention. In general, listeners find a person who speaks faster than average to be more knowledgeable, more persuasive and more enthusiastic. However, if you talk too fast, you may give the impression that you lack self-confidence and are nervous.

Speech is painfully slow if it is cluttered by long pauses and distractions such as "uhhhh" and "well." Conscious effort should be made to eliminate this word static because it conveys a lack of preparation, knowledge and self-assurance.

Poor articulation results from improper tongue and lip movement and improper breathing. If you cannot flutter a paper held six inches in front of your mouth when you sound a *p* in the word *pet* in your normal speaking voice, you are either too lazy or too weak. To get into the habit of breathing properly for forceful speech, stand erect and put your hand flat against your diaphragm, immediately below your rib cage in front. When you take a deep breath, your diaphragm will move down, and your hand will be pushed out, meaning you are breathing correctly. Too many people have lazy lips. Without proper lip movement, words can sound mumbled.

Vowel sounds should not be emitted through the nose because your voice may sound unpleasant and irritating. You can perform a simple test to determine whether your vowels are nasal. Say the same sounds holding your nose closed that you do when your nose is open. If the sounds sound different, you're sounding your vowels improperly through your nose. You must try to direct more air out of your mouth as you talk.

THE SUBCONSCIOUS MESSAGES
IN WRITTEN COMMUNICATION

What most people completely overlook in writing notes, memos and letters, or even in merely signing their names to typed communications, is the appearance of their handwriting and signature. As with your voice and personal appearance, your writing can have a positive or a negative effect on the image you portray to the party who is looking at your note or signature and can even reveal your personality to people who understand handwriting analysis.

On a sheet of paper, write down in your natural handwriting the closing sentence of a hypothetical letter. ("I look forward to seeing you in the near future.") Then write "Sincerely," below and your signature underneath. We will now interpret your handwriting and determine what changes, if any, are needed to improve your image.

If your vowel and consonant loops are primarily circular, as shown in Figure 6.5, then you are basically a Feeler and have a combination Natural and Adaptive Child ego state, which are personality types described in Chapter 7. You seek affection and approval, and you are not hostile, aggressive or competitive. If you also have circular accouterments and additions to your letters, such as the *I, e, d* and *t* of Figure 6.6, rather than as part of the basic letter form, you have a Manipulating Child ego state because you tend to be self-indulgent, possessive and jealous.

If your letters are primarily squared off, such as in Figure 6.6, you are basically a Thinker. You are a security-motivated individual; you are logical and practical; you accumulate information and have patience to build on facts and ideas.

If your handwriting is basically triangular, with pointy, wedge-shaped lettering like that in Figure 6.7, you are basically a Sensor. You have sharpness of thought and keen perception; you want to arrive at solutions quickly; and you are curious and exploring, producing ideas and solving problems independently and impatiently while leaving burdensome details for others. You can be a dynamic producer but also can jump to conclusions too quickly and have a potential to be misguided and destructive.

If your handwriting is squiggly and imaginative, such as that shown in Figure 6.8, you are basically an Intuitor. You have a unique and idealistic philosophy that may not always be in touch with reality. You are a visionary with aesthetic values and the ability to create, whether in the arts or the sciences.

As with everything else, handwriting interpretation is not all black and white. Everyone has some squared, triangular, circular and squiggly letters in handwriting, even though one or two of the four types may dominate.

For instance, if your writing is basically squared, with quite a bit of triangular letters and hardly any squiggles at all, you are practical, logical, intelligent, aggressive when necessary to insure your security, willing to compete and fight for something, and act more on reason than emotion, making you more often a winner than a loser. If, however, your lettering is

I look forward to seeing you in the near future.

Figure 6.5. The feeler.

I look forward to seeing you in the near future.

Figure 6.6. The thinker.

I look forward to seeing you in the near future.

Figure 6.7. The sensor.

I look forward to seeing you in the near future.

Figure 6.8. The intuitor.

I look forward to seeing you in the near future.

Figure 6.9. The personal writer.

I look forward to seeing you in the near future.

Figure 6.10. The introvert.

Sincerely,
Phil Sperber

Figure 6.11. The aggressor or important person image.

Phil Sperber

Figure 6.12. The important person image.

Dear Mr. O'Holloran:

Figure 6.13. Dislike and disrespect.

Dear Mr. Fang:

Figure 6.14. Respect.

Dear Mr. O'Holloran:

Figure 6.15. The enemy.

more squiggly than circular, it means that you use more of your imagination to develop plans and ideas further, you respond to challenges and enjoy solving creative problems and you gain great satisfaction from personal achievement. On the other hand, if your writing is mostly squiggly, then triangular, then circular, and least of all squared, then you are truly a dynamic individual, possessing all the qualities of success and leadership. Your mind is always generating new thoughts and images and creating and solving planned projects and challenges; you are competitive and do not worry about security; and you enjoy people but spend little time on social needs and companionship. If your lettering is more squared than circular in this same situation, then you are the same dynamic individual just described, but you are even more self-oriented and independent, with less need for compassion, patience and relationships with others.

Your handwriting also gives other messages. If it slants forward, as shown in Figure 6.9, you have good emotional relationships with others, you respond quickly to people, and you are basically a loving and affectionate person who also has a need for affection from others. If your writing is upright, as shown in Figures 6.6 and 6.7, you are neutral in your attitudes toward people, you meet them with objectivity and reserve and you guard against emotional involvement until you get to know someone, sacrificing the pleasure of spontaneous feelings. If your writing slants backward, regardless of whether you are left handed or right handed, such as in Figure 6.10, you are basically an introvert. You hide your feelings; you are involved with your own particular needs; and you draw away from people. The significance of the direction of your writing can be illustrated with the following example. If you are writing a sentence, telling someone that you like him or her, you want to see this person and you can be trusted with respect to the proposal you have outlined, your actual intent and candor will be suspect if your forward slant throughout the letter is suddenly altered in this sentence so that it appears more upright or even backwards in places, revealing your true feelings.

If you grip your pen or pencil strongly and forcefully bear down on the paper with strong pressure, you will normally produce a broad, dark stroke in your handwriting, creating indentations that can be easily felt on the reverse side of the sheet. This suggests that you are forceful, aggressive and competitive and have self-confidence and an abundance of energy. An extremely light handwriting, with no indentation, suggests just the opposite. If your forceful writing is combined with a forward slant and basically triangular and squiggly writing, you are a person with abounding energy, active in both thought and emotions. Nothing can stop you or get in your way when you are meeting goals and solving challenges.

Although this is beyond the scope of this book, there are other aspects of your handwriting that will tell a graphologist about other traits of your personality, such as morality, generosity, frugality, sense of humor, wit, sarcasm, stubbornness, flexibility, resentfulness, consideration, optimism, shyness, ostentatiousness, ambition, determination, laziness, pride, vanity, humility, procrastination, absentmindedness, maturity, deceit and honesty. The last two traits are important enough to explore further, and they will be mentioned in Chapter 12. Graphologists can even tell from your handwriting whether you suffer from headaches, have abdominal problems, have a limp or leg injury, have arthritis, have a nervous condition or are depressed, under extreme tension, fatigued, or sexually repressed or aggressive.

Your signature reveals the type of person you try to appear to be in front of others, whereas the body of your writing in your memo or letter reveals the real you. If you wish to appear more aggressive than you are, the capital letters of your signature will be substantially larger than those in the body of your letter, as shown in Figure 6.11. When you underscore your signature, as shown in Figure 6.11, you are emphasizing its importance, as if you need to stand out in the crowd.

If the last stroke of your name is drawn out, it means you feel your signature is an understatement of who you are, and that there is more and more . . . and more, as shown in Figure 6.12. If your signature slants differently than the writing in the body of your letter, it indicates that you are attempting to convey emotions that you don't actually feel.

What you think of others is revealed in how you write their name. When you think little of a person, his or her image is reduced in your mind and correspondingly reduced when writing his or her name, as shown in Figure 6.13. When you hold someone in high esteem, you subconsciously enlarge the name as shown in Figure 6.14. When a person considers someone an enemy, there is a tendency to want to destroy the person whenever the opportunity presents itself, and this can take the form of subconsciously crossing out the person's name, as shown in Figure 6.15. How you compare yourself with the person you are writing to is quite often determined by whose name you write larger.

The one-letter word *I* is one of the most highly personal words in the entire dictionary, and the way you write it tells a lot about yourself. *I* blown up out of proportion with the rest of your writing indicates that you are insecure and hungry for attention. A small and obscure *I* indicates that you think little of your own importance. The ideal *I* should be the same as or slightly larger than the other writing to give yourself the importance you deserve but not so much as to be pompous.

Other specific letters also are significant in showing your personality. For instance, if you cross your *t* with a shallow or umbrella-like curve with light pressure, it is a sign of weak willpower. Crossing the *t* with a straight line that is firm under pressure indicates a more forceful personality. The longer and darker the stroke, the greater your image of determination and aggressiveness. Also, if your *t* crossing climbs upward from left to right, it shows enthusiasm, physical energy and optimism on your part. Positive thinking is also reflected by lines of writing that slant slightly upward from left to right.

Adolph Hitler's unclear letters, fading word ends, weak *t* crosses and other handwriting giveaways of an emotionally unstable person indicated he was incapable of keeping a promise. Had Neville Chamberlain understood graphology, he never would have trusted the Dictator at Munich, and the course of world history might have been different.

Graphology is routinely used to evaluate employment applicants by 85 percent of all companies in Europe, and at least 2,000 American firms currently retain outside graphologists as personnel consultants, according to Chicago's International Graphoanalysis Society. At $50 to $125 per analysis, graphology is more economical than psychological testing and, some say, more accurate.

HUMOR AS A NEGOTIATING TECHNIQUE

At the right time and with the proper delivery, the correct form of humor will bring laughter or at least smiles from your listeners. This is physically and psychologically beneficial because humor puts people in a good mood, relaxes them and, in general, is good for their health and your presentation.

Humor creates sociability and cooperative behavior on a subconscious level because we all enjoy laughing together. It may be the only common ground you initially have with the other side. As already pointed out in Chapter 5, humor gets attention and keeps your listeners' minds focused on what you are saying if the humor ties in with the rest of your presentation. Humor can prevent or at least relieve embarrassment because it reminds others that they also are not infallible when it comes to blunders. In addition to relieving tension, humor can even show the absurdity of the other party's contention with greater impact than direct reasoning and without the problem of allowing the other party to save face. Humor can be used to put forth trial balloons on matters that you would not seriously take a stand on without knowing your listeners' feelings.

In short, you can effectively use humor for just about any purpose, whether it be to loosen up a stockholders' meeting, clinch a deal, overcome your nervousness at a public meeting, lighten an after-dinner speech, break a deadlock, avoid a strike or simply establish your wit and give yourself a favored position with your listeners.

Many executives are afraid to tell jokes—and with good reason. Even the experts say that if a joke is not well told—and most times it is not—it can hurt you more than it can help, ranging from boring your listeners to insulting them. Your humor should always make others feel superior, and no one should be the brunt of the fun. It is better to let people laugh at you than take the chance of deflating their egos. You, of course, must be certain that your humor is in good taste, it fits the situation and ties in with your talk, it will not offend and others will be receptive to it. Your humor should be short because people, unless they are your personal friends, do not have the time or patience to listen to long yarns. Never apologize or ask to be stopped if the joke has already been heard before. Assume no one has ever heard of it, and tell it in your own personal style to accomplish the specific business purpose you have in mind. Even if the humor has been heard before, it was delivered in a different manner, in a different context and for a different purpose.

The Humor Arsenal

The basic types of humor that you can draw upon are puns, incongruous things, hyperbole, "daffynitions," satire, sarcasm, irony, epigrams, stereotypes, anecdotes, tall tales and the Freudian slip. You should avoid spoonerisms (the twisting around of syllables for a humorous result), parody (substituting the words of a song, poem or prose with different words for a humorous result) and situational humor (such as farce, slapstick, buffoonery and mimicry). These forms of humor appear frivolous and tend to lower your stature. Below are examples of the various forms of humor available to you when starting off a presentation before a group of people.

Puns are humorous statements that involve plays on the sounds of words. An example is starting off your talk by telling the audience about the oil industry's formula for speech making: "If you don't strike oil in twenty minutes, stop boring."

Incongruous humor involves bringing together two unrelated things that are totally unexpected. An example is starting off your presentation by telling the audience that you asked the program chairperson what you should talk about, and the reply was, "About twenty minutes!"

Hyperbole is an exaggerated statement that produces colorful visual imagery. Sometimes the opportunity for hyperbole presents itself when you are built up as a great speaker or a highly successful businessperson by the person introducing you to the group. You can simply start off saying, "This all sounds so exciting; I can hardly wait to hear me speak!"

Daffynitions are humorous definitions. An example is starting off your talk by telling the audience what the three basics of a good speech are: "Stand up and be seen; speak up and be heard; shut up and be liked!" Another beginning line is to tell your audience what the definition of a successful speech is, based on the last one you made: "It was soothing (the people slept); it was moving (half of them left); and it was satisfying (they didn't come back)."

Satire is good-natured ridicule that permits people to laugh at their foolishness. If your talk is about venture capitalism, you might start off by remarking, "Conservative bankers view high technology entrepreneurs who request financing for high risk ventures as serious businesspeople with their feet firmly planted in mid-air!" For another example, assume that you are presiding at the annual stockholders' meeting of your firm, an oil company. In response to a heckler who makes reference to your exorbitant profits and the high price of gas, you say, "Don't knock the rich. When was the last time you were hired by somebody poor?"

Sarcasm is ill-natured ridicule that normally has an intended victim. Sarcasm is a damaging weapon because once you and others laugh at the victim of the remark, the victim's ego is deflated and he or she has no more fight. One of the best uses of sarcasm is in defending yourself against hecklers. Some examples are as follows:

1. "Sir, to have an open mind does not mean that you have to have an open mouth."

2. "I would like to get on the right side of you, but I cannot find it."

3. "I would like to bend your ear for a moment—bend it with a baseball bat."

Irony is a mild form of sarcasm wherein the statement means something other than the words said. For instance, if you are late for your presentation, you might tell the listener that you feel like the man who was on a field hike who came puffing up to a little store to ask if a group of Scouts had come by recently, explaining, "I'm their leader."

The epigram is a witticism making a universal comment or witty remark, based upon a particular situation. As example is starting off your talk by letting the listeners know you understand the essence of a good presentation: "Have a good beginning and a good ending, and keep them close together!"

Stereotype humor is based on the prediction that a person will act in a predetermined manner. An example is starting off your talk with the following recollection: "There was once a teacher who dreamed he was lecturing. When he awoke, he was!" If you are talking about management by objectives and delegating functions, you might wish to start off with the story about the boy who asked his dad what executive ability was. "Son, executive ability is the art of getting credit for all the hard work that somebody else has done!"

An anecdote is a humorous tale about a person. An example is beginning your talk on consumerism with the following: "If Robin Hood were alive today, he would be no cheap crook. He would be heading up a militant consumer help organization and would probably be busy with a book on the general theory of wealth distribution."

The Freudian slip is the seemingly accidental utterance that appears to come from your hidden thoughts that you dare not express. An example is in your role as toastmaster when you rattle off a half-dozen impressive features about the speaker you are introducing, sheepishly ending up with, "And he's free of charge."

The tall tale involves an exaggeration that emphasizes the impossible. An example is beginning your presentation by asking your audience for forgiveness if you seem a little exhausted: "The thunder and lightning during my flight up here was so terrifying that the clouds came right down out of the sky and hid under the plane!"

Tactical Humor
The following examples illustrate how different forms of humor can be helpful in dealing with another negotiator.

1. *Anger and threats:* If the other party explodes into a rage or gets unnecessarily emotional through error or fear that you are trying to take advantage of him or her, the following example of incongruous humor may calm this person: "A full length New York Hilton ballroom mirror was smashed, and a man was severely cut on his right hand. Arrested on a charge of intoxication, the wounded fighter indignantly insisted that he had walked into the room and saw the other guy looking at him 'very nasty.' " After calmly relating this account, assure the other person that there is no intent on your part to be unfair.

2. *Balancing the equities:* If the other party complains that your proposal means too much work, an epigram is one way to respond: "An unknown philosopher once remarked that the trouble with opportunity is that it always comes disguised as hard work." It reminds this person only too clearly that we cannot expect something for nothing.

3. *Breaking the deadlock:* Hyperbole is one type of humor that can be used to show your conviction: "An infallible method of conciliating a tiger is to allow oneself to be devoured." When you have to retreat from a position or when you have to concede something that you previously claimed was nonnegotiable, a pun can do the trick: "Eating words has never given me indigestion." In one brief utterance, you illustrate your courage and strength and do not lose face as the weak negotiator that had to back down.

4. *Avoiding profanity:* No matter how angry you get, remember the reflection theory. Do not fly off the handle and heap abuse on the other person. It will only further escalate a difficult situation. Hyperbole is one approach to conveying a vivid picture of your feelings without resort to harsh words. For instance, you might dictate the following note to the offending party: "Mr. Smeagle: My secretary, being a lady, cannot type what I think of you. I, being a gentleman, will not dictate it. But you, being neither, will know what I mean."

5. *Aspiration level:* If you feel you are being low balled or the price being asked is way out of line, one approach is to tell an anecdote. For example, you could say that the price reminds you of the story about a seasoned manager who was instructing a new salesperson on how to price the line of stamping machines: "When the customer asks what the charge is, you say, 'Two thousand dollars.' If the customer doesn't flinch, say, 'For a used press. A new one will be $3,300.00.' Then you pause again, and if the customer still doesn't flinch, say 'With an installation charge of $500.00' " This humor lets the seller know that you are no patsy and you are aware of the fair market value of the property to be purchased.

There are many ways in which humor can be used when dealing with subordinates:

1. *Requests for a raise:* The pun can be very dramatic when an unhappy employee gives you an ultimatum that you either give a raise or count him or her out. You can say, "One, two, three!" If one of your people feels he was overlooked when a younger employee was promoted and you must be honest and lay it on the line, a pun with a different twist can be used: "Jim, you haven't had 20 years of experience. You've had one year of experience twenty times."

2. *Encouragement and motivation:* Incongruous humor can be used to prop up the demoralized salesperson by talking about your own disappointments when first starting out: "On my first day out as a salesperson I got two orders—'Get out' and 'Stay out.' "

3. *Conveying messages:* If you are president of a company presiding over a staff meeting and want to subtly tell your technical director to get her act together and tell your publicity director to do more thinking and less releasing, a little satire can do the trick: "If only we could invest things in our laboratories one-tenth as quickly as we do in our publicity department!" On the other hand, if you want to get a message across that you feel very strongly about, you can use the direct approach with satire. "All officers opposed to my plan will signify by saying 'I resign.' "

Humor can be an even more effective tool on the job when used by the employee in dealing with the boss:

1. *The insecure boss:* Are you a hard worker? Is your boss suspicious of your motives? Does your boss think you want his or her job? Relate the following satire about the author of this book: As a young engineer with Dupont, your author was the last to leave in the evening, never took a day off, slaved through his lunch hour, and finally one day was called in to his boss's office. "I have been watching the hours you keep very carefully, Phil. Just what the hell are you up to anyhow?!"

2. *Complaints:* Does your boss expect too much of you? Are you supposed to be infallible? Are you supposed to do the dirty work? If you are an administrative assistant or an executive secretary, hyperbole can let the boss know how you feel without a direct confrontation: "A secretary looks like a woman, thinks like a man, and works like a dog." Hopefully, your boss will reflect on that statement and realize that there is a problem. Instead of getting angry, your boss will discuss with you how things can improve. If, on the other hand, you are an executive who feels you are being slighted because you are too young or because you are too old, the following satire is a good response: "People these days are only looking for alert young people between the ages of 25 and 35—with 40 years of experience."

3. *Failure and excuses:* If you are in a high risk job where there is a lot of uncertainty, always have this type of comic definition handy: "The definition of a successful corporate planner is someone who is able to foretell what will happen next month, next year and in five years—and then explain why it didn't happen."

4. *Persuading the boss:* A little incongruous humor can go a long way in getting your point across when you find your logical reasoning being resisted. For instance, if you feel your president is too isolated and isn't in touch with company employees enough, you might relate the following: "One night Conrad Hilton checked in at one of his hotels. In the morning, he wrote out his signature across the bottom of the bill and gave it back to the cashier. She studied it for a moment and then asked, 'Tell me, Mr. Hilton, with what organization are you connected?' "

Another example of incongruous humor in response to an illogical request made by your boss is relating the following story: "A busy maintenance supervisor in a large industrial complex delegated to the groundskeeper the job of watering the grass every day at 4:30 P.M. The groundskeeper did this diligently for weeks until one day there was a terrific thunderstorm. The supervisor happened to see the groundskeeper in the snack bar at 4:30 and, visibly irritated, asked what was going on. The groundskeeper, looking confused, said, 'It's raining.' 'So what!' yelled the supervisor. 'You've got a raincoat, haven't you?' "

THE UNSEEN IMPACT OF QUOTATIONS

At the proper moment, reciting a quotation of a famous person or a historical figure or giving a biblical quotation can reinforce your proposals and mend differences of opinion. People are subconsciously moved by the thoughts of those they respect or hold in reverence. Many quotations bring to mind the importance of tradition, custom and other standards of conduct that fulfill the aesthetic needs of the listener. On a conscious level, it is hard to argue against wise sayings that are centuries old or observed by millions of people. Quite often, a quotation can accomplish your objective without insult or offense where even an indirect personal statement by yourself would have undesirable implications and give cause for anger and resentment.

ERROR OR MISTAKE.   When the other party has committed a blunder that becomes apparent, any one of the following quotations may be appropriate as a face-saving remark, thereby avoiding an intimidating accusation, showing the other person that he or she still has your respect and need not fear disclosing the truth:

1. *The errors of the wise man make your rule / rather than the perfections of a fool.* (William Blake, 1811.)
2. *Error of opinion may be tolerated where reason is let free to combat it.* (Thomas Jefferson, First Inaugural Address, 1801.)
3. *The errors of great men are vulnerable because they are more fruitful than the truths of little men.* (Nietzsche, 1867.)
4. *A life spent in making mistakes is not only more honorable, but more useful than a life spent doing nothing.* (George Bernard Shaw, *The Doctor's Dilemma*, 1913.)
5. *A man should never be ashamed to own he has been in the wrong, which is but saying that he is wiser today than he was yesterday.* (Jonathan Swift, 1711.)

CREDIBILITY.   If your reliability or honesty is in question or if the other party has reason to be suspicious as a result of the matter being discussed, one or more of the following quotations may be appropriate to show the importance you attach to integrity and responsibility:

1. *Seek not proud riches, but such as thou mayest get justly, use soberly, distribute cheerfully and leave contentedly.* (Francis Bacon, 1625.)
2. *Suspicion is a thing very few people can entertain without letting the hypothesis turn, in their minds, into fact.* (David Cort, 1963.)
3. *I would prefer even to fail with honor than win by cheating.* (Sophocles, 409 B.C.)

4. *He who wishes to be rich in a day will be hanged in a year.* (Leonardo da Vinci, 1500.)

5. *The best way to keep one's word is not to give it.* (Napoleon, *Maxims*, 1815.)

6. *He that does not speak truth to me does not believe me when I speak truth.* (Thomas Fuller, 1732.)

7. *If you want to be thought a liar, always tell the truth.* (Logan Pearsall Smith, *Afterthoughts*, 1931.)

8. *Often, the surest way to convey misinformation is to tell the strict truth.* (Samuel Clemens [Mark Twain], 1897.)

9. *He who believes in nobody knows that he himself is not to be trusted.* (Auerbach.)

10. *Honesty is the best policy.* (Cervantes, *Don Quixote*.)

CUSTOM, TRADITION AND STANDARD OPERATING PROCEDURE (POLICIES AND RULES).   When your hands are tied because of policy, matters beyond your control or guidelines you feel compelled to follow, a selection from the following quotations may help the other party understand your situation:

1. *We accept the verdict of the past until the need for change cries out loudly enough to force upon us a choice between the comforts of further inertia and the irksomeness of action.* (Judge Learned Hand, 1942.)

2. *Custom creates the whole of equity, for the simple reason that it is accepted.* (Pascal, 1670.)

3. *Custom determines what is agreeable.* (Pascal, 1670.)

4. *You will always find those who think they know what is your duty better than you know it.* (Emerson, *Self-reliance*, 1841.)

5. *Habit is stronger than reason.* (George Santayana, 1900.)

6. *Habit is habit, and not to be flung out of the window by any man, but carried downstairs a step at a time.* (Samuel Clemens [Mark Twain], 1894.)

7. *I know of no way of judging the future but by the past.* (Patrick Henry, 1775.)

8. *The law is not made for a righteous man, but for the lawless and disobedient.* (*1 Timothy* 1:9.)

FAIRNESS.   Quotations can show that you have a cooperative, problem-solving attitude and will not try to take advantage of the other person:

1. *Life should be a humane undertaking. I know. I undertook it. Yet have found that in every move, I prevent someone from stepping where I step.* (Thom Gunn, 1967.)

2. *Nothing is politically right which is morally wrong.* (Daniel O'Connell.)

ASPIRATION LEVEL.   Any one of the following quotations can be used as a response to unreasonable demands and unrealistic requests:

1. *We are all in the gutter, but some of us are looking at the stars.* (Oscar Wilde, 1892.)

2. *If you aspire to the highest place, it is no disgrace to stop at the second or even the third place.* (Cicero, 55 B.C.)

3. *Slight not what's near to aiming to that's far.* (Euripides, 455 B.C.)

4. *A journey of a thousand miles must begin with a single step.* (Chinese proverb.)

5. *Men go shopping just as men go out fishing or hunting, to see how large a fish may be caught with the smallest hook.* (Henry Ward Beecher, 1887.)

6. *A wise man will make more opportunities than he finds.* (Francis Bacon, 1625.)

7. *Weeping may endure for a night, but joy cometh in the morning.* (Psalm 30:5.)

8. *He that loveth silver shall not be satisfied with silver; nor he that loveth abundance with increase.* (Ecclesiastes 5:10.)

9. *Let us not be desirous of vain glory, provoking one another, envying one another.* (Galatians 5:26.)

CAUTION, FOREBEARANCE AND DEADLINES.   When you are being rushed into something by the other side, when the other person is impatient or is offended by your reluctance to take his or her word without further study of the matter, one of the following quotations can be used:

1. *There are some frauds so well conducted that it would be stupidity not to be deceived by them.* (Charles C. Colton, 1825.)

2. *Trust in God, but tie your camel.* (Persian proverb.)

3. *Adversity is the first path to Truth.* (Byron, *Don Juan*, 1824.)

4. *What is a man if he is not a thief who openly charges as much as he can for the goods he sells?* (Mohandes K. Gandhi, *Nonviolence in Peace and War*, 1948.)

5. *Desire to have things done quickly prevents their being done fairly.* (Confucius, sixth century B.C.)

6. *Patience and diligence, like faith, remove mountains.* (William Penn, 1693.)

7. *Patience accomplishes its object, while hurry speeds to its ruin.* (Sa'Di, 1258.)

8. *The cautious seldom err.* (Confucius, sixth century B.C.)

9. *No one tests the depth of a river with both feet.* (Ashanti proverb.)

10. *There are two times in a man's life when he should not speculate: when he can't afford it, and what he can.* (Samuel Clemens [Mark Twain].)

11. *A wise man does not trust all his eggs to one basket.* (Cervantes, *Don Quixote*.)

12. *Caution is the oldest child of wisdom.* (Victor Hugo.)

13. *Be courteous to all, but intimate with few; and let those few be well tried before you give them your confidence.* (George Washington, 1783.)

14. *A fool and his money are soon parted.* (George Buchanan.)

15. *Skeptics are never deceived.* (French proverb.)

16. *Great intellects are skeptical.* (Nietzsche.)

17. *Time is precious, but truth is more precious than time.* (Disraeli.)

LYING.   If you detect a lie, one of the following quotations may avoid the permanent damage that may be caused by a direct confrontation:

1. *When the eyes say one thing, and the tongue another, a practised man relies on the language of the first.* (Emerson, *The Conduct of Life*, 1860.)

2. *Use what language you will, you can never say anything but what you are.* (Emerson, *The Conduct of Life*, 1860.)

3. *A prudent man concealeth knowledge.* (Proverbs 28:13.)

4. *Deceit is in the heart of them that imagine evil.* (Proverbs 12:20.)

5. *Bread of deceit is sweet to a man; but afterwards his mouth shall be filled with gravel.* (Proverbs 20:17.)

6. *No man, for any considerable period, can wear one face to himself and another to the multitude without finally getting bewildered as to which may be the true.* (Nathaniel Hawthorne, *The Scarlet Letter*, 1850.)

7. *Whatever satisfies the soul is truth.* (Walt Whitman, *Leaves of Grass*, 1892.)

8. *Would that I could discover truth as easily as I can uncover falsehood.* (Cicero, 44 B.C.)

9. *Irrationally held truths may be more harmful than reasoned errors.* (Thomas H. Huxley, *The Origin of Species*, 1880.)

10. *We perceive an image of truth, and possess only a lie.* (Pascal, 1670.)

11. *To be wiser than other men is to be honester than they; and strength of mind is only courage to see and speak the truth.* (William Hazlitt, *On Knowledge of the World*, 1839.)

12. *It is always the best policy to speak the truth, unless of course you are an exceptionally good liar.* (Jerome K. Jerome, 1892.)

13. *To be believed, make the truth unbelievable.* (Napoleon, *Maxims*, 1815.)

14. *I can believe anything, provided it is incredible.* (Oscar Wilde, *The Picture of Dorian Gray*.)

15. *If you tell the truth you don't have to remember anything.* (Samuel Clemens [Mark Twain].)

16. *Round numbers are always false.* (Samuel Johnson.)

17. *Any fool can tell the truth, but it requires a man of some sense to know how to lie well.* (Samuel Butler, *Note-Books*.)

CHANGING THOSE WHO HAVE CONVICTION OR ARE STUBBORN.   There are many quotations you can choose from to motivate a concession from somebody who is acting on principle or clinging to old ideas:

1. *Convictions are more dangerous and a maze of truth than lies.* (Nietzsche, 1878.)

2. *The fact that an opinion has been widely held is no evidence whatever that it is not utterly absurd; indeed in view of the silliness of the majority of mankind, a widespread belief is more likely to be foolish than sensible.* (Bertrand Russell, 1929.)

3. *Man is a credulous animal, and must believe something; in the absence of good grounds for belief, he will be satisfied with bad ones.* (Bertrand Russell, *Unpopular Essays*, 1950.)

4. *Man can believe the impossible, but man can never believe the improbable.* (Oscar Wilde, 1891.)

5. *Discontent is the first step in the progress of a man or a nation.* (Oscar Wilde, 1893.)

6. *We owe almost all our knowledge not to those who have agreed, but to those who have differed.* (Charles C. Colton, 1825.)

7. *The hearts of the great can be changed.* (Homer, *Iliad*, ninth century B.C.)

8. *A wise man changes his mind; a fool never will.* (Spanish proverb.)

9. *The essence of being human is that one does not seek perfection.* (George Orwell, 1950.)

10. *If we value the pursuit of knowledge, we must be free to follow wherever that search may lead us. The free mind is no barking dog, to be tethered on a 10 foot chain.* (Adlai Stevenson, 1952.)

11. *A man, though wise, should never be ashamed of learning more and must unbend his mind.* (Sophocles, 441 B.C.)

12. *Where there is an open mind, there will always be a frontier.* (Charles F. Kettering, *Profile of America*, 1954.)

13. *Change is the law of life, and those who look only to the past or present are certain to miss the future.* (John F. Kennedy, 1963.)

14. *Progress is a nice word, but change is its motivator and change has its enemies.* (Robert F. Kennedy, *The Pursuit of Justice*, 1964.)

15. *The pace of events is moving so fast that unless we can find some way to keep our sights on tomorrow, we cannot expect to be in touch with today.* (Dean Rusk, 1963.)

16. *Conformity is the jailer of freedom and the enemy of growth.* (John F. Kennedy, 1961.)

17. *He who does anything because it is the custom, makes no choice.* (John Stewart, 1859.)

18. *In practice, such trifles as contradictions and principle are easily set aside; the faculty of ignoring them makes the practical man.* (Henry Adams, 1907.)

19. *Man like every other animal is by nature indolent. If nothing spurs him on, then he will hardly think and will behave from habit like an automaton.* (Einstein, 1950.)

20. *Continuity does not rule our fresh approaches to fresh situations.* (Dean Rusk, 1963.)

21. *Every great advance in natural knowledge has involved the absolute rejection of authority.* (Huxley, *Lay Sermons*.)

22. *All things must change—to something new, to something strange.* (Longfellow.)

23. *Habit, if not resisted, soon becomes necessity.* (St. Augustine.)

24. *An obstinate man does not hold opinions, but they hold him.* (Pope.)

LOGIC.   When the other person is using faulty reasoning to persuade action or agreement on your part, one of the following quotations may be useful in supporting your rebuttal and getting the other side into the right frame of mind:

1. *There is no such thing as a convincing argument, although every man thinks he has one.* (Edgar Watson Howe, 1911.)

2. *Arguments that make their point by means of similarities are imposters, and, unless you are on your guard against them, will quite readily deceive you.* (Simmias, in Plato's *Phaedo*, fourth century B.C.)

3. *I do not resent criticism, even when, for the sake of emphasis, it parts for the time with reality.* (Sir Winston Churchill, 1941.)

4. *The grand aim of all science is to cover the greatest number of empirical facts by logical deductions from the smallest number of hypotheses or axioms.* (Einstein, 1950.)

5. *The wise man recognizes the convenience of a general statement, but he bows to the authority of a particular fact.* (Oliver Wendell Holmes, 1872.)

6. *You will find that the truth is often unpopular and the contest between agreeable fancy and disagreeable fact is unequal. For, in the vernacular, we Americans are suckers for good news.* (Adlai Stevenson, 1958.)

7. *Nothing is more dangerous than an idea, when it is the only idea we have.* (Alain, 1914.)

8. *General and abstract ideas are the source of the greatest errors of mankind.* (Rousseau, 1762.)

9. *Error flies from mouth to mouth, from pen to pen, and to destroy it takes ages.* (Voltaire, *Philosophical Dictionary*, 1764.)

10. *That is a bad bridge which is shorter than the stream.* (German proverb.)

11. *If the blind lead the blind, both shall fall into the ditch.* (*Matthew* 15:14.)

12. *To be proud of knowledge is to be blind with light.* (Benjamin Franklin, *Poor Richard's Almanac*, 1757.)

13. *The greater our knowledge increases the greater our ignorance unfolds.* (John F. Kennedy, 1962.)

14. *If thou thinkest twice before thou speakest once, thou wilt speak twice the better for it.* (William Penn, *Some Fruits of Solitude*, 1693.)

15. *Fury helps us to bear our ignorance of facts.* (George Santayana, 1896.)

16. *The utmost abstractions are the true weapons with which to control our thought of concrete fact.* (Alfred N. Whitehead, *Science and the Modern World*, 1925.)

17. *Man does not live by words alone, despite the fact that sometimes he has to eat them.* (Adlai Stevenson, 1952.)

18. *Men willingly believe what they wish.* (Julius Caesar.)

19. *Nothing is so firmly believed as what we least know.* (Montaigne.)

20. *Penny wise, pound foolish.* (Burton.)

STALEMATE. When both parties have exhausted their arguments, no agreement is in sight and it appears that the deal may fall through, one of the following quotations may be appropriate in relieving tension and taking a more light-hearted view of the situation:

1. *The drowning man is not troubled by rain.* (Persian proverb.)

2. *An appeaser is one who feeds a crocodile, hoping it will eat him last.* (Sir Winston Churchill, 1954.)

3. *Great is the art of beginning, but greater the art is of ending.* (Longfellow, 1881.)

4. *There's time for departure even there's no certain place to go.* (Tennessee Williams, 1953.)

5. *Compromise is an adjustment of conflicting interest as gives each adversary a satisfaction of thinking he has got what he ought not to have and is deprived of nothing except what was justly his due.* (Ambrose Bierce, *The Devil's Dictionary*, 1911.)

6. *If you cannot catch a bird of paradise, better take a wet hen.* (Nikita Khrushchev, 1958.)

7. *He that can't endure the bad, will not live to see the good.* (Yiddish proverb.)

8. *Flops are a part of life's menu and I've never been a girl to miss out on many of the courses.* (Rosalind Russell, 1957.)

9. *Quarrels would not last long if the fault was only on one side.* (LaRochefoucauld, *Maxims*, 1655.)

10. *There is no success without hardship.* (Sophocles, *Electra*, 418 B.C.)

11. *The first thing we do, let's kill all the lawyers.* (Shakespeare, *Henry IV*, 1598.)

12. *Is there anything in life so disenchanting as attainment?* (Robert Louis Stevenson, *The Arabian Nights*, 1882.)

13. *There is no education like adversity.* (Disraeli.)

MANAGEMENT AND EMPLOYEE MOTIVATION. Sometimes you can increase a subordinate's outlook, enthusiasm and cooperative spirit by using a simple quotation rather than a five-minute lecture:

1. *The house praises the carpenter.* (Ralph Waldo Emerson, 1836.)

2. *The reward of the thing well done is to have done it.* (Ralph Waldo Emerson, 1844.)

3. *If you tell* [count] *every step, he will make a long journey of it.* (Thomas Fuller, 1732.)

4. *Let the end try the man.* (Shakespeare, *Henry IV*, 1598.)

5. *To be conscious that you are ignorant is a great step to knowledge.* (Disraeli, *Sybil*.)

6. *To achieve great things we must live as though we were never going to die.* (Vauvenargues, *Reflections and Maxims*, 1746.)

7. *Eat to please thyself, but dress to please others.* (Benjamin Franklin.)

8. *Nothing is impossible for the man who doesn't have to do it himself.* (A.H. Weiler, The New York Times.)

9. *Behind an able man there are always other able men.* (Chinese proverb.)

10. *Who is not satisfied with himself will grow; who is not sure of his own correctness will learn many things.* (Chinese proverb.)

11. *Victory belongs to the most persevering.* (Napoleon.)

12. *All you need in this life is ignorance and confidence, and then Success is sure.* (Samuel Clemens [Mark Twain], 1887.)

MANAGEMENT AND DELEGATION.   At times you will receive resistance, resentment and even anger from those to whom you have delegated tasks. One of the quotations below can be effective in replying without the danger of escalating the matter out of proportion:

1. *The heights by great men reached and kept/Were not attained by sudden flight,/But they, while their companions slept,/Were upward in the night.* (Longfellow, 1858.)

2. *Once begun, a task is easy; if the work is done.* (Horace, *Epistles*, 8 B.C.)

3. *What is worth doing is worth the trouble of asking somebody to do it.* (Ambrose Bierce, The Devil's Dictionary, 1911.)

4. *The way to rise is to obey and please.* (Ben Jonson, 1603)

5. *Genius is one percent inspiration and ninety-nine percent perspiration.* (Edison.)

6. *There is no success without hardship.* (Sophocles, *Electra*, 418 B.C.)

7. *Strange how much you've got to know—before you know how little you know.* (Anonymous.)

8. *Men are born with two eyes, but with one tongue, in order that they should see twice as much as they say.* (Cotton.)

WORKAHOLISM.   Every employee, from the president of the company down to the lowliest clerk, must cope with the pressures of the job and especially the demands of those they are accountable to. Below are some quotations that will make your superior think twice when he or she asks you to increase your aspiration level further, perhaps even at the expense of your personal and family life:

1. *Who cares about great marks left behind? We have one life, rigidly defined. Just one. Our life. We have nothing else.* (Ugo Betti, *The Enquiry*, 1945.)

2. *He who begins too much accomplishes little.* (German proverb.)

3. *A man dies still if he has done nothing, as one who has done much.* (Homer, *Iliad*, nineteenth century B.C.)

4. *Blessed is he who expects nothing, for he shall never be disappointed.* (Alexander Pope, 1727.)

5. *There is only one success, to be able to spend your own life in your own way.* (Christopher Morley.)

6. *Most men who do thrive in the world do forget to take pleasure during the time that they are getting their estate, but deserve that till they have got one, and then it is too late for them to enjoy it.* (Samuel Butler, 1666.)

7. *A man who raises himself by degrees to wealth and power, contracts, in the course of his protracted labor, habits of prudence and restraint which he can not afterwards shake off.* (Alexis de Tocqueville, *Democracy in America*, 1839.)

ON FINDING AN EMPLOYEE OR PARTNER.   If you are meeting with candidates for a position on your staff or as a partner, the following story and quotation may be appropriate if the candidate or his or her agent expresses undue concern about the benefits to be obtained in relation to the contributions that you can expect from the candidate: A group in South Africa wrote to David Livingstone, asking if he found a good road leading to him so that other men may join his efforts. Livingstone replied, "If you have men who will come only if they know there is a good road, I don't want them. I want men who will come if there is no road."

ON HANDLING YOUR BOSS.   When your supervisor is reluctant to delegate more responsibility or does not appreciate your true talents, a quotation may open his or her mind to your opinion:

1. *We judge ourselves by what we feel capable of doing, while others judge us by what we have already done.* (Longfellow.)

2. (If you are a woman.) *A woman's guess is much more accurate than a man's certainty.* (Kipling.)

WOMEN.   When encountering sex bias or sexist thinking, a quotation can do the talking for you, thereby avoiding permanent damage in your relationship.

1. *Suffer women to arrive at an equality with you, and they will from that moment become your superiors.* (Cato the Censor.)

2. *The female of the species is more deadly than the male.* (Kipling.)

3. *Those who always speak well of women do not know them sufficiently; those who always speak ill of them do not know them at all.* (Lebrun.)

EMOTION, ANGER AND DISRESPECT.   In addition to remaining calm and collected under the brunt of shouting, crying, threats and he like, you may find one of the following quotations appropriate for the situation:

1. *It is not he who gains the exact point in dispute who scores most in controversy, but he who has shown the most forbearance and the better temper.* (Samuel Butler, 1902.)

2. *Justice is always violent to the party offending, for every man is innocent in his own eyes.* (Daniel Defoe, 1702.)

3. *Men are apt to mistake the strength of their feeling for the strength of their argument.* (Gladstone.)

4. *All men who reflect on controversial matters should be free from hatred, friendship, anger, and pity.* (Julius Caesar.)

5. *When Bishop Berkeley said, "There was no matter," and proved it—'twas no matter what he said.* (Byron, *Don Juan.*)

6. *It is much easier to be critical than to be correct.* (Disraeli.)

7. *One man's word is no man's word; we should quietly hear both sides.* (Goethe.)

8. *Fitting hospitality must be shown even towards an enemy arrived at the house. The tree does not withdraw from the wood-cutter the shade at its side.* (Hindu proverb.)

9. *If a traveler does not meet with one who is his better, or his equal, let him firmly keep to his solitary journey; there is no companionship with a fool.* (Buddhist scripture.)

10. *Do not speak harshly to anyone; those who are spoken to will answer thee in the same way. Angry speech is painful; blows for blows will touch thee.* (Buddhist scripture.)

11. *Anger is momentary madness, so control your passion or it will control you.* (Horace, *Epistles.*)

12. *Men in general judge more from appearance than from reality. All men have eyes, but few have the gift of penetration.* (Machiavelli.)

Chapter 7
PDC FOR
FAILSAFE NEGOTIATION

SECURITY

A person's security needs include economic and social position (money, possessions and power), autonomy (freedom of action) and conservation (preserving and protecting the status quo due to fear of change and the unknown, which might be detrimental to a person's job and career).

You can satisfy a person's security needs when you are in a position to use the words *proven, approved, accepted by, certified* and the like with respect to the high quality of the products you are promoting if your statements are supported by the favorable reports of independent testing laboratories, professional bodies and government agencies. This enables the purchasing agent to be assured that a blunder will not be committed and his or her position jeopardized because of buying a poor product.

If you are attempting to persuade someone to enter into a joint venture with you, you can play on security and esteem needs by pointing out how this person's image, reputation and career will be enhanced by being the person with foresight enough to invest in a discovery that will revolutionize the entire industry. If you are dealing with a purchasing agent, you can point out how that person's status within the company will be elevated because of the dramatic cost reduction that will be effected by the new machinery.

You can fulfill security needs without even saying anything. By carrying a briefcase or having a desk set bearing the company's name, you are building an image that suggests you have stability. Similar items, such as diaries, calendars and pens embossed with the company's name can be given away to make people feel they are important. Calling a deal that is set forth in writing an understanding is much more comforting than calling it a contract or agreement. It is a plain fact that contracts scare people because of the legal mumbo jumbo they represent. Likewise, a person will feel more secure with a simple, brief understanding drafted in lay terms and, better still, handwritten instead of formally typewritten.

115

People feel secure when they are dealing with people who appear successful and who seem to be winners. How many times have you wondered what you are doing in a restaurant that is practically empty? On the other hand, why does a restaurant that fills to capacity for dinner always have a waiting line? Success breeds success. Whether people are dealing with a restaurant, a company or a professional, they want to deal with someone who is in demand by other people. The inconvenience of waiting to deal with winners is overshadowed by the fulfillment of security needs. Similarly, the small business manager who first has a receptionist answer the phone, then the secretary and finally the administrative assistant, is conveying the image that he or she is an important executive in a large operation. This conveys an atmosphere of security to the calling party, who values reliability and responsibility.

People feel more secure when they are obtaining high quality work and expect to pay more. Before charging lower prices than normal for your goods or services, give thought to possible suspicion you may be arousing in the mind of the buyer. In the same vein, people feel more secure dealing with a party that has plenty of money. If you are advertising in a national publication, such as the *Wall Street Journal, Business Week, Fortune, Forbes,* or *Newsweek,* you are telling people that you are a winner and you are financially well off because of the demand for your product or services. The average reader who sees your full-page ad in *Time* magazine does not realize it was inserted on a regional basis at a fraction of the cost of a national campaign.

Understatements are more effective than exaggeration because they are more believable and breed confidence. Before making a point that the other party may disagree with, you may wish to use Benjamin Franklin's technique of prefacing your statement with an assurance phrase, such as one of the following:

1. "This may sound too good to be true. . . ."
2. "I wouldn't be surprised if you questioned it, however. . . ."
3. "You are going to think this is crazy, but. . . ."
4. "Many people were skeptical when I first told them this, yet. . . ."

An assurance phrase makes a definite and straightforward appeal to the other party's skepticism. It is reassuring and prepares the other party to accept the proposition put forth more quickly.

When discussing personnel, financial, personal and trade secret matters, you satisfy the other party's need for security by using a low, confidential tone of voice in a private location where his or her secrets will not be heard. You are gaining even more trust if you lean forward toward the other person and talk as if he or she were the only person in the world that mattered.

Going back to the reflection theory that was discussed in Chapter 1, perhaps the best way of obtaining the trust of another party is to be genuine:

1. Don't be afraid to reveal your true feelings and your true self.
2. Be spontaneous in your actions and relationships rather than controlled.
3. Be willing to be viewed by others on the basis of your natural behavior.
4. Don't be overly concerned with what other people think.
5. Don't worry about losing dignity and being rejected.
6. Enter into intimate relationships on a personal level. During Henry Kissinger's first journey to Peking, Premier Chou En-lai emphasized the need to remove the mystery associated with their respective countries in order to build confidence between them. They had long and deep talks, presenting their respective views of the world with a frankness rarely achieved among allies. This was repeated during President Nixon's visit. These intimate relationships no doubt hastened normalization of relations between the nations.

Some parting comments about security needs. Don't gossip about others because listeners, if wise, will know that you will tell others things about them. You will only breed suspicion and mistrust with a loose tongue.

Don't ask a person to violate principles or integrity in order to consummate the deal. You will lose respect and trust because your own efforts are put in issue regarding your dealings with that person.

People want to avoid the insecurity that comes from surprise and change. If you see an unfavorable trend or situation developing, try to prepare the other party in advance. This person will respect you for your frankness and trust you for your sincerity.

ESTEEM

Esteem is a powerful need for most of us. Answer the questions below to find out what role esteem plays when you negotiate. Rate yourself from 0 to 5, with 0 being *no* and 5 being *yes*. Put down your true feelings, not what you think the ratings should be because there are no correct answers. An interpretation of your responses follows.

1. Do you leave a meeting while others are still interested in talking to you?
2. You let poor English or mispronunciations pass without mentioning them.
3. Do you always thank people for even minor courtesies?
4. Do you always listen with interest when others talk?
5. Do you usually anticipate what people are going to do?
6. Do you laugh at attempts to be humorous?
7. Do you say "thank you," even to immediate family members?
8. Are you pretty sure people would like to do things before asking them to?
9. You never interrupt others when they are talking.
10. Do you make your visits short?
11. Do you try to encourage people?
12. Do you follow the interests of others?
13. You never talk about things that embarrass someone present.

14. Do you let others get most of the attention?
15. Do you say "please" frequently?
16. Do you frequently compliment people, even on something minor?
17. Your voice is soft and pleasing.
18. You do many thoughtful little things for others.
19. You let irritating opinions pass without arguing.
20. You are always constructive and helpful to others.
21. You show respect for just about everyone.
22. Do you normally do what others are interested in doing?
23. Do people feel happier after talking with you?
24. People think they are having their own way when dealing with you.
25. You take things gradually, without seeming insistent.
26. You are not bossy.
27. You have no hangup about being touched during conversation.
28. You talk easily with others, including strangers.
29. You look at people when conversing.
30. You treat other people as equals, even those you supervise.
31. You want people to think highly of you.
32. People find you easy to understand and get along with.
33. When talking to a stranger, you convey the feeling that he or she has special qualities.
34. Soon after being introduced to a stranger, you try to get this person to talk about him- or herself.
35. You laugh at yourself in appropriate circumstances.

Add up your ratings. If the sum of your ratings falls in the 120–130 range, you are average in your respect and regard for others.

If you are in the range up to 150, you recognize the value of making others feel good.

If you exceed 150, you consciously go out of your way to satisfy the esteem needs of others.

If you are below 120, you probably have some degree of difficulty in dealing with others, particularly in persuading people to go along with your requests, demands and objectives. In short, people will not like interacting with you if you appear or you actually are discourteous, disrespectful and not interested in them.

Sigmund Freud said that everything we do springs from two motives: "The sex urge and the desire to be great and important." Even famous people have a craving for importance. George Washington wanted to be called "His Mightiness, the President of the United States"; Columbus pleaded for the title "Admiral of the Ocean and Viceroy of India"; Victor Hugo tried to have the city of Paris renamed in his honor; Shakespeare sought to enhance his name by procuring a coat of arms for his family; and Richard Nixon was obsessed with winning a second term as President of the United States with the widest margin in history.

You can satisfy a person's esteem needs by showing respect, giving compliments and praise, and showing recognition for the individual's accomplishments, status, intelligence, wealth, possessions and style. Your message must be sincere, and one way to convey sincerity is to become genuinely interested in other people. Ralph Waldo Emerson was able to give sincere compliments because of his philosophy: "Every man I meet is my superior in some way." Direct or blatant flattery to a comparative stranger, unkind flattery, general flattery, flattery bluntly given and followed by a pause that suggests insincerity or fishing for a compliment in return may embarrass, arouse suspicion and make the recipient uncomfortable. Flattery should be definite: "The mahogany paneling is breathtaking," instead of "What a pretty office." A compliment should be woven into the conversation as you continue to talk to give the impression that your flattering comment is not a spur-of-the-moment thought that you conveniently convert to a compliment, but stems from your true outlook.

If you need a favor, respect the person's intelligence by taking the time to give a reason, even if it is of no benefit to the person.

There are many ways to fulfill people's esteem needs without saying a word. Be a good listener and encourage others to talk about themselves. Make others feel that what they are doing or saying definitely matters by avoiding interruption, nodding attentively and smiling appropriately to assure them that they have your undivided attention and your interest. When asked to give the mathematical equation for success, Einstein said: "If A represents success in life, the formula is $A = X + Y + Z$, where X is work, Y is play, and Z is keeping your mouth shut!" If your business sells a product or service of high quality that has a status in the marketplace, you will fill the esteem needs of your customers and others who do business with you merely by their association with you and purchase of your goods and services. If you walk into someone's office, together with two professionally dressed secretaries and your staff executive, who is also impeccably dressed, you are telling this person that he or she is important and warrants the presence of your entourage and the time and money their presence represent. By exercising patience and allowing others to make up their minds, present their positions or simply take a break in your discussion, you convey the impression that you view them with importance. Likewise, when you enter someone else's office, you should hold off lighting a cigarette until invited to do so. If someone offers you a cigarette, accept it and don't belittle the other person's taste by reaching for your own brand. Put back magazines and papers that you read while waiting and don't litter the reception room. Keep your briefcase and other items off the other person's desk, unless you first ask permission. Finally, anything you hand to someone should be placed carefully in his or her hands to show respect for both the person and the item.

The best way to satisfy esteem needs after people voice an opinion you disagree with is to avoid argument. If you must say something, give them the impression that they are having their own way even though you actually disagree. Start off in a soft tone of voice and with a pleasant smile of agreement. Give in on something that is unimportant enough to be a concession even if you don't agree on that either. Don't be negative.

Start out by saying any of the following:

1. "Based on your assumptions, I can understand your conclusion. Suppose . . ."
2. "Of course, you are right, and have you considered that . . ."
3. "That is an excellent point. May I make a comment?"
4. "I thought so too, until suddenly . . ."
5. "That makes sense and sounds logical to me. Can we look at it from another angle?"
6. "I see you have thought it out very carefully. Now, what happens when . . . ?"
7. "We're actually not very far apart in our thinking because . . ."
8. "Would you agree that this is subject to more than one interpretation?"

Starting out in the above manner allows others to save face and makes it easy for them to agree with you because you did not reply as an arguer, adversary or opponent. Loss of face is a powerful factor that has blown many deals and cannot be stressed enough. Richard Nixon was so fearful of being rebuffed that he always constructed an excuse for failure in advance.

Another technique allowing someone to save face is to spread out or transfer the blame or embarrassment. Make it the fault of the person's accountant, lawyer, associate who is no longer with the company or corporate policy or procedure.

A strong technique of filling people's esteem needs is making them think you need them and giving them a chance to prove it. Ask a favor. Better yet, ask a favor that will require them to demonstrate their knowledge or superior abilities. This tactic can involve something as simple as getting someone's opinion on a matter of importance to you.

Perhaps two of the most potent ways of appealing to people's esteem needs are to give them a fine reputation to live up to and to stimulate competition between them and others. People do not think of themselves as losers and will rise to the occasion to show that the challenge can be met or that they are better than someone else. In fact, if you treat a thief as an honorable person, he or she may be so flattered by your trust that he or she will live up to the reputation.

The story is told that Lowell Thomas once motivated Dale Carnegie to learn the game of bridge, and even though he had never played it and had no interest in it, Thomas merely said, "There is nothing to bridge except memory and judgment. You once wrote a chapter on memory. Bridge will be a cinch for you. It is right up your alley." In short, Thomas threw a challenge and at the same time treated Carnegie as if he had the abilities to easily do what Thomas suggested.

During Israeli Prime Minister Golda Meir's visit to Washington, she hailed President Nixon as an old friend of the Jewish people. This surprised many people familiar with Nixon's ambivalences on that topic. Meir shrewdly gave Nixon a reputation to uphold.

Another tool in the esteem arsenal is bestowing authority, responsibility and honor on the other person. Napoleon distributed 15,000 Legion of Honor Crosses to his soldiers and made eighteen generals "Marshalls of France" in the "Grand Army." The same thing is done by the old widow who makes a teenage gang leader her "detective" or "sheriff" to keep other members from bothering her and vandalizing her property. A seller can apply this technique to get a purchasing agent's or design engineer's support by showing how he or she will become visible and an important and respected person in the organization by saving money, manpower, time or returns as a result of the decision to buy from the seller.

Etiquette is one area where many of us work against the esteem needs of others. Most of the time we do not even realize how our manners are offensive, rude or discomforting. During introductions, for instance, the lower age or rank is always presented to the greater age or rank. During negotiation, avoid chewing gum, noisy eating, nose picking, head scratching, finger or pencil tapping, fingernail cleaning, knuckle cracking, tooth picking, lip biting, looking at your watch, rubbing your eyes, inspecting the floor, dry hand washing, counting fingers, coin jiggling, and scratching in various areas of the body.

There are a number of common courtesies we often forget that are quite important in fulfilling a person's esteem needs. For instance, someone's own name is the sweetest and most important sound in any language, and it should be used during your conversation, as well as in writing, when you wish to make key points and hold the person's attention. Remember to frequently say "please," "may I," "thank you," and "I appreciate." When someone attempts to be amusing, laugh in appreciation. Don't talk down to another person. Don't call attention to someone's mistakes unless it is absolutely necessary. Try to talk about your own mistakes before criticizing another's. If both you and the other person came up with an idea or a new approach to solving a problem, give the other person credit for it and make this person feel that it was his or her idea. Try honestly to see things from other peoples' points of view and at their levels. Be sympathetic and understanding regarding their ideas and desires. As already hinted above, never tell people who have expressed an idea that they are wrong. If at all possible, do what the other person is interested in doing. In short, be the reverse of the constant critic who leaves people with negative feelings about themselves and the type person who unconsciously leaves people feeling inadequate due to little things that add up to disrespect.

Talk in terms of *you* and other personal pronouns. When people feel you are interested only in them, even for the moment you are conversing, they feel important. As already mentioned, calling people by their names while presenting your case adds to the respect you are showing.

It is reported that Napoleon made it a practice to memorize the biographies of his soldiers as well as their names. Andrew Carnegie, the steel entrepreneur, is credited with selling many trainloads with the use of "namepower." He simply named his steel plants after important buyers. Pullman did likewise, naming his cars after well-known customers.

There are various memory systems you can learn from books, courses and seminars; however, the basic formula in improving your memory to utilize namepower is impression, repetition and association. When coming into contact with someone new or hearing his or her name for the first time, it is important to get the impression correctly and fixed in your mind at once. Be able to view it clearly, spell it accurately, say it audibly, write it and picture it. Generally, people cannot remember a name because it never made any impression in the first place and no effort was made to make it stick. Repetition is important in making the impression permanent. Repeat the name silently to yourself after meeting the person. The association stick is important for recall. Unfamiliar things can be remembered more easily when they are hooked up with familiar items and ideas. A name can be associated with almost any mental hook, such as an animal for Mr. Finn, a vegetable for Ms. Croot, a color for Mr. Breen, an occupation for Mr. Carpenter and appearance for Ms. Small.

Another way to make your message personal and appeal to the individuality and esteem needs of the other person is to express your personal feelings. There's nothing that makes a person feel more important than hearing you confide your true feelings on a confidential and personal basis. At times, you will want to take advantage of this and throw logic, analysis and reasoning out the window. Just tell the person how you really feel about things. This will work especially well with people who are Feelers and Sensors (discussed later in this chapter).

FRIENDSHIP

People really have a need for love and belonging. They want friendship, sympathy, empathy, nourishment, attention and amusement, and they want to be wanted. When the friendship need is satisfied on the part of both sides, the negotiators establish a harmonious relationship, or *rapport*.

Not only does friendship attract and hold the other person's attention, but it also brings out the better side of human nature. People really do enjoy working with someone who understands them and likes them. Even the seemingly mean and grumpy negotiator wants to be liked. People generally expect highly successful men and women to be very serious and abrupt because they carry so much responsibility and power. The executive who conveys friendship will win people over at once because they can identify with the executive even though they have nothing in common with the tycoon except for the warm atmosphere that is established.

At their first meeting, Soviet Ambassador Anatoly Dobrynin greeted National Security Advisor Henry Kissinger with a friendly smile and suggested they deal with each other on a first-name basis. At the close of their conversation, Dobrynin again smiled and conceded that not all the mistakes impeding relaxed tensions in past years had been on the American side. It is no surprise that, before leaving, Kissinger promised Dobrynin that he would have an early meeting with newly elected President Nixon.

Will Rogers summed up the reflection theory on friendship very well when he said, "People like people who like them and will do things for people who will do things in return." This was confirmed by a study conducted at Harvard University. A psychologist gave students different literary selections to read from. They were told that various writers had written different selections. The selections that were attributed to an author that the students liked were rated "fine" and "excellent." The selections that were accredited to an unpopular author were rated very low in literary ability. All the selections were written by the same author, Robert Louis Stevenson.

President Nixon was especially considerate when it came to relations with France. For instance, it was a thoughtful gesture for Nixon to attend a dinner in New York in French President Georges Pompidou's honor after hostile demonstrations in Chicago. Subsequently, he flew to Paris for de-Gaulle's memorial service. Notwithstanding his doubts and suspicions regarding Americans, Pompidou grew to like Nixon, and relations with France improved. Without a doubt, the reflection theory was responsible when Pompidou helped arrange Henry Kissinger's secret contacts with the North Vietnamese, even making his own jet available for Kissinger.

You learned in Chapter 1 that friendship is a prerequisite to establishing cooperative behavior and the benefits that flow from it. Suppose you don't feel friendly or you have reason not to be friendly? Unfortunately, people are pretty good at detecting phony feelings.

Perhaps the easiest way to be friendly and make people like you right off the bat is to develop a genuine and sincere interest in them. Be relaxed, address people by name, listen patiently, compliment people, show a good sense of humor, use contractions and other informal jargon, greet people with a warm smile, be humble and show your human side. Even if you hate someone's guts, there is some goodness and something interesting in everyone. As Will Rogers said, "I never met a man I did not like." Abe Lincoln refused to get mad at people who abused him, ridiculed him and tried to discredit him. His philosophy was that people's actions spring from their character and many factors beyond their control are created from early childhood. He felt, "You shouldn't become angry with a person who blocks your goal any more than with a tree which the wind blew across your path."

In summary, be participating and not withdrawn, be enthusiastic and not melancholic, be adventurous and not fearful, and be accepting and not suspecting. The following list shows the various components that make up each of these attributes. Although you are probably somewhere between the extremes shown, you should adopt the attributes in the left-hand column and consciously eliminate those on the right from your personality during negotiation.

Participating	*Withdrawn*
Adaptable	Aloof and timid
Cooperative	Cold
Friendly	Cynical
Good-natured	Obstructive
Optimistic	Pessimistic
Trusting	Rigid

Enthusiastic	*Melancholic*
Changeable	Aloof and timid
Cheerful	Habit-bound
Lively	Quiet
Sociable	Sad
Spendthrift	Thrifty

Adventurous	*Fearful*
Carefree	Cautious
Frank and open	Cynical
Friendly	Secretive
Grateful	Self-distrustful
Idealistic	Thankless
Self-confident	Unfriendly

Accepting	*Suspecting*
Cheerful	Cold
Grateful	Sad
Sentimental	Suspicious
Trusting	Thankless

AESTHETICS

Satisfying a person's aesthetic needs of fairness, balance, order, and harmony, sensuality, beauty and drama can be advantageous in obtaining acceptance of your position. People wish to be thought of as honest, considerate, equitable and responsible and appreciate that which is pleasing to the senses. When you ask someone to agree to cultural, institutional, noble and even individual ways and customs of doing things, you are appealing to aesthetic needs.

It is sometimes amazing how a person's desire for fulfillment of these needs induces him or her to accept your way of thinking when it is presented as your company policy or the standard industry practice. The aesthetic need appeal is illustrated by getting someone to "split the difference," to take a "fifty-fifty split," to round the purchase price of a piece of machinery from $2650 to $2500, and so on, based upon precedents, rules, norms of reciprocity, legitimacy and fair play.

Many people aren't interested in long, drawn out explanations based on lots of data and software. These people would rather see the big picture on a colorful graph or slides because of their aesthetic need to visualize something dramatic. As you will learn later, these people are called Sensors. You want to give them pictures, models, things to smell and touch and anything else that will make your idea or presentation interesting and exciting.

One of the most effective and seductive appeals to the aesthetic needs of the others is the Parent slogan. The story is told of the general who amassed a great deal of data and was attempting to reach a logical decision on whether to go to the help of a friendly neighboring country that was being invaded by another power. He could not make up his mind until an advisor said, "General, I cannot believe it is taking you so long to go to the rescue of our neighbors. What are friends for if they cannot be counted on?" With that question, the general committed his nation to a war that lasted twelve long, hard years. The general, like many people in moments of stress, abandoned his Adult (logic) ego state and was swayed by the sloganlike Parent (emotional) message because it fulfilled his aesthetic needs for fairness and responsibility. Catchy Parent slogans have always been used by politicians, military leaders and other managers of large groups of people. Parent slogans provide simple concepts for followers to identify with and support. When you are running into a stone wall in using logic, try to sway the other person with such slogans as "Stick to the company policy," "Don't change horses in midstream," "Don't mix business with pleasure," "Never abandon your principles," "Fight fire with fire," and "Never let anyone take advantage of you."

SELF-ACTUALIZATION AND KNOWLEDGE

Self-actualization is the inner motivation to become everything one is capable of becoming in light of natural and taught physical and mental abilities and talents. One of the best ways of making this need work for you is merely to make a suggestion or throw out an idea that you are not sure about something instead of arrogantly ramming your opinion down the other person's throat. People like to make up their own minds and draw their own conclusions. Benjamin Franklin used to say: "The way to convince another is to state your case moderately and accurately. Then scratch your head and shake a little and say that is the way it seems to you, but that of course you may be mistaken about it . . . which causes your listener to receive what you have to say and as like as not turn about and try to convince you of it." In short, appeal to others' self-actualization need so that they will wind up arguing your case for you and feeling that the idea was actually theirs.

Franklin's advice brings us to the theory "Dumb is smart and smart is very dumb." It is not smart to be decisive, brilliant, quick, witty and completely rational when you are engaging in a negotiating session. You will probably get more concessions and far better answers if you act slow to understand, less decisive and somewhat irrational because you permit others to satisfy their esteem and self-actualization needs. Forget that you want to look good and force yourself to say, "I don't know" or, "Tell me this again."

When people participate in a decision, they tend to accept and support it. Without such involvement, a person's natural tendency is to judge, evaluate and approve or disapprove the statement of another. Evaluative judging can be avoided by enticing someone else to state your own case through proper questioning.

For instance, you should regularly remember to ask, "Does this sound logical to you?" and "How does this strike you?" Another questioning ploy is to say, "You know my reason for saying that, don't you?" The other person will say, "Of course. You think. . . ." Then you ask, "And why is that important?" In response to this, the other person will again help you state your own position.

This questioning technique is known as the "saying is believing" phenomenon. The research shows that the greater the discrepancy between what people think and what they say, the greater is the likelihood that their opinion will change. Thus, if people disagree with you, do not be satisfied with a "no" or other brief response. Draw them out with questions and get them to give logical explanations that will force them to see the fallacy of their own opinion. Persuade them to write down their reasoning. Nothing exposes faulty logic quicker than attempting to convert abstractions into clear details on paper.

The need to know and to understand arises from our basic drive to explore and to explain the unknown and satisfies our most basic needs regarding the application of reason and logic. The more you tell the other party about yourself and your goals and plans for both of you, the better the climate will be for trust, cooperation and decision making by the other party.

In fact, knowledge is so important that information obtained from indirect sources has more credibility than that provided openly. Lost memos, stolen documents, and notes thrown in the wastebaskets where the other side can find them is one way to convey your position or information without taking responsibility for it and without creating a deadlock and risking termination of negotiations. Another technique is to let the other side read your thoughts by deliberately writing so large that it can be easily seen upside down. Remember, if a negotiator forgets his or her attache case in your outer office, don't trust everything you read. It may be a deliberate plant designed to mislead or test out what concessions you are willing to make.

THE SIX EGO STATES

When dealing with people within your company or with outsiders on a continual basis, you will have the additional advantage of knowing exactly what their emotional needs are, in contrast to the general rules of thumb regarding need satisfaction outlined above in this chapter. You can use transactional analysis to analyze the Parent, Adult and Child ego states from which the person you deal with transacts, their consequences and the best way for you to take advantage of them.

The three basic ego states of transactional analysis are the Parent (dominant), Adult (detached) and Child (dependent) modes. Each person exhibits varying degrees of Parent, Adult and Child behavior at various times and in different situations. Usually, an individual's personality is dominated by one or two of these ego states.

The Adult

The Adult ego state is fact oriented, organized, objective and reflected by realistic reasoning and logical decision making. The Adult state results from independent thinking in early life and its subsequent development during maturity. Verbally, the Adult is inclined to speak of probabilities, exchange facts, offer suggestions, opinions and options, avoid words like *never* and *always*, and use phrases such as "I see your point," "I recognize . . . ," "How do you feel . . . ," "So far the facts seem to indicate . . . ," and "Possibly. . . ." The Adult's vocal tone is relaxed, somewhat deliberate and self-assertive. The Adult will also be revealed by body language: straight, relaxed stance, slightly tilted head, appearance of active listening (alert body movements, such as nodding the head), regular eye contact, and confident appearance.

How do you handle the Adult? Of all the personality types, this one is most affected by the logic of your argument and least swayed by emotional appeals, except for self-actualization and knowledge needs.

The Child

How do you identify the person who is in the Child ego state? Child behavior reflects the toddler before age three, who attempts to avoid pain, adapts, is dependent and tries to win approval. The Child ego state actually has three parts: the Natural Child, the Manipulating Child and the Adaptive Child.

The Natural Child enjoys life, craves affection, is curious (reflected by touching, pushing and gripping everything in range), acts freely and openly with others (creative feelings of warmth, friendliness and acceptance), and expresses playful and joking activity. The curiosity and playful behavior of the Natural Child can spark outstanding performance, achievement, creativity and discovery. Typical expressions of the Natural Child are "Wow," "Oh boy!" "Golly," and "Did I do OK?" The vocal tone is generally cheerful, and body language will reflect a friendly, happy childhood when the child had a twinkle in his or her eyes, went skipping and enjoyed hugging. Needless to say, the Natural Child is best handled if you display a warm, friendly and caring attitude, which will go a long way toward satisfying his emotional needs. This person is inclined to react negatively if you put constraints on his or her creativity outlets, if you present the cold facts without emotions from your Adult ego state or if you express disapproval or anger from your Parent ego state.

The Manipulating Child uses his or her understanding of people and their tolerance to manipulation-playing for tricking and conning people into doing what he or she wants. The Manipulating Child is a master strategist who toys intuitively with ideas and relationships that can trigger inspiration, creation and insight. Some of this individual's typical expressions are, "I wish . . . ," "If only . . . ," "One of these days . . . ," and "It's not my fault. . . ." The vocal tone frequently has a complaining, nagging, indignant, protesting and grumbling quality, and body language will show scowling, pursed lips and sadness.

The Manipulating Child can be dealt with effectively by avoiding a response directly to what he or she says, thereby not playing the game that this person has in mind. By responding to the Manipulating Child's feelings and not the words, you can trick this person out of the manipulating ego state. Once you understand, based on body language, choice of words and tone of voice, how this person feels, you can respond with a statement that is devoid of any child implications by using neutral words, such as, "You look like . . . ," "I notice that . . . ," "I hear you saying . . . ," "I am aware that . . . ," "I perceive that you . . . ," and "I feel as. . . ." This type of response, using neutral words on the feeling level, provides the Manipulating Child with a mirror image of what he or she is and feels. This reality feedback exposes and ends the manipulating game. It also forces the Manipulating Child to face his or her real concern, problem or objective on an Adult level.

A typical example of this is when a boss asks a secretary to get a ruler and pen and prepare a simple chart that the boss lays out. The secretary says, "Ms. Cohn, I'm no good at drawing. Why don't you get Debbie to do it?" Instead of getting disgusted and either insisting the secretary do it or being manipulated into using Debbie, Ms. Cohn responds on the feeling level by saying, "You look disturbed and dejected. Seems like you are depressed about something." The secretary, faced with reality, confirms that she has some personal problems she's coping with and thanks Ms. Cohn for being understanding. The boss nods with a smile and walks off, leaving the secretary in a better mood and ready to tackle that chart because her hidden need for friendship, love and understanding has been satisfied.

The Adaptive Child is concerned with acceptance by others, conformity, obedience to authority, and the need to please others. This individual is fearful of pursuing his or her own inner needs and wants because he or she may fail or be rejected. Typical expressions of the Adaptive Child are, "I'm sorry" and, "How am I doing?" In place of spontaneity, flexibility and initiative are inhibition and conservatism.

It is not difficult to understand how to deal with the Adaptive Child. In the above example, if Ms. Cohn actually detected her secretary's true fear of drawing the chart, she would have responded with encouragement and reassurance that it would be OK for her to fail because making a mistake or doing a bad job is a legitimate part of learning.

The Parent

How do you know when a person is negotiating with you in the Parent ego state? The Parent personality is pretty well established by the time we are six to eight years old and is based on all the rules of living, as observed and taught by one's parents. There are actually two Parent ego states: the Nurturing Parent and the Critical Parent.

The Nurturing Parent encourages, supports, guides and looks after the physical and emotional needs of others. Some typical expressions are "I'll protect you," "I'll take care of it" and "Don't worry." Vocal tone is generally soothing and comforting, and body language quite frequently is expressed by patting other people on the back and giving them a reassuring smile.

One obvious way of effectively dealing with the Nurturing Parent is to assume the role of the Child who asks the parent's help, permission, and the like. For instance, assume you are trying to sell something to a purchasing agent who is dealing with you in the Nurturing Parent ego state. He or she states, "We've done it this way for many years, and I don't see changing to your equipment at the present time." By playing the role of the child and asking permission to show the features and the reasoning why the status quo should now be changed, you will appeal to the purchasing agent's desire to give you a fair shake and demonstrate that he or she is not being arbitrary. If, on the other hand, you say that the purchasing agent is wrong or display other aggressive behavior, you risk switching this person's ego state into the Critical Parent, which is discussed in the following section.

Critical Parent behavior is reflected by narrow mindedness, a superior attitude, commands, demands, and criticism. Typical expressions are, "You should . . . ," "You must . . . ," "Don't tell me . . . ," "You disappoint me" and "Don't do that." Typical vocal tones are harsh, judgmental, indignant, commanding, confusing and condescending. Common body language of the Critical Parent consists of looking down over the rim of glasses, pointing an accusing finger, hands on hips, head leaning or straining forward and raising a hand in a punishing gesture.

How do you deal with the Critical Parent's inherent position that he or she is always right, regardless of the data and the circumstances? If this person is blaming you for something, revoking your responsibility, giving you a stern look or raising his or her voice, you must respond from your Adult ego state, calmly, but firmly, with logical reasoning to encourage the person to switch back to the reality of the situation and his or her own Adult. If you agitate or excite this person further, then you reinforce Critical Parent behavior, which the person considers necessary in order to put you in your place due to your discourtesy and insubordination.

The Transaction

In the language of psychotherapists, an exchange between two people is called a transaction. The success of your transaction with another person will depend on your respective ego states and whether the transaction is complementary, crossed, ulterior or angular.

In complementary transaction, you get the response you are expecting, as shown in the example below:

> *Dave:* I need some help on Monday in making a sale of our VMOS 200 to IM. Can you go with me?
> *Sales Manager:* Sure, I'll be happy to go with you.

In the above example, the Adaptive Child is receiving the support he wanted from the Nurturing Parent.

The crossed transaction occurs when an unexpected response is solicited, as shown by the following examples of the sales manager's responses to Dave:

> *Sales Manager:* When are you going to stop using me as a crutch for difficult sales?

> *Sales Manager:* Just look at all the work on my desk. Why does everybody have to come with their problems at the wrong time?
>
> *Sales Manager:* I wish I could help you, Dave. I simply have too much work piled up. But I know you'll pull through OK. You always seem to pull some trick out of your hat in the clinch. (Chuckling.)

Above are responses of the Critical Parent, Manipulating Child and Natural Child, respectively.

The ulterior transaction involves hidden psychological messages between ego states that are different from the surface or apparent social messages. Normally, the literal verbal message will be from one ego state, and body language (pounding on the desk, a grimace, a sigh) or the course of dealing with each other conveys the ulterior message from a different ego state. The actual words spoken comprise the social transaction, whereas the ulterior message is the psychological transaction between different ego states from one or both persons. Below is an example of an ulterior transaction initiated by Dave in the business situation already discussed above:

> *Sales Manager:* Yes, I'll change my schedule so I'll go with you on Monday.
>
> *Dave:* Thanks, a two million dollar deal is riding on this meeting.

At first glance, it would seem that Dave and his sales manager had an Adult–Adult transaction. However, it was actually a Critical Parent–Manipulating Child ulterior transaction. The sales manager agreed to help out in a tone of voice conveying disgust and in effect saying, "When will you ever learn to solve your own problems?" Dave responded in a sarcastic tone of voice which in effect is saying, "It's about time you got off your ass and did something important."

The ulterior transaction causes even greater resentment than the crossed transaction because the participants aren't being open with each other.

The angular transaction is a variation of the ulterior transaction where the sender's message is deliberately expressed in a way that allows the sender to appeal to two ego states in the receiver. In this manner, if the receiver is not manipulated into the desired course of action, the sender can feel safe by saying that he or she was misunderstood. The angular transaction can be used to sound people out about their feelings and intentions or get them to say something that they later regret. The following example is based on the business situation already discussed above:

> *Dave:* I'm shooting for a two million dollar VMOS 200 deal with IDM on Monday. Too bad you can't come and help me close the deal. I understand Sol Fein doesn't want you in the field any more.
>
> *Sales Manager:* I don't give a damn what Sol says. I'm going.
>
> *Sales Manager:* I agree with Sol. I shouldn't be going out in the field because I have more important things to do here.
>
> *Sales Manager:* You are incorrect about me not being able to go into the field. However, I have other things to do that would keep me from joining you.

In the above example, Dave's Manipulating Child has conveyed a seemingly adult message in order to draw forth a Child response that would probably be detrimental to the manager. If instead of the first response given in the above example, the Sales Manager gives the second response, that of an Adult, Dave has not been hurt by the sales gambit. In the third response, also an Adult communication, Dave has at least been successful in finding out some inside information on how free a rein his boss has with Sol Fein, the marketing vice-president.

None of the complementary, crossed, ulterior and angular transactions discussed and illustrated above have been productive. Below is an example of the sales manager who sees through the sender's social message and recognizes Dave's fear of handling the major sales opportunity all alone. This is the sales manager's response as both an Adult and Nurturing Parent, solving Dave's security and knowledge needs.

> *Sales Manager:* I won't be able to join you on Monday because of my work backlog. However, I think you'll have an excellent chance of closing the deal if you take some suggestions that worked for me when I handled the IDM account. O'Brien doesn't really warm up to anything 'til after his Martini after lunch. Also, I wouldn't see Johnson, the manufacturing manager, in the afternoon until O'Brien suggests it. Just have a good, friendly getting acquainted meeting in the morning and don't talk business during lunch. When you get back to his office, he should be quite receptive to your proposal. If there are any concerns you have about your Monday meeting, go ahead and shoot. I'm all ears.

THE FOUR LIFE SCRIPTS

A person's life position determines to a large extent his or her dominant ego state behavior and the kinds of transactions he or she makes with other people. A person's life position, called a script in psychological terms, is formed during childhood, reinforced by parents and justified by subsequent events. It is the dominant one of four basic life positions that will influence an individual's action perhaps 70 percent of the time.

The four life scripts involve how people feel about themselves and others in general, outlined as follows:

1. I'm OK–You're OK.
2. I'm OK–You're Not OK.
3. I'm Not OK–You're OK.
4. I'm Not OK–You're Not OK.

Unlike the other three scripts, which are solidified by the time a person is three years of age, Script 1, I'm OK–You're OK, is finally decided upon during maturity. People with this script are free of hangups because they see themselves as pretty much always doing things right, they feel OK about themselves, they accept themselves as good and sound, they feel worthwhile as a person, they feel no great need to demonstrate to others or to themselves that they are in fact OK and they have no need to play psychological games. In short, they are confident and constructive in their dealings with other people. These totally OK people have a winning attitude about life that allows them to live up to their capabilities and achieve their objectives.

Not only do OK–OK people lack the internal need to manipulate others to achieve ulterior goals, but in addition, these individuals have the capacity for intimacy and a sense of concern for others. They care for people, accept them as they are, treat them as OK regardless of how they may see themselves and are willing to risk becoming emotionally involved with others in unconditional relationships based on mutual respect, openness and honesty.

OK–OK employees communicate openly, accept delegation readily, develop independently, learn willingly, resolve disputes with cooperative behavior, solve problems by consulting others and trusting themselves, are productive, have initiative and treat others fairly and as equals.

People in the script of I'm OK–You're Not OK tend to act superior, arrogant, distrustful of others and as a persecutor. This life position usually involves the Critical Parent or Manipulating Child and stems from the child who has been abused by his or her parents and grows up thinking that everyone is against him or her and it's all right to strike back in the name of survival.

OK–Not OK employees communicate defensively and aggressively, accept delegation with procrastination, bickering and bargaining, develop and learn with difficulty, handle disputes by blaming others, solve problems by rejecting the ideas of others, boast, provoke and play persecutor, perform assignments when absolutely necessary and feel superior to peers and even the boss.

The OK–Not OK script is characterized by psychological games that unconsciously offer rewards that motivate and reinforce the script itself. The pay-off of these games is in feelings, such as anger, sulking, superiority or disgust, resulting from practices such as blaming, criticizing and putting people down. Such practices are called negative strokes because they produce bad feelings. They are in direct contrast to the positive strokes of an OK–OK script, which produces the feelings of happiness, elation and self-satisfaction.

Games that result in negative strokes, called "discounting" in psychological terms, quite often descend from the early childhood games of "mine is better than yours," which is another way of saying, "I'm better than you" or, "I'm OK, and you're not." Such games as NIGYSOB (Now I got you, you son of a bitch), Blemish, Critic, Rapo and Tricky Switches will be discussed later.

How do you handle people whose life position is I'm OK–You're Not OK? People of this type will react indignantly if efforts are made to change them. In fact, although they play the persecutor toward others, they actually see themselves as victims of people out to take advantage of them. You must persuade them that you are not out to "get" them by means of complementary Adult and Natural Child transactions that win their respect and allegiance.

Probably the most difficult thing for people to do when dealing with OK–Not OK individuals is to remain in their Adult ego state in order to establish an atmosphere of OKness to achieve those individuals' trust and encourage them to be open regarding their feelings. For instance, although the temptation is great, the last thing you want to do is to tell them that you think they are playing a psychological game. They may not understand and may resent your accusation, and, even if they do understand, it may simply reinforce their feeling that they are victims and you are Not OK.

One way to stop the game playing of OK–Not OK people is to withhold the pay-off and instead use your Adult in calling upon them to use their Adult to change their behavior. Thus, when these people have been waiting for something to go wrong in order to pounce on you and play NIGYSOB, instead of playing the victim, acting helpless or admitting error, you should break the game up with a neutral Adult response, such as, "I'll think about it," or, "That's an interesting point you made."

The I'm Not OK–You're OK script reflects a person who is basically depressed and feels inferior. This is the most common of the four scripts and stems from all the negative strokes that a child receives growing up: "You are lazy," "You are too slow," "You can't do anything right," "This is the way it's supposed to be done" and many other discouraging statements that are accepted by the child as truth.

Not OK–OK people have a kind of servile, self-demeaning stance in relation to others and are unlikely to be happy even when achieving some success. Regardless of what happens, they just can't seem to feel good about themselves. For instance, people of this type have difficulty enjoying compliments about themselves or their work. They are generally discouraged about things and have a tendency to withdraw from other people. Their Not OK Child ego state fears failure and rejection and throws up defenses.

Not OK–OK employees communicate defensively and self-deprecatingly, accept delegation timidly, develop slowly with reassurance and coaching, handle disputes by focusing on their inadequacies, depend on others to solve problems, brood or overcompensate for their perceived weaknesses with constant activity, are motivated by praise and admonition and consider peers superior.

How do you handle Not OK–OK people? You must give them encouragement that they are really OK by conveying reassurance, showing recognition and satisfying their esteem, security, love and self-actualization needs. When you do have to criticize these people, you should talk about their undesirable behavior rather than attacking them as a person. Instead of saying, "You're _____ (and therefore you are not acceptable to me)," you should say, "Doing this is not acceptable to me because _____." Needless to say, criticism should be done in private so that Not OK people are not embarrassed before others, therefore losing what little esteem they have in the first place. Although Not OK people may play Stupid, Kick Me and other victim-oriented games, you must withhold the pay-off of confirming Not-OKness by not saying they are acting dumb or deserve to be punished. Instead, you should use your Adult in calling upon them to use their Adult to change their behavior.

People with the script of I'm Not OK–You're Not OK feel hopeless and futile. This life position stems from the Not OK–OK child who is abandoned by his or her parents or simply loses their affections at an early age. The child realizes not only that he or she is Not OK because of inability to do grown up things, but also that other people are Not OK because, after all, they don't provide recognition, friendship and love.

These people are basically losers because they are so negative toward themselves and others. They distrust most people and see little good in work and life in general. Not OK–Not OK employees communicate with hostility and abruptness, avoid responsibility, delegate upward, repeat errors and develop with difficulty, escalate disputes, don't solve problems, withdraw, play psychological games, are motivated by reprimand or threat and feel despondent and alienated.

How do you handle Not OK–Not OK people? Extreme negativity should be treated by a professional therapist. Otherwise, with sensitivity, patience and understanding, the distrust and lack of confidence of these individuals can be overcome.

THE FOUR COMMUNICATING STYLES

If you assume that everyone is an introvert, you will be right two-thirds of the time. Introverts' main interests are in concepts, ideas, abstractions and detail. They are normally private, withdrawn and happy in such jobs as lab technician, researcher, bookkeeper, repairperson and machine operator.

The extrovert is primarily interested in people, things and external realities. Extroverts have a high degree of interest in factors that personally influence people and can be found in positions requiring characteristics such as persuasiveness and people interest; these positions include jobs as sales people, public relations people, politicians and lawyers.

In addition to the three ego states, four basic life scripts and two people-interest levels discussed above, there are four distinct communication styles. If your style is not the same as the other person's, you may each be talking past each other and even offending each other, all without realizing or intending it. The four styles are generally known as the Thinker, Feeler, Intuitor, and Sensor.

The Thinker is organized, structured, logical, concerned with facts and figures and cautious in drawing conclusions and making decisions. Thinkers are inclined to have a conservative, well-tailored look, an orderly living and working environment, an accurate checkbook, points that they itemize in conversation (such as first, second . . .) and occupations like engineering, data processing, law, accounting and teaching.

About one out of every four Americans we talk to or negotiate with is a Thinker. How do you handle these individuals?

The style of the Thinker is close to that of the Adult ego state. This person is swayed by arguments and other things that are well planned, are the result of thought and analysis and are arrived at cautiously.

Introverted Thinkers, who have a High Adult–Low Parent–Low Child ego state, are good at organizing facts, not people, because of their difficulty in communicating and quiet, reserved and sometimes withdrawn personality.

Extroverted Thinkers, who have a High Parent–High Adult ego state, can get bogged down in details and can be rigid, dogmatic and boring. These people will stick to their decisions tenaciously and are inclined to reflect Critical Parent behavior. They must be calmly but firmly switched back to their Adult ego state with sound logic. On the other hand, many of these High Parent–High Adult–Low Child people are our industrial high achievers.

Feelers are emotional, spontaneous, introspective, sociable and empathetic. Feelers value human interactions, are known for their love of people, adventure and involvement, are warm in their speech and letter writing as well as their choice of styles and colors, and base most of their decisions on feelings, saying such things as, "The way I feel about it is . . . ," "Wow!" and "Exciting!"

About one out of every four Americans is a Feeler. These people are warm and friendly, have personal charm and intuition, are self-indulgent, are partial to the bright, sunny and outrageous, and are inclined to be a nuisance to others: impulsive, irrational and cavalier. They turn up in such fields as acting, sales, writing, social work and nursing.

Extroverted Feelers, with the profile of a High Natural Child–Nurturing Parent–Low Adult ego state, tend to be impatient with long, slow jobs or complex tasks, especially when they require solitary effort, and tend to jump to conclusions before thinking through all of the facts. Because they ignore unpleasant circumstances, they can be insensitive to potentially explosive interpersonal situations. They are also loyal to their superiors and the company.

Introverted Feelers are similar to the extroverts, except that their High Natural Child–Low Parent–Low Adult gives them a tendency to be overly sensitive to criticism, to suffer a sense of inadequacy and to be a poor administrator.

The manner in which you treat Feelers is sometimes more important than the facts you bring out and the logic of your argument. Before you are halfway through your presentation, Feelers have already made their decision about you and about what their response will be. They will be receptive to you if you treat them warmly, if you present your argument in terms of your own and their own feelings and if you get to the point quickly, with a minimum of background and facts.

Intuitors are imaginative, futuristic, visionary and inclined to value and produce ideas, concepts, long-range thinking and complicated solutions.

Only about one out of every ten Americans is an Intuitor, and these individuals tend to be inventors, scientists, researchers, architects, artists, writers and planners of some sort.

Extroverted Intuitors, with High Child–High Parent–Low Adult, are able to stimulate and persuade others to accept their ideas. Introverted Intuitors tend to be blinded by their ideas and fail to see circumstances, realistic factors and other matters of judgment. They find criticism uncomfortable and have difficulty getting acceptance of their ideas, appearing to be impractical geniuses indulging in fruitless fancy.

How do you handle Intuitors? These people are basically interested in the big picture. The technical details often elude or bore them. This can be illustrated with a story about the famous Intuitor Albert Einstein. He misplaced his train ticket, and the conductor reassured him that he recognized Professor Einstein and would not require him to pay the fare a second time. Einstein said, "Young man, you may not worry, but without my ticket, how will I know where to get off?"

It is important to fulfill Intuitors' esteem needs. They get impatient with anyone who doesn't respect or see the immediate value of their ideas. Intuitors may very well be rigid, uncompromising and impractical, deemphasizing the importance of the pertinent factual details. Instead of countering the Intuitor's disposition with factual analysis, you should talk in terms of the new angle or create a new approach. Intuitors are inclined to be receptive to such thinking and will consider the proposition even though it is different from their own.

Sensors are realists oriented toward performance and results and attuned to the concrete and factual. They absorb facts, are perceptive and use good judgment most of the time; they value acting, getting things done and attending to the immediate; they are spirited; enjoy a fast pay-off and are interested in the bottom line. Almost half of the American population is composed of Sensors, whose dominant ego state is the Natural Child. Quite often, Sensors will switch into the Critical Parent ego state. They may demand total loyalty. If they fail in a task because of hasty decisions, they have a tendency to blame others for not being as aggressive or devoted as they were.

Extroverted Sensors tend to have an Average Parent–High Adult–Average Child ego state and to arrive at solutions others find satisfactory, but they have difficulty seeing the value of new ideas and concepts.

Introverted Sensors, who have a lower Child, are more thorough and patient with detail and make good administrators, but they tend to be impersonal and passive with others.

How do you handle Sensors? Unlike with Thinkers, you must get right down to the point with Sensors. They don't want to waste too much time with a lot of facts and figures. They must be given the proposal in as brief and sensible a format as possible and in a manner that will allow them to quickly decide to go for the deal or make a counterproposal.

Some people seem to have an innate ability to use the right approach at the right time in dealing with these four basic personality or communication styles originally defined by Carl Jung. Most of us don't realize we have to adjust to another person's communication style. Even if we were aware, we would not know how to adjust. We wonder why it can be so difficult to talk to some people and so easy with others. Why, when we are getting nowhere in a conversation, do we all of a sudden get through to a person when we change our communication style?

WHAT'S YOUR COMMUNICATION STYLE?

Once you have determined your own primary and back-up styles and have become familiar with the behavior associated with each, you are then ready to "read" the other person's styles quickly and effectively. The following two tests will help you understand what your own communicating style is and start you off on the right track toward understanding the styles of others and how to relate to them. Rate yourself from 0 to 5, with 0 being *no* and 5 being *yes*. Put down your true feelings, not what you think the ratings should be because there are no correct answers. An interpretation of your responses follows the second test.

I appear to others as:

1. practical.
2. emotional.
3. astute.
4. intellectual.

I like my projects to be:

5. results oriented, so that my time and energy will be justified.
6. stimulating, with other people involved.
7. well planned.
8. designed to contribute something new.

My time is important, so I make sure that:

9. what I do today counts.
10. my actions will be meaningful to my grandchildren.
11. I plan well and follow my plan.
12. I am ready for the future.

I feel satisfied when I:

13. get more done than planned.
14. can help a friend.
15. can solve a problem by thinking it through.
16. can tie one idea in with another.

I enjoy others seeing me as:

17. a person who gets things done.
18. warm and creative.
19. knowing where I am going.
20. bright, with a vision.

When others pressure me, I:

21. react immediately.
22. get "carried away" by my feelings.
23. am critical of them.
24. step back into my own world of thought.

Now, to determine your personal communication style, choose twenty characteristics from the following list that you think best describe your personality.

adaptable	diplomatic	logical	reliable
agreeable	disciplined	loyal	reserved
analytical	dominant	mature	responsible
bold	easy going	modest	sensitive
calm	efficient	objective	serious minded
cheerful	energetic	observant	sincere
clear thinking	enthusiastic	open minded	soft spoken
committed	factual	organized	stable
confident	forward looking	painstaking	stimulating
conscientious	frank	patient	tactful
considerate	friendly	perceptive	thorough
controlled	idealistic	persevering	tolerant
cooperative	imaginative	persistent	thoughtful
creative	independent	persuasive	understanding
curious	ingenious	practical	warm
decisive	intellectual	quick	
dependable	intelligent	quiet	
determined	involved	realistic	

In the first test the sum of your ratings for 1, 5, 9, 13, 17 and 21 represents your Sensor score. The sum of 2, 6, 10, 14, 18 and 22 is your Feeler score; 3, 7, 11, 15, 19 and 23 are your Thinker score; and 4, 8, 12, 16, 20 and 24 are the Intuitor in you. Any communicating style that exceeds others by at least five points can be considered dominant. It is not unusual to have two primary styles of communication. The well-balanced communicator will probably be surprised to find that all of his or her scores are within five points of each other.

To evaluate your responses to the second test, match each of the six personal communicating styles below with the characteristics you selected. Your dominant communicating style or styles will have at least four more characteristics than those in other styles.

Extroverted Sensor	*Introverted Sensor*
Calm	Conservative
Considerate	Dependable
Diplomatic	Effective
Easy going	Factual
Efficient	Objective
Factual	Painstaking
Friendly	Persevering
Open minded	Practical
Persuasive	Reliable
Quick	Serious minded
Realistic	Stable
Tactful	Systematic
Tolerant	Thorough

Extroverted Feeler	*Introverted Feeler*
Agreeable	Committed
Cheerful	Controlled
Considerate	Cooperative
Cooperative	Independent
Enthusiastic	Loyal
Friendly	Modest
Gracious	Patient
Idealistic	Sensitive
Loyal	Sincere
Sympathetic	Soft spoken
Tactful	Sympathetic
Understanding	Tolerant
Warm	Understanding

Extroverted Thinker	*Introverted Thinker*
Analytical	Adaptable
Bold	Analytical
Confident	Clear thinking
Conscientious	Curious
Decisive	Disciplined
Determined	Efficient
Disciplined	Independent
Dominant	Intellectual
Energetic	Logical
Logical	Organized
Objective	Persistent
Practical	Quiet
Responsible	Thoughtful

Extroverted Intuitor	*Introverted Intuitor*
Confident	Creative
Energetic	Determined
Enthusiastic	Frank
Forward looking	Ingenious
Imaginative	Intelligent
Innovative	Observant
Involved	Patient
Mature	Persevering
Perceptive	Persistent
Persistent	Reserved
Persuasive	Sincere
Serious	Soft spoken
Stimulating	Understanding

Chapter 8
OBTAINING ACCEPTANCE

In this chapter, you will see how your basic approach to negotiation, pre-negotiation planning and maneuvers, your position strategy and the psychology of presenting your position all come together in the form of various ploys and techniques for speeding up agreement.

Some of the tactics discussed in this chapter repeat principles already brought out elsewhere. However, this chapter contains three of the toughest topics that every negotiator faces in virtually every deal he or she concludes: saying no to a person's demands, persuading the other person to make a concession that will break the deadlock and closing the deal.

The negotiating ploys that are covered in this section are important, but even new techniques discussed here are not meant to replace the various tactics already treated in previous chapters.

PLOYS THAT CHANGE *NO* TO *YES*

Nonverbal Techniques

Nonverbal signals form an important part of your arsenal of counter tactics. Much can be accomplished without speaking a single word. One of the most important nonverbal signals, and the one that is most often abused, is listening. When someone is making a point or presenting a position, do not interrupt. Do not attempt to knock it down until the speaker is clearly finished. His or her expertise, status, reputation and esteem are tied up in the presentation. Being an attentive listener will subconsciously give the recognition and praise that the speaker seeks.

One of the best ways to counter demands is to show your interest in and understanding of the points made. In addition, you should cock and nod your head in interest or briefly smile as the speaker's points are being made. Periodically, ask a question to show you are interested (but do not switch subjects or issues), and repeat some of the things said to introduce your own ideas without opposition and to prove that you have taken the other side's reasoning into consideration. There is no one more competitive and hostile than negotiators who feel that their best arguments were ignored, misunderstood or dismissed.

Even if the other person is your assistant, resist the temptation to cut this person off because the subject is unpleasant or you feel you understand what he or she is getting at. Unpleasantness and resentment will not go away simply because you will not permit them to be voiced. Also, you may have incorrectly anticipated the point.

Studies show that the average person remembers only about half of what he or she heard immediately after the speaker stopped talking, no matter how carefully the listener paid attention. As long as it is tactically important to show your interest and to show that you are carefully listening, you might as well follow a few simple rules at the same time that will actually help you maximize the benefit you get from what the other person is saying. In this manner, you will not have to pretend and risk the appearance of phoniness.

First of all, if you find the subject dull and would normally go off on a mental tangent, recognize that you are trapped into listening anyway and force yourself to tune in for any new knowledge that you can perhaps sift out. On the other hand, the subject may not be boring, but rather difficult and hard to comprehend, perhaps because it is too technical or detailed. Do not allow your mind to wander merely because distractions are more fun than the topic under discussion. Try to develop an interest and grasp the meaning of the broad things being said.

Second, we tend to dismiss statements if they come from people we consider unimportant. Withhold judgment until your comprehension of the speaker's proposal is complete. The good listener will hear out the other person before passing judgment and framing rebuttals.

Third, do not turn yourself off simply because the speaker's delivery is poor or unintelligible. The speaker may still know a lot more about the subject than it appears. Make every effort to understand what is being said. If necessary, interrupt and ask the speaker to repeat something. This person will appreciate your interest in not wanting to miss anything. The same attentiveness applies when the speaker is using emotion-laden words that would otherwise create a barrier between the two of you. Do not let negative imagery prevent you from carefully listening to the actual substance of the message. One of the problems every listener has is the ability to think at the rate of about 400 words a minute—almost four times faster than the average speaker talks. Do not let your mind drift. Instead, anticipate the speaker's next point and give thought to what you hear while waiting for the next idea.

When taking notes, get down the concepts and principles. If you have time, write down the facts, but do not let them overwhelm you to the degree that you are missing important points. Not only does note taking force you to listen carefully, but it also psychologically throws the speaker off balance when he or she sees you nodding and furiously writing away and having a record of all the facts and basically everything said. A further benefit of note taking is that you have the perfect excuse to avoid eye contact if you are afraid to reveal your reactions to someone's proposals.

Nonverbal signals can play an important role in counteracting unreasonable demands. One distraction ploy that can be used is for members of your team to change their seating arrangements after breaks in negotiation. Or one or more members of your team might deliberately pay no attention as the party is making demands, or you might get up in the middle of a presentation and walk around the room, still maintaining a posture of listening. You can punctuate your displeasure by dramatically ripping from the pad the page you were taking notes on and take no further notes. These signals are designed to subtly distract and subconsciously suggest your displeasure.

Perhaps the classic example of distraction is Henry Kissinger's description of his first encounter with the Soviet Union General Secretary, Leonid Brezhnev. Brezhnev's hands were in continuous motion, twisting his watch, flicking his ashes, and tapping his cigarette holder. He would rise from his chair, walk around the room, and even leave temporarily without explanation. At one point, he fired a toy cannon that went off with a roar.

One of the most effective techniques of showing disagreement is frozen silence after the other person is finished talking. Without saying a word, you are working against this person's aesthetic need for fairness by indicating the proposal is one sided, inequitable and unacceptable. All of a sudden, you have dramatically shifted the burden back to the other party. There is emotional pressure on the other party to say something that will hopefully lead to acceptance of a better solution to break your self-imposed deadlock.

Although not as forceful as frozen silence, there are other nonverbal reactions that can be used immediately after people complete their proposals to you. For instance, after hearing the price, you flinch, raise your eyebrows or drop your jaw slightly no matter how good the price sounds. It is your silent way of saying "Wow, that's high!" and setting the seller up for a price reduction. The flinch-eyebrow technique also protects you against a low-ball price that does not include certain components or services that you want. In other words, price may actually be high without the extras. Another example is waiting a few seconds before actually responding to the other person. Your listener will see that you are giving the ideas careful thought and that your reply is likely to make more sense than if you blurted out the first thing that came to mind.

In fact, when there are three or more negotiators involved, you might wish to take Abraham Lincoln's advice: "Better to remain silent and be thought a fool than to speak out and remove all doubt." Your opinion carries greater weight if you have the patience to wait for its solicitation. Your previous silence also adds an element of suspense and impact to what you say and certainly draws greater attention.

Last, but not least important of the nonverbal tactics, is making sure you are talking to the right member of the negotiating team. One of the first things you should do is to find out who in the meeting room has the greatest authority and responsibility. You should try to talk with that person, even if he or she is there primarily for observation. If the other negotiators on the team are specialists on the subject matter and are doing most of the talking, when responding, look at the person with the authority. By rebutting the experts' arguments with common sense persuasion directed to this person, you will have given that person a tremendous amount of recognition and esteem. After a while, this person will tend to dismiss the complex arguments of his or her own team members in favor of your simple logic.

The Response

After a speaker has expressed feelings, ideas and demands, this person will then be ready to listen to what you have to say, provided you have been a good listener. No matter how much you may disagree with what you just heard, it is bad practice to come out with a "no" response. It gives the impression that you are not interested enough to take the time to really seriously consider the other party's reasoning. In fact, it is smart to restate the other person's position and objectives. People like to know they were understood. Sometimes after they hear what they said, they recognize the inequity or fallacy of their thinking without you saying another word.

You should almost always start off with agreement after describing your understanding of what was just said, even if it has to be on the most trivial aspect. By so doing, you are saying, "I like that too," and "I am somewhat like you." It is human nature to like people who agree with us. This flattery and affiliative behavior will set the stage for cooperative behavior in considering your ideas.

Thus, disagreeing with someone or criticizing or finding a mistake will only alienate the person you want to convince. This person's judgment, pride and sense of self-importance will have been personally attacked. If you say, "I'm going to show you what the problem is with your reasoning," you present a challenge to resist your point of view, no matter how objective and logical. This does not mean that you are stymied. Fortunately, there are a number of ways to get your diametrically opposed point of view across without having the other person lose face and want revenge even at the expense of his or her company's interests.

After agreeing with and giving recognition to some of the good ideas that are not detrimental to you, introduce your own viewpoint with a phrase that does not threaten or tarnish the other person's esteem. For instance, you can say, "We are not that far apart. This is what I have in mind . . . ," or, "I may be wrong about this, but let's look at it again. . . ." Then you state your case calmly, logically and accurately. Be for a point of view, never against it.

Then express your feelings on an emotional level. For example, "Asking us for another \$200,000 leaves me disappointed, concerned and just feeling bad." Next, specify what you are willing to do, if anything, in the way of compromise. Finally, spell out the positive consequences that will benefit the other party for going along with your views.

How do you counter the person who is being sarcastic with you? Again, you rely on the standard counter, which includes a restatement of what the person said, a description of the facts, an expression of your feelings, specifying what your position is and relating the consequences of agreement with you. However, this time you must start off by telling the other person that the sarcasm is not appreciated instead of thanking the person and finding partial agreement with what was said. For instance, if in response to your inquiry about whether the person read your report, he or she says, "I don't want to wear out my eyes any quicker than necessary," you should reply, "That is not funny. I agree that the report was lengthy, but the topic and its importance required a thorough treatment. I'm hurt that you did not read it and with your flippant and offensive behavior. I want to discuss the report with you later this afternoon after you read it. By the end of the day, we should be able to solve the problem that I addressed in the report and take action tomorrow morning to head off any embarrassment for the department."

The person who psychoanalyzes you can be handled in the same manner as if you were dealing with someone sarcastic. For instance, assume you are trying to get the cooperation of one of your peers, who replies, "You are trying to manipulate me because you are worrying I will get the promotion and not you." Instead of starting off with the response that the statement is not funny, you say, "Do not try to analyze me. I know myself better than you do, and I know why I act the way I do. Are we going to tackle this assignment, or do I have to do it by myself?"

How do you counter frozen silence after you make your proposal? There are two approaches. First, you can ask questions, such as, "Do you agree with my observations?" or, "Do you understand my feelings?" The other approach is to ignore the silence and interpret it favorably for supporting your own position. For instance, you can say "I am glad that you have no objections to my opinion on this matter. This is an important point for us to be in agreement on. Now, with respect to the topic of. . . ." Since you are now switching to another issue or subject, the other person will have to break out of this silence if he or she does object to your position and will be forced to negotiate with you.

One of the most effective ways of getting your position accepted is to have the person participate in the reasoning process that leads to the point of view favorable to you. The key to this tactic lies in satisfying self-actualization and knowledge needs. The person who makes contributions toward the resolution of a problem will become committed to the logical solution. As long as you can formulate the problem, given known facts, you should be able to guide the other person through the alternative solutions to the one that is best for you.

An important consideration in negotiation is preserving the status quo by not asking the other party to do or say anything after you state your position on something. Resistance to change is automatic, and people need time to get used to ideas that are unpleasant or foreign. In short, people need acceptance time to reconcile themselves to a proposal. This tactic can be implemented easily in conjunction with trial ballooning. Your sales administrator informally tells buyers that a price increase can be expected in the next month. If there is no serious adverse reaction, you send out a formal announcement with the revised price schedule five to six weeks later. By this time, customers have accepted the fact that it's coming and are already in suspense wondering why it hasn't happened yet.

Face Saving

If someone takes a strong stand on an issue and is clearly wrong, your response requires a considerable amount of skill and tact because it is against human nature for a person to admit an error or a false statement. You must overcome the problem by leaving the door open so that the person can escape from the previous position without losing face. You might call this rescuing the negotiator from his or her own logic. There are a number of good face saving techniques that can be used in a sensitive situation.

First, there is the technique of finding or creating a good excuse for incorrect views or conclusions. Say, "I would have thought the same thing had I been in your shoes without knowing that such-and-such took place a week ago," or say, "Perhaps your secretary or some other member of your department called in the order without your knowledge," in response to a denial that an order was placed for the delivery of goods. In this case, your sales office jotted down the verbal order in the ordinary course of business and the party's name was taken down by your sales person. By giving the party an out and presenting the evidence that an order was indeed received, you then provide an escape by allowing him or her to check and come back with an affirmative answer that the order was indeed placed.

The face-saving techniques discussed so far also apply to dealing with other personnel in your own company. In this situation, you should also remember to give constructive criticism in absolute privacy after you have given a kind word or a compliment. Do not forget to make the criticism impersonal. Attack the act, not the person or the ego. As in negotiating with outsiders, remain calm and unemotional and end on a positive note with a smile so that future cooperation is assured. For instance, say, "I know this is a difficult task, but I am confident you will master it if you just keep on trying."

Every once in a while, humor may be used as a face-saving technique. The story is told that in one labor negotiation a while back, the 5 P.M. deadline for calling a strike was rapidly approaching, and tension was building up without much progress as the last hour slowly ticked away. With minutes to go, the negotiator for management held up a large sheet of paper with a big clock drawn on it with the numeral 5 missing. Both sides chuckled; it was decided to continue discussions beyond the deadline, and the atmosphere became considerably more relaxed.

Another type of face-saving technique involves a drastic restructuring of negotiating personalities. This can take the form of a new negotiator, a mediator or having an issue decided upon by specific members of both negotiating teams. If it is your judgment that a person is in danger of losing face no matter how much skill and tact you exercise, you may be wise to bow out and let one of your colleagues, who is new to the negotiation, take your place. Since the new member will not be privy to previous strong positions and commitments made by that person, this will give the person an opportunity to make concessions more gracefully without loss of esteem.

A shrewd face-saving technique that could be used more often by negotiators is playing dumb and simply saying, "I don't understand your point," or, "I'm sorry, would you repeat that please." Not only does this slow the other person down because the person has to think about how to clarify the statements, but it also forces the person to further analyze the logic of his or her reasoning. Quite often, this person will see the problems with the proposal as he or she tries to amplify on a position.

Questioning

During negotiation, there will undoubtedly be times when you need to have more information before you can intelligently evaluate views advanced by the other person. This calls for informational questions. The trouble with questions is that they raise anxiety in the minds of those who must answer them. They will immediately think, "What are they trying to find out?" or, "How can I avoid giving away information they shouldn't know about?" It is an established fact that answers to direct questions are unreliable because people do not generally give truthful responses and do not always have the ability to give correct information, even when they think they do.

There are two ways to assure a high degree of reliability for answers to your questions. One way is to lay the foundation for asking them. By letting someone know why you want to ask the question, you reduce his or her anxiety level and consequent evasiveness. There will be less inhibition in giving the true facts that first come to mind. For instance, you are doomed before you start if you ask your vendor, "How many of these machines has our competitor X bought?" Instead you should say, "I respect your ability to analyze the needs of companies like mine. How many of these machines do you feel a company of our size should have?" This is a "nondirective question" that puts people at ease and allows them to express themselves with sincerity. You will probably get a straightforward answer that will very possibly include the exact information you want to know with respect to the number of machines your competitor has.

The second method of assuring the reliability of answers to your questions is through the use of the tactic called "bipolar questioning." Basically, this technique asks the answerer to make a choice or express a preference between two diametrically opposed features of the subject in question. Such questioning is indirect. The answer will shed light on how the person feels about the subject matter as a whole, even though the answer merely pertains to a feature of it. For example, if a manufacturer is offering you the right to take on the distribution of a new product it has developed, do not ask, "Will this product be compatible with others we are selling in the such-and-such market area?" The manufacturer, in its enthusiasm, may mislead you with a "yes" answer. Instead, ask "Will this product be in the $25 to $100 range, or in the $5 to $25 range?" "Will it be socially acceptable to lower-class families or upper-class families?" "Would more of these be sold to teenagers or adults?" or, "Is this of high or low quality in comparison with the closest substitute products now on the market?" Getting answers to such questions before indicating the area of market introduction you have in mind will get you truthful and unbiased answers from the manufacturer, to the extent that the manufacturer has already conducted some degree of market studies.

Because uncertainty is one of the prime factors in making poor or bad deals, you must force yourself to ask questions that make you uncomfortable. Have the courage to pry into the other person's affairs if the facts you are looking for are important to your decision. Have the courage to ask what may seem to be dumb questions. Have the courage to ask questions that you feel will be evaded. Evasion itself will give you information you need to know. Be quiet after you ask your question. Make silence your tool for encouraging the other person to talk more and more and more. Be persistent in following up your questions when they are evaded.

How do you counter questions? Always give yourself time to think. Never answer until you clearly understand what is being asked. Do not be embarrassed to answer a question with another question: "What do you mean by that?" Some questions do not even deserve answers, especially if they are antagonistic or rhetorical. Do not be afraid to plead ignorance based on incomplete knowledge or not being able to remember. If he asks "Why?" to every second thing you say, do not play his game. Say, "That is the way I feel," or "Those are my values." "If justifying everything is so important to you, how about justifying why you disagree with me so much."

Probably most important of all, anticipate what questions will be asked so that you can plan ahead whether you are going to answer them and if so, whether you are going to answer truthfully. It is easy to spot a false answer when the question catches the person by surprise. Even if the other person is barraging you with questions one after the other with lightning speed, do not hesitate to slow him up with each question by giving background information you feel is necessary. For instance, "You have to understand the history of the problem, which began . . ." or, "I'm going to have to give you the detailed procedure before we can even consider your question."

Whenever you can, avoid hypothetical questions because it is easy to construe your generalized answer against you when applied to the specific factual situation. Responses to the hypothetical can be, "I cannot agree with the statement on which your question is based," "I cannot talk about that because . . . ," "It is really not the way you have laid it out," or "We are going to have to get more specific than that."

Tactics
If you are having trouble getting sufficient information to respond intelligently or if you wish to preserve the status quo and make the negotiations drag on, you will want to use the tactic of "forebearance." This is a delaying ploy to maintain the status quo for a more successful outcome than would happen if decisions were made in a rush. An illustration of forebearance is when you receive a demand to cease manufacturing a product that infringes someone else's patents. You attempt to stall for a half-year or so by studying the matter and preparing a response in an attempt to settle the dispute. In the meantime, not only do you preserve the status quo to fulfill

your need for security, but you also attempt to improve it by putting yourself in a better bargaining position. One way to do this is to design around the allegedly infringed patent claims and score a fait accompli.

Sometimes, when there is no other way to obtain the information you need to determine if a concession should be made, you can use the ploy of pure guesswork. The story is told of a labor-management dispute that was bogged down. A management negotiator decided to chart labor's demands to take a look at the trend. He then extended the curve and drew a red circle around the figure for which management was prepared to settle. He put a capital *F* here, standing for Final Offer. He then extended the curve further to a higher pay increase figure and drew a red *X* with a vertical red line going down to the horizontal axis of the chart. Here, next to the *X* mark, he put the letter *S*, standing for strike. This was the absolute maximum to which management was prepared to go. The chart was left in the negotiating room, and when labor rejoined management, they noticed the chart. After a whispered consultation, they said, "All right, no need to continue. We will settle at that figure," pointing to the red circled figure on the curve. Later, management learned that labor figured inside information had leaked out about what its final figure was going to be. Also, upon seeing the nonverbal signals of the red *X* and red *S* at the end of the curve, they probably reasoned that no management concession would be made at this point and that the final offer would be the one circled in red. Thus, by guessing, management was able to quickly settle what could have turned out to be a long negotiation and an eventual strike.

There are seven important ploys you can use that are based on working against a person's need to know. They are trial ballooning, feinting, play acting, bracketing, misstatement, discounting and secrecy.

Feinting is a mock action designed to distract attention from the point of real concern. For example, a purchasing agent gives a new vendor the false impression that the agent possesses more information and knowledge than the vendor regarding the vendor's savings for a large-volume purchase. This has a tendency to divert the vendor's plans to play down the fact that there will be savings and stick with the price. A modified approach would be for the purchasing officer to say, "With your volume discount price in mind, we will accept delivery in 30 days." The ensuing conversation between them continues without mention of price because the officer has convinced the vendor that the firm is entitled to a discount and the officer already knows what it will be and has taken it for granted. Feinting is often implemented on a more basic level whenever you have to leave to use the bathroom, become starved for lunch, supply an overwhelming amount of files or data or suddenly introduce a new complication in order to change, delay or cloud an issue of concern.

Trial ballooning is the tactic of taking a controversial position on an issue without others knowing it. It may be in the form of a rumor that you leaked or through a statement made by your assistant as his or her own views. If reaction is favorable, you openly take a firm stand on the issue. If unfavorable, you don't have to lose face in reversing your views.

Play acting is used to convey sincerity, friendliness, fairness and cooperative behavior by working against the person's need to know. An example is when you make a concession based on a contingency that you know, in all probability, will not take place. Thus, you agree to take a reduced payout from a company acquiring you if your key people should quit within the next two years. You know they have contracts to stay; the company does not. You convey cooperative behavior and sweeten the deal for them without any detriment to yourself.

Bracketing is a tactic of shooting beyond and then short of the point where you feel you can reach a settlement to let a party know that you are aware of the midpoint where both parties will wind up settling. For instance, in the example discussed above, the vendor says, "I know that you are too experienced to pay $500 per unit with the volume you intend to purchase, and I know you couldn't buy it for $400 no matter how large your purchasing volume is." The vendor has clearly bracketed in the agent, who knows that the vendor knows exactly what is being discussed. The vendor then brackets further: "If I were to offer this to you at $475, it would still be no good for me if you could purchase from our competitor at $450." In the agent's eyes, the vendor has superior knowledge of the competition, and an agreed-upon price at the midway mark or slightly below is facilitated.

The tactic of misstatement is based on the element of surprise by incorrectly stating that a party does not have knowledge of a fact in the hope that this will reveal that the party does indeed know. In the example above, the vendor says, "I know you are paying $500 for this." Quite often the buyer will interrupt, "What do you mean? I'm only paying $460." The vendor then says, "I'm terribly sorry. I heard the price had gone up." The buyer replies, "No, it's still the same." Thus, through misstatement, it is sometimes possible to get competitive information to help you know at what point to close the deal without the other person thinking that he or she has been taken advantage of or tricked.

Sometimes, feinting can be used in combination with the tactic of abdication. Abdication is the technique of giving up further argument or persuasion with the request that the other person work out a fair solution for both of you. In the example discussed above, it would be a fairly safe tactic to have the purchasing officer decide on a fair price after the vendor finished the bracketing routine.

When responding to a demand, you may wish to use the common tactic of balancing by appealing to the aesthetic need for fairness. You ask for one or more concessions as a trade-off for those that the other party is demanding.

Too many negotiators give in on minor things when it is not tactically necessary. Soviet Premier Krushchev made famous the tactic of nibbling. If a person gets enough minor concessions, one after another, eventually the slices add up to a large portion of what is to be shared. If someone is asking for a small concession here and a small concession there, notwithstanding agreement on major terms, resist the tendency to give in simply to appease. If necessary, make the person feel "chintzy."

Although you will emphasize the necessity of balancing concessions when you give up something, do not fall for this equity argument when you are insisting on a concession. Tit-for-tat concessions are not necessary. Do not let the other party play against your aesthetic need for fairness. If the party wants to split the difference, say, "I can't afford to."

A tactic almost the exact opposite of participation is mirage. This involves the technique of telling someone not to do a specific thing to create the desire to take that action. Thus, instead of participating with you, the person is induced to act unilaterally in noncompliance with your request. This may be illustrated by the seller who can provide a fancy package for a product but does not want to be pressured as to the delivery date. He or she tells the buyer, "Don't ask us for fancy packaging at that price." The buyer makes it a point to negotiate for the fancy packaging. The seller reluctantly agrees to the additional cost, provided the buyer allows sufficient time for delivery.

Another tactic that induces acceptance of a position favorable to you without the use of participation or mirage is called good guy–bad guy. You have two diametrically opposed negotiators, one who takes an extremist or hard-line position and the other a more moderate or soft position. The extreme position is presented first, and then the moderate position is presented. The soft position will seem reasonable by comparison and certainly more palatable to the other party, who will be inclined to accept it.

If you anticipate that others are going to say legitimately damaging things about you or your company, state them before the opportunity arises, and you will steal their thunder. This is called the "straw man" technique of arguing for their position so that their bargaining power seems even stronger than previously contemplated. Then you make a concession of some type in light of their strong position before any discussion ensues. In many instances, they will be content with the concession you made even though it might be less than they might have asked for. Thus, the straw man technique has diverted them from using bargaining power to extract a more injurious concession.

When the other party sticks to a price as reasonable, the going rate or what is necessary to bring a fair profit, the tactic of discounting can be used to motivate price reduction. You or your technical assistant examine the equipment more carefully and find it is tarnished or deficient in some way. Maybe it has an unwanted projection formed during molding. Maybe it does not completely meet your strict tolerances. You can also offer to buy in greater volume in order to reduce the seller's costs. You can even bargain for a lower price by installing it yourself, or offer immediate cash up front.

If you cannot think of any logical reasons for discounting, you can bring discussions to a close by the tactic of saying, "This is all I have" or "This is all we can afford." In effect, you are telling someone, "Take it or leave it." At this point, the person will do one of three things. *One*, he or she will make a final price concession, meeting you part way or accepting your offer. *Two*, the party will restructure the deal and cut corners to reduce his or her own costs in order to stay within your budget. This applies when you discover items built into the cost that are not essential to your needs or that you can take care of yourself at nominal cost. *Three*, the person will walk away. At this point, you must use bland withdrawal to close, knowing that the other party will not budge further and you have the best deal possible; or you deal elsewhere.

One of the most important considerations in working against the other party's need to know is to keep your true goals and bottom-line feelings to yourself. Play out your strategy and options close to the vest to keep the other party guessing, off balance and constrained from taking risks, without knowing in advance your likely reaction. After Iranian revolutionary students took fifty-three Americans hostage, demanding that the Shah and his money be returned, President Jimmy Carter publicly said that his most important concern was the safety of the hostages and ruled out military action that would risk their lives. Once it became clear that a negotiated settlement was the only U.S. option other than economic boycott, the Iranians grew bolder. Ayatollah Khomeini put the Iranian government stamp of approval on the actions of the students. In fact, Iran was now so confident about the minimal risk of holding the hostages that they did not bother to scatter and hold them in different locations until after the aborted rescue mission.

Had President Carter kept his thinking to himself, he would have enjoyed much greater bargaining leverage. The potential risks, even in the absence of threat, would have weighed heavily in the eyes of Iranians each time they rebuffed American negotiators. The importance of secrecy was dramatically illustrated by Ronald Reagan's election victory. Up until the time of his inauguration, he was conspicuously vague about how he would get the hostages back. He did, however, express very strong feelings about the "barbarians" holding them. There were even jokes about "What is flat and glows, one day after Ronald Reagan takes office?" The uncertainty of risking a military confrontation with President Reagan, who was not limited to Carter's peaceful options, motivated the Iranians to settle the matter before Carter left office.

BREAKING DEADLOCKS

In a deadlock situation, a mediator can help reduce irrationality, facilitate communication and provide opportunities for graceful retreat or face-saving by taking responsibility for concessions strongly urged or imposed. The research conducted by investigators showed that intervention by a mediator enables bargainers to make concessions without viewing themselves as weak for having done so. Simply, a bargainer will not look weak or unwise if the blame for a reversal of a previously strong position can be placed on the mediator.

A situation that calls for even greater control on your part occurs when a person becomes angry and starts shouting or threatening you. How do you react? (See Figure 8.1.) There is one sure solution. Remain calm and keep your voice soft, but firm. Take several deep breaths before you speak to calm yourself and prevent your voice from quaking and taking on an unnatural pitch. This will prevent you from becoming angry also. Use the

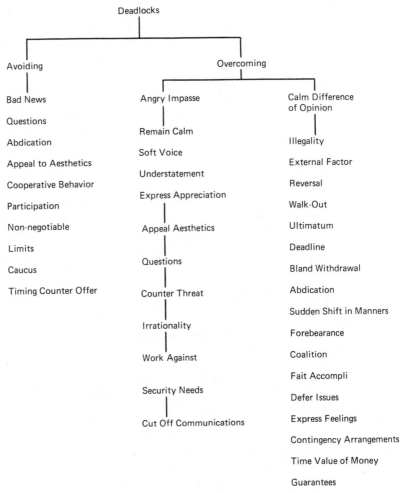

Figure 8.1. Breaking deadlocks.

same techniques you would had the bargaining not become volatile with additional points in mind.

When giving your viewpoint, do not be forceful or exaggerate, since this will tend to fuel anger. You may even express doubt as to whether you are correct. If you react in this manner to anger, the other person will be receptive to your thinking without damage to his or her ego, and this person's anger will be deflated.

You can exploit the threatener's aesthetic need for civilized conduct by calmly pointing out that the behavior is immature, unreasonable, manipulative, domineering, violent or barbaric. Many people will become embarrassed and receptive to what follows.

If the shouting continues, threaten to walk out or to drive an extra-hard bargain because of the insulting manner in which you are being treated. In fact, you don't have to say anything. Put your papers and pen in your briefcase, turn toward the door, stand up, start walking and finally leave if the rude behavior doesn't stop. When spelling out the positive consequences of going along with your position, you can imply or point out the negative consequences of disagreeing with you, which could be the injurious consequences stemming from a counter threat carried out by you.

In many instances, a series of well-formulated questions will diffuse anger by pinpointing irrationality. Your questions should be designed to elicit obvious answers that are favorable to your viewpoint. For instance, if you are divesting a division of your business and the acquiring company is complaining about the high asking price, your questions could go something like this: "Why is it high? Why is it unreasonable? Isn't the same multiplier being used for other businesses in our industry? Why should we sell for less? Are we less profitable? You do feel we have potential for growth, don't you? Then why are you negotiating with us?"

You may also wish to use questions that require a choice in order to pin him down. For instance, in the example above, you could ask, "Would you prefer to use LIFO or FIFO? Do you want to stick with the managers we have now or bring in your own people if you are not happy with our growth potential? Do you want us to continue negotiating solely with you or look around for other suitors?"

Perhaps the best way of getting someone to see your viewpoint is to ask a series of questions that create a "yes" mood. For instance, with respect to the above discussed example: "Isn't this a great product?" "Should be easy to market, no?" "Wouldn't you say it has a good profit potential?" "You think you could build this business up rapidly?" "Then you think this could become a major division for you?" Finally, you pop the really important question after a half-dozen "yes" responses: "Isn't it worth the price we are asking?"

One simple technique that has been effective in cooling down an angry person is pausing for a couple of moments and then expressing thanks for the person explaining his or her position. For example, say, "I very much appreciate your willingness to spell out in detail your assumptions and conclusions in this matter. Not everyone is so considerate." It is amazing how a calm and sincere "thank you" will make someone feel too foolish to continue being angry.

One technique used to escape an early deadlock situation is the ploy of working against the other side's aesthetic need for legality. For instance, a manufacturer offers you the exclusive right to sell in a specified territory. You had not planned to be so geographically constrained in your marketing efforts. You quickly blurt out that this is horizontal market allocation among dealers and therefore an illegal restraint of trade since the market is being divided up among competitors. Even though the manufacturer's counsel may be able to explain that such geographical division is an ancillary restraint to a patented product that is considered reasonable, the manufacturer's chief negotiator has already been scared into submission to whatever reasonable alternatives you propose.

Another technique of bringing a demanding party into line fast is reversal. If you were pressured into making too many concessions, you simply go back to a harder line and withdraw some of the concessions. This works against the other person's need for security because it becomes harder to get what was contemplated as assured concessions. The person will be more appreciative and satisfied with the original concessions that were taken for granted once you reverse your position back to a softer line. Another example occurs when you are having a contract dispute for failure to pay for goods you sold. Bill the buyer for a larger amount than due as a fait accompli. The buyer will probably call to dispute your figures and verify the correct amount, at which time you can probably settle the debt quickly.

Play acting can be used quite effectively in a deadlock situation. For instance, if talks are bogged down and you genuinely feel that the other party should be more yielding, you can culminate the meeting in a "walk-out" coupled with an ultimatum. The ultimatum should sound final but should always be worded in a vague manner with regard to content, firmness and consequences so that you will be able to retreat gracefully from it if you miscalculated in testing the strength of the other party's bargaining position.

For example, the ultimatum may be the setting of a deadline for making further progress. If there is none, you will terminate negotiations. If the other side calls your bluff, you can use the tactic of apparent withdrawal. You actually terminate negotiations to appear firm in your stand. The other side will hopefully have serious thoughts about what has occurred and will urge you to consider reopening negotiations. If the party does not approach you after a period of time, you can always come back and say that the recess has been long enough and you are ready to continue. Your graceful escape from embarrassment and weakness is bland withdrawal. You say that you only meant to terminate negotiations for a recess period, not completely.

The deadline tactic is indeed very effective. The research findings show that time pressures increase the likelihood of agreement and tend to be manifested in reductions in bargaining aspirations, demands and the amount of bluffing that occurs.

You can use to your advantage even deadlines that you do not set. For instance, claims agents can generally get acceptance of lower offers at tax time, before vacations and after Christmas. Insurance companies will generally pay out the best settlement after the lawsuit has been initiated or the jury selected. A plane schedule, vacation, holiday, funeral or other legitimate event can be used to move an indecisive party toward a quicker settlement or acceptance.

In combination with a walk-out, you may wish to take a less drastic approach. This can be done through the use of abdication. Instead of setting a deadline or giving some other ultimatum, simply throw the burden to come up with a better solution to the other party.

Another moderate technique short of ultimatum is play acting a change in your manners. Upon hearing that someone will not budge from certain demands, you, who have been mild-mannered and soft-spoken during the negotiations, suddenly change your mannerisms. This involves the conspicuous alteration of the tone of your voice, rate of speech, facial expression and hand gestures to visibly show irritation and dramatically make your point.

Sometimes it makes sense to react in a more dramatic fashion when you are being threatened with legal or other detrimental action. A good defense to a threat is irrationality. By showing a person that you are having a lapse of self-control over your reasoning power and that your emotions are telling you to resist the threat, even at great injury to yourself, the threat becomes meaningless in its intended result.

Instead of remaining cool and trying to calm down a person who is acting irrational, you may try another approach if you think it's just a tactic. Denounce the irrationality loudly and get your concern regarding the behavior across to this individual's peers and superiors. They may be just as disturbed as you appear to be. Even if they are not, you will put the person on the defensive and make him or her think twice about continuing the behavior, which could be detrimental to his or her own security needs.

There are a number of other tactics that can be employed against a threat. You can use fait accompli by taking action and then talking. You can counter with the threat of forming a coalition to soften the blow should the threat be carried out. You can logically show the threatening party that it has more to lose than it has to gain, aside from emotional satisfaction. You can cut off communications so that the threatening party is not sure that its threatening messages are being received.

If someone's demands cannot be met because the required concession is nonnegotiable on your part, you should not keep this information to yourself too long. Delaying bad news only weakens your position because most people find surprise disappointments intolerable. You, of course, should not immediately say that you cannot comply with the demands. As discussed above, you should calmly and logically explain the inequity of your compliance.

There are many ways of persuading the other side that something is not negotiable through the skillful employment of authority limits due to custom and policy. For instance, you can convey financial limits, such as a maximum capital expenditure, the need for signature authorization, the requirement of staying within your budgeted figure, the need to stay within standard cost limits and the necessity of remaining under the government approved limit. You can convey limits with respect to terms and conditions, such as a limit on advance payment, standard quantity discount schedules, fixed warranty conditions, standard liquidated damage terms and most favored nation limits. Your limits can involve procedure and policy, such as the way changes can be approved, rules against revealing cost and other information, your make or buy procedure and the policies of the company salary review committee.

If the other party does not believe that certain things are nonnegotiable, there are other methods of breaking an impasse. You can change the payout terms to a shorter or longer period, depending on the person's cash flow situation. You can change to another negotiator or call in a mediator.

You can postpone agreement on the stalemated issues and start dealing with each other within the framework you are able to establish for the time being. This is exactly what Egypt and Israel did with the Camp David accord. Difficult issues that the parties were deadlocked on, such as the Palestinian problem and a divided Jerusalem, were left for renegotiation at a future date. You can change the degree of risk taking. If there is uncertainty regarding the losses or gains, you can offer to share the unknowns based on certain contingencies. You can also offer guarantees or grievance procedures if there are concerns about performance or assurances. You can state your true feelings—namely, that you feel frustrated, stymied or irritated that neither party really wants to get down to the bottom line and try to work the differences out instead of playing games with each other. Expressing your honest feelings in this manner often will galvanize both sides into action.

An effective approach to avoiding situations leading to deadlocks is the caucus. Too many negotiators continue discussing issues and making decisions no matter how much new information is learned during the meeting. It is not necessary to have to analyze new data on the spot. In fact, it is dangerous. Calling a recess and holding a caucus will allow you to review what has been heard or learned, think of new questions, develop new tactics and strategy, confirm new information, consult experts and analyze how things are going.

Even if you cannot improve your bargaining position as a result of dilatory actions, a counter offer to resolve the negotiation after a period of forebearance is much more believable as your bottom line than if you had made it initially. In fact, if your previous position was stated as your final offer or nonnegotiable, your concession now will be more believable as your bottom line or even below it.

In summary, common counter-tactics to obtain acceptance are:

1. Nonverbal signals:
   a. listening well,
   b. distraction,
   c. frozen silence,
   d. flinching,
   e. pausing,
   f. looking at the right person.
2. Initial remarks:
   a. appreciation,
   b. flattery,
   c. restating the other person's position,
   d. agreement.
3. Working against need to know:
   a. discounting,
   b. secrecy,
   c. feinting—abdication,
   d. bracketing,
   e. misstatement,
   f. play acting,
   g. trial ballooning.

4. Balancing concessions and nibbling.
5. Guessing.
6. Questions to others:
   a. obvious,
   b. choice,
   c. affirmative ("yes"),
   d. informational (bipolar and foundation).
7. Employing face-saving:
   a. creating an excuse,
   b. injecting humor,
   c. changing negotiators,
   d. playing dumb,
   e. using a mediator.
8. Questions to you:
   a. answering with a question,
   b. pleading ignorance,
   c. your feelings in place of logic,
   d. requiring justification,
   e. taking your time,
   f. frozen silence.
9 Maintaining the status quo.
10. Participation.
11. Your position:
   a. facts (calmly),
   b. feelings,
   c. position (logic),
   d. consequence.

THE CLOSE AND BEYOND

Closing is your ultimate goal. Knowing when and how is critical to your success. Too many negotiators overclose. They never know that they reached the point where the matter was settled long ago. Continuing only complicates matters and may change agreed-upon items to disputes once again, given enough time. Negotiators typically tell each other to "think it over." This is a mistake if the time for closing is ripe. Urge the other person to take a stand before leaving the session. You may never get another chance.

You are ready to close when it is apparent that the other party will not make any further concession and you are satisfied with the deal that has been hammered out. As a general rule, it is a good idea to sum up the key points in principle, looking at the other person with a pause after stating each point. This will afford a final opportunity to disagree.

You should project a positive attitude about closing. You can lead into the closing with such casual but confident statements as, "Well, it looks like we know everything necessary to agree," "I think we can wrap this deal up now," and, "Is there anything else we need to discuss before concluding this matter?"

In general, when you assume your product is excellent, the price is just and the customer is a rational person who will buy from you once he or she has all the facts at hand, the customer will be put at ease and reflect your own confidence in your product, service or other deal being offered. In fact, the ideal sales close requires no words. After you have stated the benefits and made your recommendations, your silence in conjunction with confident body language will encourage the other person to take favorable action.

There are many other techniques of closing. You can emphasize the possible loss of benefits now available if agreement is not reached by a certain deadline. You can provide a special inducement for immediate closing, such as a price reduction, favorable credit terms or other special services. You can tell a story that shows what a good deal this is and how somebody else lost out by passing it up or made a killing by accepting the deal. In short, you can make the closing an interesting and even exciting experience for the other person.

You can also use the assumption technique of leading into the close with statements or questions such as, "I would suggest this model for you," "Do you want this billed on a cash or credit basis?" and, "Where would you like the machine installed?" Each of these closings is made in a manner to suggest that you are confident in your assumption that the other party is ready to close the deal with you.

If you have used several closing techniques to no avail, you should ask the other person what the problem is. The party may be reluctant to tell you the truth, but ask this person to be honest with you so that you at least know the real reason why the two of you will not be working with each other in the future. No matter how discouraged you get, remember that a professional negotiator expects to get many *nos*. Finding out the reasons for those *nos* is the key to turning objections into opportunities and the final closing.

If the closing reached is more than a simple agreement on price, items and time and a formal contract will be needed, it is a good idea to write a memorandum outlining the understanding of the parties before they leave their meeting. A jointly signed memorandum of understanding will keep the parties from changing their minds if later on they get second thoughts about the deal. It also prevents misunderstandings and loss of memory later on. In fact, you will find that the exercise of writing down the understanding you and the other party reached will spur further negotiation, either because there is a misunderstanding between the two of you or the understanding wasn't specific enough. It is better to resolve the differences that crop up when the memorandum is being written out than a week or a month later when the attorneys get involved and opposing positions are solidified. You must have the courage to open an issue that both parties thought was definitely taken care of if the proposed wording bothers you or can be interpreted differently.

When the parties finally get down to drafting the final agreement, an advantage can usually be obtained by being the one to prepare the draft for several reasons:

1. The one who prepares the agreement from scratch usually takes a more comprehensive approach in considering all the ramifications to a greater degree than the one who simply reviews the agreement that has already been prepared.
2. Clauses favorable to you that might have received protest if they were inserted after a draft had been prepared can initially be put in.
3. You can take approaches favorable to you, such as tax consequences—for example, selling an undivided part interest in product rights rather than granting a nonexclusive license, so that the payments you receive will be treated as long-term capital gain.

If you cannot meet the other party's demands or the party cannot make the concessions you require, the deal will fall through, but the negotiation could be an initial step toward a future closing. The party may have second thoughts and get back to you. Now that this person knows you, he or she may contact you at a future time with respect to a different deal. The person may even consider you as a second source should some other party default or break off relations for some reason. The moral of the story here is that it is to your benefit to part on good terms with no hard feelings. You never know when you might cross paths again. If the failure to close was the result of hostility or produces hostility on the part of either party, you will never know what future opportunities you lost.

Even after a closing and the signing of a formal contract, many skilled tacticians continue to negotiate for better terms. For instance, even the best drafted agreement will have procedural and substantive gaps and ambiguities. You can plug a gap or clarify a term or condition by writing a letter to the other party stating that the contract clarification will become effective by a specific date in the future if no objection thereto is received. Quite often, you can take an interpretation that is to your advantage and unilaterally make it a part of the contract because the other party does not spend the time to study your change carefully or simply overlooks it until the deadline for objection has passed. An example is when your vendor gives terms of net thirty days. You write back saying it is your company policy to pay cash in fifteen days and take a 2 percent discount. You indicate your expectation that this is acceptable and that any objection should be received in writing within ten days. Sometimes the formal contract will have a clause that requires modifications to be executed by the officers of both parties. In this situation, you can still rely on the unilateral understanding even though it is technically unenforceable. If the other party does not object in time, he or she may be too embarrassed or feel it unfair to make an issue of the matter. An alternative approach is to request the other party to sign at the bottom of your letter and return it in a self-addressed, stamped envelope that you enclose. Although this approach can no longer rely on the other party's default in making a timely objection, you convey a note of confidence when asking the other party to sign the modification. The party will feel compelled to go along with you to avoid making waves if your revision is not terribly unreasonable.

When it comes time to perform under the signed contract, many skilled negotiators use the tactic of nibbling. Nibbling involves minor breaches of contract or other actions that are not technical breaches but are not in the spirit of what the parties had intended. For instance, sellers nibble by making overshipments, supplying lower quality goods, avoiding promised services, delivering late, or adding unforeseen charges. Buyers nibble by paying bills late, taking unearned discounts, requesting special services, reports and certification, getting consulting and training assistance without payment, and getting better quality than contracted for. Nibbling may involve small bites, but they add up and can take a big chunk out of your profits.

A counter tactic to use against the party who does not live up to a promise is the squeaky wheel. The squeaky wheel gets the most grease. These are the customers who complain the loudest and the most. In essence, they make nuisances of themselves, and the other party will ultimately do what they want just to get rid of the problem. The squeaky wheel that is polite and courteous, not nasty, is most effective because the other party will become increasingly guilty with each call or visit until his or her conscience forces him or her to take the requested action.

Chapter 9
THE MANAGER AS NEGOTIATOR

STRATEGY AND TACTICS FOR THE SUPERVISOR

Over the long run, the crucial difference between competitors regarding their success in the marketplace does not lie with tangible resources, but rather depends on the performance of individual employees. The degree to which employees are trained and motivated to help achieve broad company goals often provides the margin of superiority of one company over another since it must be assumed that competing firms employing hundreds or thousands of employees will wind up with the same general calibre of talent due to the law of averages.

An American Management Association survey found that 39 percent of top management and 46 percent of middle managers considered interpersonal activities their most important function. In fact, almost one-fourth of top management spends up to half their time and one-half of management spends up to one quarter of their time on the specific task of motivating employees.

Yet, most managers are not really sure of the best way to motivate their people. They do not know which of the many management theories popularized in the literature should be employed. For example, the following two management views of people are adapted from Dr. Douglas McGregor:

McGregor "Theory X"

1. People are naturally lazy and do only what they must.
2. People work mostly for money and status rewards, and fear is what keeps them productive.

McGregor "Theory Y"

1. People are naturally active, set goals and enjoy striving.
2. People seek satisfactions in work, pride in achievement, a sense of contribution, pleasure in association and the stimulation of new challenges.

162

McGregor "Theory X"	*McGregor "Theory Y"*
3. Most people remain children and are naturally dependent on leaders.	3. Most people normally mature beyond childhood. They crave independence, self-fulfillment and responsibility; are close enough to a situation to know what is needed, and are capable of self-direction if given goals, policies and the big picture.
4. People need supervisors to praise good work and reprimand errors.	4. People need respect for being capable of assuming responsibility and self-correction.
5. People naturally separate work from leisure activities.	5. Most people naturally integrate all activities when possible. When work and play are too sharply separated, people are unhappy, and initiative and production suffer. The only reason a wise person prefers leisure to work is the greater satisfaction of the work he or she can do during leisure.
6. People naturally resist change, preferring the status quo.	6. People naturally tire of monotonous routine and enjoy new experiences.
7. People are selected, trained and fitted to predefined jobs.	7. Jobs should be designed for and fitted to people.
8. Given the opportunity, most people will be inclined to take advantage of you.	8. Given the opportunity, most people will be inclined to treat you fairly.

Often, managers will simply use their own instinct and on the job experience in dealing with the people they supervise. At times, managers will reflect the supervisory style of their own bosses in combination with the policies and climate generated by the company personnel department.

EMPLOYEE MOTIVATION

If we take a look at what was brought out in Chapter 7 about PDC, it is clear you can produce a climate that in general fulfills the most important emotional needs of your employees, and you must vary your style in dealing with individual employees in accordance with specific personalities, life scripts and ego states. This specific work climate and the proper one-on-one style of communication will result in employees who are motivated to produce their best work regarding creativity, initiative and output.

Before you can create the right work environment and deal effectively with individuals you supervise, you must know the real reasons why people motivate themselves for maximum achievement. Following are twenty-five factors that can result in motivation:

1. Agreement with organization's objectives.
2. Attending staff meetings.
3. Being told by my boss when I do a good job.
4. Chance for promotion.
5. Change to turn out quality work.
6. Congenial work associates.
7. Fair company policies and administration.
8. Feeling I am responsible for something significant.
9. Feeling my job is important.
10. Financial security.
11. Getting along well with others on the job.
12. Getting a performance rating so I know how I stand.
13. Good pay.
14. Good physical working conditions.
15. Having an efficient supervisor.
16. Knowing what is going on in the organization.
17. Knowing I will be disciplined if I do a bad job.
18. Large amount of freedom on the job.
19. Opportunity for self-development and improvement.
20. Opportunity to do interesting, challenging work.
21. Outlet for my creativity and originality.
22. Participation in planning and decision-making that affects me.
23. Pensions and other security benefits.
24. Respect for me as a person.
25. Work you can make a game of.

A 1980 survey of more than 100,000 employees produced surprising re-sults. Before I tell you the results, find out whether you are in tune with what turns your employees on. Pick what you think are the most important factors of the twenty-five listed above.

The survey found that most employees checked the same six of the twenty-five items, differing only in how the items were ranked in impor-tance. The factors were 9, 13, 18, 20, 22, and 24.

The most significant result of the survey was the deemphasis of finan-cial security, good physical work conditions, the chance for promotion, agreement with organizational objectives and getting a performance rating to know where the employee stands. With the exception of getting good pay, all six factors relate to inherent characteristics of the work and do not involve external incentives, such as fringe benefits and other working con-ditions and incentives.

These results confirm the applicability of McGregor's Theory Y and the studies of Frederick Herzberg, who suggests that true motivators are factors such as achievement, recognition and responsibility that are intrin-sic to the job in producing job satisfaction. Herzberg feels that such motivators provide long-lasting employee satisfaction and are less costly than hygienic factors that are extrinsic to the job and include security, wages and physical working conditions. The term *hygienics* is used because these factors merely clean up the work environment, are temporary, more costly and lacking in true motivational value.

Investigators agree that the combination of challenging work and the achievement in getting things accomplished that an employee can take pride in is the most important motivator that brings job satisfaction and high performance. If the work is sufficiently interesting, challenging and varied, an employee will get great satisfaction out of performing tasks even in the absence of supervisory recognition. If we look back to the principles learned in Chapter 7, you will see that the employee's craving for challenging and interesting work and satisfaction with achievement stems from an emotional need for self-actualization.

The second most important motivator is respect and recognition for one's capabilities and achievements. In essence, you must satisfy the esteem needs of the people you supervise.

The third most important motivator is responsibility for important work with the freedom to achieve goals under minimum supervision. Such responsibility not only satisfies an employee's esteem and self-actualization needs, but also the emotional need to know and learn since greater responsibility goes hand in hand with increased knowledge about the big picture of the project or the company business as a whole.

Challenge and Achievement

How do you create a climate of challenge, interesting work and achievement? You can start by giving some of the work you enjoy doing to people on your staff. Do not dump routine and boring work on any employee in particular. Spread it out so that it creates no burden for anyone and at the same time makes all the employees appreciate the more important things that they do.

Instead of each employee handling a specialized area or piece of the work to be completed, consider expanding the role each person plays so that the individual can see how the various parts fit together and have variety throughout the day. Thus, instead of having four workers completing different tasks for a single job or project, reduce it to two workers or even one worker completing the entire project so that four different projects are being tackled simultaneously by the four workers. Not only does this add variety, interest and challenge, but it also gives each of the employees a sense of achievement to see the finished results of their sole efforts. Enlarging the job (sometimes called job enrichment) satisfies the employee's emotional needs, regardless of whether the employee is an attorney who now handles depositions, attempts to negotiate a settlement of a dispute, prepares briefs and argues the case at the trial in addition to his or her former job of specializing in legal research, or whether the employee is a production worker who now puts the electronic components onto the chassis and fits the chassis into the cabinet of an instrument after inspecting it per electrical specifications in addition to the old job of merely wiring the chassis.

The achievement that an employee can attain can be heightened for even greater job satisfaction through the employment of MBO (management by objectives), which will be discussed in connection with the question below of how to give employees respect through more responsibility. The climate of achievement, challenge and interesting work can be created and maintained through the employment of a technique that can be called MBP (management by participation), which will be discussed below in connection with the question of how to give recognition to the people you supervise.

Respect and Recognition
How do you show your employees that they really do have your respect and are sincerely recognized for their talent and achievements? You can start off by maintaining the right image. If you get in late and leave early, if you have long lunches, or if you do personal reading or other nonwork things at the office, you are showing disrespect for the people you supervise if you expect them to work long hours and keep their nose to the grindstone. You show respect for your people by being serious, competent, efficient, productive and a pacesetter for them to model. Not only does a slovenly, uninterested, opportunistic or incompetent boss show disrespect for the people he or she is supervising, but in the process the boss also quenches motivation because the employees will tend to behave in the same manner, in accordance with the reflection theory discussed in Chapter 1.

Certainly, your employees will not feel respected if you reprimand any of them in the presence of others, if you show favoritism to certain individuals for reasons other than performance, if you use any of them as a scapegoat for your errors, if you refuse to admit mistakes, if you do not support and fight for your people, if you are overly critical of their work, if you play psychological games such as those discussed later in this chapter, if you gossip about your people or if you fail to emphasize common courtesies such as those discussed in Chapter 7 in connection with the emotional need for esteem.

The quickest way to deny respect to your people is to treat them as inferiors instead of as associates working wtih you towards common goals. In fact, the author has intentionally refrained from using the term "subordinate" in this chapter because of its demeaning and dependency-laden connotations. IBM actually went one step further and redefined the supervisor's or foreman's job by labeling that person as an "assistant." The role of the IBM supervisor or foreman is to be an assistant to workers by making sure they know their work and have the tools to discharge their functions. By not being their "boss," the assistant must get the respect of the workers in order to carry out his or her responsibilities, and this means that this person is forced to inherently respect the people he or she is trying to help. If you display too much "brass" or never let anyone forget you are the boss, you are making your people feel subordinate in more than the traditional management sense, and they will not feel respected.

One of the best forms of flattery that makes your people feel important and have respect is to share information with them. Business information, company projects, corporate procedures and other knowledge of what is going on afford a certain prestige to those who have access to such information. Many supervisors maintain their information leverage, their superiority and their security by doling out pieces of information to their people only on a need-to-know basis. Conspicuously withholding information generates mistrust. In accordance with the reflection theory, you can expect your people to withhold information from you. By sharing your information with your people, you give them a chance to prove that they can handle it in a mature and responsible way, and they will return your trust and respect in a climate of productive and cooperative behavior. Withholding information is the reason rumors are generated because people tend to assume the worst when they have to fill in information gaps.

Supervisors lose the respect of new employees if they do not spend sufficient time to explain clearly what is expected, what the organization stands for, how it is organized, how it operates, something of its history, personnel policies, what the person's particular tasks and functions will be, how they relate to those of his fellow workers, what authority the person has, where the person can get materials, supplies and equipment, how the quality and quantity of his or her work will be evaluated and measured, the best techniques and methods of doing work and other things that will allow the employee to feel wanted, important, part of the team and respected for his or her abilities. The employee should be given an organization chart, office rules, job descriptions and explanations and a company policy manual that outlines everything that is verbally communicated to the employee and more so that this individual feels he or she has the opportunity to be an important, productive and cooperating member of a team effort.

Whenever possible, you should try to get your people into on-the-job training programs and other programs where they can attend outside educational and professional functions to develop their capabilities to the fullest. Not only does this satisfy their esteem needs, but it also satisfies their need of self-actualization and need to know, understand and learn. Even if a worker does not care why he or she is doing the job, this employee will be pleased that you bothered to explain everything about it and how it fits in with everything else. Knowing the department business goals and the specific objectives of his or her work will enable the employee to use initiative and creativity and to think of possible improvements since no instructions and no training can cover all contingencies. This employee is more likely to take the right actions if unforeseen circumstances occur.

The desire for self-expression and communication to management from a position of respect is one of the reasons employees organize and join unions. One-way communication is not good enough. You must create a climate of open communication, flowing up as well as down, with your people. Do not discourage your people from asking questions or conveying bad news. The employee who feels able to ask a question without embarrassment, humiliation or punishment will let you know the areas in which he or she is weak or needs to learn more information. This employee will also be open to your help in avoiding wasted time and costly mistakes. An employee who can trust you to give a straight answer to a question that you may have already explained in the past without worry about reprisals or anger knows he or she has your respect. Remember, as brought out in Chapter 5, even people who pride themselves in being good listeners only grasp about half of what they hear. Also, if your explanation or instructions are handed down to more than one level in the chain of command, realize that about 30 percent of the message is lost or distorted after passing through the first two people or levels in the communication chain. Even when a person delivers unpleasant or irritating news, perhaps about a problem that you had not anticipated, be sure to thank the person for being frank and alert and bringing it to your attention.

You can, of course, use your discretion in discouraging visits and chats from people who make a nuisance of themselves, but if you, or even your body language, tell people only to come to you with good news or things you want to hear or that confirm your already-stated feelings or positions, you will simply groom a bunch of "yes men." If your people know you are open minded, they will come to you even after you have committed yourself to a certain course of action if they find a better approach or a basic fault with your approach. By encouraging an atmosphere of trust that it is OK to be controversial, you can expect the truth and you can be sure that your ideas and orders are sound if they are being carried out by your people without voicing doubt or objection. In short, giving your people permission and the freedom to experiment and share their ideas with you without censure or bad feelings should they be mistaken is one of the most important ways of showing respect and being able to rely on the responsible advice of the people you supervise in contrast to hearing them protect or defend your own preconceived or prestated positions. When candor is discouraged, behavior and upward communication become political because employees must seriously worry about the consequences of their actions.

Probably the ultimate action that shows respect goes beyond the mere sharing of information with your people and rewarding them for asking questions and giving their honest opinions, good or bad. By applying MBP (management by participation), you personally involve each of your people in the planning stage of a project or other responsibility that they will be working on. Not only do they help plan the assignments, but they also participate in formulating strategy to achieve the objectives and ultimate goals. Many top-level managers resist the idea of giving up authority and power to middle management and even production workers in order to practice MBP. However, in actuality, Japanese companies and many progressive U.S. corporations, such as IBM and Texas Instruments, have found that they abdicated no authority or power but actually strengthened top management's authority and effectiveness by making it more capable of doing its primary tasks instead of focusing on day-to-day details.

Furthermore, companies like Texas Instruments have found that employees set tougher goals for themselves than any manager would dare to set alone. They are in the best position to judge their own performance and invariably come up with excellent suggestions for improving productivity. In fact, most major companies today have successfully adopted the same principle with decentralization of subsidiaries and divisions that are individually responsible for coming up with budgets, business plans and strategies for implementing them for review, discussion and acceptance or revision by top managements of the parent corporation and profit centers. As already brought out in Chapter 6, the employee who seriously participates in the planning stage will have a greater interest in the work that must be done, will have less fear and resistance, if any, to the changes to be brought about and will have greater initiative, enthusiasm, imagination, entrepreneurship characteristics and productivity. If you isolate yourself with the attitude that, "I'm up here and you're down there," and "I give the orders and you do the work," not only do you lose a valuable tool for fulfilling others' esteem needs, but you also increase your work load since you have to make all the decisions, big and small, yourself and miss out on valuable contributions from people closer to the work and perhaps more knowledgeable of the work than you. A further benefit of MBP is that if your people are involved in decision making most of the time, it will be acceptable for you to be dictatorial at times in crisis situations where there is no time for discussion since there is already mutual respect established with the people you supervise.

In implementing MBP, there are two important considerations you should keep in mind. First, you will not get true participative planning from your people if you tell them in advance what your tentative position is since people inherently do not like to disagree with their boss once they know where he or she stands. Second, your people will consider participative planning a sham if you involve them when it is almost too late to make changes in a proposal that you are scheduled to present to higher management. Employees are generally loath to make changes in what seems like the final version because there's so little time to do anything constructive.

Researchers find that annual performance appraisals are of questionable value in helping employees improve their performance. People accept suggestions for improvements when they are given in a less concentrated form periodically throughout the year. As the number of criticisms mount in an annual review, experiments show that employees are more inclined to reject the negative evaluation, probably because of an "overload phenomenon." Studies of the learning process clearly point out that feedback is less effective if much time is allowed to elapse between performance and the feedback. Frequent discussions with each of your people emphasizing one or two weaknesses to be strengthened at a time when problems and mistakes are fresh in the minds of manager and nonmanager will not only lead to improved performance, but also will show the employee that you are interested in how he or she does and respect him or her for his potential. Limiting performance reviews to once a year makes the employee feel that you are doing it because of personnel policy procedure and not because you are really interested in helping him or her as an individual. Also, frequent informal performance reviews are far less threatening than an annual appraisal on which salary and promotion aspirations usually hinge. The employee will be much less defensive and much more amenable toward accepting a supervisor's suggestions to improve performance on these informal occasions.

It cannot be emphasized too much that, as learned in Chapter 5, your criticism should be directed to the facts of the improper action or omission and not the employee directly. Instead of accusing an employee of carelessness, say "My June memo asked you to phone Mr. Birnbaum by July 20 at the latest, yet he tells me that he did not hear from you until August." A person is less defensive when presented with observed facts, a concrete situation rather than a personal opinion that may be based on an incorrect interpretation or actual understanding. You are not open to a charge of subjective or biased thinking and there is a greater chance of the criticism being constructive and leading to improved performance.

If you are going to convey considerable bad news, it is probably best to do so at the beginning of the day and not at the end of the week. This allows the employee time to think the problems over and have the opportunity for a second discussion later on in the same day to concentrate on ways to overcome the problems. A second meeting can help stabilize the situation and soothe the employee's bad feelings. It is better than leaving the employee depressed at the end of the day to brood at home during the evening or weekend at which time things may get completely blown out of proportion. It is better to convey bad news informally in the employee's own office where he or she will feel more secure and there will be less of a sting.

There are many other ways of showing respect for your people. You can make sure that high performers receive various types of recognition. For instance, employees will appreciate their visibility to other members of management and your own boss. When one of your people does an outstanding job, consider copying in other members of management in a memorandum outlining what was achieved by this person. Copy in personnel also so that it will go into the employee's permanent file. For each person reporting to you, think about what this individual does that is uniquely superior or that no one else can do and what would happen if he or she left your employ. Periodically, tell each person you supervise why he or she is a cornerstone of the department or organization, based on what the employee does best and its impact on the business. The employee will certainly feel respected for his or her talents and contributions. Recommend your employee for write-ups in the house organ, for publicity in news media, honorary dinners, certificates, plaques, membership in elite groups and professional and honorary titles such as the IBM or RCA Fellow. Give your people time off for trips to seminars or to publish a paper or give a speech. The various rewards, forms of recognition, and types of preferential treatment that you can give are almost limitless. The important thing, however, is that you do not dole out such recognition indiscriminately regardless of employee performance. Your people should know that you only give such recognition for achievement. The traditional signs of respect, of course, are promotions and raises.

In short, respect means that employees can exist as people, not pawns. With respect, employees can feel good about themselves because they feel good about what they are doing and because they receive good, positive strokes.

Responsibility and Freedom

Responsibility, work that is of great importance to the company and freedom to achieve goals without someone looking over the employee's shoulder every hour or day are strong job satisfying factors. In fact, the respect, recognition, freedom and responsibility associated with MBO (management by objectives) tends to motivate the employee's initiative, enthusiasm, imagination and entrepreneurship, whether the person is an assembly-line worker or an engineer. With MBO, workers are given sufficient information to know what must be accomplished and how their efforts will be measured towards reaching those goals. They are given high standards of performance in contrast to minimum or normal acceptable output or achievement, which inherently tends to destroy motivation. People are happy and satisfied with the responsibility of being able to focus their vision on a high goal and having the information needed to guide and evaluate their own efforts without close supervision. They like the opportunity MBO gives to exercise their ingenuity and show what they are capable of accomplishing. MBO actually makes people more responsible, self-disciplined and independent. They're more devoted to their work, are more ambitious and have broader, higher and more definite goals. They crave the freedom, trust and respect MBO gives them. They crave seeing an idea through from a goal to completion. MBO also discourages office politics, which thrives when people are subjectively evaluated in the absence of goals and performance criteria.

The ultimate job satisfier is combining MBP with MBO so that the employee first participates in formulating the goals and then actually carries out the necessary responsibilities for achieving those goals. It must be remembered that one of the important aspects of implementing MBO and MBP is the manager's attitude. If you start out with the assumption that your people are weak, irresponsible and lazy, you will get weakness, irresponsibility and laziness. If your behavior, actions and communications assume strength, responsibility and initiative, you will receive few disappointments. Again, the reflection theory discussed in Chapter 1 clearly applies in this situation. If you treat people as adults with your own adult behavior, they will in turn act as adults and can be expected to switch out of their Parent or Child ego states.

Hygienics

Except in a recession or depression, the fulfillment of a worker's physiological and security needs are fairly easily satisfied for the most part by salary, company benefits, opportunity and advancement. A person can normally switch jobs in today's business world without great difficulty and usually with a better position and salary to be had. Because financial security, although a basic need, is rather easily satisfied, the emotional needs of job satisfaction (motivators) take on greater importance. This is why the 1980 survey mentioned above found that respect, challenge, interesting work, responsibility, freedom and participation in decision making are so important to workers today. Sometimes, salary, promotion, bonus and other financial incentives, when improperly administered, actually have a negative effect on motivation and have been called hygienic factors extrinsic to the actual job or work itself from which the motivators are derived. For instance, a salary that a person feels is too low, given his seniority or responsibility level, will create unhappiness. A person who feels there is too little difference between his or her salary and that of a recent college graduate will be dissatisfied.

Another problem with salary rewards is that, as salary increases, the incremental incentive effect of rewards decrease. People tend to become immune to new raises unless they take on successively higher magnitudes in the same manner that an individual takes for granted the pats on the back received after a certain point because they no longer mean much. One interesting finding of the investigators is that company pay secrecy has a highly negative impact on people who are paid well and get good raises. There is a general tendency for workers to overestimate the pay of their peers and assume that others are making more or receiving the same or better increases in pay. In one study, a company that became more open about pay showed a significant increase in the employees' perceptions of the relationship between pay, raises and performance, allowing them to have an accurate performance feedback and be effectively motivated by good pay. Of course, an open-pay policy makes no sense if pay is not tied to performance, but rather is based on seniority, bias or other factors. Thus, although the researchers categorize salary and raises as hygenic factors that can reduce motivation, the 1980 survey shows that employees feel pay is important in motivating them and can be effective if properly handled.

Another example of a hygienic factor that could be an effective motivator if properly handled is fringe benefits, such as bonuses, insurance and vacations. Company profit sharing and stock ownership plans are not effective financial incentives in motivating personnel to perform at higher levels because of the tenuous profits, which depend also on the efforts of hundreds or thousands of other people. Furthermore, pay incentives to workers for exceeding norms of performance have the disadvantage of not coinciding with the maximum profit objective because they induce workers, regardless of their output capabilities, to turn out a little more than the minimum requirements for some bonus money, but not so much as to show that the greater output is easy to achieve and that the standard norms are at too low of a level. Sometimes, more money is not even important to employees. They want other things. For example, one factory found that time off was a greater motivator than additional money in increasing productivity. When assembly-line workers in one plant were told they could go home after a certain amount of work was done, output exceeded all earlier attempts that relied on incentive pay. In fact, there are even a substantial number of workers high in "external control" who feel that they have little control over what happens to them and have little ability to influence their environment. The external control people do not normally feel they can influence their pay, regardless of what they do and what kind of pay system the organization employs. People high in "internal control," on the other hand, feel they can influence their own destiny and tend to be much more highly motivated by a properly administered financial incentive system.

The success of financial reward is determined by the degree and manner in which the employee's individual contribution to company profits and growth is objectively measured, the degree to which the reward is received simultaneously with or soon after the contribution and the degree to which the reward is proportional to the contribution relative to rewards given to others so as to be fair. In short, if bonuses are personal to and under the direct control of employee, they will not sit back and leave it to others in the company to work hard because their incentive depends only on their or perhaps their small department's performance as opposed to the performance of many, many strangers they do not even know.

Possibly the ideal financial benefits plan is to let each employee choose the combination of benefits, pay and time off within the constraints of the total benefit package cost. As of 1980, only 1 percent of 582 companies surveyed actually gave employees a "cafeteria benefits plan" from which they could pick and choose within an overall dollar limit. Only 6 percent of the companies let employees take extra cash in lieu of vacation time.

Qualified stock option plans of the 1950s and 1960s have all but disappeared as long-term incentives today simply because options did not pay off and stock prices did not always reflect company growth and profits. Companies are wisely replacing or at least supplementing stock options with performance plans that reward executives for meeting long-range growth targets. Performance plans award performance shares or units to executives for the degree to which they meet or exceed specific economic standards that executives have control over, such as earnings per share, return on assets, return on shareholders' equity and increases in capital spending. Some progressive companies, such as Champion International Corp., are even going one step further. They feel that in order for economic goals to have meaning, they must be compared with how the competition is doing in the rest of the industry. Thus, if a company beats the industry average for earnings-per-share growth, executives will receive a performance reward even though the arbitrary company goal for earnings-per-share growth may not have been reached because of external factors such as inflation, energy and shortages.

Even promotions on the job can demotivate if handled improperly. Since the vast majority of people are bound to be disappointed in their hopes for further promotion, it is unwise to focus on promotion rather than the satisfaction of doing the job itself. In fact, when promotions are too rapid and become the accepted reward for a good job, employees become dissatisfied when they finally rise to a level or peak above which promotions are few and far between.

There is actually a lot of seriousness behind the old joke about banks and other organizations having so many officers at the assistant vice-president, vice president, Senior vice-president, Group vice-president, executive vice-president and senior executive vice-president levels. The more rungs on the ladder, regardless of actual changed responsibility, the easier it becomes to give recognition in the form of a promotion in job title. Of course, the additional esteem associated with the more prestigious title also benefits the employer because the fancy title helps the employee in dealings with outsiders.

Even the most basic need extrinsic to the job itself, security in being able to hold onto the job, can be turned from a hygienic factor into a true motivator. For instance, the Lincoln Electric Company of Cleveland, Ohio has encouraged its people to find ways to eliminate their own jobs. If they are able to increase productivity by doing so, they do not have to worry about being laid off. They get promoted instead. The firm has a job security agreement with its 2,600 employees and has not laid one person off since 1951, when the contract was signed. Work productivity at Lincoln is 100 percent higher than the U.S. industry in general, and the sales price of its products has not increased in several decades.

Even when times are difficult, worker productivity and morale can be kept high and recruiting of the best people can be facilitated by not laying off employees and pursuing alternative approaches to the problem of declining sales. Jobs can be saved by eliminating overtime, initiating a work sharing program whereby employee hours per week are reduced by 20 percent or so for a staggered 4-day work week, leasing or contracting out personnel to neighboring businesses that are shorthanded and so on.

PDC

Although this chapter has treated the general principles of dealing effectively with the people reporting to you, you should be aware of the life script, ego state and personality of each person reporting to you and adapt your management style to fulfilling his or her needs, even if it means throwing out some of the general rules of supervision.

Figure 9.1 shows the various personality characteristics employees might have. The spokes of the personality wheel separate the four general personality categories of typical people you supervise. All of the characteristics illustrated in the personality wheel are discussed in detail in Chapter 7.

By identifying the life script, ego state, behavior and communication style of each individual reporting to you, you will be able to utilize PDC (see Chapter 7 for a discussion of personality dependent communication) to modify general principles of employee motivation. For instance, if one of your people has a Not OK–OK life script and an Adaptive Child ego state, financial incentives, such as big bonus money, will not motivate him or her to take risks on the job that might result in rocking the boat. This person is more concerned with acceptance by others, conformity, fear of failure and rejection and depends on others to solve problems. Instead of being motivated by bucks tied to performance goals, this person will be motivated to take on new responsibilities and achieve higher goals if he or she receives encouragement, reassurance that it is OK to fail as long as he or she tries to the best of his or her ability and is given plenty of praise, even for little things, to build up confidence and courage to change the status quo.

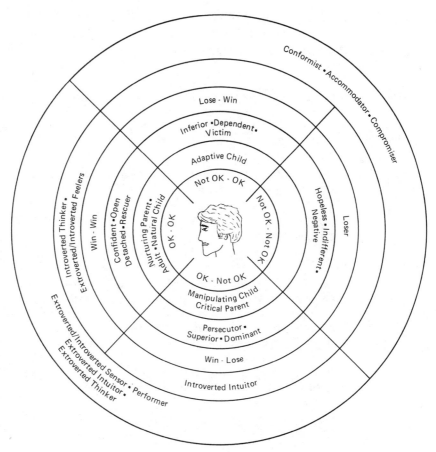

Figure 9.1. Personality wheel.

NEGOTIATING TECHNIQUES OF HIRING
THE BEST PERSON

The major mistakes managers make when interviewing job applicants are:

1. Ignoring prenegotiation planning (failure to read the résumé before the applicant is brought into the office and failure to understand the kind of personality needed for the opening).

2. Failure to establish the agenda (not planning ahead on how to structure the interview and haphazardly asking questions that come to mind on the spur of the moment).

3. Cold behavior. (If warm, friendly and cooperative behavior is not dis-

175

played from the beginning, the applicant will become tense, defensive and close-mouthed. From then on, the applicant will not be sincere in expressing true feelings about things. He or she will say what you want to hear.)

4. Not working against the applicant's need to know. (Too many managers tell the applicant all about the company, the job and the needs and requirements before questioning the applicant to determine if his or her interests, personality and capabilities match the opening. Do not bias the applicant before questioning. Keep the applicant in the dark so that he or she will not know what you are looking for and will be honest in answering your questions.)

5 Too much emphasis on first impression. (Although it is an important factor in your evaluation, do not let the applicant's appearance and initial mannerisms and responses bias your analysis for the rest of the interview.)

6. Emphasis of job know-how over personality fit. (All the experience in the world won't do much good if, for instance, the applicant is an introverted thinker with a Not OK–OK Adaptive Child ego state and the opening is for an engineering manager.)

7. Working against the applicant's need to know about you. (Too many managers are afraid to tell the applicant negative things about themselves and their companies. You should give the job applicants as much information about the working environment as you are trying to extract from them about themselves so that they can make an intelligent decision also should an offer be made. If you are honest with applicants regarding working conditions, opportunity and so forth, you may be able to save a lot of wasted time and aggravation in case you misjudge one applicant's suitability, offer him or her a job and then receive a rejection of the offer because the applicant was given sufficient information to know in his or her own mind that it would not work out.)

As already learned in Chapter 7, we always want to hire a confident, OK–OK employee. But what other traits are best suited for th opening? Do you need an introvert or an extrovert, a Sensor, Feeler, Intuitor or Thinker, a Parent, Child or Adult?

Many managers seek out assistants and executives where the "chemistry" is right. This can be dangerous for managers who have a superior OK–Not OK life script and Critical Parent ego state because they tend to seek out depressed Not OK–OK employees, whose obedience and inferiority complex match the managers' management style perfectly.

If you are trying to fill an opening for a research scientist, you may want to look for an engineer or physicist with a Low Parent–High Adult–High Child ego state who scores high as a Thinker and Intuitor. If you are trying to hire a manufacturing manager, you may wish to look for a manager with a High Parent–High Adult–Low Child ego state who scores high as a Thinker and Sensor. If you are trying to hire a secretary, you may wish to hire a person with a Nurturing Parent–Low Adult–Adaptive Child ego state who scores high as a Sensor and Feeler.

If you are searching for an entrepreneur, general manager, marketing director or other top executive who must be innovative, a leader and responsible for P&L, you may wish to look for someone with an average Parent–High Adult–High Child ego state who scores high as an Intuitor and Sensor.

A typical agenda might start off with some casual, relaxed conversation, at which time you will have the opportunity to observe the applicant and get an initial impression while encouraging him or her to be open with you. Probably the most important aspect of your initial reaction is that you can be pretty sure others who first meet the job applicant after he or she is hired will probably also have the same first impression you do. If you are hiring someone to be a sales person, you will recognize that the first three minutes in which a customer will form an initial impression may be the only three minutes the person has to make the sale, and this should certainly be a heavy factor in your decision whether or not to screen out this person.

The second stage of the assessment process is asking questions to determine the applicant's occupational expertise and specific job know-how. The third stage of the assessment is asking appropriate questions to evaluate the applicant's personality and suitability for the work environment, assuming you decided he or she has sufficient experience for the job. The fourth and fifth phases of the assessment are psychological testing to confirm desirable personality traits and the medical examination, respectively. The fourth and fifth phases will be discussed in more detail later, especially with respect to their importance in choosing the right applicant.

Questioning the Applicant

Probably the most abused part of the job applicant's assessment is the interviewer's questioning and, in particular, how the interviewer asks the questions and what the questions are. Following are the five main categories and specific characteristics that should be identified during the interview:

Rating factors for job applicants

1. Aspiration level:
   a. What are present and future salary desires?
   b. What future promotions and responsibilities are expected?
   c. Is the candidate likely to switch jobs, companies or careers in the future?
   d. Will this person aggressively seek the best deals for the company?
   e. Is the applicant competitive?
   f. Is the applicant ambitious?
2. Initiative:
   a. Is little praise needed due to inner job satisfaction, interest and enthusiasm?
   b. Does this person recognize problems and opportunities before they occur?
   c. Does the applicant have the courage to suggest change, make important decisions involving risk, persist, fail, face rejection and take criticism?
3. Responsibility:
   a. Can the individual assume heavy delegation of responsibilities?
   b. What quantity of work output can be expected?
   c. What quality of work can be expected? Does the individual show good judgment, and can few mistakes be expected?

    d. What is the rate of learning and development? Will this person profit from his or her mistakes and not make the same one twice?

    e. Will the individual cooperate with others, be liked and be influential?

    f. Can the applicant see the big picture, set priorities, plan and organize well?

    g. Is the person mature?

4. Dependability:

    a. Does this person meet deadlines no matter what?

    b. Is the individual adaptable and flexible regarding boss's quirks, changes, new procedures and working on many tasks simultaneously?

    c. Is little supervision needed?

    d. Is the applicant loyal to a boss?

    e. Is the applicant honest?

    f. Can this person work well under pressure and remain cool under stress, and does the candidate have a confident nature?

5. Capabilities:

    a. What is job knowledge?

    b. What are analytical reasoning and logic abilities?

    c. Is the candidate strong in abstract thinking?

    d. Is the candidate concise and clear, with organized writing and speaking abilities?

    e. Is this a good manager whose subordinates will be motivated? (Does he or she understand the use of praise, participation, goal setting, freedom, delegation and so on?)

    f. Is this person creative and able to follow intuition and hunches without forcing things to be logical?

    g. Does the candidate show tolerance for ambiguity and think in terms of probabilities, instability and change?

Many managers make the mistake of asking direct questions in order to find out what makes an applicant tick. Questions such as "Do you consider yourself an introvert or an extrovert," immediately tip off the applicant to what is at stake and what the interviewer wants to hear. Questions must be open ended, general so that they do not bias answers and worded in a manner so as to encourage lengthy responses rather than short yes and no responses.

    The following list, Scientific Questioning Techniques for Interviewing Job Applicants, illustrates questions that can be used for each applicant. The second column of the list lists what those questions are designed to reveal with respect to the traits of the Rating Factors for Job Applicants list above. Several questions regarding the same trait should be phrased differently and asked at different times in order to establish any inconsistency in answers that would indicate insincerity by the job applicant. The questions can be asked in any random order, not necessarily in the order given here. The important thing to remember is that the same questions and the same order in which they are asked should be uniform with all job applicants in order to make an intelligent comparison of their answers. When going through the questions, you will see that, beyond traditional fact-gathering questions, there are three kinds of questions. Bipolar attribute association questions require a choice ranging somewhere between two extremes, utilizing a range from 0 to 5 (using the principle of the Likert attitude scale). More sophisticated questioning techniques involve thematic apperception wherein a partial sentence or story must be completed by the applicant. The third type of question involves unlimited projection of the applicant's true feelings. This is done by asking the person to tell a story based on a picture or to state what the consequences of a hypothetical set of facts would be.

For any particular position you are interviewing applicants for, certain of the outline traits of the Rating Factors list will be more significant than others, and you may wish to direct more questions to those important factors. For instance, if you are hiring an assembly-line worker who can learn how to do the job in thirty minutes and that is what the job will be for as long as the individual stays with the company, it is unnecessary to ask questions involving the traits of 2b–c, 3a, d, f, d, 4f and 5b and g.

On the other hand, if you are looking for a new president of one of your profit centers, you will want to ask more questions regarding certain critical traits. For instance, the person with the potential to be a successful entrepreneur and chief executive officer of a corporation is:

1. Unafraid of bigness. (Large-scale projects are not intimidating, and the rewards of tackling something big are worth the risks.)

2. Capable of setting simple objectives to meet the overall goals you set, based on the big picture. (He or she is not distracted by facts, problem areas, circumstances and tasks that do not advance the central purpose of his or her plan.)

3. A good abstract thinker who can mentally manipulate and structure a complex undertaking and then implement it and see it through from the abstract dream to reality. (Trial-and-error experiments are avoided because they are weeded out during the mental analysis process.)

4. Someone with tolerance for ambiguity so that decisions are confidently made on the basis of incomplete information before problems get worse and opportunities vanish. (These people are able to use good judgment in weighing contradictory data and opinions and in guessing what the actual circumstances are or may be, and they're willing to gamble and are not afraid to fail in order to be the first to reach the prize.)

5. Totally responsible for everything that happens regardless of how much he or she has delegated to others. (People of this sort know that no one can ever delegate responsibility, only authority to perform the task. If something goes wrong, they know that they are responsible for the blame just as they are responsible for the glory as a result of their plans and their wise delegation of functions.)

6. Not fearful of success and suffers no guilt from greed. (He or she is comfortable with the idea that he or she deserves and has the right to obtain the wealth, power and success he or she is looking for).

With the preceding in mind, choose from the following questions to interview applicants:

Question number	The answer to the question gives information about the following traits in the Rating Factors List	Question
1.	1–5	What do you look for in a job?
2.	1–5	Why do you wish to leave your present position?
3.	2–5	What types of people seem to rub you the wrong way?
4.	2–3	What kind of guidance did you get from your boss?
5.	2–4	What is the nature of your typical work day?
6.	2–5	What can you do for us that someone else cannot?
7.	1–5	Describe your closest friend and tell me how you differ from him or her.
8.	2–3, 5a	What do you know about our company?
9.	2–3, 5e	Do you usually speak to people before they talk to you? Rate yourself from 0 to 5, with 5 being you always speak first.
10.	1–2	How would you describe the essence of success?
11.	2–5	Why should we hire you?
12.	2a	How did you happen to get into this field of work?
13.	3–4	Can you work under pressure? Rate yourself from 0 to 5, with 5 being under tremendous pressure.
14.	2, 3, 5	In your present position, what problems did you identify that had been overlooked by others?
15.	2–4, 5e	What is your philosophy of management?
16.	1–4	What traits do you feel you can most improve upon?
17.	1–5	Aside from money, what do you want from your next job that you are not presently getting?
18.	1	What do you consider satisfactory earnings progression from this point?
19.	1–5	Are there certain things you feel more confident in doing than others? What are they, and why do you feel that way?
20.	1–5	Will you be out to take your boss's job?
21.	5f	Are you creative? Rate yourself from 0 to 5, with 5 being extremely creative. If you rate yourself anywhere from 3 to 5, give an example of your creativity.
22.	5b	Are you analytical? Rate yourself from 0 to 5, with 5 being excellent reasoning and logic abilities. If you choose anything from 3 to 5, give an example of your analytical abilities.

23.	1	What kind of salary are you worth?
24.	2c, 3d, 4f	What is your usual reaction when chewed out by your boss for doing something wrong?
25.	2–5	What were your 5 biggest accomplishments in your current job?
26.	1–5	What irritates or displeases you most in other people?
27.	3–4	How do you feel about working overtime without pay?
28.	1–5	Tell me about the reputation you have as an employee.
29.	1–5	What are some of the things in your job that frustrate you and what do you do about those frustrations?
30.	1	What do you see yourself doing five years from now?
31.	2–5	How long will it take you to make a contribution if you join us?
32.	1, 2, 3, e–g 5d, e, g	Are you a leader? Rate yourself from 0 to 5, with 5 being a born leader. If you choose anywhere from 3 to 5, give an example of your leadership.
33.	1c	How long would you stay with us?
34.	5e	How do you feel about people from minority groups?
35.	1–5	Tell me about the last incident on the job that made you angry and what you did about it.
36.	2a	If you could start again, what would you do differently?
37.	1, 2, 3f	How have you changed the nature of your present job?
38.	1–5	Would you describe a few situations in which your work was criticized?
39.	1–4	Would you object to working for a woman?
40.	2–5	Are you a planner or a doer? Why?
41.	2c, 4f, 5b, c, f	Pretend that I am Thomas Edison interviewing you for a position at laboratory. How would you go about measuring the volume of air in one of the electric light bulbs I just built? (The right answer is explained in the text following.)
42.	2b, 3f, g, 4f, 5b–d, f, g	What are all of the things you think would happen if a pill was discovered that satisfied a person's daily food needs? (Typical responses and their significance are discussed in the text following.)
43.	1–4	How would you describe your own personality?
44.	1–4	How many hours a week do you feel a person should devote to the job? Why?
45.	1–3, 5e	What do your subordinates think of you?
46.	1–5	What other types of jobs are you considering right now?

47.	5g	Do you make decisions quickly or only after thorough research of the facts? Rate yourself from 0 to 5, with 5 representing thorough research, and explain your rating.
48.	1–5	What are some of the things you and your supervisor disagree about?
49.	2b, 3f, g, 4f, 5b–d, f, g	How would it affect you if it was suddenly announced in the news media that regularly scheduled passenger service to the moon would start in one year? (For typical responses and their significance see the text following.)
50.	1–5	What do you feel are your boss's greatest strengths?
51.	1	What do you think you will be doing fifteen years from now?
52.	3e	Does it bother you to work for a younger person?
53.	1–5	Which person in this picture is you? Tell me a story about what is happening right now, based on what you see in this picture. (A typical picture that can be used is Figure 9.2.)

Figure 9.2. Unlimited projection testing.

54.	1–5	Do you prefer staff or line work and why?
55.	1–5	What are your five weakest areas?
56.	1–2a	If you had your choice, what would you most like to do?
57.	1–5	What is wrong with your present company?
58.	1–4	How do you feel about the way your boss treats you and others in your department?
59.	2b, 3f, g, 4f, 5b–d, f, g	Think of everything that would probably happen if a drug was discovered that would wipe out all disease. (For responses and their significance, see the text following.)

60.	2–4	Describe your ideal boss.
61.	2–4	Have you been successful in working with people you dislike, and how do you do it?
62.	3e	Do you like working more by yourself or with others? Rate yourself from 0 to 5, with 5 being your greatest enjoyment in working alone.
63.	2b, 3f, g, 4f, 5b–d, f, g	Tell me ten ways in which a spoon can be used. (Some responses and their significance are discussed in the text following.)
64.	2b, c, 3d–f, 4b, 5f, g	Are you a person of very strong convictions? Rate yourself from 0 to 5, with 5 being an extremely opinionated person.
65.	2b, c, 3d, 4b, 5g	How does it feel when your boss hands you vague instructions?
66.	1–4, 5f	Is business before pleasure a hard-and-fast rule in your life? Rate yourself from 0 to 5, with 5 being first priority to business.
67.	1–5	What things or activities do you most hate to do?
68.	2–4	What kind of people do you like to work with?
69.	1–5	What do you regard as your major assets?
70.	1–3, 5b, c, f, g	Do you like to play around with a new idea just for fun even if it doesn't benefit you in the end?
71.	1, 4f, 5b, c, f	Here is a picture (show Figure 9.3) of three rows of three dots. Is it possible to join all nine dots with four straight lines without removing your pencil from the paper? (If applicant says yes, give applicant three chances to do it. If applicant is unsuccessful, ask the question again. If applicant says no, say that other applicants have done it and ask if applicant thinks he or she can. If he or she responds in the affirmative, proceed in accordance with the interview procedure above. See typical tries in Figure 9.4 and the solution in Figure 9.5.)

Figure 9.3. Nine-dot problem.

72.	1e, 2b, c, 3e, 5f	Do you occasionally voice opinions in groups or meetings that seem to turn some people off? Rate yourself from 0 to 5, with 5 being frequently voicing such opinions.

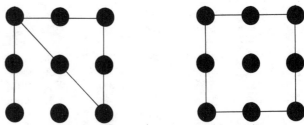

Figure 9.4. Wrong solutions to nine-dot problem.

73.	1e, 2c	When someone gets ahead of a few people in front of you in line, will you ask him or her to go to the end of the line if no one else does? Rate yourself from 0 to 5, with 5 being your choice if you always demand that the person go to the rear of the line.
74.	1–5	Tell us about the kind of person for whom it is difficult to do your best work.
75.	2b, 5c, f	Would it be nice to act more spontaneously more of the time? Rate yourself from 0 to 5, with 5 being acting spontaneously much of the time.
76.	2b, c, 3e, g, 5e	Do you feel that you do not have the right to criticize others because you, as well as they, have your own failings? Rate yourself from 0 to 5, with 5 being no criticism.
77.	2a, c, 3e, g, 4f, 5e	Do you often wonder what others are thinking about you? Rate yourself from 0 to 5, with 5 being that you often wonder.
78.	1, 2c, 5e	Are you frequently conscious of being too materialistic? Rate yourself from 0 to 5, with 5 being frequent consciousness of being too materialistic.
79.	1e, 2b, c, 5b, c, f, g	Are you prouder of your ability to solve rather than unearth difficult problems? Rate yourself from 0 to 5, with 5 representing pride in your ability to solve.
80.	1, 2, 4f, 5b, g	Do you take larger financial or investment risks than most? Rate yourself from 0 to 5, with 5 being larger risks. Explain why.
81.	1, 2c, 4f, 5e	Do you always avoid talking about things that will embarrass someone? Rate yourself from 0 to 5, with 5 being avoidance of things that will embarrass.
82.	3e, 4b, 5e	Do you frequently find yourself complimenting other people? Rate yourself from 0 to 5, with 5 being frequently complimenting others.
83.	1–5	Do you usually impress others as someone who is practical rather than intellectual? Rate yourself from 0 to 5, with 5 being practical.

84.   1, 4e, f, 5d, e   Are you always the person you appear to be? Rate yourself from 0 to 5, with 5 being yes. Explain.

ANSWERING THOMAS EDISON'S QUESTION.   This is a question actually used by Thomas A. Edison when he interviewed people to work for his company. He wanted to determine if they could wade through the various details and see the big picture, using intuitive and creative thinking.

Many applicants would immediately become flustered and confused when asked to state how they would arrive at measuring the volume of air in one of Edison's electric light bulbs. They did not have the trait known as field freedom, ignoring irrelevant facts and poor approaches to solving a problem.

They would think of measuring the diameter of the bulb and then performing laborious arithmetic calculations, for instance.

Applicants that were hired intuitively thought of the big picture, which meant a simple solution–namely, filling up the bulb with water and then pouring it into a tube graduated in milliliters for a volume readout.

RESPONSES TO FOOD PILL QUESTION.   Manufacturers and processors of basic foods that people eat more because of nutritional value than because of taste and flavor would see a sharp decline in sales if people switched to the pill. These companies would have to obtain a license to produce the pill or design around the patent protection held by the company that developed the pill. Without a license or research to come up with a new type of pill to compete with the original pill, these food manufacturers and processors would die off just like the carriage manufacturers did with the advent of the automobile.

Manufacturers of delicacies, desserts, snacks and other good tasting and feeling foods will not immediately be impacted because pills do not offer the emotional gratification that people want from such foods. However, these manufacturers cannot simply sit back and do nothing. The next generation of consumers will be growing up with the pill and may be less attached to snack foods. Furthermore, second- and third-generation pills may be developed that will offer the flavor and crunchy feeling or other characteristics of luxury foods.

Supermarkets will have to diversify into other retail goods in order to survive the decline in food items. On the other hand, the development could be a bonanza for pharmacies and possibly health food stores.

Business lunches, dinner parties and most social occasions that center around breaking bread with others will no longer have the same traditional meaning.

People will have more leisure time since it only takes a minute to have a meal. It is also possible that the typical work day may be compressed since people do not need as much time for lunch anymore. However, it may be found that people still need three-quarters of an hour or an hour to relax and break up the day.

Unless somehow built into the pill's characteristics, the roughage needed by internal organs and the biting pressure needed to properly exercise the teeth and gums may be lacking.

Animals such as cows, chickens, ducks, pigs and the like will proliferate since they will no longer be raised for human consumption.

Farmers, who supply the animals and crops for our food needs, will become extinct.

The world food problem will be solved. Underdeveloped and poverty stricken countries can import or establish local manufacture of the pill for their populace.

These responses show creativity because the more practical consequences a person can anticipate within a limited period of time and the more realistic detail that he or she can supply in describing those consequences, the more a person is able to use imagination and intuition in foreseeing key trends resulting from circumstances never thought of before.

ANSWER TO MOON PASSENGER SERVICE QUESTION.   Typical responses are willingness to visit or take a vacation up there, complete indifference, finding the idea of going to the moon foolish, ridiculous, childish or scary, and thinking about how to benefit from the news, such as starting a tourist service, opening up a business on the moon, opening up an import business to sell raw materials excavated on the moon or fad products, such as moon rocks.

People's answers will reflect how aggressive and competitive they are, whether they recognize opportunities, whether they have immature views on life, whether they are adaptable to change, their degree of confidence in themselves, their abstract thinking skills, their creativity and their tolerance for ambiguity.

RESPONSES TO THE MIRACLE DRUG QUESTION.   The entire health care establishment would be drastically affected. With the exception of old age, birth, accidental injuries and the like, people will no longer need physicians, nurses, other drugs and hospitals.

With disease eradicated even in the underdeveloped and poverty stricken nations, world population will be sure to increase more rapidly, causing food shortages and other problems.

Pharmaceutical companies and pharmacies would take a beating because many drugs used to treat, contain and cure illness will now be obsolete.

The pressure to find ways of taking care of senior citizens will become even more acute.

These responses show creativity because the more practical consequences people can anticipate within a limited period of time and the more realistic detail they can supply in describing those consequences, the more they are able to use imagination and intuition in foreseeing key trends resulting from circumstances never thought of before.

Ten possible uses for the household spoon are:

1. screwdriver,
2. gardening tool,
3. child spanker,
4. shoehorn,
5. eye-gouge weapon,
6. infant toy,
7. drum stick,
8. catapult,
9. door knocker,
10. stirrer.

Ability to immediately think of ten uses for a common implement depends on how flexible or rigid someone's thinking is. If people are creative and imaginative, they allow their mind freedom to come up with ideas. If the task leaves them stymied, they need to loosen themselves up intellectually.

ANSWER TO THE NINE-DOT PROBLEM.   Most people who try to join all nine dots with four straight lines spend ten minutes or so and produce nothing but frustration and doubt that it can be done or the feeling that they are not as creative or smart as they thought. They feel boxed in, either way.

The person who is not limited and exercises intellectual freedom is able to use intuition and creativity regardless of existing beliefs, tradition and expectations. A person who has these characteristics will shortly realize that the problem can only be solved by drawing beyond the outside perimeter of the nine dots, as shown in Figure 9.5.

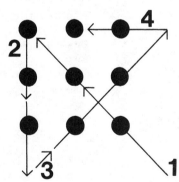

Figure 9.5. Solution to nine-dot problem.

Testing

There are numerous tests the applicant can be asked to take for a penetrating look at the kind of person and how well he or she will perform on the job. For instance, there is even a test that has been developed to measure the degree to which the job applicant will be motivated by pay raises and bonuses. There are the standard ability tests for math, logic, communication skills, vocabulary and so forth. There are the personality tests that will give the manager a pretty good idea of the applicants's life script, ego state, communicating style, maturity, responsibility, initiative, aspiration level, dependability and so on.

The medical examination, aside from the obvious purpose of assuring the health of the applicant, can also determine various characteristics that indicate high performance. For instance, applicants with high levels of uric acid tend to be successful in whatever they do. Applicants who suffer from bruxism (gritting or gnashing the teeth) and who consequently develop strong jaw muscles also tend to be prosperous and successful. The use of an electroencephalograph can show which hemisphere of the brain the job applicant relies on the most. It is well known that the left side of the brain handles the logical, linear and verbal functions, whereas the right handles the emotional, intuitive and spatial functions. A left-brain dominated job applicant is probably a Thinker or Sensor with a high Adult ego state, quite suitable as an engineer, attorney, administrator, or other staff technician. The right-brain dominated job applicant may well be an Intuitor, which would be desirable for positions as president, research scientist and marketing director.

The use of polygraph instruments, commonly known as lie detectors, to check the honesty of job applicants has spread quickly in industry. The instrument produces a graph of the subject's heart and respiratory rate and skin changes in response to questions. Its accuracy can be more than 95 percent, depending upon the expertise of the operator who interprets the graph. The instruments generally range in price from $1,000 to $4,000. The typical polygraph test takes between sixty and ninety minutes, at a cost to the employer of from $50 to $200 per subject. Because the instrument monitors pulse and blood pressure, electrical changes in skin caused by sweat gland emissions or muscular activity indicative of tension, it is difficult for a subject to control what is being measured when lying—hence the deadly accuracy of the test if the subject is first put at ease to establish normal behavioral response to test questions.

Another type of lie detector that is becoming more popular is the voice stress analyzer, which can cost up to $6,000, for measuring microtremors in the voice indicative of hard stress by means of a pen that inscribes tremors on graph paper. During the great debate of 1980 between Jimmy Carter and Ronald Reagan, the International School of Polygraph Science used a voice stress analyzer, which showed particular stress when Carter denied any aid deal in the works with Iran to get the hostages back and when Carter promised the Social Security system will not go bankrupt, as well as when Carter made his concluding statements (at which time the pen jumped off the paper). According to a vice-president of the school, Carter did not believe what he was saying in those instances. A week later, the newspapers carried headlines that President Carter had indeed offered to trade $140 million in military equipment for the immediate release of the hostages.

In determining an applicant's intuitive capabilities, a company may consider testing his precognition. Studies over the last two decades reveal that there is a close link between a chief executive officer's above-average precognition powers and the above-average profits yielded by his or her company. Simply stated, the high precognitive executive is able to correctly rely on hunches in predicting what will happen and in taking the right courses of action in guiding the company toward future successful growth and profit.

Chapter 10
NEGOTIATING YOUR WAY TO CAREER SUCCESS

THE FIVE STRATEGIES FOR JOB ADVANCEMENT

There are five key prerequisites to success on the job. *One*, you want good people below you who can assume your responsibility so that you can be promoted. This is covered in Chapter 9. *Two*, you want to help your boss perform well and make him or her look good. In short, you want to push your boss up because it's a lot harder and more dangerous to push a boss out. *Three*, you want to exploit your supervisor's emotional needs so that you will be selected for a promotion and a good raise over the competition. *Four*, you want your performance to excel. *Five*, you want to produce a good image and make it visible to your boss and your boss's superiors.

In order to push your boss up so that you can take his or her spot, you need to know what your boss's most important goals are and what is important to his or her superiors. Otherwise, you can work twelve hours a day and outperform everybody else in the office and eventually find out your boss has no interest in the results you achieved. One way to find out where your boss's interests lie is to look back at the advertisement you responded to for the job and also ask the personnel department for your job description if there is one in the files. Chances are more than likely that your boss had a hand in drafting the functions and responsibilities considered important. An astute person will talk with the boss's secretary and a senior person in the department to find out what problems the boss gives top priority to. Sometimes, during an informal chat with your supervisor, you will be able to subtly bring out what this person considers his or her most vexing problems. It is particularly important to find out where your boss's weak areas are so that you can help strengthen his or her own performance, assuming some of these weaknesses are your strengths.

In addition to working hard and giving the right things the right priorities so that your boss's performance will be good, there are other things you can do to make your boss look good. One of the most effective

190

techniques is allowing the boss to take credit for your great ideas, reports and projects. Not only is this difficult for most people to do because of their pride in their work, but it is also dangerous. Unless you have a pact or understanding with your supervisor that you want to do whatever you can to advance his or her career, provided the supervisor will bring you along, you will have sacrificed the opportunity for visibility and recognition for nothing. Whenever you can, whether it be a social, professional or business occasion, praise your boss in high places. Defend your boss whenever your boss or his or her projects are being attacked by people from other departments. In the same way you find out what your boss's problems are, you should also find out who your boss's enemies are so that you can put into proper perspective what you hear from them and also exercise discretion regarding information they directly or indirectly receive from you that can in some way be used against your supervisor.

Hand in hand with helping your boss perform well and look good are the principles of PDC learned in Chapter 7 and emotional need satisfaction (Chapter 5). If you, more than anyone else, help satisfy your boss's security, esteem, friendship, physiological and knowledge needs, you will be a giant step ahead of the competition for advancement.

Supervisors' needs for security encompass many things. They do not want to have to worry all the time about whether an employee is going to slip up and make them look bad, since they are ultimately responsible for their work. In fact, you satisfy a boss's need for security when you are willing and have the courage to tell the boss when you think he or she is doing something wrong before his or her superiors discover it. At the same time, your supervisor will want your 100 percent loyalty to do things his or her way after he or she has heard you out and disagrees with you. After all, your supervisor has the big picture, and you do not want him or her to have to worry about whether you will continue to be supportive once a decision is made. As already mentioned in connection with helping your boss perform well, even if you are not able to solve the most pressing problems, your boss will still regard you highly for having tried because you have demonstrated your loyalty and dedication. A supervisor will feel even more secure when your praise and compliments regarding his or her accomplishments and your defense of any attacks trickle back down. Perhaps the ultimate appeal to your supervisor's need for security is making it clear that your goal is to do whatever you can to help this person do well, look good and move up.

Appealing to the esteem needs of your boss and your boss's superiors cannot be emphasized too strongly. As already mentioned, when your boss realizes that you have gone out of your way to pay him or her compliments, this individual will feel very good about the respect and esteem you show. You also satisfy esteem needs by respecting your boss's idiosyncrasies and catering to his or her desires. For instance, if your boss prefers verbal reports to lengthy memos, you do not want to be irritating by doing otherwise. Likewise, if someone does not want people to smoke in his or her office, you should respect this. In connection with learning which are your boss's weaknesses and strengths in order to improve his or her performance, you want to have maximum interaction regarding your boss's strong areas, where he or she enjoys and feels comfortable discussing things. You do not want to work against your supervisor's esteem needs by continuously going over weak areas where ignorance or faltering may become conspicuous and embarrassing. By subtly picking up responsibilities in the areas where your supervisor is weak and taking care of them without bothering him or her in these areas, most of your meetings will involve areas where he or she can look good because of knowledge and strengths in them. Your boss will associate smooth-running meetings and the pleasant communication with you. Another technique of filling esteem needs is to emulate or quote your boss in some manner. Even something as little as adopting one of your supervisor's favorite phrases is a genuine form of flattery.

It is human nature that the better people know you, the more time they spend with you, and the friendlier you are to them the greater will be their interest in you. As quite often happens, satisfying your supervisor's need for friendship may tip the scale in your favor when you are being considered with one of your peers for a promotion and both of you have equal track records. There is a certain intimacy about having dinner together with your boss out of town. Times like these are when he or she really gets to understand you as a person and not just another worker in the department. If possible, invite your boss to be your guest at a dinner meeting or an annual meeting of your professional or trade association. Many times, a supervisor will not hesitate to accept such an invitation, whereas he or she would be reluctant to accept an invitation to your home, which would have a stigma of socializing with an employee. One of the best techniques of appealing to your supervisor's friendship needs is to volunteer to do bad news assignments and other dirty work that no one else wants to help out on. People have a built-in bias against running errands and doing other things that seem like apple polishing, but that is exactly what it is and it can be used to cultivate an excellent relationship with your boss.

Finally, satisfying your boss's need to know what is going on is greatly appreciated. Although it may seem petty, many supervisors will even value tidbits of gossip you can bring them about what people are saying within and outside of the department. After all, most supervisors are shielded from what is going on in the rumor mill, especially if it indirectly or directly involves them. Furthermore, just hearing your thoughts on trends and developments based on information you have come across that your boss has not will be valued.

What abilities do you need and should you cultivate in order to perform well beyond the level of your peers? For most executives, the major abilities needed to excel are initiative, a high aspiration level, intuitiveness, thinking big, a high tolerance for ambiguity, abstract thinking skills, understanding people and hard work coupled with responsibility for tasks tackled.

With initiative, you become the type of person that will make and then take advantage of opportunities. You look for potential problem areas and then take whatever action is necessary to avoid fires before they start. You look for ways to take some of the load off your boss's shoulders. In general, you do things before requests to take care of them are made. In short, you are a self-starter.

People with high aspiration levels have enough confidence and courage to always shoot as high as they reasonably can. People like this consider themselves winners, and as you learned from Chapter 4 they usually get more than the next person because they ask for more. Likewise, these ambitious people usually accomplish more because they try to do more than the next person. In short, people with a high aspiration level usually try to do the best they can whenever the matter they are tackling is important or interesting, whether it be exceeding the sales quota or designing a better piece of equipment at less cost.

Intuitive people are able to see the big picture and set simple objectives. They are normally creative because they do not get confused with irrelevant details and facts. If you are going to have a clear understanding of what your boss's goals are and what is important to his or her superiors, you have to have a good understanding of the company as a whole. This is where your intuitive abilities come into play.

You must not shy away from thinking big merely because major undertakings and big deals proportionately involve a greater risk than more routine, safer matters.

Your tolerance for ambiguity must be high so that you can make timely decisions regardless of the uncertainties involved. After a certain period of time, you are going to have about 80 percent of the factual information you need in order to make a decision. If you wait a long time, you may acquire another 5 to 10 percent. In general, you will never be sure about that final 10 percent of information. People who do not act after they obtain the 80 percent of knowledge relevant to the problem or task at hand are procrastinators and will consistently let opportunities slip through their fingers because they do not act fast enough or act at all.

You should develop your abstract thinking so that you can visualize complex situations in your mind and make trial-and-error experimentation in real life unnecessary. Things get speeded up; decisions can be made more quickly with less uncertainty; and problems get solved quicker. Get into the habit of thinking negatively because constructive worry to foresee problems ahead of time is important to good planning.

If you work hard and assume total responsibility for your functions, your progress will not go unnoticed. If you volunteer for even more and accomplish more than is expected by your supervisor, your feats give you visibility at the desired levels of power. In fact, if you always perform at a higher level than you are hired for and are being compensated for, you make yourself continuously underpaid in relation to your performance and responsibilities and almost force management to give you promotions and raises commensurate with your progress.

Being open and honest with people and understanding how to win their attention, interest, support and active help for achieving your goals without injuring theirs is essential to success. Nothing is impossible for a person to achieve if he or she has the necessary people to help achieve it. The necessary people can mean those above you, those below you, and/or your peers. Mastering the fundamentals and advanced techniques of PDC is probably the single most important benefit you can get from reading this book for career success.

The last prerequisite is producing the right image and making it visible to the people above. Everything you learned about sensation transference in Chapters 5 and 6 regarding your appearance, demeanor, voice, gestures, apparent success on the job and so on must be taken seriously to achieve career success. In fact, one study shows that 83 percent of fired executives surveyed all shared the common problem of not aggressively calling their superiors' attention to their achievements, preferring that they be rewarded without doing so.

YOUR IMAGE IS YOUR FUTURE

Before we get into the detailed aspects of what image you want and how to project it, you may wish to rate yourself. For each of the 100 statements below, respond with a rating from 0 to 5, with 0 representing your true feeling that the statement is always false and 5 representing your true feeling that the statement is always true, and a number between 0 and 5 representing somewhat mixed feelings on your part. Do not take this questionnaire thinking that your answers will be reviewed by a potential employer. This questionnaire is strictly for you to experience your true feelings so that you can learn something about yourself. Later on in this chapter, you will find out how image conscious you are and what you need to do about it. As a matter of fact, you should be going through the rest of this chapter determined to improve your image in light of the common agreement by experts that people in positions of leadership are really no brighter and no more decisive, alert or informed than many of those reporting to them. The only reason they are in command is that they had a better image.

1. The boss is always right.
2. It is smart to flatter important people.
3. Power is one of life's most precious commodities.
4. If you are even one-fourth Protestant, list it as your religion on your résumé (assuming you believed it would increase your chance of getting the job).
5. I ask my boss's opinion about personal matters (such as investments or real estate) although I don't need the advice.
6. If I had the skill, I would help my boss or his or her boss with his or her antique car hobby on Sunday afternoons.
7. I will wear uncomfortable clothing to the office if it gives me a successful look.
8. If I discovered a fellow executive pilfering office supplies, I would use that information against him or her in asking for favors.
9. I would invite my boss to a party in my home even if I didn't like him or her.
10. A woman should take advantage of her sex and flirt with male executives in the company to gain advantage.
11. You should know why people are your friends.
12. If my boss were a prominent person, I would start a scrapbook about him or her.

13. Given a choice, choose only those assignments that make you look good.
14. I would tell my boss what some of my co-workers really thought about him or her, if it was negative.
15. If someone higher up on the organizational ladder offends you, say nothing.
16. I like the idea of keeping a "blunder file" about my peers for potential future use.
17. I would not have an affair with the company president's spouse, even if I were attracted to that person and he or she wanted to.
18. Most people at work cannot be trusted.
19. You should tell the truth, or not, depending on how others are affected.
20. Before taking any action at work, think how it might be interpreted by key people.
21. Never tell anyone at work anything that can be used against you in the future.
22. You should personally select the subordinates upon whom your success greatly depends.
23. If you have to punish somebody, do it all at once.
24. Act and look cool even when you don't feel that way.
25. Bluffing, in the long run, will actually be beneficial.
26. It is necessary to lie once in a while in business.
27. If you disagree about something important with your boss, it would be a poor strategy to complain to an acquaintance on the board of directors.
28. Given the opportunity, I would help my boss's secretary put up some shelves in his or her apartment even though I don't like him or her.
29. Why bother cultivating the minnows in my company? It's the big fish I'm after.
30. It is important to have lunch with the "right people" at least twice a month.
31. People will remember you longer if you do nice things for them. Therefore, I try to be as nice as possible to everybody.
32. I would attend a company picnic even if I had the chance to do something I enjoyed much more that day.
33. If necessary, I would say rotten things about a person to get a promotion.
34. If a customer was pleased with the way I handled his or her account, I would ask this person to write a complimentary note to my boss.
35. If you will make a poor showing, it is not worthwhile to compete.
36. If I worked for a jean manufacturer, I would never wear another brand to work.
37. If you have important confidential information, release it only to your advantage.
38. Accept advice willingly, but take the risk of asking why you are being given advice.
39. The best policy is to tell people what they want to hear.
40. Honesty is really not the best policy in many cases.
41. How you accomplish something is much less important than what you accomplish.
42. Do not simply wound a rival. Get this person demoted or fired.
43. If your rival for a promotion is making a big mistake, why tell him or her?
44. A person who is able and willing to work harder than peers will not necessarily succeed in business, even some of the time.

45. If I wanted to show someone up, I would be willing to write memos documenting that person's mistakes.

46. If I had a legitimate gripe about my company, I would air my views publicly (such as a letter to the editor of a newspaper).

47. Before you write a final report to your boss, find out what your boss really wants to see included in that report.

48. I would be willing to say nice things about a rival to get him transferred away from my department.

49. I stay late or come in early just to impress my boss.

50. Why teach your subordinate everything you know about your job? The subordinate could then replace you.

51. It is better to be important and dishonest than to be humble and honest.

52. Do not enter into a cooperative venture with someone you like if it means that you are going to risk personal advantage.

53. I use gossip for personal advantage.

54. While on vacation, I remember to pick up a gift for my boss.

55. Don't be a complainer. It may be held against you.

56. Past promises do not stand in the way of success.

57. It is necessary to instill fear to keep some people in place.

58. It is wise never to let one's reputation be fully tested.

59. I would get drunk with my boss if I thought it would help me get ahead.

60. Reading about office politics is more fun than reading an adventure story.

61. One good way to be a hero is to create a crisis for the company and then resolve it.

62. I go out of my way to cultivate friendships with powerful people.

63. I frequently raise questions about the capabilities of my peers.

64. Keep job know-how secrets in your head. It is foolish to put procedures and other important work ideas in writing.

65. If you have an acid tongue, conceal it at work.

66. If I were a tournament-level tennis player and my boss an overweight hack, I would gladly team with him or her in a match.

67. I would have an affair with a powerful person if I thought it would help my career.

68. I take credit for someone else's work when it is to my benefit to do so.

69. Only a fool would correct mistakes made by the boss.

70. If I discovered a co-worker looking for a new job, I would tell my boss.

71. Even if you made only a minor contribution to an important project, get your name associated with that project.

72. It is necessary to play office politics even if you are extremely competent.

73. If you have injured a rival, get that person removed from the scene if possible.

74. There is nothing wrong with blowing your own horn.

75. I try to use some of the same jargon my boss does, even if I don't particularly like some of my boss's favorite phrases.

76. I keep my office free of personal mementos, such as things made by my children, even though my office seems cold and businesslike.

77. Once you offend someone, never entrust that person with something important.
78. One should take favorable action regardless of whether it is morally correct.
79. If someone compliments you for a task that is another's accomplishment, smile and say thank you.
80. I would purchase stock in my company even though it might not be a good investment.
81. I use personal influence whenever possible to gain a promotion.
82. If I wanted something done by a co-worker, I would be willing to say, "If you don't get this done, our boss might be very unhappy."
83. If I thought it would help my career, I would take on a hatchet-man assignment.
84. It is much safer to be feared than loved by your subordinates.
85. If I were looking for a new hobby, I would think first of trying out my boss's favorite.
86. Most people act out of self-interest.
87. Although you have to resort to speculation, make up some financial figures to prove the value of your proposal when necessary.
88. Once you become the boss, transfer from your department anyone you suspect does not like you.
89. Even if you dislike a particular person in your firm, send him or her a congratulatory note when he or she receives a big promotion.
90. I laugh heartily at my boss's jokes even if they are not funny.
91. It is difficult to get ahead without cutting corners here and there.
92. I learn of my boss's political preferences before discussing politics.
93. If you do somebody a favor, remember to cash in on it.
94. I would not hire a subordinate with more formal education than my own.
95. Never tell anyone the real reasons you do something unless it is useful to do so.
96. A wise strategy is to keep on good terms with everybody in your office.
97. People generally try to win favorable comparison over others.
98. All forms of office politics boil down to more than just ass kissing.
99. If apple polishing helps, do it.
100. My primary job is to please my boss.

There are five basic categories of image consciousness: the innocent lamb, the straight arrow, the survivor, the politician and the Machiavellian.

Innocent lambs honestly believe that competent people are rewarded for their efforts and eventually rise to the top. Their view on how things work is best described by the biblical quote "By their works ye shall know them." In short, these people naively think they will be rewarded for their hard work and therefore have no concern at all about their image.

Straight arrows essentially believe that people are honest, hard working and trustworthy and that politics is unnecessary for advancement. Their basic strategy is to demonstrate competence on the job, assuming that other strategies, such as cultivating influential people, are not as important as an image as a good worker. Although straight arrows are not political, unlike the innocent lamb, they are image conscious enough to periodically educate their boss about the tasks they are performing, how well they are doing them and how goals are being met sooner than anticipated as a result of foreseeing and handling various problems.

Survivors are a little more political than straight arrows. Not only do they actively present an image of competence, but they also make sure they do not irritate their boss and other superiors, and they consciously try to take advantage of opportunities to please higher-ups. Thus, they laugh at the boss's jokes and compliment the boss after he or she has successfully completed a tough negotiation. In short, survivors are aware of the benefits of satisfying his or her boss's needs for esteem, friendship and security when the occasion permits it.

Politicians are sensitive at all times about their image. They want their superiors to recognize that they can motivate subordinates and produce outstanding performance because of ability to get along with them. They want the boss to see that they are industrious, ambitious, self-starters, creative and able to see the big picture. They also want superiors to believe without a doubt in their integrity. All of these traits are found to be the most important characteristics that 782 executives, in a recent survey, said they considered when looking at which subordinates to advance up the corporate ladder.

Politicians also understand the necessity of and the way to push the boss up by helping the boss's performance and making him or her look good. They recognize the benefits of showing respect, loyalty, friendship and intimacy toward the boss, regardless of whether they really feel that way. They are shrewd enough to know that if the boss perceives them as trying to advance the boss's career, liking the boss as a person and respecting him as a manager and businessperson, it is only logical that they will be selected over peers who are not as image conscious.

What are some of the things politicians will do to make their image favorable and visible to superiors? They will buy company-brand products and make sure they use or consume them in the presence of superiors. Likewise, they will purchase company stock and bonds and make a point of subtly mentioning the fact if they are in a large corporation instead of a small company, where it would become known immediately. Politicians appreciate the importance of cultivating peers in addition to subordinates and superiors. By always saying good things about the people they work with and especially making flattering comments in their absence, they in turn will find themselves being liked by these people. Although one person saying good things about you does not mean much, when a lot of your peers have positive things to mention, the word gets around, and your superiors will hear about the esteem you are held in by co-workers.

If politicians are able to associate themselves with a powerful person in top management, they will take advantage of the opportunity to imply that they speak for that person, that they are chummy with the person and discuss business matters together, that they are on their way up because of that association and so on. Recognizing the impact that association can have on other people, politicians can frequently be seen holding a directorship or office in a trade or professional organization or an institution or company in a noncompetitive area. They know that this gives them the image of a winner and the stature needed to advance further in their own organization.

Unlike survivors, who are more worried about not making blunders and maintaining job security, politicians can frequently be seen establishing new trends and presenting new ideas in order to get favorable publicity and visibility in high places. For instance, a politician may be the first manager to let people set their own working hours because they are motivated under him or her and act mature and intelligent under this person's guidance. He or she may be the only executive to have refreshments served at staff meetings. When presenting a new idea the politician is shrewd enough to minimize the risk that it will bomb by getting advance support from peers or the concurring viewpoint of an outside expert who has credibility.

If the politician should make enemies—and this normally happens as one is jockeying one's image to aggressively advance up the corporate ladder—he or she befriends a superior who acts as a buffer with the hostile department or executive. The buffer acts as an intermediary and prevents a direct fight that can tarnish the politician's image because the politician has shown the buffer how he or she can benefit from the politician's rise. In order to make sure their image gets to the right people, politicians will find out who the power people and influence peddlers are. If they discover that an executive who wields a lot of power relies heavily on the opinions of his or her secretary, they will not hesitate to exploit the secretary's emotional needs with the hope that a favorable image will be conveyed by this person to the boss.

Machiavellian executives are obsessed with grabbing more and more power, and they will do anything short of breaking the law to advance in the organization, even if it means deceit and ruthlessness. They are fully aware of everything the politicians knows regarding a favorable image, but they go one step further because they lack the morals of the politician. Their job is in constant peril because they have created many enemies on the way to the top, and these people are probably plotting revenge and lurking in the background to stab them in the back at the slightest indication they are slipping from power. Because they are so preoccupied with power, politics and image, it is difficult for them to perform their functions well, especially when they have to remember thousands of self-serving lies on a weekly basis.

Machiavellian executives would just as soon push bosses out as push them up if they felt that the former would help them advance quicker. They are not strangers to back-stabbing and discrediting rivals while pretending to be nice to them face to face. This executive is too shrewd to directly denounce peers as incompetent. Instead, he subtly asks the boss if the co-worker is overloaded or more of a specialist than a generalist. When the boss inquires as to the meaning of the question, the Machiavellian vaguely talks about the co-worker's exhaustion lately and preoccupation with his technical specialty to the exclusion of other matters. A common tactic is to take credit for work performed by others and shrug off responsibility for the failures of subordinates. The Machiavellian will gladly use sex to his or her political advantage if an affair with a superior or the secretary or assistant who reports to that person can help the Machiavellian's goals.

Machiavellians will even create a crisis so that they can be assigned the job of resolving the problems they create. They will resort to blackmail if they feel that information of a negative nature must be used against a person for advantage. It should come as no surprise that Machiavellians will commonly tell superiors what they think they want to hear. Giving bad news is not a good image maker. Every now and then, a Machiavellian will even hold a gun to the boss's head for a promotion or raise by threatening to quit at a key stage in a project or during a crisis when he or she is needed. The Machiavellian will play the ulterior and other dishonest psychological games covered in Chapter 10. A final example, and one that should come as no shock, is that the Machiavellian will typically keep poor records and tell no one about the details of his or her job so that he or she becomes indispensable.

Let's take a look now at how you rated yourself in response to the questions above. Add up your scores. If you scored 450 or more points, you are probably a Machiavellian. Because your tactics will probably result in your downfall sooner or later, you should consider taking actions to control your obsession for power. Restrain yourself from devious tactics and courses of action that will seriously injure others around you. If you can become more like the politician, who will probably score somewhere between 375 points and 450 points, you will still be a shrewd maneuverer and will not have the liabilities and risks of a Machiavellian. In fact, a person who scores somewhere between 375 and 425 points will most likely have the best chance of success in climbing the organizational ladder. If you had a score of 250 to 375 points, you are probably a survivor. You should give serious thought to why you are so concerned with security and are not willing to take risks in advancing your career more aggressively. Is it because you are a Not OK—OK person? If your score is between 175 and 250 points, you are most likely a straight arrow. You now know that you have to do more than just project job competence. Below 175 points, you are an innocent lamb, and this chapter may be the turning point of your career if you are able to recognize the problem and you have the capability to change and become image conscious. If you can't or are unable to change your thinking, it may be that you have an introverted Thinker or Intuitor personality. In this situation, your only hope is to invent something equivalent to the transistor, laser or recombinant DNA (gene splicing) so that people will be forced to recognize your accomplishments.

MANAGING YOUR BOSS

In the same manner that the manager must go beyond the general rules of supervision in dealing with people according to PDC, you must analyze your boss's particular personality and formulate the proper strategy of dealing and communicating with your boss based on that analysis. There are as many supervisory types as there are personalities in the personality wheel of Figure 9.1. Below are the types of people you will have the most problems reporting to.

Bosses with the I'm OK–You're Not OK life script persecute the people reporting to them. Some of their favorite games are NIGYSOB (Now I Got You, You Son of a Bitch), Blemish, Critique, Rapo, Tricky Switches, You're Not Good Enough, I'm Only Trying to Help You, and You Got Me Into This.

NIGYSOB is the common game played by the Critical Parent supervisors, who set difficult or even impossible goals for subordinates and then angrily explode when they fail to measure up. The payoff of this game is confirmation in the supervisor's mind that the employee is unreliable and Not OK. Quite often, the employee will play complementary victim games, such as Stupid and Kick Me, as a result of an I'm Not OK–You're OK life script. As a result, both players win the feelings they are playing for, but they and the company lose out in the long run because the supervisor is not able to properly delegate tasks, and the employees are motivated to fail.

In the game of Blemish, the Critical Parent supervisor does not relax until he or she finds the employee's fault or blemish. This is the type of boss who must have everything 100 percent perfect.

When the Critical Parent boss spontaneously feels the need to pick on someone to relieve his or her own pressures or bad feelings, he or she plays the game of Critique. Here, the supervisor reviews a subordinate's progress, behavior or attitude in order to criticize the employee, using the process as an excuse to make him- or herself feel better.

Quite often, the Critical Parent boss who plays Critique will move directly into the game of You're Not Good Enough. In this game, the supervisor explains why the employee is incompetent and why the supervisor is worried that the job will not be done properly. The supervisor then states that he or she will have to do it for the employee to make sure it's done right. Many times, the game of You're Not Good Enough is used by supervisors who see delegation as losing control and fear the consequences of mistakes their people may make while learning. Unfortunately, this creates a situation in which none of the subordinates ever learns anything important.

When the employee complains about not having enough responsibility or being picked on so much the Critical Parent supervisor then switches to the game of I'm Only Trying to Help You in a hopeless attempt to maintain loyalty. If the Critical Parent boss performs the task for the subordinate and fouls up in some manner, he or she then will probably play the game of You Got Me Into This, denying responsibility and dumping the whole mess and credit for it back on the subordinate.

The game of Rapo involves an ulterior transaction described in Chapter 7. For instance, the Critical Parent boss makes a verbal statement from his or her Child to the subordinate's Child. The employee responds as if it were a Child-to-Child transaction. Then, the boss pounces on the employee in a Parent-to-Child reply. An example is when your boss comments how nice it is to have spring here again. You say, "Yes, it's great to see the flowers and trees budding." Your boss replies, "How about getting back to work? You can look out the window after five!"

Tricky Switches is another game that leads to employee resentment quickly. The boss keeps changing procedures and policies. Employees become confused, then mad. They finally quit and end the game.

There is even the type of Critical Parent boss who persecutes him- or herself. These people must meet high standards of competitiveness and performance at all times or lose their peace of mind. They may very well be workaholics because of the extent to which they continually drive themselves.

Another major category of supervisors are the I'm Not OK-You're OK bosses. They assume the role of a victim and play such games as Stupid, Kick Me, If It Weren't for Him, Harried, Poor Me, Look How Hard I'm Trying, Let's Not Rock the Boat, and Why Does This Always Happen to Me?

The boss who presents to his or her own supervisor a report with several obvious errors is playing the game of Kick Me by inviting a Critical Parent put-down for carelessness. The supervisor gets angry and chews the subordinate out, which directly or indirectly confirms that the subordinate is not OK, and he or she gets the desired kick. Although many of us do not realize it, there are many people (those with Not OK-OK life scripts) who feel good when they are criticized and put down because of the pleasure they derive from feeling sorry for themselves and for garnering sympathy from others. In a more subtle form, the same game of Kick Me is played by the boss with subordinates. It is commonly achieved by failing to tell employees about important deadlines or other key information they need to do their jobs right and well. An atmosphere is created where the employees are openly complaining to their boss or showing dissatisfaction in other ways. The end result is that the boss is able to get the necessary put downs and sorry feeling for him- or herself, even if they are not as acute as those from a supervisor. The Child supervisor who plays the game of Kick Me or Stupid is dangerous because this person can make subordinates look bad and gives a poor image of the department. He or she is unpromotable, does not accept delegation well, and presents a barrier to subordinates who want to advance in the organization.

The Not OK-OK Child supervisor who is continually handing in budgets late and falling down in other areas and then blames the problem on someone else or extenuating circumstances is playing the game If It Weren't for Him. This person uses task avoidance to get the sympathy of subordinates or superiors and collect the self-righteous feelings that keep him or her happy.

The game of Harried is played by bosses who are always taking on more and more responsibilities, come in early, work late at night and work during lunch and even on weekends. In short, they make themselves so busy that they eventually collapse with depression, a bad back, ulcers, hypertension or a heart attack. These victims often leave things in a mess for others to straighten out, feeling overburdened and self-righteous and wallowing in sympathy from others. Quite often, they will be viewed by others as workaholics who never seem to have time to relax or get on top of all the work to be done. They are always getting the sympathy of others because they always have to work so hard and because of the headaches or indigestion they frequently have as a result of being harried. This can go on for months or even years before victims bring themselves to a physical or mental breakdown, at which time they are able to collect an even greater degree of sympathetic feelings as they play out their game and get a chance to relax at home or in the hospital at the same time.

Another major category of supervisors consists of the rescuers, who feel compelled to make people dependent on them. These Nurturing Parents actually have an OK–Not OK life script, even though, from appearances, they seem to have an OK–OK life script as they try to help their people tackle their responsibilities. But in actuality, the rescuers strive to make sure that subordinates fail to develop their full potential or even think they can be successful without them because they assume the subordinates' responsibilities and hold back company information to assure that the subordinates do not develop and gain confidence.

Rescuers may even set people up to fail if they try to break out of their continued dependence on them. Quite often, they give people the image that they are the only thing between the employees and a cold, hard management that cares nothing about them. Games that the rescuer plays include I'm Only Trying to Help You, Why Don't You and Let's You and Him Fight.

The Adaptive Child and Manipulating Child supervisors are concerned with doing the least amount of work necessary, hesitate to innovate or make changes because they seek acceptance from everyone, are conservative and try to avoid offending people, are apologetic and defensive and are buck-passers and fault-finders when things get tough. They tend to delegate responsibility upward and play such games as See What You Made Me Do, If It Weren't for . . . , Yes, But . . . . Why Don't You and Him Fight and Let's Not Rock the Boat.

The game of Yes, But is used by this Child supervisor to give an excuse to any request and any sound reason for granting the request to the point of absurdity. For instance, an employee asks his boss if he can sign his own name to an opinion that will be read by his boss's superiors. The boss replies, "Yes, you can sign your name to it, but I'm going to revise and amplify the report before it goes upstairs under my own signature." The employee says, "If it goes up with my own signature, this is my chance for some visibility and will make a possible raise this year easier for you to secure." The manager replies, "Yes, but if management does not like your report, your visibility will backfire, and a raise will become even more difficult to justify." The employee says, "Why can't you review it and suggest changes so that there's little risk of that happening?" The boss replies, "Yes, I can revise it to assure its favorable acceptance, but then it would be my work product and should have my own signature on it." In the Yes, But game, nothing the employee says is going to influence his boss, who can give excuses, no matter how ridiculous, for as long as necessary.

The insecure boss manipulates people with the game of Let's You and

Me Compete. The boss can keep subordinates from growing and maturing by competing instead of managing them. That way the boss can keep them from becoming confident and competent enough to threaten his or her own job.

The boss who manipulates people in the game of Tell Me What I Want to Hear guarantees that intimacy and frankness will not occur. This boss and the subordinates have a secret contract wherein they must lie, if necessary, in order to avoid bad news. Because the employees fear the wrath of their boss should they breach their part of the bargain, the boss is effectively cut off from useful input merely because employees worry that it may be upsetting or have repercussions regarding their own job security. The employees, of course, feel stifled because they see problems getting worse and are afraid to propose solutions since they cannot have an open relationship with their supervisor pursuant to participatory management.

As brought out in Chapters 7 and 9, there are many more categories of management personalities that we could cover, but the above illustrate the most common supervisor types and the psychological games they play. Chapter 7 explains in detail how to identify these personality types and how to effectively deal with each.

Probably the most important aspect of handling game players is to understand what they really want. For instance, victims who are always missing a deadline or committing errors or expect a hard putdown basically want recognition and attention. If you give them the attention they crave by acknowledging that they are stupid or chewing them out in the game of Kick Me, then you are giving them their attention and recognition. If, on the other hand, you do not give them the expected pay-off with criticism and only give them positive strokes (praise) when they do OK and you use your Adult to call upon their own Adult to map out a satisfactory plan for change, people can be motivated to gradually eliminate their role as victim.

People who report to a boss victim sometimes find it very natural and easy to play the role of persecutor and eventually take the victim boss's job. This can backfire if not done subtly because the Not OK–OK victim boss may decide that you are Not OK either in view of the nuisance or abuse you cause. In this situation, the Not OK–Not Ok boss will give you a very negative image with his or her superiors. It is always easier to advance by making your boss look good and pushing him or her up to a better position than by having your boss ousted or fired in a power struggle. Try to change your boss's inferior life script into a confident one by refusing to play victim games and encouraging your boss to manage with confidence and for results as a way of getting recognition.

The same strategy in dealing with the victim should also be used in dealing with the Critical Parent OK–Not OK boss. When he or she pounces on you for something you apparently did wrong, instead of giving him or her the satisfaction of persecuting you and feeling good about it, you respond from your Adult ego state (rather than as a victim who confirms the need for punishment and a put down). Thus, you can stop the NIGYSOB game by responding, "I'll think about it," or "That's an interesting observation you made." Likewise, when your boss keeps on saying, "Yes, but" to your suggestions or requests, stop trying to persuade him or her and bounce the ball back into your boss's lap with the abdication tactic by saying, "What do you think would work?"

If you get hooked into a supervisor who plays I'm Only Trying to Help You, you can stop the game by refusing to play along with his or her Nurturing Parent ego state. Your reply can be, "I prefer to do this myself," "You do not have to supervise me this closely," or, "Please give me a chance to show you what I can do." If you are reporting to a Manipulating Child supervisor who plays Why Don't You and Him Fight, you can reply, "I prefer not to hear the gossip" or, "It's best if you handle it directly yourself, not through me."

NEGOTIATING RAISES AND PROMOTIONS

Everything you need to know about getting a better raise and promotion and getting it quicker than the other guy is already contained in previous chapters of this book. The purpose of this chapter is not to provide a comprehensive strategy and checklist, which can probably be obtained from entire books written on the subject, but rather to point out how key considerations already covered in this book specifically apply.

Timing
Executives frequently make their first mistake in the timing and location of the salary or promotion discussion they initiate with the boss. Certainly, you do not want to talk about your personal circumstances in front of your boss's boss or your peers, regardless of any leverage you feel it will give you, because of the embarrassment it will cause your boss. Just as important is restraining yourself from the common practice of bringing up the subject with your boss when you are together on an out of town trip, at a lunch or dinner meeting or at a party or other social occasion. Salary and promotion discussions should be done on company time; otherwise, your boss will feel you are trying to take advantage of him or her during the informal setting.

The ideal time to raise the issue is when your boss comes into your office for a relaxed chat about something. Take advantage of the opportunity because you're on your home turf and feel most comfortable behind your desk with your boss out of his or her dominant surroundings. If you have a boss who rarely comes into your office, then you have little choice but to get this person into a neutral place, such as the conference room, or walk into his or her office. Never initiate a discussion of your salary and future with the company by memo. These are things that should be discussed in person, verbally and face to face, for reasons brought out in Chapter 6.

Another untimely ploy that is fatally executed by too many executives is confronting the boss for a raise or promotion or both during a crisis. When the boss, department or entire company is trying to survive a bad turn of events, everyone becomes conservative. In such a climate, a promotion request is viewed far more dramatically and appears as a sign of disloyalty. The ultimate death knell is when you are one of the key people needed to overcome the crisis and you threaten to quit if your salary and promotion demands are not met. On the other hand, after all the stress and strain of successfully overcoming a crisis or consummating a major deal is a perfect time to bring up the subject. Very simply say that this last project or event has convinced you that you should be working at a higher level in terms of responsibility, title and money. Assure your boss that you will not quit or anything like that, but you feel you should be getting an additional $5,000 and should be elevated to Assistant Director for worldwide research and development. Say you do not need an immediate answer, but ask when your boss thinks he'll be able to give it to you.

Prenegotiation Planning

Before bringing up the subject with your boss, you must put yourself in his or her shoes, as discussed in Chapter 2. What will be your boss's reaction? If your supervisor has a dominant Parent ego state or is an OK–Not OK manager, this person will view your request as a challenge to knock you down or at least whittle down what you are asking for. If your boss views you as too competent and a threat to his or her own security, this individual may see this as an opportunity to say no and hope you quit. If your supervisor is a Not OK–OK person, he or she may look upon the prospect of getting approval for your request from his or her own superior with horror. If your boss is an introverted Intuitor, this person will probably shy away from giving you any immediate answer and hope that you will just stay away and not bother him or her with personal details like this that cause discomfort.

Even if you have a confident boss, he or she will immediately be thinking about how to justify your demands, especially if they are unusually high. Your boss will also be thinking about what your peers will say if they find out how much less they got. The superior will also be looking at industry standards to see where you fit in for your age and experience. Also, he or she will be concerned if your request would upset the apple cart as far as the salary progression for everyone in the department. Certainly, the boss will immediately be thinking about whether your performance warrants granting your request.

You must plan in advance for any one of these responses by your boss and many more than just these examples. Likewise, if you cannot anticipate your boss's reaction, then you will not know the best approach to use in asking for the promotion or raise.

Tactics

If you have performed well on the job, then obviously you will want to highlight your accomplishments. As learned in Chapter 5, you do not start off with your conclusion or request when making a proposal if it involves bad or unpleasant news. Emphasize that you like the freedom and responsibility that have been delegated to you, but you think now might be an opportunity to simply go into some of the details of how you achieved the goals that were set over the past year and about the things you plan to do over the next six months to improve operations even further. At this point, you might also bring up the various accomplishments that your boss complimented you for as well as those he or she is not even aware of. At all times, you should keep in back of your mind the fact that your boss is thinking about the cost of your extra pay and wondering if this and future increases will be a worthwhile investment. Thus, you should emphasize monetary savings in specific dollars and cents, statistics supporting your claims of increased productivity, new skills mastered, new sources gained, hours of labor saved, improved morale, new developments, benefits you initiated that will continue for the good of the company over the years and so on.

Another approach is to appeal to your boss's aesthetic needs for fairness of living a reasonable existence. You can emphasize that your present compensation doesn't seem to meet your living expenses since you moved from Lincoln, Nebraska, to New York City. Give the impression that you don't like talking about your personal problems, but make it clear that your head is barely above water and you really need that raise. Although both you and he know that a raise cannot be justified by your personal needs, it can be the extra factor that tips the balance, or it can motivate Parent opinion that, when considered with your accomplishments, spurs him or her to act favorably on your request.

Another approach is to point out the small differential between your present salary and those of your subordinates. Normally, a differential should be significant enough to delineate management status and motivate those reporting to you to perform well with the hope of eventually moving up to your job. If you vigorously pursue greater compensation for superior performance by your key people, and if this has closed a gap between their salaries and yours, you have your case for a good raise and, at the same time, for drawing attention to your superior performance as a manager.

Another approach that can be used, which is particularly attractive when you feel significantly underpaid, is to put everything up front by describing the situation, expressing your feelings, specifying what you want and pointing out the positive consequences of meeting your request. An example might be as follows: "It has been fifteen months since my last raise; my salary is $3,000 below the median for electronics engineers in this area with my experience and in this size company; and I am still only acting manager for design engineering even though Jack Weinberger left five months ago. I feel unfairly treated. I have worked conscientiously; the design group has higher morale than ever before; and our interfacing with research and applications personnel is much smoother than it used to be. I want to discuss a $5,000 pay raise and my formal promotion to manager of the design group. Will you discuss these with me tomorrow after work? I want to continue working here because I enjoy what I am doing and the responsibilities that have been delegated to me."

In less than two minutes, you spelled out the inequities, expressed your unhappiness, and told your boss what you feel you need in order to continue with the company. At the same time, you have not issued any threat to quit that would make the boss angry and put him or her on the defensive to retaliate in some manner.

A tactic that can be used in conjunction with this approach is the fait accompli. You can arouse interest on the part of another department head. It is ideal if you can tell your boss that so-and-so wanted me to come over and join her team, but I turned her down cold. In this situation, your boss knows you can revive the other department manager's interest any time you want.

Another technique to remember is the straw man tactic. After stating that $6,000 would be a reasonable increase warranted by your performance, you then bring out certain arguments you expect your boss to use against you. For instance, you say, "However, I realize the department recently had a budget cut and the company hasn't been doing well lately. I therefore would be willing to settle for a $4,500 increase." You know full well that the boss would probably have used that argument to counter offer at $2500 or $3000. On the other hand, if your performance hasn't been great, you might bring out the one or two blunders that you caused rather than wait for your boss to do so. Put them on the table, make them sound even worse than they really were, get your boss's sympathy, explain what you did to prevent anything like that from happening again, and state the tough goals you are setting for yourself over the next year. Then ask if your boss has any other problems about your performance. If not, you can ask for the raise with the premise that no one is infallible and nothing more can be expected than your doing your best in the future. Most bosses are not going to bring up your blunders after you have been so tough on yourself, and many bosses are more sympathetic toward giving raises to a person who honorably admits mistakes and has laid out clear plans for avoiding them in the future. In effect, you have argued for your boss and then subtly dismissed the point as a reason for not getting a good raise.

Counter Tactics

Once you decide on your approach, how much do you ask for? This is where the know-how of Chapters 4, 5 and 7 come into play because you need to know what kind of person your boss is, and you need the discipline and confidence of understanding how to make a high demand and how high to go. If your boss is a highly competitive person who likes a fight and will try to whittle your request down, then you must start at a higher figure than that which you would be happy with, knowing that you will have to compromise in order to satisfy his or her emotional needs of winning the best deal possible. If, on the other hand, your boss is primarily in the Adult ego state, pick a figure that is high, yet reasonable, and stick with it. "That is what I should get, Ryan. You are going to say it is a lot, and I am not going to argue with you; and I even sympathize with that feeling. But I do not want anything less." If a boss asks what will happen if he or she cannot get or give what you want, simply persist. "I feel that raise is justified, and I am sure that after you give this some thought, you will feel the same way." By remaining firm and cool under the boss's questioning, you show that your position is nonnegotiable, and you show your seriousness about your position, thereby implying your willingness to leave if your request cannot be met.

What do you do when the boss appeals to your aesthetic needs for fairness and uniformity? For instance, your boss tells you that your peers are not asking for half the raise you are. Your counter will be that "Everyone knows his or her own value best. I am surprised that Robin and Milt do not feel their performance warrants greater compensation. Now that I think of it, however, I guess the problem is that they simply haven't been producing the kind of results you look for, huh? What exactly are the problems with them? It is probably a good opportunity for us to see exactly how I stack up against them. (Rip off a piece of paper and start writing down comparative points.)"

Another aesthetic appeal that the boss may make is for trust—you will eventually get your raise, but not right now. Your boss asks you to count on him or her and go along with a delay for the time being. Your supervisor has put this request on a personal basis. If you disagree, you are working against this person's esteem needs, need for friendship and loyalty and view of your character as a person who believes in fairness. The only smart way to combat this response is to reply on a personal level yourself. "I do trust you, Fran. That is why I am going to level with you when I say I really need this raise now. I cannot go into all the personal reasons, but you can understand that I would not be asking you for it if I did not have a real serious need. I hope you will believe me and will go to bat for me this one time when you yourself have reasons to delay."

In the situation where the boss asks for a delay but does not tell you or want to tell you the reasons, you can instantly assume the worst. "Oh boy! It looks like we really are in trouble this time. Just how bad is it? I'll have to break the bad news gently to Jeff, Stan and Kate. It wouldn't be fair to hold this from them, right?" Here, you make the boss realize that if he or she does not give you the true reasons for delaying a response to your salary raise request you will panic the whole department and eventually it will get to his or her superiors. This is nothing but a variation of the assumption technique in dealing with frozen silence. You simply choose to threat the party's failure to respond in the way that is most favorable for you.

Another way to respond to the boss is graciously to agree to trust and wait, yet at the same time set a time limit on that trust. "Sure, Al, I know that problems crop up from time to time and you do not have to give me an answer right now. Just forget about it and we will get back together in three weeks." The boss then says, somewhat embarrassed, that he was thinking of a much longer delay than that. You then tell him that you feel you have a right to know what the problem is that is delaying consideration of your request. You feel that if it concerns your raise you should have the opportunity to help out and cooperate and that you can be trusted to keep it entirely confidential. Here, you are testing your boss, determining whether there really are reasons for delay and finding out how much this person is willing to trust you—and you're testing your friendship for each other.

Another approach is to exploit your boss's emotional needs regarding how he or she views himself as a decision maker. For instance, if your boss is basically a Sensor, he or she is proud of being decisive and reaching conclusions rapidly. You could say, "I'm counting on your answer now,

Jane, whether it is yes or no. If I did not know you were the kind of manager who will lay it on the line, I would go along with the delay. But you know as well as me that at times any answer is better than no answer, and I just do not want to dangle, anxiously awaiting your reply." If the boss still wants to delay, then assume the worst, as already mentioned. With a look of disappointment and bewilderment, say, "I always thought that you had the authority to approve raises for executives such as myself?" If the boss has a lot of pride, she may decide to give you a response to your raise request right there on the spot in order to avoid the image of having less power than she really does. If she still refuses, say "If it isn't your authority, I guess there are things that I have been doing poorly or haven't paid attention to. At least for my own benefit, won't you tell me what they are so that I can try to improve?" Here, you are trying to smoke out the boss's real objection to giving you an answer right away.

Once you find out what the real objection is, then you have the opportunity to turn it to your advantage by using the appropriate counter ploy discussed in Chapter 8. For instance, the boss tells you it is simply a matter of your not being experienced enough to take such a large jump to the salary level you are looking at. The first thing you do is make sure that this is the only reason the boss cannot grant the raise and there is nothing else between you and that raise. Once you qualify this as the only reason, then you can start asking choice questions to zero in on faulty logic or the absurdity of the reason itself. "Do you feel experience is just a matter of being around for a certain number of years, or are there other factors? You say experience is the maturity to know how to handle problems and get guidance from others rather than tackling things all by yourself. I always work that way, and I think I am successful at it—for instance, the time when Baker Enterprises cancelled their order and I got your boss's advice on who at Baker to have a personal meeting with and what strategy to use to get them to reconsider. It would not have done me any good to have had even twenty years of experience. Even you yourself were not sure how to handle the problem. Do you agree that it is not experience itself, but how you call the experience into action that is the key to being a good executive? In that case, can we wrap this discussion up and give me my raise?"

Another example of countering an objection is when the boss states that the budget will not permit anything like the raise you are asking for. Again, you ask questions that require a choice that is rather obvious so that you can show your boss that his or her reasoning really is not sound as justification to deny your request. "The budget is already set for next year? It will not allow change of any kind? If it can be revised, then are there situations in which the budget would be modified if there were good enough reasons for it? If there is the flexibility for meeting a large order like the X745 from DOD, does that mean the budget would also allow for change to hire more bodies? Then I guess that means the budget can be modified to take care of changing needs regarding people as well as equipment and inventory? I am glad we agree because that is exactly my point. My situation has changed, and the following are the reasons why I think the budget should be modified to include my raise."

Another way of dealing with a weakness is to plan in advance and use the tactic of timing. For instance, if your boss has consistently complained about you always being late in answering your correspondence, do not point out your improvement the moment you eliminate the backlog. Keep it for the salary negotiations when the boss brings this up as the reason to deny your request. But do not bring your turn-around, improvement or solution to a continuing problem up until you give the boss the opportunity of telling you how great you are in the other areas and asking you to take care of this one problem spot before he or she grants you the increase. In effect, you have persuaded your boss to put all his or her eggs in one basket through the tactics of forebearance, advance planning and good timing and working against the boss's need to know. Once you disclose that you have eliminated the reason for denying your raise request, the boss has little choice but to grant it because he or she already said that there were no other reasons for denying it.

If you anticipate the boss complaining about your lackluster performance, you can use the tactic of playing against his need to know by capitalizing on your seeming weakness. For instance, you can bring out the fact that you made a hectic job routine, you did not make waves or cause the boss headaches, you kept problems away from him and the very fact that it does not look like you do much shows just how effortlessly you do handle your job.

One tactic that is commonly used by managers is to replace a raise with or seek a compromise by holding out the carrot of esteem. They offer to give you a new title, new responsibilities, new furniture, your own secretary and any one of a number of other things that will appeal to your need for esteem. You should show your gratitude for such recognition but remain persistent on the money. "The bottom line is that you can call me anything you want. To me, how much I earn is the ultimate measure of my worth and recognition by my employer. How much I earn also is important for computing my life insurance and how much credit I can get from a bank, and it plays heavily in creating my image as an important executive."

If your boss brings up or believes in the theories of Dr. Frederick Herzberg, the leading industrial psychologist who propounded the "hygienic" theory of what motivates and what does not (covered in Chapter 9), you have your work cut out for you. Herzberg concluded that salary increases do not really motivate workers to work harder or become more efficient. Herzberg feels that the real motivators are responsibility, accomplishment, inner job satisfaction, participation and recognition. In this situation, state that Herzberg does recognize money can represent recognition of achievement as long as raises are really given for performance and not just for seniority or reasons of favoritism. If all else fails, you may wish to consider threatening to quit, but before you do, ask yourself a number of questions in accordance with Chapters 2, 3 and 4. How is business now? Could they get along without me? Would the boss welcome the opportunity to cut the payroll? Can someone else easily fill in for my responsibilities? How much does the boss really want to keep me? Will the boss hold a grudge against me? How can he or she make things tougher for me? Will the jobs I have lined up or hope to quickly get be substantially better than the one I now enjoy?

Many of the closing techniques learned in Chapter 8 apply to raise and promotion negotiation. For instance, you can use the assumption technique by saying, "Well, we've gone over everything pretty thoroughly. I assume that if nothing negative turns up between now and next week when you get back to me, I can count on getting the raise." This technique is also good in smoking out any objections the boss really has but has chosen to conceal. He or she has been forced to reveal them; otherwise acquiescence in what you just said makes it difficult to bring up things later that he or she should already have been aware of during your present discussion. If the boss is delayed longer than what he or she originally indicated, another twist to the assumption technique is saying, "You would have let me know by now if the answer to my request was no, so I am not really worried. If there is any further information I can provide to expedite the process, please do not hesitate to confide in me."

When your boss finally agrees to the raise, show immediately that he or she made no error and prepare for next year's negotiation: "This increase means more than just additional income. You and the company really do appreciate my efforts, and I feel that I have a good future here. I'll do my best to be worthy of your confidence in me, and I will do everything I can to earn more money by increasing my abilities and assuming more responsibility from you."

NEGOTIATING PRINCIPLES FOR THE PERFECT RESUME

Many books, some good and some bad, have been written on how to write the ideal résumé. There are many seminars and career counseling firms that you can spend your money on. Again, some are good and some bad.

The purpose of this chapter is not to replace a comprehensive treatment of résumé writing, but rather to highlight the fundamentals that the reader has already learned and show how they can be applied to a specific goal, such as drafting a résumé that will get a high percentage of interviews and eventual job offers.

The number one fatal defect of résumés is failure to do prenegotiation planning and specifically researching and understanding the person who will be reading the résumé.

The manager, personnel specialist or headhunter may be receiving anywhere from fifty to 500 responses to the ad that was placed. In order for your résumé to obtain the interview, it must attract the reader's attention and interest within a period of ten seconds.

By stepping into the shoes of the other person in accordance with what you learned in Chapter 2, you suddenly realize that your résumé must be simple, attractive and favorably suggestive, pursuant to techniques discussed in Chapter 5.

It should dawn on you that ten seconds is no more than a quick scan for a two-page résumé. This means that appearance may actually become more important than substance in forming the reader's initial, and in many instances final, impression of the applicant. To put it another way, the subconscious sensation received in the first ten seconds from the résumé is transferred to the applicant's personality and abilities.

Needless to say, you want to produce a quality, professional image of yourself. You want a 100 percent rag bond paper of a 20–50 pound weight, with a lightly textured linen or pebble finish. Your typing should be neat and letter perfect. Your résumé should be printed by offset, not photocopied. Paper color should be off-white or light cream, beige or gray. You should consider a borderline a quarter of an inch from the edge of all four sides of the résumé sheet because it produces an impressively framed subject and subconsciously encourages the scanner to slow up and take a closer look at what appears to be more important than the run-of-the-mill résumé.

Your résumé must set forth your experience and abilities in simple terms because there is no time for lengthy discussions and detailed chronologies of your career. If you do your homework, you will come to the conclusion that your employer is primarily interested in your future: what you can do and what you will probably accomplish. He or she is less interested in particular facts of your past.

Now we come to another fatal flaw of many résumés. Because the experts in the recruiting business place emphasis on your most marketable skills, there is a tendency for job hunters to come across fast and hard. Unfortunately, as learned in Chapter 5, hard sell, the appearance of bragging or overstatement, does not attract. Instead, the reader is put on the defensive and subconsciously may consider it a challenge to find flaws in the résumé, real or fictional, that will destroy the forceful claims made by the job applicant. Thus, the proper goal of the job hunter is to set forth the interesting and impressive facts in a manner that will sell the applicant without the reader being aware of the sale. Although this is not the time to be modest and use dull words, serious consideration should be given to understatement while listing a series of progressively important accomplishments in terms of sales, profits, cost control and so on. To summarize, do not come across as too brash and confident that you're "the man" the company needs because it tends to turn off the recruiter or company manager reading your résumé. After all, how can you be so presumptuous as to know enough about the position from a two- or three-inch ad to be advising the reader that he or she needs you more than anyone else who responds?

So far, we have talked about making your résumé stand out from the pack because it is simpler, more attractive and more unique in appearance. There is also another plus in producing a résumé that projects a winning image. We learned in Chapter 7 that people feel secure when they are dealing with people who appear to be successful. You are satisfying the personnel or business manager's need for security with a high quality résumé because this person feels comfortable calling you in for an interview.

You can also satisfy security needs by carefully reading the advertisement and making use of key phrases that describe the position. These phrases were obtained by the personnel department from the company manager who is looking for somebody, or the phrases represent what the personnel department or the headhunter feels describe the activity needed. In either case, if your résumé does not include these phrases, it may not be considered further. If the reader sees that your résumé contains the exact items of activity and functional responsibility that were put into the advertisement, his or her need for security will be fulfilled by setting up an interview for you to meet him or her and the company manager.

Is there a way to make your résumé personal to the recruiter? Yes, by talking in terms of *you*. Your standard résumé cannot do this, but a cover letter can as long as it is not a mass-produced sheet starting off with the standard "Dear Sir:" or having the name and company name and address typed above an obvious form text. When a letter is individually typed, the recipient looks upon it as more personal and feels more like reading it. The same stationary, coloring and other considerations in appearance and image apply to the cover letter as to the résumé. Because four out of five résumés will be sent without a cover letter and four out of five cover letters will not project a good image, you immediately have a competitive edge over 96 percent of others responding to the ad.

There are basically two types of cover letters. The first is a brief letter that does not get into details of your abilities and experience because your résumé so closely matches the advertised position. The second type of cover letter is lengthier because the advertisement covers specifics and details your résumé does not get into.

Figure 10.1 shows an ad for a director of external affairs, and Figure 10.2 illustrates a typical brief cover letter that should accompany the ré-

Figure 10.1. External affairs director job advertisement.

DIRECTOR, EXTERNAL AFFAIRS

Recognized leader in the manufacture of consumer products seeks experienced Executive to direct the legal and external affairs at our New Jersey Corporate Headquarters.

Background must include a B.S. Law Degree, with a demonstrated record of business accomplishment covering at least 10 years in Operations, Legal, and Business Finance.

You will take immediate charge over all ongoing work, dealing with Public Utilities, Regulatory Agencies, Leases, Product liability and other matters requiring formal agreements. Reporting to the Chairman of the Board, you will provide counsel to all Management Personnel and coordinate outside legal assistance.

For prompt consideration, send résumé to:

Corporate Personnel Director

Z 7122 TIMES

An Equal Opportunity Employer M/F

```
Box Z 7122 Times
The New York Times
229 West 43d Street
New York, New York 10036

Re: Director, External Affairs

Dear Personnel Director:

My operations, legal and financial experience span fifteen years of
business accomplishment and professional achievement.

Although I think the enclosed resume demonstrates the record of
success that your advertisement emphasizes, there is much more to
relate. I would appreciate the opportunity for a personal meeting.
I am confident that it would be both interesting and mutually
profitable.

Sincerely,
```

Figure 10.2. Résumé cover letter for External Affairs Director job.

RETAIL LAW
GENERAL COUNSEL
VICE PRESIDENT

A billion dollar retail organization headquartered in New York City seeks 2 senior legal executives to establish and administer house counsel functions at two of its principal companies.

The candidate should have substantial legal experience with a law firm and/or corporation and must have demonstrated leadership and administrative skills. Ability to deal effectively with top management is essential. Salary and benefits will be highly competitive.

Please send your résumé, including salary requirements, in strict confidence to

BOX 201 LRG

Suite 307, 1200 Park Avenue
New York, New York 10020

We are an Equal Opportunity Employer M/F

Figure 10.3. General Counsel job advertisement.

sumé responding to this advertisement. Although the temptation is great to send a short, handwritten memo, resist the thought. A handwritten note suggests that you did not consider the matter important enough to have a cover letter typed. Also, you may think your handwriting is neat and easy to understand, whereas the reader, who is alloting fifteen seconds to both your cover letter and the résumé, may find your handwriting an irritation. Figure 10.3 shows an ad for a general counsel, and Figure 10.4 shows a brief cover letter transmitting the résumé in response to the ad. Figure 10.5 shows an ad for division president, and Figure 10.6 shows the cover letter transmitting the résumé in response to the ad. Figures 10.7–10.9 illustrate more detailed cover letters that add key points of interest to the advertiser but are not covered in the résumé.

Now, turning to the résumé itself, most people have obsolete ideas that a résumé is supposed to give a chronology of experience. This "obituary" type résumé ties you to the past, hinders a proper presentation of your true talents and potential and prevents the person reviewing your résumé from getting a true picture of your potential for the position in the short time he or she is looking. So what can you do about it?

If we turn back to Chapter 5 we will see that, for the situation where the reader has minimal time to catch the essence of your messages, the most important approach is to start your résumé off with the most important things and leave the minor details for the middle and end. Thus, the top half of the first page of your résumé is the hot zone that will receive the majority of the reader's attention. This is where you want to summarize your ability and potential. You have the rest of the résumé to bring out the

Box 201 LRG
Suite 307, 1200 Park Avenue
New York, New York 10020

Re: Retail Law General Counsel Vice-President

Dear Madam/Sir:

After receiving my law degree in 1968, I rose to partner in a
Washington, D.C., law firm. I subsequently built from scratch the
legal department of a consumer products company where I functioned
as vice president and general counsel and am presently group counsel
for a family of retail companies in a multi-billion-dollar
conglomerate.

Although I am happy with my present responsibilities and my progress
to date, I would again welcome the challenge of establishing an in-house
legal function in a major company.

For your convenience and to save time, I have marked, in yellow, key
portions of the attached resume that may be of particular interest to
you.

My current salary is $52,450, and I would expect a reasonable increase.

I am looking forward to the opportunity of discussing in detail your
needs. In the meantime, thank you for your thoughtful consideration.

Sincerely,

Figure 10.4. Résumé cover letter for General Counsel job.

```
┌─────────────────────────────────────────┐
│                                         │
│           DIVISION PRESIDENT            │
│                                         │
│  We're a solid, aggressive corporation  │
│  with an extraordinary growth record    │
│  and a promising future in multi-       │
│  national markets.                      │
│                                         │
│  One of our fast-moving divisions has   │
│  tripled its sales to $65,000,000 in    │
│  the past four years and is already     │
│  number three in its industry. The cur- │
│  rent division president is moving up    │
│  to a key position at corporate head-   │
│  quarters, and this creates an unusual  │
│  opportunity for the right person.      │
│                                         │
│  The position of division president     │
│  demands a seasoned pro with broad      │
│  executive skills and P&L experience.   │
│  It offers a very high degree of        │
│  decision-making autonomy, excellent    │
│  pay and fringe benefits, and room for  │
│  future personal growth at the          │
│  corporate level.                       │
│                                         │
│  Inquiries will be held in strict       │
│  confidence.                            │
│                                         │
│    Box M-950, The Wall Street Journal   │
│                                         │
│        An Equal Opportunity Employer    │
│                                         │
└─────────────────────────────────────────┘
```

Figure 10.5. Division President job advertisement.

facts that support your beginning statements. Therefore, contrary to what many placement agencies and counseling experts say, you do not start off your résumé with education and personal details (birth, health and so on). You do not even start off with your employment history. Instead, you start your résumé off with your immediate career objective and then a summary of your main selling points.

Another fatal mistake people make in their résumé is ignoring the technique of low-balling. The résumé serves the initial purpose of screening you out. There are certain things that recruiters and personnel people always look for to make their screening job easy. If you are too young or too old, then you do not want to put your age or date of birth in the résumé. If you are with a small company and looking for even more responsibility with a large corporation, do not put in the annual sales volume of your present employer.

If you have an embarrassing period of unemployment, make the résumé functional and deemphasize the chronology of the various jobs you held. In short, the résumé is no place for a confessional, even if you have good reasons for negative items. There is simply too much competition and too little time for the recruiter to be interested in explanations.

Although a cover letter helps bring out your experience and abilities that are closest to those required by the advertised position, nothing makes a better impression on the reader than seeing a résumé that closely matches the job specifications. Thus, if your experience is such that you would be capable of assuming responsibility in a number of different jobs, you should have a different résumé geared to each one. For example, if you

```
Box M-950
The Wall Street Journal
22 Cortlandt Street
New York, New York 10007

Re: Division President

Dear Madam/Sir:

As Vice-President of a leading manufacturer listed on the American
Stock Exchange with annual sales of $50,000,000, I hold P&L and
administrative responsibilities that encompass: (1) planning, co-
ordinating and managing the operations of a dozen subsidiaries and
divisions; (2) plotting and implementing the future product/market
mix of the corporation; and (3) administering general corporate
affairs.

An engineer and lawyer by training, I have a background that is heavy
in marketing and finance. I am people- and profit-oriented and am
second in command in the general management of my present company.

Frankly, I am now looking for the opportunity of running my own show.
You truly need a skilled, mature and dedicated professional and self-
starter of exceptional stature to continue your current division
president's obvious success and outstanding performance. I would be
pleased to meet with you and discuss your future growth and how I
may play a part in continuing your record of success.

Sincerely,
```

Figure 10.6. Résumé cover letter for Division President job.

Dear Mr. Jones:

The enclosed resume broadly covers my responsibilities as Marketing Director and previously as Sales Manager and Regional Manager in the chemical industry. However, I would like to comment on certain aspects of my experience that may be of interest to you.

At Polystrand, I played a major role in forming a marketing division for providing in-house direct sales report to a number of subsidiaries and divisions that were independently selling products through different outlets in similar markets.

In my present position I have improved division margins with new pricing and customer relations strategy favoring high-volume customers and by cutting 40 percent of customer orders from company rolls with only a slight decrease in sales volume.

When you read my resume, I think you will recognize that I am quite familiar with your products, distribution and markets.

I would be glad to discuss in a personal interview additional details of my background and how I can spearhead your future marketing and sales program.

Sincerely,

Figure 10.7. Résumé cover letter for Marketing Vice-President job.

Dear Mr. Smith:

I advanced from Division Counsel to Corporate Counsel to Vice-President of an $80,000,000 health care manufacturer. One of my major functions is to ensure the safety and efficacy of our products, both from the viewpoint of government compliance and product liability.

I am responsible for the pleading, discovery, trial and settlement strategy for an average of a dozen cases annually, ranging in exposure from $10,000 for minor injuries to $8,000,000 for death. Probably of greater importance have been the internal company programs I developed for liability-proofing our products through proper labeling, well-controlled laboratory and clinical testing and investigations, and good manufacturing processes, as well as formal product-hazard brainstorming sessions.

I believe that your key executives would find me to be mature, energetic, a product liability pro, a doer and the type of person who could help company managers increase product safety and efficacy and facilitate the successful defense of lawsuits.

Sincerely,

Figure 10.8. Résumé cover letter for Products Liability Attorney job.

Dear Chairman of the Board:

My background, abilities and interests appear to match your requirements for a chief operating officer.

I am President of the major subsidiary of a multinational manufacturer. I held previous positions in product engineering, sales, general management and consulting.

My experience covers every aspect of managing a business, and over the past five years my market research, corporate planning, cost analysis, new product development financial controls and advertising strategies have led my subsidiary to a four-fold increase in gross revenue, a doubling of return on investment to above the industry average, and a six-fold increase in after-tax net income.

I feel it is time to move on to a more responsible position where I can lead a larger business on to new profit and growth achievements.

Sincerely yours,

Figure 10.9. Résumé cover letter for President job.

started out as an engineer, went into sales and worked yourself up to manager of a marketing subsidiary, you would want to tailor your résumé differently for each position if you are applying for jobs as sales manager, marketing director, general manager, company president and director of sales engineering. Personnel staff and company managers like to feel that the candidate most suited for the position has his or her primary experience in that area. If the résumé indicates that the experience required has only been secondary, you will more than likely be screened out.

Figures 10.10 to 10.14 illustrate various résumés that lend a professional and outstanding image to the job applicant. Note that Figure 10.10 gives the job hunter's objectives and summary of his or her experience and talents in the hot zone (top half of first page) and ends with personal data and education (which the reader will become interested in only if the hot zone and subsequently the employment history look interesting). Another myth that seems widespread is that a résumé should be one page and certainly not more than two pages long. The three- and four-page résumés in this chapter amply demonstrate how effective a long résumé can be if properly designed and drafted to get and hold the reader's interest. Figure 10.11 shows the entire first page as the hot zone. This can be done when lots of space is used around and between text so that the reader's attention is actually drawn to each selling point on the page. As previously mentioned in this chapter, the frame effect of the border also subconsciously makes the reader want to see what's inside because things that are framed usually are important. Figure 10.12 illustrates a functional résumé, which emphasizes the job hunter's categories of experience and ability and merely lists the employment history briefly. Figure 10.13 is also a functional résumé, with an additional page so that the employment history can be treated more fully. The first page illustrates how important making use of space can be. The reader's eyes are literally pulled to the three paragraphs in the center of the page. Figure 10.14 is a four-page résumé typeset and printed on a 11 × 17 inch sheet of paper folded in half to give the effect of a brochure. The manner in which this résumé was prepared and put together is pleasing to the eye, impressive, uncluttered despite a large amount of information, and especially a good image maker for someone in marketing, sales or advertising.

TACTICS THAT PRODUCE JOB INTERVIEWS

The first thing a job hunter wants to do after preparing a résumé and cover letter is to go to the library and review the job ads that appeared over the last ten weeks. Executive and top management positions typically take as long as three months and longer to fill, even though they are only advertised once or twice. This is because job applicants are called back from anywhere from three to six interviews in addition to one or two further meetings for psychological assessment before a decision can be made. You want to search through major newspapers such as the *New York Times* and the *Wall Street Journal*, as well as technical, trade and newsletter publications

ROBERT MORRIS

310 Boyleston Avenue   Home: (204) 555-2123
Boston, Massachusetts 02345   Office: (204) 555-2000

> *Objective:* Qualified for Assistant to Chief
> Executive or as *Director* of such
> functions as Corporate Planning,
> Marketing Services, Market Devel-
> opment and New Products.

Summary. Presently *Director of Corporate Planning* with a major New York
Stock Exchange Company. In a smaller company, I was Vice-President of
Marketing. Previous to this, I was Assistant National Brand Manager
with a large liquor company. With the same company, I was Operations
Manager for the Western Division. My accomplishments in every position
are substantiated by rapid salary growth.

Personal qualities include strong analytical and creative ability,
outstanding managerial skill, great initiative and an ability to get
things done. I am well traveled and experienced at making presentations
and working with the highest levels of management.

> *Present Employer (since April 1977). Director of*
> *Corporate Planning* with manufacturer. During the
> last 10 months, I also served as consumer products
> Assistant to the President. This involves
> traveling with him, briefing him on marketing
> developments, participating in profit planning
> and budget review of divisions, handling marketing
> questions from the financial community and working
> on corporate-wide marketing problems.

As *Director of Corporate Planning* of this $100,000,000 company, I am
responsible for extensive work in the areas of corporate strategy,
new products, market development and acquisitions. Some specific
accomplishments are as follows:

Designed and created the company's first formal one-year and
five-year Planning System and Guide.

Assisted the President and other officers in developing both
corporate and divisional objectives and plans for their achievement, including rate of return, rate of increase in sales and
product-line objectives.

Figure 10.10. Résumé of Corporate Planner.

Supplied direction and coordination in the preparation of each major function's objectives for conformity with corporate objectives.

Conducted continuing assessments of corporate performance, as compared with corporate plans, analyzing variances to identify strengths and weaknesses in coping with the present and future business environment.

Formulated Action Programs for the purpose of in-depth analysis of the entire scope and nature of our business. This planning technique has resulted in new and efficient operating procedures and involvement with two major acquisitions. I am presently involved in our expansion programs, spearheading the planning for the start-up of production and marketing of both these companies.

Instituted business plan monitoring systems that resulted in earlier product-line freeze dates, saving the company over $500,000 in tooling expense.

Instituted a complete marketing intelligence system and procedure for data usage of new product development.

Revamped personnel function and benefits program--involvement with management development programs, wage and salary administration, establishment of succession programs, personnel inventory, employee stock purchase prgram--and wrote Company Personnel Manual.

> _Previous Employer (1974-1977)_. Vice President of Marketing, University Teaching Corp., New York, New York. Company engaged in marketing educational computer programs involved in the location and identification of both scholarships and colleges.

Major accomplishments included the following:

Arranged acquisition of both College Choice and Scholarship Search.

Developed and executed national marketing program, including advertising, promotion, pricing, public relations, research, geographical coverage, price schedules and packaging resulting in 150% increase in sales.

Secured nationally recognized endorsements of services with 65 major banks nationally.

Arranged for company's private placement and public offering.

Established nationwide distribution network.

Figure 10.10 (continued).

225

Marketing methods included multimedia advertising, purchase and selection of media, direct mail campaigns, seminar guidance sessions, guest speaking engagements, creation of point-of-purchase material.

From 1970 to 1974, I was with National Liquor Corp., New York, New York. Completed Executive Marketing Management Training Program, became Operations Manager Western Division for the import company, and then Assistant National Brand Manager.

Major accomplishments included the following:

Completed 18-month Executive Marketing Management Training Program in one year.

As Operations Manager for Western Division, maintained effective controls and records for $8,000,000 volume.

In-depth analysis of brand distribution, pricing, advertising, and promotion resulted in implementation of my recommended programs, creating a 34% increase in sales in 2 years.

Developed overall objectives for the marketing of the products, including volume and profit objectives, sales and share-of-market forecasts, geographical quotas, advertising plans and programs, coordinated merchandising and promotion plans.

Coordinated and administered advertising agency activities and plans and media selection and maintained $3,000,000 advertising budget.

Established prices, terms and discounts for brand at competitive profitable levels.

Coordinated distributor sales planning and forecasting, created specific market promotions and prepared and executed the national brand budgets.

Instrumental in creating new marketing philosophy and brand image with dynamic new packaging and promotion attack.

Personal Data: *30; married with two children, 6', 180 lbs., excellent health*

Education: *Masters Business Administration, Rutgers University Graduate School of Business, New Brunswick, New Jersey. Major: marketing.*

B.S. Degree, Fairleigh Dickinson University, Madison, New Jersey. Major: marketing. Minor: finance.

Figure 10.10 (continued).

9 Hickory Lane   Home: (201) 555-1343
Short Hills, New Jersey 07821

RESUME

OF

NORMAN E. BAUM

Qualified at

SENIOR MANAGEMENT LEVEL

***   Successful experience as Executive Vice-President
        of military/industrial manufacturer of complex
        instrumentation and controls.

***   Competent in all phases of management: production,
        finance, marketing; qualified electrical
        engineer with solid earlier experience in devel-
        ing navigation and computer systems.

***   Played major role in better than 1,000 percent
        expansion of present employer in revenues and
        profitability through innovative marketing,
        pricing and engineering and manufacturing
        controls.

***   Profit-conscious decision maker with talent for
        leadership, motivation, harmonious relationships
        at all levels. Accustomed to effective planning
        for rapid growth. Qualified for major position
        with medium-sized company or division of large
        company.

Figure 10.11. Résumé of Executive Vice-President.

BUSINESS EXPERIENCE:

<u>1972-present</u>   GUARDIAN ELECTRONICS CORP., Hanover, N.J.

EXECUTIVE VICE-PRESIDENT, SECRETARY, MEMBER of BOARD of DIRECTORS
(1977-present) of approximately $5 million O-T-C listed manu-
facturer of shipboard fire-control systems, digital computer
interface equipment and industrial controls. Corporate Vice-
President for Marketing and Engineering (1972-1977).

Responsibilities include finance, engineering, manufacturing and
marketing, with supervision of V.P. Manufacturing, Purchasing,
Production Control, Sales Managers and Sales Representatives.

Achievements and most significant responsibilities include:

- Primary responsibility for growth of Company from $250,000 in
  1972 to nearly $4 million by 1977.

- Primary responsibility for increase in value of Company's stock
  from $0.45 to $12.00 in a five-year period.

- All pricing and funds flow requirements.

- Establishment of all budgets for marketing, manufacturing and
  engineering.

- Supervision and preparation of annual and other reports to
  stockholders and government.

- Participation in one acquisition and continuing search for
  suitable merger/acquisition possibilities.

- Direction and coordination of all engineering activities:
  electromechanical and solid state digital systems and sub-
  systems for computation, display and control in military and
  industrial applications.

- Relocation and merger of two separate operating divisions,
  included all power and mechanical layouts while maintaining
  operations during move.

- Scheduling all production; organization of inventory control
  system.

- Establishing purchasing policies and vendor payment plans.

- Conception and direction of marketing plan of corporation;
  development of long-term corporate plan.

- Bid successfully on large Navy procurement of MK53 attack
  consoles formerly restricted to major suppliers, amounting to
  $5 million over a period of 4-5 years. Program provided the
  company with credentials to become a major supplier to the
  Navy for more advanced systems.

Figure 10.11 (continued).

- Generated the need for and set up license agreements with foreign and domestic manufacturers of aircraft and flight instruments, resulting in sales of more than $2 million in three years.

1967–1972   DEFENSE SYSTEMS CO., Brooklyn, N.Y.

PROGRAMS MANAGER (earlier PROJECT MANAGER), responsible for all activities of division in the development and manufacture of equipment for navigation, display and computer systems. This included customer liaison, contract negotiation, preparation of proposals, cost estimates, budget controls. Utilized PERT program management techniques.

Customers included all major aerospace manufacturers.

1962–1967   GLOBAL ELECTRIC CORP., Philadelphia, Pa.

Successively, JUNIOR ENGINEER INDUSTRIAL TRAINING COURSE, ASSOCIATE ENGINEER, ENGINEER, SENIOR ENGINEER.

- Responsible for basic electronic computing building block concept development with applications to airborne missile fire control computers for use with various radar systems.

EDUCATION:

M.B.A., Columbia University, New York, N.Y., 1974.
B.S.E.E., New Jersey Institute of Technology, Newark, N.J., 1962.

PROFESSIONAL MEMBERSHIPS:

I.E.E.E. (Senior Member)

PERSONAL DATA:

Born 4/6/83, married, three children, excellent health.

REFERENCES AND FURTHER DATA ON REQUEST

Figure 10.11 (continued).

OBJECTIVE:

    Corporate Counsel

LEGAL EXPERIENCE:

    Corporate: Negotiations and drafting of acquisition agreements, buy-outs, liquidations, distributions and dissolutions. Closings of taxable and tax-free mergers, stock and asset sales and purchases. Preparation of qualified and nonqualified savings, profit sharing, pension and stock option plans. Employment agreements with stock purchase and deferred compensation provisions. Preincorporation and shareholder agreements, including buy-out provisions. Subscription agreements. Loan financing, indemnification, and guarantee agreements. Warrant agreements. Convertible and subordinated debentures. Preparation and closings of bulk sales and secured transactions, including UCC filings. General corporate and practice including drafting of minutes and miscellaneous agreements and documents.

    Securities: General familiarity with the Securities Act of 1933 and the Securities Exchange Act of 1934 and the rules and regulations promulgated under each. Preparation of registration statements and prospectuses. Underwriting agreements. Private placement memorandums and syndication of limited partnership interests. Responsible for compliance with reporting requirements and preparation of necessary reports, including 8-Ks, 10-Ks and review of company's annual report to stockholders. Preparation of proxy material and solicitation of proxies. Analysis of exempt transactions and exempt securities.

    General: Equipment leasing, including purchase-lease and sale-leaseback transactions. Short-term, finance and net leases. Purchases and sales of real estate and leasehold estates. Triple-net real estate leases. Sale and leaseback of real estate, developed and to be developed. Purchases of condominiums and cooperatives. Partnership, limited partnership and joint venture agreements. Premarital and separation agreements.

EMPLOYMENT HISTORY:

    Golden, Rose & Greene, 450 Park Avenue, New York, New York;
    August 1975 to present.

    Osterman, Eisen & Marcus, 315 Madison Avenue, New York, New York;
    September 1973 to January 1975.

Figure 10.12. Functional résumé of Law Firm Associate.

EDUCATION:

    LL.B. Brooklyn Law School, 1973.
    B.A. Long Island University, 1970.

    Continuing Legal Education Courses:
    General courses in accounting

BAR MEMBERSHIP AND ASSOCIATIONS:

    New York State (1973); United States District Courts, Southern
    and Eastern Districts of New York (1974); United States Supreme
    Court (1977); United States Tax Court (1979); American Bar
    Association (Banking, Corporation and Business Law Section);
    New York State Bar Association (Banking, Corporation and
    Business Law Section).

PERSONAL:

    Born September 20, 1949; married; two children.

References available on request.

Figure 10.12 (continued).

PAUL F. WEISS
48 Pippin Road
Cincinnati, Ohio

(308) 555-0257

Manager with extensive profit responsibility as
DIVISION GENERAL MANAGER and MANUFACTURING
EXECUTIVE of single and multiple operations in
the plastics and packaging industries. Broad
experience and background include the achievement of profit, manufacturing and sales objectives,
and their dramatic improvement.

POSITIONS OF RESPONSIBILITY

General Manager, Vice-President Manufacturing,
Technical and Engineering Manager, Production
Manager (multioperations), and Plant Manager.

AREAS OF RESPONSIBILITY

Manufacturing, sales, engineering, commercial
development, business planning, financial control,
industrial relations, union negotiations, production control, scheduling, purchasing, warehousing,
traffic and quality control.

Figure 10.13. Functional résumé of General Manager.

MANAGEMENT EFFECTIVENESS

GENERAL MANAGEMENT and SALES

Successfully instituted, as General Manager, turn-around programs that substantially improved profits and increased sales. Considerable losses were eliminated, and actual profits were made within four months. Major parts of the program consisted of establishing a job and product costing system to evaluate profitability. This resulted in changes in sales emphasis and product lines. Accounting procedures were instituted to provide rapid determination of manufacturing effectiveness. The total effort, including other changes, resulted in an annualized division profit improvement of $500,000, while providing reserves for bad debt and inventory. Established sales policies and actively worked with salespeople to increase prices and bring in new customers. Sales for the division were increased by 50 percent within a six-month period, while affecting an increase of 7 percent in average selling price.

MANUFACTURING

Managed total plant and engineering activities for multi-plant operations in the capacities of Vice-President Manufacturing and Engineering and Production Manager. As Plant Manager, have profitably operated union and non-union plants with 50 to 350 hourly employees on seven-day operation. Responsible for profits of total operations with standard costs and budgetary controls. Prepared operating and capital budgets. Conceived and developed specifics of cost-reduction programs, and prepared requests for expenditures. Numerous programs resulted in annual savings of up to $350,000 via: productivity increases, hourly labor and overhead reductions, technological changes allowing automation techniques, increased material efficiency, purchasing and shipping practices, and revisions to scheduling production. Negotiated numerous union contracts. Started up two new plants, bringing them from empty buildings to fully operating multiprocess plants. One served as a model for other divisional plants, and the techniques and efficiencies developed were used by them. As Production Manager, made a complete analysis of the business, which was experiencing $350,000 annual plant losses. Recommendations for plant consolidations and product-line eliminations were implemented, and the resultant business, reduced in size, turned profitable.

TECHNICAL

Responsible for specifying, purchasing, installing and releasing for production all equipment for products in polyethylene film and bags, bottle and large blow molding, thermoforming, extrusion, structural foam molding, printing, decorating and auxiliary plant services. Performed and responsible for commercial development on production equipment for the manufacture of new products involving new processes. Successfully developed new techniques in bottle blow molding, thermoforming containers and heat sealing. This work resulted in my authoring six U.S. Patent applications and having four patents issued.

Figure 10.13 (continued).

BUSINESS HISTORY	United Packaging, Inc., from October 1970 to the present. General Manager of a division engaged in the extrusion of blown polyethylene film and manufacture of bags. Sales are approximately $5½ million.
	Previous assignments include Vice-President Manufacturing of division producing above products and converting and printing. Operations located in two plants. Was also Technical Manager of division, with complete technical and engineering responsibilities.
	BBO Industries from August 1969 to July 1970. Business Manager, with manufacturing and sales responsibilities of a PVC bottle-blowing operation.
	Blow Molding, Inc., from February 1968 to August 1969. Plant Manager of a household chemical liquid filling and captive polyethylene bottle-blowing plant.
	American Plastic Corporation from 1963 to 1968. Production Manager of fabricated plastics products with manufacturing operations in three plants. Manufacturing and engineering responsibilities in the areas of large blow molded items and structural foam molding. Plant Manager of a multiprocess plant engaged in high-density polyethylene in-line thermoforming, PVC and polyethylene bottle blowing, large blow molding and structural foam molding. The development of production equipment and techniques for manufacturing in these areas was performed at this plant.
	Formed Nupack Corporation, subs. of Crown Chemical, Inc., from 1960 to 1963. As Plant Manager started a new facility for the manufacture of a new packaging concept. Processes included extrusion coating, flexographic printing, in-line thermoforming and heat sealing.
	Garden Container Company from 1954 to 1960. Plant Superintendent of a plant initially engaged in pipe extrusion, injection molding and bottle blowing. Major reemphasis and expansion programs built up the bottle blowing and decorating areas, minimized injection molding and eliminated pipe. Concurrent with the expansion program, started up a thermoforming operation and a metal-end polyethylene container production line. Major cost reductions and new techniques resulted in a highly profitable bottle manufacturing plant.
PERSONAL	Age: 47 Married; three children
	Bachelor of Chemical Engineering Massachusetts Institute of Technology, 1954.

Figure 10.13 (continued).

234

DAVID SCHUSTER

A PROFESSIONAL MANAGER QUALIFIED FOR POSITIONS AS:

- Marketing Manager
- Director, Corporate Planning
- Director, Operations
- Senior Staff in above areas

7100 Georgia Avenue
Silver Spring, Maryland 03689

202-555-4000 (office)
301-555-2548 (residence)

ACCOMPLISHMENTS	Organized a new product and industry planning department for a billion-dollar corporation.
	Managed a $2,000,000 budget . . . reduced costs by 24% while maintaining constant output.
	Coordinated the successful development of a long range plan for a $400,000,000 firm.
	Derived a forecasting system to measure market demand for certain industrial commodities.
	Purchased $2,500,000 in automotive assets in highly competitive environment at 5% below market value.
	Developed national policy for food industry good manufacturing practices.
	Published reports that were quoted by the President and the Secretary of the Air Force.
	Achieved academic rank of Assistant Professor of Business and Public Administration at age 28.
STRENGTHS	Has extensive supervisory experience with environments requiring a self-starter.
	Functions effectively with management at all levels.
	Possesses a true appreciation and desire for P & L responsibility.
	Has comprehensive background in marketing and corporate planning.
	Extremely energetic and dynamic . . . known as being a prime mover.
PERSONAL DATA	AGE: 33 Married—2 children HEIGHT: 5'10" Honorable Discharge WEIGHT: 165 Top secret clearance HEALTH: Excellent Willing to relocate
EDUCATION	BA, New York University, 1968, Business Administration. MBA, New York University, 1970, Business Administration.
REFERENCES	On request.

Figure 10.14. Brochure résumé of Government Executive.

235

PROFESSIONAL HISTORY	
11/78–present	EXECUTIVE OFFICE OF THE COMMISSIONER, Food and Drug Administration • Deputy Director, Food Industry Liaison Division Exercised line management responsibility for developing policy and accomplishing policy-related actions for the food industry.
12/76–10/78	UNITED STATES AIR FORCE, Office of the Comptroller • Operations Research Analyst Derived procedures for cost estimation and assessment of billion dollar weapon system programs for implementation at the major subordinate commands. Selected by the Comptroller for two special high level assignments.
4/74–11/76	UNITED STATES AIR FORCE • Captain Administrative Officer to a four-star general. Managed $2,000,000 budget. Supervised 54 civilians. Received Joint Service Commendation medal and perfect efficiency report.
2/73–3/74	NATIONAL ELECTRIC CORPORATION • Marketing Specialist Responsible for planning marketing strategy at the Group level and analyzing trends in industrial markets that would have an impact on the marketing effort. Acted as consultant to the 7 operating divisions and the centralized field sales force to rationalize the difference in sales forecasts by major industry, evaluate these forecasts in light of industry trends, and establish realistic industry sales objectives.
10/72–1/73	NUMACH, INC. • Marketing Analyst Designed a short run forecasting system to project market demand and set quarterly production schedules.
12/71–9/72	RAWMAT CORPORATION • Assistant to the Director, Corporate Planning Initiated a long range planning activity for the corporation and coordinated implementing sub plans. Recommended alternative courses of action in matters as capital facilities planning, disposal of assets and new business opportunities.
1972 to present	ACADEMIA • Assistant Professor, Lecturer and Instructor Taught over 50 courses in business administration (evening divisions) at New York University and Columbia University.

Figure 10.14 (continued).

AS OTHERS SEE HIM	
As a Manager	"Mr. Schuster's greatest skills lie in the area of business management. He is responsive to the needs of his superiors and the problems facing the organization. He is able to organize resources, delegate assignments, follow up progress of work, and schedule work to meet deadlines. He sees that details of personnel management, progress reports, monitoring of new developments, and potential problems are fully covered under his direction in managing his branch. I would not hesitate to recommend Mr. Schuster for similar supervisory positions." From an official government performance appraisal dated July 3, 1980
As a Subordinate	"He has the exceptional capability to see the needs of management and works well with General Officers and executive level civilians." From an official government performance appraisal dated November 10, 1978
As an Innovator	"My Special Assistant has informed me of the many new ideas and concepts which you contributed to the project and the overall excellence of the cooperation and willingness to participate which you displayed. Your special contribution to the final material to be used for approaching and eliciting responses from top managers; your efforts in the pilot tests conducted and other preparatory actions for the survey; and the analytical work you performed in summarizing and interpreting survey results are all worthy of special note. The high level interest displayed in the results and analyses provided by the project is a reflection upon you and a credit to your efforts and resourcefulness." From a letter of commendation by the Comptroller dated January 16, 1977
As a Catalyst	"I particularly want to acknowledge your contribution to the scheduling and preparation for the May Advisory Committee meeting. The coordination of presentations by 25 outside organizations before national television news cameras went extremely well and you can take pride in the part you played in its success." From a congratulatory letter by my supervisor dated September 18, 1979
As a Leader	"Mr. Schuster has earned the respect of all by his demonstrated good judgment, tact and competence. He has shown an uncommon ability to derive from subordinates a full measure of their inherent abilities." From an official government performance appraisal dated May 25, 1976, and signed by a four-star general

Figure 10.14 (continued).

237

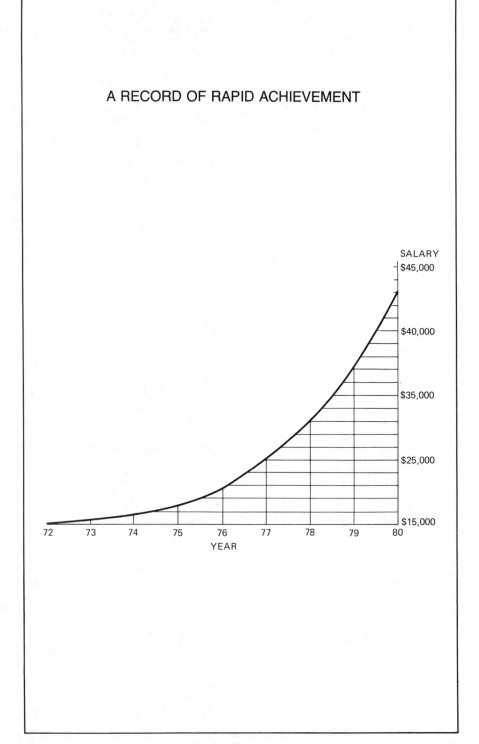

Figure 10.14 (continued).

that advertise positions available, and, especially, the executive opportunity digests, which clip out and publish display advertisements for positions from newspapers and other publications throughout the country.

Although you do not want to waste your time applying for positions that do not closely match your talents, you should not restrict your replies only to advertised responsibilities you know you can handle. Most ads exaggerate the experience needed for serious consideration and success in the position. You should answer ads even though requirements may sound above your level of industry experience and degrees are preferred that you do not have. If you do not force yourself to increase your aspiration level, you cannot hope to land something challenging and beyond your present ability so that you can grow in your career. Furthermore, there may be no other job hunter possessing the advertised specifications. Even if there are better candidates, you may be more attractive to the employer because of your lower salary and your potential to quickly pick up the responsibilities. Finally, the individual who is hired for the advertised position may take a look at other résumés received for it and choose from them a deputy or assistant, which may still represent a good opportunity for you.

Many people are under the impression that blind ads should be skipped over because they are phony or might possibly be from their own company. Blind ads should be considered seriously because they are placed by executive search firms and corporations that do not want to be bothered with phone calls and having to reply to everyone's résumé out of courtesy, that want to maintain secrecy in light of competitors and employees, and that want to avoid a poor image because, for one reason or another, they are advertising heavily for the same positions due to frequent turnover, promotions or transfers. The chances of applying to your own employer's advertisement are slim since there is usually enough information in the ad to tip you off as to whether the company is in the same industry, location, market and so on.

Whenever possible, you want to identify what company is placing the blind ad so that you can directly contact the hiring executive, thereby bypassing the personnel department that placed the ad. Thus, if the ad mentions that the company is a quarter-billion dollar energy resources conglomerate headquartered in Texas and the opening is for a national sales manager, then you can research the *Dun & Bradstreet* or *Standard & Poors* directory in your library and send your résumé directly to the vice-president of marketing of the half-dozen or so firms that you will find match the advertised description.

Between one-half and two-thirds of all résumés responding to an advertisement will be received in the first week. After two weeks, 90 percent of the résumés have been received. Few companies react quickly to the barrage of résumés and actually interview and offer a job to someone within the first few weeks. Most personnel departments and business managers use the first couple of weeks to screen out the bulk of the candidates and then start setting up the interviews. After one or more candidates have been interviewed, hiring executives are in a knowledgeable and confident position to make a quick decision. By this time, they know what they want and know what areas they have to compromise on. As time goes on, they also become more interested than ever to fill the position. Thus, as you learned in Chapter 3, you want to delay sending your résumé for a couple of weeks after the advertised position appears so that your credentials and abilities will be reviewed at the best possible time, which in particular means having the least amount of competition the day your résumé is looked at.

As long as you are being selective in choosing advertisements for sending a well-prepared résumé, you should follow up within three weeks if you have no response from the firm that placed the ad. The follow-up letter should restate your interest in the position and the contribution you feel you can make. Many times, your résumé will be pulled from a stack that has not even been reviewed yet or from a stack that has been screened out. As the one applicant in fifty or 100 that expressed a greater interest in the position, you may be called in for an interview for that reason alone, even if you are already rejected.

Unadvertised Jobs
Ninety percent of your competition for a job will be for advertised openings, and it's said that 80 percent of all openings are not advertised. This means that only 10 percent of all other job hunters looking for a similar position will be competing with you for 20 percent of the unadvertised openings. But how do you learn about openings if they are not advertised?

Most people think that letter mailings, placing advertisements regarding their availability for a position and other techniques of asking for a job ferret out the unadvertised openings. This is incorrect. Research shows that over half of all unadvertised executive level openings are filled in some manner as a result of personal contact. Contacts frequently include friends, acquaintances, business associates, association and professional society colleagues, alumni, family members, members of Congress and fellow social and business club members. Because trade and professional organizations are the best places to meet future employers, you should go through the *Encyclopedia of Associations* or one of the other trade directories and pick out those organizations in which you would expect your superiors and yourself at some future point in your career to be members. These are the organizations you want to join, not those that you and your peers presently belong to because the contacts you can make there that will lead to a job are minimal. Thus, if you are presently the manager of a small profit center and you want to become president of a company or major division, you should become active in groups like the Financial Executives Institute, Young Presidents' Organization, Chief Executives Forum, World Business Council, Sales Executives Club, International Executives Association and the American Management Association's President's Association.

As you already learned in Chapter 4, people like to feel that they are getting a bargain or something that is hard to get. Thus, employers find an active job seeker less desirable than someone who is content where he or she is and not actively looking. The rationale seems to be that people who aren't looking are probably doing a good job where they are.

What all this means is that the ideal way of obtaining an interview for an unadvertised job opening is to be solicited by the employer, its headhunter or someone else who thinks you would be a good candidate for the position. It sounds great, but how do you get yourself solicited?

The easiest way to be contacted for a position without asking for a job yourself is to have visibility in the industry and your profession. Keep your name in print through articles, news releases, speeches, awards, promotions, achievements, *Who's Who* directories and so on. Furthermore, there is no reason for you to depend on chance that publicity about you will be caught by leaders in your industry or companies in your local area (assuming you do not want to relocate). In other words, you should consider sending reprints of your speech or article or copies of the release to industry executives, local company management and executive search firms.

The techniques of making personal contacts with company presidents and other top executives are only limited by your imagination. For instance, if you already have a responsible post in industry, you may consider the tactic of feinting by phoning company presidents and board chairpersons to tell them of your availability and interest in serving on their board of directors at the appropriate time in the future and suggesting a get-acquainted meeting.

Another indirect approach of making personal contacts is to invite executive search firms and company personnel directors to attend a seminar or speech you are presenting in an area of interest to them. Whether they come or not, you'll have the opportunity of giving them a write-up on your background with the letter of invitation. Along the same lines, you could phone these people to set up appointments to interview them for research you're conducting for a forthcoming article or book. As mentioned in Chapter 7, people, even important people in industry, are flattered when someone wants to hear their opinions. As an extra added inducement, you can offer to give them a complimentary copy of the article or book when it is published. These techniques of satisfying esteem needs can be used to get to know most of the presidents and other important executives of the companies in your metropolitan area.

Although these various techniques of making personal contact with potential bosses and headhunters that can recommend you to your future boss do not involve asking for a job, some of these people, impressed with you and your background, will think of contacting you when there is a suitable job opening. However, at some point in the future, you can cash in on your contacts by phoning and asking their opinions on opportunities in their industries and asking that they keep an eye out for any suitable positions in the industry because you have decided to move on to greater responsibility elsewhere, again appealing to their esteem needs and using the tactic of mirage, making it seem that you are calling for their advice and not to ask them for a job. Obviously, if they have an opening in their own organization, they will consider you for it, but there is no sense in putting them on the spot and causing possible embarrassment by asking them for a job.

As already learned in Chapter 6, your initial contact in implementing approaches such as those mentioned above should be by phone, whenever appropriate and possible, rather than mail. You can either set up an appointment to meet the executive during your phone conversation or offer to send a letter or literature on what you are doing, subsequently followed up by another phone call from you to set up the interview. You do not want to start off by mail because the response rate will be low due to secretaries screening out mail, mail being junked before it is read and a variety of other reasons.

In the phase of your job hunting campaign when you are directly telling people you are available, you can greatly expand the number of personal contacts you have by using the tactic of association in contacting complete strangers. For instance, if you are looking for a top management position, you can phone presidents and board chairpersons who are listed in your alumni directory, relying on your common bond of schooling when introducing yourself and immediately getting their attention and interest. You can pick out presidents and board chairpersons from directories in your library, based on their residence in your town, their membership in the same professional or social organizations and so on. No matter how important a person is, when he or she finds out that both of you have a common ground, this person tends to warm up to you and help you out if possible because you in some way are alike. People like to help people whom they feel some kind of kinship for, especially when their need for esteem is being satisfied at the same time.

Another technique of establishing a personal contact and being on the ground floor when a position becomes available is to congratulate executives when their promotion, job transfer or job change is announced in a newspaper. At the same time, you take the opportunity of offering to assist them in meeting their new responsibilities. This is most effective if your letter is sent to them two to three months after they assume their new position. In the beginning, they are under so much pressure that your letter would become junk mail. After they settle down and are in the swing of things, they may actually be looking for help, and your letter will be timely. Even if they have no present staff requirements, by congratulating them and appealing to their esteem needs, you can be sure that many of them will keep your letter on file for the appropriate moment.

A slightly modified approach can be used when a merger is announced in the papers. You should consider sending a letter to the surviving company. Quite often, management in the merged company, if they haven't already done so, will leave for jobs elsewhere. Sometimes, present management of the merged company is fired because of conflicting interests or a hotly contested fight against the merger. In either case, mergers often represent an opportunity for high-level executive jobs.

In addition to contacting people at their new comapnies after they switch jobs, you should consider contacting the former employer. There is a good chance the former executive has not been replaced, even months after his or her departure.

Figure 10.15 illustrates a letter sent to a recently appointed public official, congratulating him, asking him to consider the writer's qualifications to be a member of the official's team and wishing him a rewarding future in his new post. Figure 10.16 shows the reply letter from this important leader, who felt compelled to take time off from his busy schedule to personally respond as a result of the appeal to his esteem needs. Figure 10.17 shows a much briefer cover letter transmitting a résumé.

December 29, 1976

Joseph A. Califano, Jr., Esq.
839 17th Street N.W.
Washington, D.C. 20036

Dear Mr. Califano:

I read with great pleasure and interest of your appointment as the next
Secretary of Health, Education and Welfare. I would like to take this
opportunity to personally congratulate you.

During the campaign, I lent my active support to Jimmy Carter. For the
most part, his views on resolving and administrating the nation's
health concerns and programs coincide with mine. I would be honored if
you would consider my qualifications, enclosed, as a potential member
of your team.

My broad legal, business and bio-medical engineering background in
government, private practice and the health care industry (currently
as an officer of a major medical manufacturer and a national trade
association) has given me a unique insight regarding the interdependence
and problems of HEW, industry and the public.

A perusal of the attached resume, showing my business accomplishments
and my published books and papers over the past year (circled items
relate to health matters) will show the extensive experience I have
already had in health care policy, health legislation and Congressional
relations, complying with FDA and Bureau of Radiological Health regulations and product standards and handling general legal matters peculiar to the health care area (such as informed consent and medical liability).

The elected and appointed posts I have held this past year include:
vice president, medical, and a director of the UIA, Inc.; director of
the New Jersey State Bar Association Food, Drug and Cosmetic Section;
Standards Committee co-chairman of the Association for the Advancement
of Medical Instrumentation; chairman of the Medical/Surgical Section
of the American Society for Testing and Materials; United States Delegate to the International Electrotechnical Commission Medical Committee;
and chairman of the New York State Bar Association Food, Drug and Cosmetic Law Section Committee on Medical Devices.

Best wishes for a joyous holiday and a prosperous and rewarding year
ahead as the new Secretary of HEW. I look forward to hearing from you.

Sincerely,

Philip Sperber

Figure 10.15. Congratulatory letter.

THE SECRETARY OF HEALTH, EDUCATION, AND WELFARE
WASHINGTON, D. C. 20201

January 24, 1977

Dear Mr. Sperber:

Thank you for your letter of congratulations
and your interest in working for the Department.

I deeply appreciate your willingness to assist
me as I take on this enormous responsibility.
While it is too early to tell just what our
needs will be, I will keep your resume on
file to be considered as we develop our
staffing requirements.

Sincerely,

Joseph A. Califano Jr.

Secretary

Figure 10.16. Reply to congratulatory letter.

Mrs. Kimberly Mazur
AMAX INTERNATIONAL
35 Van Nuys Drive
San Diego, California 92109

Dear Mrs. Mazur:

Congratulations on your recent promotion and assumption of Mr. Hart's responsibilities as Vice-President and Controller of AMAX INTERNATION-AL.

I feel that I could make a contribution to AMAX in assisting you in successfully carrying out your new functions.

I look forward to a personal meeting should there be an appropriate opening on your staff as a result of your promotion.

Sincerely,

Figure 10.17. Brief congratulatory letter.

Just as there are many imaginative approaches to making personal contacts, there are also many creative techniques that can be employed to immediately find out where job openings are and even where positions will open up in the future. For instance, you can place a display advertisement with a box number to indicate your availability, your major qualifications and your job objective. Another example would be putting an ad in for a position more responsible than the one you are looking for, together with a box number. The managers responding to your advertisement will probably be in positions that you are presently looking for. This tips you off as to openings that will become available in the near future when these people change jobs.

No hunt is complete without a trip to the library to get directories of executive search firms. A cover letter with two résumés should be sent to search firms specializing in your area of work. The best approach in this situation is to write a few brief paragraphs of "soft sell" in the cover letter, which should be worded in a manner that you are not actively seeking a position at this time or you have been solicited by someone else and are now surveying the market to see what else is available. You will also get a better response if you initially include your salary and state whether you are willing to relocate. Figure 10.18 illustrates a letter that shows that the applicant is actively looking for a position, but only because this person was initially solicited by another executive research firm. Figure 10.19 is a more detailed letter sent without a résumé. The significant thing is that the first paragraph appeals to the esteem needs of the search firm by mentioning they are only one of a handful that you are writing to and that you are writing to them to seek their advice as to whether you should leave your present position.

The same approach that is used with executive search firms can be adapted to letters mailed to company senior executives. However, it is absolutely critical that the cover letter be personally addressed and tailored to the particular individual and the particular company being written to. Without this personal touch and without precisely tailoring your letter and résumé to that particular company, you drastically reduce the probability of being called in for an interview. When writing to the president or other senior officer, you should mark the outside of the envelope *private* and *confidential* in the hope that the secretary will hesitate to open it and send it automatically to the personnel department. To be doubly safe, you may wish to hand write the address and private and confidential markings on the envelope. The secretary will assume that this is indeed personal and perhaps from a family member or a friend because the envelope is not typed. Figure 10.20 illustrates an unsolicited letter sent to a manufacturer.

When sending out large mailings to executive search firms and private industry, you take the risk that word will get back to your present employer and jeopardize your job. To eliminate this problem, you may wish to use the third-party letter technique wherein a colleague is the one who actually writes the letter for you. Figure 10.21 is an example.

Dear Madam/Sir:

I am currently vice-president and chief counsel of a diversified manufacturer listed on the American Stock Exchange and was previously a partner in a Washington, D.C., law firm.

As a result of being contacted by another executive search firm, I am having my initial interview for associate general counsel of a 1.5 billion dollar steel and chemical conglomerate in Pittsburgh on December 22, and I am going back for my second interview to be group counsel of a 1/2 billion dollar consumer products manufacturer in Indianapolis on December 26.

I would like to be considered for other openings before making a decision to accept any offers. If any of your Fortune 1000 clients have a need within the next few months for a senior-level counsel (I am presently at the $55,000 level) with outstanding credentials and broad business experience, please consider my qualifications, enclosed in duplicate.

Thank you for your time and thoughtful consideration.

Sincerely,

Figure 10.18. Brief letter to search firms.

Dear Madam/Sir:

You are one of a dozen prestigious consultants to whom I am sending confidential information to determine if a new position as chief counsel, as vice-president for administration or corporate planning, or as chief operating officer of another company is in my best interest.

I would like to discuss your clients' needs in the coming year if they are looking for a youthful (mid-forties) and energetic self-starter who is a profit- and results-oriented executive of exceptional stature, with a salary now approaching $80,000.

I am presently an officer and chief counsel to the president of a diversified public company where I have both staff and P & L responsibility for: (1) the administration of corporate and legal affairs; (2) planning, coordinating and helping to implement the operations of a dozen subsidiaries and divisions; and (3) plotting and consummating the future product/market mix of the corporation as a member of a three-person acquisition/divestment team with the president and another officer.

An engineer and lawyer by training, I am now a market- and financial-oriented management generalist. My past includes a line, staff, small business ownership and consulting background, and I am recognized in my profession and in industry as an authority on corporate legal and business strategy.

My legal and business experience includes: product planning; merger analysis; R&D; patent procurement and enforcement; trade secret protection and company security; market research; manufacturing, cost analysis and inventory control; government compliance (FDA, BRH, CPSC, EPA, OSHA, FCC, DOD, FTC, SEC, IRS); test marketing; pricing policies, distribution, dealer network practices, advertising strategies, sales, brand name promotion, public relations and trademark and copyright procurement, usage and enforcement; trade regulation and antitrust prevention programs; negotiating and drafting agreements (licensing, joint ventures, acquisitions, consulting, research, vendor, distributorship, leasing, financing, commercial transactions, labor, realty); insurance, product liability, litigation and arbitration; and accounting, budgeting and financial controls, including evaluation of alternative investments and allocation of resources.

If any client needs a skilled, aggressive and dedicated legal pro or general manager with a demonstrated record of success, I would be pleased to provide my resume and personally meet with you. Thank you for your time and thoughtful consideration.

Sincerely,

Figure 10.19. Letter without résumé to search firms.

Ms. Sherry E. Bloom
Senior Vice-President
ATCO Corporation
13 Franklin Street
North Scituate, Massachusetts 02060

Dear Ms. Bloom:

As general counsel for a multibillion dollar conglomerate, you no
doubt need an attorney of exceptional stature from time to time.

I advanced from division counsel to corporate counsel to vice-
president of a smaller conglomerate over the past six years since
leaving my law firm partnership. I feel it is time to move on to
a larger organization, and ATCO is one of two dozen firms I am now
contacting because I believe I can make a significant contribution
to your company in the years to come.

My track record and accomplishments over the past eleven years
earned me recognition as one of the youngest leaders of our profession, locally and nationally. In addition to being an officer
of the state bar association, I am the ABA corporation, banking and
business law committee chairperson and antitrust committee vice-
chairperson, author of two books on corporate law and strategy that
can be found in the libraries of many Fortune 500 firms, vice-
president for government relations of a national trade association,
the recipient of an American Law Institute commendation and a bio-
graphee in Marquis' Who's Who in American Law.

I believe that you and your key executives would find me mature,
energetic, a legal pro, a doer and the type of person who could
help company managers achieve their business objectives while avoiding unfavorable legal implications. I welcome the opportunity to
personally meet with you sometime over the next year.

Sincerely,

Figure 10.20. Unsolicited letter to industry.

Mr. Corey Newman
Dynacomp, Ltd.
1050 George Street
New Brunswick, New Jersey 08903

Dear Mr. Newman:

A business associate of mine with twenty years of marketing and financial experience asked me to contact you on his behalf.

He has a solid background in sales engineering, promotion, budgeting,
forecasting, EDR systems, records retention, contracts, presentations,
new product planning and market research.

He has the demeanor, maturity, initiative and managerial skills to
bring prestige, dignity, cost reduction and increased sales to any
organization.

There is much more that could be said about his abilities, and there
is detailed information, including his resume, available at your request. If you would like to pursue this matter further or arrange an
interview, I would be delighted to hear from you.

Sincerely,

Figure 10.21. Third-party letter.

NEGOTIATING WITH THE JOB INTERVIEWER

All the basic and advanced principles and techniques learned so far are applicable almost without any modification to the interview and job offer situations. For instance, you want to make a good initial impression by wearing a dark to medium blue or gray suit, with a solid white shirt and solid tie; by carrying your brief case in your left hand so that you can smoothly offer the interviewer a firm handshake; by establishing good eye contact, with a warm smile at the appropriate time; by angling your chair at 45 degrees so that you can lean toward the interviewer without appearing to stage a frontal attack; and by not placing your brief case on the floor between you and the interviewer, thereby subconsciously causing it to become a barrier in the interviewer's mind.

In order to show your interest in the interviewer's company, you want to listen attentively, ask questions about the job and the company at the appropriate time, and home in on some of the company's problems and how your past experience and abilities would be relevant in solving these problems. Researching the organization will help you prepare an intelligent list of questions and analyze where the organization's weaknesses lie and how you can make significant contributions.

An applicant who asks good questions will appear more interested, more mature, smarter and more of a self-starter than other applicants who are interviewed. At the same time, the applicant will acquire sufficient information to make an intelligent decision should a job offer be extended. Questions should not be asked until there is a lull in the interview or the interviewer asks if there are any questions. At this point, you can ask such questions as the following:

1. Is the opening a result of growth or because someone left?
2. What was the reason for the previous employee's departure?
3. What are the company's future plans for the division that will be employing me?
4. What are the probabilities of being transferred to another location?
5. (Where the interviewer is the future boss.) What are your short-term and long-range goals?
6. (Where the interviewer is the future boss.) Can you describe your ideal assistant?
7. (Where the interviewer is the future boss.) Can you tell me what kind of management style you have?
8. (Where the interviewer is the future boss.) Where do you and the department fit in as far as the company organization chart is concerned?
9. Do you have any objection to me calling the last person in the job should I receive an offer so that I can have a more complete picture before accepting or rejecting the offer?

Before each interview, you must prepare yourself in advance to answer questions such as those listed in Chapter 9. Regardless of how a question is phrased, there is usually a standard reason for asking it. For instance, if interviewers ask you to tell them about yourself, they simply want to know what you have to offer the company. If you go off on a tangent and do not zero in on your main selling points and how they relate to the job that is open, you are making a negative impression. Below are some common questions and the kinds of answers that you can consider giving:

Q. Tell me about your major weaknesses.

A. Quite a few people consider me to be a perfectionist, impatient to demonstrate my abilities, a person who works a little too hard, rough on my people because of my high standards (although I consider myself a fair supervisor and do my best to help my assistants reach the objectives we jointly set) and prolix in my writing. (The strategy here, of course, is to give an answer that lists weaknesses that are either trivial or actually positive points and strengths probably desired by the interviewer and the company.)

Q. What things or activities do you most dislike or hate to do?

A. I dislike wasting time due to incorrect priorities, insufficient delegation of responsibilities and other practices that can be made more productive. I do not like to dwell on tasks that are not challenging as far as my analytical, creative, business and professional capabilities are concerned.

Q. Which past jobs did you like the most and why?

A. I liked my position with Parker Systems Corporation the most because my boss gave me the freedom to show what I could do. He had extremely high standards for performance and results, and I found it very satisfying to run the show and still be able to please him.

Q. What types of people seem to rub you the wrong way?

A. I have always had an inherent dislike for persons who lacked integrity or masked their true feelings about serious subjects. In particular, I could not tolerate a subordinate who was a "yes" man, telling me what he or she thought I wanted to hear instead of what the actual problems are so that we can mutually solve them.

Q. How did you happen to get into this field of work?

A. I always knew and the counseling tests confirmed that my writing, speaking and people-oriented abilities were high. I therefore chose a career in marketing, and I made the right decision. I find my responsibilities very satisfying, and work is actually fun.

Q. What kind of guidance do you get from your present boss?

A. Very little, and that is the way I like it. The more I can free him for policy matters and planning and the more he delegates to me, the happier I am.

Q. What is your typical workday like?

A. I have no typical day. It depends on what I am working on and what comes up. It might be a week day or a weekend, and I might leave at 5:30 or 8:30 in the evening.

Q. How long would it take you to make a contribution to our company?

A. Less than a week. I am a quick learner and pick up new responsibilities in a smooth transition.

Q. Describe your closest friend.

A. That would be Dave Aibel. He is president of Fibratron. Like me, he is very ambitious, has a lot of drive, is outgoing, knows how to motivate his people and is a strong player on the tennis courts.

Q. How do you feel about your boss?

A. I highly respect him and have learned a lot in the short time I have worked for him.

Q. How much do you know about our company?

A. Before the interview, I reviewed your annual report and your 10-K. I also researched your biography and the biography of your boss in *Dun & Bradstreet* to know a little bit about the people themselves who run the company.

Q. How long do you anticipate staying with us?

A. I look upon this position as a growth opportunity, and I can see myself making my career here. Of course, if I am wrong and the challenge and opportunity wanes at some time in the future, it would not be fair to the company or myself to hang around as a disappointed and unhappy employee.

Q. Can you give us references to call?

A. Certainly. I would like to wait until we are both serious about each other. I do not like to bother my references prematurely. They are important and busy people. [If you have doubts about what your references will say, have a friend make a phone call in the guise of an employer who has interviewed you. If necessary, have your friend send a letter to the reference if the person hesitates to say anything on the phone.]

Q. If you join us, where do you expect to be in the next five or ten years?

A. I always work harder and accomplish more than expected of me. I believe in making myself underpaid so that raises and promotions are actually forced on to me without me having to ask for them. I therefore feel that I will be in a much more responsible position in the future. I also believe in doing everything possible to make my boss look good and hopefully push him or her up so that one day I can assume his or her responsibilities.

Q. What's wrong with your present company?

A. It is actually a great company to work for, and it has a lot of top people in management. Basically, I have outgrown my responsibilities, but there is nowhere for me to go in the foreseeable future.

Your negotiating agenda for the first job interview with a company should exclude salary and benefits topics. Your ideal position is to have the company seriously interested in you and on the verge of making an offer before discussing how much they are going to have to pay to get you. Employers are much more inclined to pay more for a person they have decided they want than for a person who has not yet been singled out as better than the few best candidates.

If the interviewer brings up the subject of compensation, you should indicate that you would prefer to hold off discussions in that area until you are sure you want the job and the company concludes you're the best person for the position. You can emphasize that there is really no sense in getting into the compensation area at this early phase of the interview process. You can also mention that you have no worries about being able to agree on a reasonable compensation package if the parties decide they want each other.

Furthermore, in no interview should you ask questions about insurance, lay-offs and other matters that give the appearance that you are looking for security. You can always get answers about benefits and the like from the company personnel department. Throughout the interview, you should show a high level of confidence in yourself as a person interested in challenge and changes necessary to improve the company's growth and profits, for in the end your only real security is your ability and the results you produce.

At all times during the interview, keep in mind the interviewer's goals as outlined in Chapter 9. Every time you open your mouth, exploit the opportunity to project the image of an executive who possesses the important attributes listed in Chapter 9.

AFTER THE INTERVIEW

Most job hunters completely ignore the importance of repetition, discussed in Chapter 5, and the importance of appealing to the esteem needs of the interviewer once the interview is over. You should always send a follow-up letter if you are interested in the position, but it should be more than the standard "thank you." Because the interviewer always concentrates on finding and remembering the negative things about each applicant, it is important that your letter refresh his or her memory about the positive abilities you possess, in addition to expressing your interest in the position. Figures 10.22–10.28 show typical follow-up letters, with Figure 10.22 illustrating a brief note and Figure 10.28 showing the effectiveness of a lengthy communication, if properly done and appropriate for the situation.

When it finally becomes appropriate to discuss salary, adhere to the principles of Chapter 5. If asked about your requirements, state your worth unequivocally, but condition it on what the bonus arrangement and other fringe benefits of your compensation package will be. You do not want what you thought was a good salary to be immediately accepted, only to find out that the bonus and other benefits are minimal.

It is not unusual for job hunters to be looking for 20 percent to a third more than what they are currently earning. Based on your estimate of how much the company wants you, what the going rate is in the particular industry for the particular position, and any hints that have already been given to you on the expected salary range, ask for the highest salary you think is reasonable. However, do not ask for something that is clearly excessive with the thought of bargaining and eventually compromising downward. You are not dealing with a rug merchant. You should pick a figure that is at the high end of the range you feel is reasonable and stick to

Mr. David B. Ingraham
Centennial Corporation
2325 N.E. 15th Street
Portland, Oregon 97212

Re: Plant Manager

Dear Mr. Ingraham:

I want to thank you again for an enjoyable dinner. Your frank and
informative explanation as to why your current manufacturing manager
doesn't fit is appreciated. Your management team clearly needs a
high-performance, results-oriented pro who has the necessary initiative, confidence and know-how.

In short, I really think that I can do an outstanding job as your
plant manager, and I would like to explore your requirements further.

Sincerely,

Figure 10.22. Thank-you letter.

Ms. Elaine Rosenthal
Manager, Personnel and
  Organization Development
American Utilities Company
Valley Industrial Park
Los Angeles, California 92951

Re: Assistant to the President

Dear Ms. Rosenthal:

I thoroughly enjoyed our Tuesday meeting. I especially want to thank
you for your discussion of operations, current and future needs for
management development and the opening, which sounds exceptionally
challenging.

I think Tuesday's Wall Street Journal feature article "Worried
Utilities" provides an excellent scenario of the increasing complex-
ities and difficulties of doing business that will confront you in
the coming years when your chairperson and president are completing
the final years of their service to the company.

I believe I am the well-rounded generalist with the necessary expertise, dedication and flexibility to be groomed within a short period
of time to carry on your outstanding growth record and financial stability, while other utilities fall victim to shortages, escalating
operating costs, rate adjustments too little and too late, consumer
and environmental oppostion, equity dilution and investor apathy.

I look forward to hearing from you next week and meeting your
president.

Sincerely,

Figure 10.23. Thank-you letter with repetition.

Ms. Thea Grossinger
Wilson International, Inc.
2500 State Street
Rochester, Minnesota 55901

Re: General Manager

Dear Thea:

I want to thank you again for your hospitality.

After learning more about your organization and its needs last night,
I became convinced that I can make a rapid and significant contribution in guiding your business along a trouble-free path for long-term
growth and profitability.

Your president and chairperson appear to need someone who can be
relied on right away, with minimum orientation and supervision. I
am confident that they will find me flexible to work with and the
"right-hand man" they are looking for. At the risk of appearing
boastful, I would like to seriously emphasize that: general management is my occupation; marketing is my skill; success is my story;
and increased profits for you are my goal.

I look forward to a congenial meeting with your president and chairperson at your facility in the future.

Sincerely,

Figure 10.24. Thank-you letter with salesmanship.

Mr. Edward J. Woodell
Vice-President, Technical
General Computing Corporation
100 Avenue of the Stars
Los Angeles, California 92951

Re: Group Project Manager

Dear Mr. Woodell:

Thank you for a most pleasant and stimulating interview. It was re-
freshing to field your questions on how I would handle some of your
current projects and problems.

You clearly have high standards for your managers. I would consider
it a privilege and a challenge to join your team and try to exceed
those standards.

After you discuss my candidacy with Mr. Petersen upon his return, I
would be happy to supply references to facilitate your decision.

Since you are going to reach a decision quickly, I would like to mention several additional things that I feel qualify me for the job we
discussed:

1. proven ability to generate fresh ideas and creative solutions to
    difficult problems,

2. experience in the area of program planning and development,

3. ability to successfully manage many projects at the same time,

4. a facility for working effectively with people at all levels of
    management,

5. experience in administration, general management and
    presentations,

6. an intense desire to do an outstanding job in anything I
    undertake, and

7. unquestioned loyalty and integrity.

Thank you for your time and thoughtful consideration.

Very truly yours,

Figure 10.25. Thank-you letter with more information.

Ms. JoAnn Stein
Executive Vice-President
Allied Enterprises, Ltd.
200 Duncan Road
Don Mills, Ontario M3B 3J5

Re: Vice-President, Corporate Development

Dear Ms. Stein:

Thank you for a most pleasant and stimulating meeting.

The inside information I learned from you gave me an insight, not
apparent from my research of Allied, regarding the advantages of
joining your team.

My philosophy and rationale in acquiring businesses is actually
quite similar to your acquisition guidelines that I received. The
basic difference is that marketing was not always a critical factor
since we were looking for businesses that our existing marketing
capabilities could handle without a large incremental increase in
overhead and labor. Our interests in direct marketing, consumer
goods marketing, size, growth, location, management, brand identifi-
cation and margins are the same as yours.

I feel that my expertise in evaluating the marketing capabilities
and competitive situation of acquisition candidates can be successfully used from day one to propel Allied Enterprises into a billion-
dollar empire. (In my first five years with Standard Goods, there
was a 400 percent increase in after-tax income, primarily due to
acquisitions.)

When looking at Allied's super track record, I find myself excited
about the challenge of performing even beyond the expectations of
the dynamic and demanding superiors I would be reporting to.

I certainly look forward to seeing you again and the opportunity to
meet Mr. Winters, the group vice-president with whom you mentioned
I would be closely interfacing.

Sincerely,

Figure 10.26. Thank-you letter with more information.

Mr. Benjamin Ivers
Vice-Chairman and Chief Executive Officer
IBB Corporation
1000 Market Street
Philadelphia, Pennsylvania 19107

Re: Vice-President, Marketing

Dear Mr. Ivers:

Thank you for the pleasant and stimulating meeting we had yesterday. You have certainly intensified my interest in the position. There is nothing more rewarding than performing beyond the expectations of a dynamic and demanding superior.

On my flight back, I carefully read through the service brochure you gave me. I was extremely impressed. It is an excellent selling piece that clearly and concisely transmits to the industry the IBB theme: rapid quality service of any industrial machine, anywhere, anytime.

I notice that both the service brochure and the advertising sheets I received from you are directed to the various industries that use machinery. I would be curious to know whether IBB has considered the prospect of offering its services directly to industrial machinery manufacturers. I would think that some of these manufacturers might find it attractive to refer customers to IBB service centers in at least some areas of the world where the manufacturers are not equipped to maintain and service machinery. There may even be some manufacturers that view maintenance and service as incidental to the profits of equipment sales. Such companies might be happy to have a reputable service organization such as IBB take care of their customers' needs.

I also noticed the absence of a customer list and testimonials. I hope you are collecting such data in anticipation of future competition from other service companies. A partial listing of IBB's most well-known and respected customers, with testimonials from some attesting to IBB's service reputation, will no doubt be needed in future advertising when competitors enter this lucrative market.

Also, in light of what you told me yesterday, it would seem that IBB's extensive experience in maintenance and repairs results in service of a higher caliber at lower cost than that provided by many machinery manufacturers. Future IBB promotional literature might emphasize this reality, especially once a computer history bank is established, containing data on how each type of repair was effected, the time it took to make the repair, and the cost.

I apologize if my comments are based on incorrect assumptions since I am not intimately familiar with your business. I do not wish to sound too presumptuous. I suppose my enthusiasm over the prospect of helping IBB double its size within the next few years is involving me prematurely with ideas for making such growth a reality.

I am looking forward to meeting with Ms. Klein on Monday evening, November 15, and taking the psychological tests the following day in Philadelphia.

Sincerely,

Figure 10.27. Thank-you letter with helpful ideas.

Leslie C. Peterson
General Counsel
Eastern Telecommunications Corporation
400 West Shore Drive
Fort Lauderdale, Florida 33303

Re: Associate General Counsel

Dear Mr. Peterson:

I feel that our initial meeting was quite productive. I especially
want to thank you for your frank discussion of the company, the legal
department and your immediate needs. I feel that we could work well
together and find myself excited about the prospect of joining your
team.

You made two key points during our discussion on Thursday. First, you
need a self-starter to aggressively manage the legal function for the
General Phone Division. Second, you had difficulty in finding the
necessary time to properly interview, evaluate and select the best
candidate for the job.

I believe that the attorney you are looking for should demonstrate
initiative and ability to assist you in every appropriate way, even
before he or she is hired. Accordingly, attached is an objective
analysis to help crystallize your thinking on whom to bring back for
a second interview. It covers three basic criteria that I use in
hiring attorneys and that you will probably find applicable also.

After reviewing the attached and the material received from me on
Thursday, I think you will find that I am mature, energetic, a legal
and regulatory pro, a doer and the type of business-oriented attorney
who can help company managers achieve their objectives while avoiding
unfavorable legal implications. I look forward to seeing you again
within the next few weeks and meeting your colleagues.

Sincerely,

Figure 10.28. Detailed thank-you letter with helpful information.

1. Which candidate has the greatest experience and ability for independently handling the General Phone legal function with the least drain on Mr. Abrahm's time?

A. Outstanding Manager.

Mr. Welt supervised staff and outside attorneys for the past 10 years in addresssing and providing solutions for complex corporate circumstances, first as a law firm partner, then as vice-president of an electronics manufacturer and finally as counsel for a group more than twice the size of the General Phone Division. Applying the techniques of management by objectives and management by participation, he motivated staffs of attorneys, paralegals and secretaries into highly enthusiastic and productive teams. Notwithstanding the fact that some lawyers reporting to him are 10 or 15 years older than he, he has not encountered difficulty in commanding respect for his expertise, competent leadership and hard work.

B. Knows the Business.

By coincidence, the companies he counseled over the past decade are in the same industry as General Phone and sell similar products and services for the consumer, industrial and government markets. Working for companies in the same business as General Phone has provided him with the type of legal experience in government compliance, contracts and trade regulation that is required for the General Phone position.

C. Proven Track Record.

At his age and salary level, Mr. Welt has an unparalleled track record of success and advancement in private practice and industry as well as recognition by bar groups of his professional achievements. A bright associate or even a partner from the most prestigious law firm represents an unknown quantity. He may not like the industry environment after all, once on the job for a half year. He may not be business oriented enough to function optimally without close initial guidance from Mr. Abrahms.

D. A Result-Oriented Achiever.

Perhaps his greatest asset is that Mr. Welt removed important burdens and administrative functions from corporate presidents and attorneys who thought them incapable of delegation. His attitude of welcoming and learning from criticism; his immediate adaptation to new circumstances, procedures and management styles; his willingness to work long hours and his total dedication to helping his boss meet objectives have normally enabled him to assume responsibilities and achieve results far beyond that expected of him.

E. A Self-Starter.

In short, Mr. Welt has the background and drive to immediately and responsibly take over the reins of the General Phone legal function and make a greater contribution starting from Day One than any other candidate available.

Figure 10.28 (continued).

2. Which candidate has the attitude and personality that will interface best with the key company executives and managers?

A. Deals Effectively with Others.

Mr. Welt established an excellent rapport and good working relatinship with headquarters, profit center and department managers in past positions. In addition to his outgoing personality and diplomacy, there are two important reasons why he was able to do this. One, being an engineer and also having expertise in marketing and finance enables him to talk the same language as the businessperson he's dealing with and also clearly understand feelings on the issues involved. Two, he enthusiastically removed significant problems from the shoulders of the various managers in order to free these executives for more important functions.

B. A Planner Steering Managers Free of Legal Problems.

By working on a daily or weekly basis with company managers, Mr. Welt was able to truly practice preventive medicine in addition to satisfying immediate legal and quasi-legal needs. For instance, within one year after joining Teletron, he initiated the first formal corporate policy manual covering various procedures and guidelines for technical, marketing, financial and management personnel, to avoid violation of the antitrust laws, covering various government regulations affecting the products, the plants and the environment and to assure contract control and protection of company inventions, trade secrets and trademarks, among other things.

3. Will the best candidate be happy enough with the work and future growth opportunity for the company to keep him for a long time?

Having been with Teletron for seven years, Mr. Welt is not one to job hop. His philosophy is that if you are good and make valuable contributions, the company will treat you favorably. He therefore has given a great deal of thought as to whether he should leave Teletron at the present time and especially for the spot to be filled at General Phone.

"I think that by the end of the interview, I had enough new information to conclude that the job would be a step up in challenge and responsibility. However, I am going to mention my thinking below so that you can also make a determination as to whether I'll have sufficient job satisfaction.

"I am most excited about the idea of handling legal services for the largest segment of the corporation and reporting directly to the vice-president and general counsel without layers of attorneys in between. The administrative red tape of getting things done at Teletron can be pretty frustrating. I believe that I would have a freer hand at General Phone to use my creativity in both achieving objectives and accomplishing things beyond what is expected of me.

Figure 10.28 (continued).

"I have found over the years that I am at my best and am happiest when reporting to dynamic and demanding executives in a pressured environment where correct decisions must be made fast and where results are what counts. Without intentionally trying to flatter you, Mr. Abrahms, my impression is that you have done a remarkable job over the past year under extremely difficult circumstances and that you probably have the kind of high standards I look for in a boss.

"Lastly, the General Phone Corporation is expanding and diversifying so quickly that the legal department may not have had time to catch up both in growth and organization. From my point of view, this represents a unique opportunity to join the company in a responsible position and immediately prove myself as an invaluable right-hand man to the vice-president and general counsel."

Figure 10.28 (continued).

it. The prospective employer will respect you for insisting on a high salary, and there is little danger of being rejected from consideration if the employer really wants you. Instead, he or she will simply ask you to consider a lower offer. However, based on the principles you learned in Chapter 4, you can be sure that their offer will be higher than the one they would have made if your aspiration level was lower.

No matter how you fare in salary negotiations, the higher your aspirations, the more the company will feel it is getting something of value and, if it is getting you for less than you want, a bargain. You also set yourself up to get concessions in selected areas. For instance, you may be able to get a salary review in six months rather than a year or eighteen months. By compromising on salary, you may have an easier time getting a contract regarding bonuses, deferred compensation, moving expenses, profit sharing, life insurance and severance pay upon employment termination. In fact, as executive dismissals become more commonplace in industry, companies expect a job applicant to demand a termination clause. It is estimated that close to 90 percent of all executives taking jobs paying over $100,000 a year get some type of termination agreement, compared with only 50 percent in 1975. Other requests you can make are an outline of promotions you can expect for being on a fast track, a company car, privileges on the company jet, purchase or lease of a house, carry-over of your current company pension benefits, and a bonus up front as a substitute for lost bonuses earned on the present job.

In selecting your next job, there are of course things more important than salary, bonuses, benefits and "perks." Does the position represent a good growth opportunity? Does it involve the kind of work you like to do? In other words, will your capabilities be utilized and your interests satisfied? It has been estimated that four out of five people do not like their jobs. It is a lot easier to succeed in work you enjoy than in a job you dislike. What kind of personality does your immediate boss have, and will you be able to get along with this person? Is the company on a fast track or on the decline in a maturing industry? Does your boss have a large degree of freedom in deciding who gets raises and how much? Is there anyone else in the organization who can perform your job? What is the possibility and probability within a short period of time that your boss will be promoted?

Chapter 11
SPECIAL NEGOTIATING CONSIDERATIONS FOR WOMEN EXECUTIVES

MANAGING THE FAST TRACK FEMALE IN THE 1980s

The negotiating principles and tactics covered in this book apply to women; however, there are some additional fundamentals and techniques that women must be aware of in view of their minority position in the executive suite. Research shows that any conspicuous minority group making up less than one-third of a given population will be subject to special scrutiny because of their very presence in a given environment. Since women managers comprise a much smaller percentage of the business executive environment, every woman executive becomes highly visible, and her daily reality is an eggshell existence because improprieties and aesthetics are greatly amplified.

To make matters worse, studies show that close to half of all male executives have mildly unfavorable to strongly unfavorable attitudes towards women in management. Other studies show that both women and men perceive men as being more aggressive, self-reliant, decisive, confident, vigorous, responsible, objective, informed, stable and direct, as well as more of a leader, than women managers. On the other hand, women managers are perceived as being more understanding, helpful, sophisticated, aware of feelings of others, intuitive, neat and courteous than male managers.

The studies also show that people in general perceive women managers to be as intelligent, competent and creative as their male counterparts. This may be the reason why women are often placed in executive positions requiring a high degree of expertise from which authority can easily flow and that invariably involve specialized staff positions rather than line jobs. This bears out in major U.S. companies, where 99 percent of women officers hold staff positions such as assistant treasurer, corporate secretary and vice-president.

266

What actually happens in the typical company when a woman accepts or is promoted into a top management slot? Let's look at four common situations that are exemplary of the real world.

The first situation is where a woman becomes the only female department manager. Some of the men in adjacent departments and some of the men reporting to the woman executive feel that only a real man can handle her responsibilities, and their self-image is seriously injured, resulting in various destructive reactions. They may attempt to ruin the effectiveness of the woman through conscious or even unconscious sabotage. They may use her as a scapegoat for their own mistakes. They may try to isolate her and her department as much as possible. They may withhold help and information she needs to meet her department's goals.

The second situation is when the woman is perceived by top management or her boss as a token female executive. Although she has the title, she will find herself without important responsibilities, blocked from channels of information and excluded from committee and other activities that someone in her position should be participating in. More than likely, the woman executive is extremely talented; her confidence will be wasted; and eventually she will rebel, causing a morale problem for many people—she will quit, and/or she will sue.

In the third situation, the woman's supervisor actively persecutes her or subtly underminds her morale, confidence and effectiveness. For instance, he criticizes her for taking a long time, instead of praising her thoroughness; he calls her lazy for not taking care of low priority items when he should really be sympathizing with her tremendous work load; he berates her for being careless with first-time mistakes instead of pointing out that no one is infallible; he chews her out for overstepping her boundaries without getting prior permission instead of complimenting her for her initiative; he calls her stubborn when she feels strongly about a matter instead of respecting her for being firm and having courage; and when she gets a bonus or promotion, she is told it is a lucky break instead of a reward and recognition for her hard work.

In the fourth situation, the woman executive is quickly brought up through the organization by a well meaning mentor. If her rise is too fast and her relationship with her mentor too close, people will make assumptions, and rumors will spread that she is sleeping her way to the top. This is exactly what happened when Mary Cunningham, a twenty-nine-year-old single executive, became vice-president of strategic planning for Bendix Corp., under the tutelage of William M. Agee, chairman and president of the company. Three weeks later, she quit amid rumors that a romantic relationship between the two influenced her rapid rise in less than two years with the company. She claimed that the "malicious gossip . . . and innuendo" made her job impossible.

The one thing all four situations have in common is an illustration of the courage and strength women need to break out of the barriers they face in the corporate world. They must risk rejection and failure in a manner and to a degree few men ever encounter.

What can the general manager or president of a company do to promote a smooth transition when bringing into the executive ranks a woman who performs well? Four key policies should be established in order to maximize performance and development on the part of both the woman executive and her male peers and assistants, minimize organizational trauma and minimize tokenism.

First, care should be taken to assure that the woman executive is reporting to a person with positive views toward female managers and that she will be teamed with peers who likewise look upon her without prejudice. A woman should not just be thrown in with the assumption that her co-workers will accept her and work well with her in time. Heavily indoctrinated views about a woman executive that are of a negative nature cannot be changed overnight.

Second, in order to minimize the woman's isolation and prevent her from losing visibility and getting sandbagged, she should have a mentor who can closely follow her career growth and who has the power to provide opportunities and make fair evaluations. The mentor must make sure she proves herself in each position of increased responsibility, rather than artificially pushing her up at a pace faster than the organization can adjust to. The mentor should make her work visible, have her reports adequately distributed and published, encourage her to stand up in important meetings and assure that her decisions are recognized as her own and not the mentor's. Most important of all, the mentor must eliminate any appearance of intimacy to prevent suspicions that she is getting to the top through sex.

Third, people should be encouraged to bring out issues and risk trying to resolve them. If necessary and appropriate, periodic development sessions with a consultant can be established to work out the issues. Full acceptance of women as professional peers and superiors requires relearning by both sexes to dispel previously learned male/female role expectations.

One of the best ways of changing attitudes and destroying myths is simply to state the plain facts and statistics and let them sink in without any hard sell. For instance, few people realize that one out of every two Fortune 100 companies in the United States has, on the average, at least one woman officer. Chances are that she is chairperson, vice-chairperson, president, group vice-president, senior vice-president or vice-president of the corporation. Quite a few earn more than $100,000 a year. Some three million women, five times the number ten years ago, hold American Express cards. Women purchase over 40 percent of all new life insurance nongroup policies. There are more employed females than males in the United States. Women are presently buying $8 billion worth of cars on their own credit lines. The statistics can go on and on, and they all point to one thing. Times are changing. Given the same degree and amount of education as males and given the motivation to break out of stereotyped roles in society, the female MBAs, attorneys and engineers being cranked out of today's universities inevitably will become tomorrow's business leaders, along with their male alumni. Once employees and management personnel accept this as a fact and recognize that they may be just as likely to have a woman supervisor as a male boss, it should become easier to integrate females into management notwithstanding their present minority status.

Another approach is to show a training film to company personnel so that they can witness the many facets of sexual harrassment, from innuendo to blatant attack. A film entitled *Preventing Sexual Harrassment*, produced by B.N.A. Communications, Inc., of Rockville, Maryland, does just this and is accompanied by participants' manuals filled with exercises and activities that reinforce points made in the film and teach managers and supervisors how to deal effectively with a variety of situations.

Fourth, top management, starting with the chief executive, must clearly be committed to minimizing tokenism and supporting the person most qualified for a task. They should set up systems of objectives, action plans and measurements to account for performance and development to prevent discrimination against women.

SUBCONSCIOUS TACTICS FOR COUNTERING BIAS

So far, we have discussed two themes: first, the peculiar difficulties facing women executives that dictate negotiation strategy and tactics not previously covered in this book; second, what supervisors can do to effectively deal with the problem and minimize trauma to the organization while hopefully increasing productivity.

But what about you, the woman manager? How do you cope with the hostile environment you find yourself in, as part of a 1 percent minority in the corporate ranks of management?

Your company and your mentors can make an all-out effort to support your responsibility, importance and acceptance. However, in the end, you must learn to live with negative attitudes from people reporting to you, your peers and higher-ups on a daily basis. Later we will look at typical examples of statements and questions you must learn to respond to in a mature, competent, professional and confident manner.

If your dress, demeanor and gestures, as well as what you say, show that you are outside the male executive's stereotype of a woman who is not aggressive, emotionally stable, self-reliant, responsible, objective and well informed, he will treat you with the dignity an executive in your position should command. Even your voice should show toughness and stature. Referring back to Chapter 6, you will recall that lowering the tone of your voice will help endow you with the image of maturity and thoughtfulness. High-pitched (shrill) tones are associated with youth, frivolousness, and irresponsibility.

You should even attempt to use your office, furniture and fixtures to create the business executive image discussed above. Your office walls should be painted in the standard blue or beige and certainly not in a feminine color or wallpapered with a feminine or flowery pattern. Likewise, do not have a flower in a vase on your desk because this is the badge of a secretary. Do not display your husband's picture on your desk because it creates a negative image, according to the research. Pictures of children, however, appear to be acceptable. Your desk, chair, lamp base and other futniture should have straight lines, which suggest power, importance, drive and dominance. You should have solid-color, textured up-holstery fabric and solid-color wall-to-wall carpeting, which is suggestive of your independence, ambition and competence. You do not want a huge chair that overwhelms you and diminishes your stature. Your nameplate, letterhead and signature should ideally say Janet Cohen, which is better than the following names listed in order from good to bad: Mrs. Janet Cohen, Ms. Janet Cohen and Miss Janet Cohen.

Below is a list of responses designed to counter negative behavior toward you and improve your image, yet not make you seem too forceful, vicious and aggressive, thereby alienating those around you.

How Do You Confront Sexist Thinking?

Many people do not even realize they are thinking in sexist terms. Pointing out the sexist aspect of their opinion or attitude will be appreciated in many instances, as long as you do not confront them in a hostile manner. Your only goal is to show how a statement directly or by implication is based on or requires different rules for males and females in a situation where they should be treated equally.

1. *Vice president, marketing to female sales administrator:* "I think it would be a good experience for you to spend a half day or so out in the factory so that you are more familiar with our products and how they are made, especially when it comes to quality control and making them safe. My only concern is that Dan Roth, the manufacturing manager, will get irritated because when the workers see you, they are not going to be able to fully concentrate on their jobs."

Response: "Perhaps you are right, but you have to admit that the se-cretaries do not have difficulty concentrating on their work when you sit on their desks. You have to admit that you're a fairly handsome man and have as much sex appeal as I do. Are our situations really that different?" (By pointing out the sexist thinking and then asking this person to comment on whether you are correct, you are treating him with respect and asking him a question that requires an obvious answer favorable to you and that you will get because of your calm, nonargumentative and friendly attitude. The last thing you want to do is call him "sexist" or "chauvinist" because the person will only reflect back your hostility even if he realizes he is wrong.)

2. *Chief engineer to female project engineer (with sincere admiration):* "I must say you really think like a man."

Response: "Any man in particular? A physicist? A janitor? A teacher? A salesman? A policeman?" (Without making any statement at all, these ques-tions show the absurdity, without disrespect, of the chief engineer's com-pliment.)

Alternative response: "As the only Ph.D. in the department and with my track record in the brief time I have been with the company, wouldn't you say that I think better than most men? Frankly, I am hurt that you let my sex color your opinion of my worth." (Whenever the opportunity presents itself, you should remind those around you of your credentials and your right to have their respect. At the same time, do not hesitate to express your feelings. It is potent when a man expresses his true feelings. It has twice the impact when a woman does it because men are taught from early childhood to be sensitive to a woman's feelings and help her when she is in distress.)

3. *Purchasing manager to female sales representative upon her entering his office for the first time (obviously attracted to her physical appearance):* "I am most definitely pleased to have you here. I am only sorry we did not do business before with such an attractive lady."

Response: "Thank you. Your compliment is most welcome. I have come here to talk about your rubber O-ring needs." (There is no need for an oversensitive reaction to a compliment on your physical appearance when you are expecting to talk about rubber O-rings. In fact, you already learned in Chapter 5 that prebargaining discussion on casual matters is important in establishing cooperative attitudes on the part of the parties. It is only natural for a male executive to be struck with your beauty if you really are attractive. Instead of penalizing him for commenting on your appearance, take advantage of it. Women executives have a lot of things going against them. They might as well grab any opportunity that they can, even if it is simply the fact that they are more attractive and nicer to be with than their male rivals.)

4. *Chairman of the board to the female vice-president and general counsel:* "As you know, since our President passed away, we have looked at all of the vice-presidents and general managers, including yourself, to determine who is the best qualified to lead the corporation onto new levels of growth and profit in the future. You are well respected in the company and have many of the skills necessary to carry out the president's responsibilities in a heavily regulated firm like ours. Unfortunately, like many of the other people under consideration, you have a basic disadvantage. Most of the directors feel that stockholders, especially the heavy institutional investors, would become disenchanted with the company's future if you were at the helm."

Response: "Perhaps the board does not realize that it is not uncommon to have women heading businesses. There are 500 women officers in the top 1,000 U.S. companies right now, many of whom are in chairperson, vice-chairperson, president, group vice-president and senior vice-president positions. Ten percent of these women earn more than $100,000 per year. It is generally believed that it is no longer a question whether a woman can perform as well as a man, but whether she will be given the opportunity. I would like to go before the board and make them aware of these facts as well as my own impeccable credentials and track record. Personally, I believe that the major stockholders will not abandon us, but instead will invest even more heavily once they learn about my background and my capabilities, as well as the fact that I am joining a large group of women executives who are successfully running major businesses." (Referring to statistics and the simple facts is one of the best ways of fighting sexist thinking, especially when it involves fear and embarrassment regarding the possibility that a woman will get too much visibility to an organization's detriment.)

5. *Salesman demonstrating trailer hitch operation to specialty vehicle dealers:* "Although this incorporates the latest technology, any woman can hook it up and disconnect it without difficulty."

Response by female dealer: "I would say that your trailer hitch can be successfully operated by people of low mechanical aptitude. Although many women are mechanically inept, it is also true that many men also are all thumbs when it comes to mechanics."

6. *Comptroller to subsidiary manager:* "I will have my girl come come up to your plant on Tuesday to review the books."

Response from "girl" who overhears the conversation and speaks after the comptroller gets off the phone: "To refresh your memory, I am a certified public accountant; I am twenty-eight years old; I am married with three children; and I am not your girl. Since you do not call the other accountants in the department boys, don't you think it is unfair and demeaning to call me your girl?"

7. *Vice-president, administration to female personnel manager:* "Now that you are getting this raise, you can go out and start buying that fancy clothing you've probably wanted."

Response: "I wish it were true. However, like the two out of three other women managers who are single, divorced, separated or widowed, I need this money for the necessities."

8. *Junior partner of law firm to female associate:* "Susan, will you please get me a photocopy of this brief?"

Response: "I'll be happy to do that, provided you sharpen these pencils for me. Do you really want to exchange these minor errands?"

Confronting Antagonistic Remarks

How do you confront someone who is obviously being antagonistic with his sexist remarks? Since the person is probably looking for a fight and the chance to verbally abuse you even more, remember the reflection theory. Stay cool and state the facts in a logical, objective manner to get him thinking in his Adult ego state. This is the situation where it is even more important how you reply to sexist thinking than what you reply. You do not want to be argumentative and threatening to that person. You may win the battle but lose the war because he will always have a deep resentment for you in the future and never again be receptive to the thought that women should be on an equal footing with men. Sometimes humor can be used effectively in permitting the male executive to save face while simultaneously making it appear that both of you think of his remarks as an innocent joke or tease, regardless of whether they were meant to put you down.

1. *Sales manager to female director of public relations:* "I wish you would be a little less vocal in staff meetings. Aggressive women are kind of annoying to me."

Response: I am no more aggressive than some of the other department managers. It seems to me that you simply dislike women being on an equal footing with men. This is what our president wants. I would not have been promoted into this position if I wasn't ambitious and aggressive. Do you really want me to lower my performance on the job just because I wear a dress and have mammary glands?" (Remaining relaxed after an antagonistic remark, stating the facts and asking a question that shows the absurdity of the executive's thinking leaves the door open for better relations in the future. Certainly, over the long run, this type of response is much better than a slap in the face, such as, "I get the clear impression your masculinity is threatened when you have to deal with women on an equal footing.")

2. *Male accountant to female accountant:* "Will you be frank with me? Why is it so important for you to compete with men?"

Response: "Because men have the good jobs in this company. When I discover a company where women have most of the good jobs, I'll compete with women."

3. *President to female sales manager:* "Ruth, we need this order. It means a lot to me if you do whatever you have to do to get it. Sleep with your buyer if necessary."

Response: "If it means that much to you, John, I'll do it, but my call girl fee is $150 per hour. I want that added onto my regular commission. Furthermore, if your buyer proves to be a bummer in bed, I want my fee doubled. Is it a deal?" (By taking a derogatory or antagonistic statement at face value and replying to the literal meaning of the statement, you force the executive to think twice about what he just said and withdraw his remark without even asking him to.)

4. *Department chairman to female assistant professor:* "I hear you just had a paper published in the *Harvard Business Review*. That certainly is an accomplishment for a woman with three children."

Response: "Thank you for the compliment. I am beginning to feel as successful as Arthur Goldman, the most published member of the faculty, and a man who has four children." (This is another example of responding seriously to the literal meaning of an antagonistic remark and turning it to your advantage instead of reacting to the psychological meaning that was intended.)

5. *Magazine editor to female journalist in a large publishing house right after a staff meeting:* "I am going to give you a word of advice, Sally. It is not very feminine to challenge a man's ideas."

Response: "I do not feel I was hired to be feminine, but rather to apply my intellectual skills and voice and implement good ideas for the good of the firm. I do not think our publisher would be very happy with me if I always said what he wanted to hear; instead of making valuable suggestions regardless of whether they conflict with his ideas. You obviously do not think very highly of my competence, or you simply feel I am a second-class citizen. In either respect, my feelings are deeply hurt, and you can be pleased if that was your intention." (After describing the factual situation, it is a good idea to express your true feelings the first time an executive makes a sarcastic statement. Many times, the executive does it in expectation of a biting and vicious response that will give him the opportunity to escalate matters or talk about what a shrew you are to other executives. When he encounters a mature response and the shock of realizing feelings have been hurt, the psychological game is prematurely terminated in shame, and chances are that he will have a permanent attitude change.)

6. *Trade association officer to company representatives at a luncheon meeting:* "Boy, if Betty wasn't here, I would tell you a story that would bring down the house."

Response (by Betty): "Tell it, Brian. You don't have to worry about off-color jokes in front of women. Don't you realize that the most recent statistics find that 50 percent of all people engaged in heterosexual acts are women?" (Humor frequently serves to help the executive save face while the woman makes her point.)

POWER DRESSING FOR THE BUSINESS WOMAN

Your clothes send out an endless variety of messages about who you are, what you feel, and what image you are trying to fit. In fact, psychologists and psychiatrists start off their mental examination report with a description of how the patient dresses.

Although the trend is changing, the fashion industry has traditionally given women a much wider choice of styles in clothes than men. In this section, you will learn what fashions to ignore and how to dress for the job you want, not the job you have.

Some women feel they are creating a tough, authoritative image by dressing like a man. The actual effect is more like that of a little boy who dresses up in his father's clothing. He looks cute, not serious. Research indicates that a three-piece pinstripe suit emasculates a woman's authority.

A skirted suit gives you the best image of an upper-middle-class executive. The jacket should be cut full enough to cover the contours of the bust and not be pinched in at the waist to exaggerate your bustline. The jacket should match the skirt, which should fall just below the knee. Minis and midis come and go as fashion dictates, but you must discipline yourself to avoid such severe departures from your conservative business uniform.

A skirt suit of wool material with a country tweed look will give you class and stature. Solid and conservative plaid suits have also tested well. Medium gray and medium blue are the best solid suits that you can wear. Avoid green, pink, pale yellow, gold, bright red, bright orange and exotic shades that will detract from your credibility.

Your blouse should be simple and styled almost like a man's shirt, without the frills, see-through effect, plunging neckline and other features of feminine clothes. Silk, solid-color blouses make the best impression. The blouse collar should be worn inside the blazer to avoid the feminine sporty look.

A white blouse is excellent for an image of authority, for a strong sense of presence and for establishing credibility. A black blouse increases your dominance too much, and it is estimated that you would offend up to

20 percent of the male executive population, especially men over forty-five. A pale yellow blouse with a navy blue suit somewhat weakens your authority but increases your credibility and likability. A maroon blouse gives you a high sense of presence and attention from others. A pale blue blouse with a beige suit will make you appear in a cheery mood and will enhance your likability, but you will not appear as authoritative.

When you wear a vest with your suit, you draw attention to your bust, especially when your jacket is off. The more sexually attractive you are to male executives you deal with and, in particular, the larger your breasts appear to be, the less authoritative, competent, ambitious and intelligent you will appear.

It should be apparent from the above discussion of jackets, blouses and vests that it is inadvisable to go braless. Like it or not, you convey a sexy, permissive, available image and reduce your authority where the clear outline of your breasts and nipples is visible.

All pantyhose other than skin color tests negatively with executives in the business suite. Turning now to zippers, if a zipper can be seen, you are wearing a cheap skirt. It should always be concealed in the seam and, furthermore, should be the same color as the fabric.

The best shoe for the business woman is a dark plain pump with closed toe and heel. Boots and multicolored or brightly colored shoes will hurt your stature. High heels above an inch and one-half tend to give business women a "dumb blond" image and emphasize their sexuality to the detriment of their status in the business suite.

The second-best outfit for the business woman is a dark dress with a solid, plaid or striped pattern, preferably with a matching jacket or blazer. Light-colored dresses, dresses with feminine prints, such as flowers, bird and floral patterns, dresses that cling, shine, make noise when you walk, dresses that have a halter top and dresses made of sporty material, such as denim and corduroy, will make you appear frivolous and ineffective. Likewise, if you put on a sweater instead of a blazer to keep warm at the office, this garment spells nothing but "secretary." Studies have shown that the pantsuit is just as ineffective as a sweater when dealing with men in the business suite. In fact, the findings indicate that the pantsuit even makes you ineffective when dealing with other women.

In addition to wool skirt suits or those that have the look of wool, linen will be quite effective in the North in summer and all year round in the Sun Belt. Memphis is the only city in the United States where the dress tested better for business women than the skirt suit, and Miami is the only city where the short-sleeved dress works as well as the long-sleeved dress.

You should have medium-length hair—not so short that it appears mannish or boyish and not longer than shoulder length because long hair streaming down your back connotes youth and immaturity. Likewise for hair that hangs partially in your face and for hair that is too curly. Although gray hair adds authority to a man, it takes it away from a woman. The simpler and darker your hair, the more power and stature you will appear to have. Tipping, streaking and frosting have all tested as being unauthoritative and perceived as lower class.

For men and women, the hat is a traditional symbol of power, authority and position and can add height and substance to the wearer. The medium brimmed hat and fedora will add to your sense of presence, whereas the cartwheel and turban should only be worn for social occasions, and the pillbox and cloche do not test well at all.

Raincoats that will give you the best look for business and social situations are beige or black, wtih a rich artificial or real fur collar about three inches wide and with the bottom of the raincoat falling about three inches below the knees. The camel-colored wraparound winter coat tested better than any other coat for giving you authority and appeal. The coat with a conspicuous fur collar or one larger than that recommended with raincoats will convey the impression that you are frilly and flighty and definitely not serious as far as business is concerned. Fur coats can produce a negative reaction with many executives who oppose fur on ecological grounds or who will think of you as a dependent weakling who follows fashion and is insecure.

Although black and gray are acceptable, deep brown leather gloves test best for business women.

If you are under forty-five, you will have a more professional appearance and authoritative image with minimal makeup. Do not use lipstick that stands out in any way; do not use eye shadow; do not use eyeliner; avoid long fingernails and false eyelashes; stick to colorless nail polish; take great care with mascara; keep your eyebrow line as natural as possible; and avoid perfume that is not delicate or that a businessman can smell a few feet away. On the other hand, you should darken pale eyebrows if you do not wear glasses because they give your face a washed-out, weak look that lacks authority. Also, a suntan can increase your sense of presence because having a tan seems to be part of the top executive mystique.

Eyeglasses can add weight to a woman's face, resulting in a more authoritative image. The frames should match your hair if you are a brunette or be dark brown if you are a blonde or redhead. Avoid wire rims. Shaded and tinted eyeglasses reduce your credibility and likability.

Leave your handbag home, and carry a thin, executive type wallet in your coat or jacket pocket or in your attache case or slim portfolio.

FEMALE BODY LANGUAGE

Women are more sensitive to nonverbal cues than men. Women also differ in certain significant respects in the meaning of gestures that they make and in gestures themselves. In this section, we will cover only the major differences from the gestures and interpretation of gestures associated with nonverbal communication by businessmen, covered in Chapter 6.

Because of our culture, schooling and parental guidance, girls and women learn submissiveness. One result of this is that women tend to lower or avert their eyes when stared at. Women also tend to close or blink their eyes more slowly than men. A slow blink is feminine and actually flirtatious and provocative to many men. Most women are not even consciously aware of their eye-lowering and slow blinking because it is so natural, something they have been doing all their lives. If you make a conscious effort to look back at the person who is talking to you or even glaring at you, and if you consciously force yourself to blink quicker, you will project a better image with respect to your authority and power.

Women also tend to send submissive signals wtih their mouth. You should not smile when conversing with a male executive unless you are discussing something humorous. As already pointed out in Chapter 6, uncalled-for smiling detracts from your stature and power and conveys the impression that you consider yourself subordinate. You should also avoid the common habit of touching your lips with your tongue because it can be construed as a flirtatious gesture or seen as the act of a cute little girl concerned with frivolous things—a stereotype the male executive remembers from his childhood.

There are many things business women do with their hands that they should not and a few things they avoid that they should adopt. When you slowly and gracefully bring your hand to your throat, as if there were a constriction or you're checking to make sure your necklace is still there, it signals your need for reassurance. It means that you are saying or hearing something that makes you uncomfortable. It is a sign of defensiveness, and it may mean that you are hiding something or not speaking the truth. Another act of reassurance that is more common with women is pinching the fleshy part of the hand. Showing the palm of your hand when making a point, when you are about to shake hands or when you are pushing back the hair from your face or rearranging it above your ears spells femininity, flirtation and submissiveness.

What are some of the things you should be doing with your hands? You should consciously force yourself to learn to use masculine gestures to lend more forcefulness to your proposals and negotiations. Instead of keeping your hands limp at the wrist, consider putting greater movement and power into your hands as you gesture while you talk. Consider clenching a fist and even knocking or tapping it on the table when you make important points. Consider pointing with your finger to emphasize things. Men are not used to seeing women use these gestures and will subconsciously treat what you say with greater importance and view you with more seriousness and respect. On the other hand, there are times when you want to use gestures that suggest friendship, likability and courtship. One example is the woman politician who stretches out her arms and shows the palms of her hands to court her audience in body language.

When a woman is wearing a skirt or dress, how she sits and what she does with her legs can be quite revealing. A woman who sits with her legs stretched out in front of her and not crossed tends to be assured, independent and dominant. She probably heads up or will head up a department or company. The woman who sits with both feet on the floor together is a down-to-earth realist in touch with her surroundings. If she is holding her legs perfectly parallel, she is probably an organizer and "neatnick." A woman who crosses her legs at the knee is probably concentrating on a job to be done or a goal to be accomplished. If she is dangling one shoe from the free leg, she may very well be ambitious and competitive. When a woman takes both feet up off the floor and rests them on something, she is probably comfortable with the person she is with and trusts him or her.

If you sit with your legs positioned as described below, you should make a conscious effort to change your posture. If you have your legs off to one side crossed at the ankle with your knees together, you are assuming a model's stance and conveying femininity, but not authority and power. In general, if a woman keeps her legs crossed at the ankle, it is considered a containing gesture, and it may be thought that she is holding something back—herself, her ideas or the truth. If a woman's feet are both on the floor, crossed at her ankle, she is conveying a good-girl image and probably considers herself subordinate to the person she is talking to. If a woman wraps one leg around the other so that the leg in back is coming to the front, she probably would like to agree with you but finds herself holding back and restrained. If a woman sits on one leg, she probably is a conformist and not a self-starter.

In general, a woman who leans forward on her chair is being friendly or is showing interest. However, if she leans forward in a manner that exposes her breasts, the man she is talking to will either consider this a signal of sexual interest or a pleasant distraction from the point he is trying to make or the lecture he is giving. With either signal, the woman has reduced her authority in his eyes. As already pointed out in Chapter 11, the more a woman is viewed as a sex object, the more diminished her stature and power become. This also applies if a woman draws her legs up to put the heels of her shoes on the chair frame or to rest her legs on another object in front of her and thereby reveals a provocative stretch of thigh. In general, if a woman is leaning backward in her seat, she may be conveying distrust or hostility. As already mentioned in Chapter 6, the sitting posture becomes a clear signal in conjunction with other gestures, such as arms crossed about the chest and a frown.

JOB INTERVIEW STRATEGY FOR THE WOMAN EXECUTIVE

Most principles and tactics covered in Chapter 10 apply to the woman job hunter. However, things such as what she wears and how she copes with sexist thinking and organizational discrimination are addressed in this section.

Because company policies and attitudes toward women executives can make or break a woman's advancement up the organizational ladder, care should be exercised in selecting companies for a job opportunity. Probably the best prospects are those corporations where women have already risen into top management, thereby paving at least part of the way for you to follow in their footsteps. At the same time, you may be able to rely on a senior female executive to serve as your mentor and render a certain amount of protection from bias.

At the interview, you should not hesitate to question the personnel director or supervisor about the problems that can be anticipated as you are promoted into roles of increasing responsibility. If the interviewer is reluctant to talk about the matter, it may be an indication that you are the token female executive or that the interviewer really does not know what to say because the company is completely unprepared for your assault on the executive suite. Certainly, before the end of your final interview, you should establish the highest management level the company feels you will have a reasonable expectation of rising to over the next ten years. This will also give you an indication of how you are perceived and the opportunity and responsibility you will be allowed to have. You should also get a commitment that if you join the company an internal announcement giving your background experience and credentials will be distributed throughout the company with appropriate words of support from top management so that people know you are being hired because of your competence and capabilities and not to satisfy an Equal Employment Opportunity Commission body count.

If your interviewer makes sexist remarks or asks you inappropriate questions because of your sex, it may or may not be representative of company thinking. One thing you can do after receiving the job offer is to write a brief letter to the president of the company or at least the interviewer's boss. You indicate that you would like to accept the job offer, that you feel the company is offering a good opportunity, that you are very impressed with the progress the company has made in recent years and its future potential and that you would like some advice so that you can make an intelligent decision. Then you specifically mention the sexist thinking and statements and questions of the interviewer and ask if this is what you can expect after being hired. If so, you do not feel that the company is for you, and you indicate that it is your hope you will receive a prompt and sincere reply regarding your concerns.

In the meantime, how do you handle yourself on the hot seat in response to the interviewer's questions? Below are some common situations that will start you off on the right track in planning ahead.

1. *Future supervisor:* "You meet all my qualifications for the job. However, I am concerned that you may leave for family reasons after the lengthy training session is over."

Response: "Relax. Both my husband and I want separate careers. I would expect to be out no more than two months or so when having children. In short, I expect to be like the other fifteen million mothers in America who enjoy full-time jobs.

2. *Employment agency representative to woman job hunter:* "Right now, frankly, we do not have any requirements for women executives, but we will definitely phone the moment we do."

Response: "Perhaps I confused you. I am looking for an executive position. I am not concerned whether the openings you have specifically call for a female applicant. These are my qualifications, and I feel you should attempt to match them with the various requirements you now have."

3. *Personnel manager:* "I want you to know that our company has many excellent jobs for women."

Response: "I am pleased to hear that. However, does that mean that there are jobs that are not open to women?"

4. *Company president:* "You realize there will be plenty of weekends here in the office. Will this be a problem with your husband?"

Response: "We have our separate careers, and both of us work hard. I see no problem at all."

Alternate response: "My husband has agreed to allow me to eat, sleep, play and work as I see fit, providing I use mature judgment. Would you like to give him a call to confirm his approval of my weekend working hours?" (Humor here makes the company president realize his overreaching question; he will probably go on to the next matter without further delay.)

5. *Bad news personnel specialist:* "Mrs. Welt, are you still capable of having babies?"

Response: "I appreciate your interest in my reproductive system. I am still capable of having or not having babies. Would you also like to know about my data processing experience?" (Again, humor makes its point with impact, yet without hostility.)

When dressing for the job interview, you want to look as if you were applying for a position one or two steps higher in importance. The best outfit to wear in the North for most of the year is a charcoal gray skirt suit. Switch to a medium gray skirted suit for the Sunbelt and the North during the summer. In all instances wear a white blouse. If you are having more than one interview, save the less important ones for a navy blue skirt suit with a pale blue blouse (white if you are below average in height) and a light gray skirt suit with a dark blue blouse. As already mentioned carry an attache case with you, and leave your handbag home.

Most interviewers and companies are looking for a polished, professional image, yet they do not want a woman to dress like a man. A woman in a pants suit with short hair gives a mannish appearance that is harsh and projects inflexibility. On the other hand, a woman whose hair color, makeup and clothes are too dressy and extreme will not be considered conservative enough. She appears too informal and too sexual and lacks executive stature.

The woman in the skirted suit with a simple hairstyle, minimal makeup and an attractive, feminine look will project a serious, self-assured image because her attire enhances her physical attractiveness and projects her as being serious, committed and career oriented.

A few other points to remember are: do not take your jacket off during the interview; do not wear designer glasses; do not wear a vest; and do not have more than one drink during lunch. Wear plain pumps, not high-heeled shoes; wear neutral-colored pantyhose; carry an executive gold pen; and wear an overcoat that covers your skirt.

Chapter 12
EXAGGERATION, BLUFFING, LYING AND ILLEGAL CONDUCT

NEGOTIATION AND ETHICS

Time magazine recently reported a study by one psychologist which concluded that the average American lies literally 200 times a day. Another study by Cambridge Survey Research concluded that 69 percent of the public believes that the country's leaders consistently lie and that lying is an accepted part of the medical and legal professions.

The University of Michigan survey research center found that trust in the government to do what is right most of the time dropped from 81 percent in 1960 to 76 percent in 1965, 61 percent in 1970 and 38 percent in 1974, this last figure probably reflecting Watergate. Under contract for the Senate committee on government operations, Louis Harris & Associates asked members of the American public if they felt the people running the country didn't really care what happens to them. Americans agreeing rose from 26 percent in 1966 to 63 percent in mid-1974. The proportion of the American adult public that agreed that "most people with power try to take advantage of people like yourself" rose from 33 percent in 1971 to 38 percent in mid-1972 and 60 percent by June, 1974.

Do these statistics sound ridiculous? Let's take one specific business situation as an example: excuses given by companies late in paying their bills and their daily ramifications. Checks are intentionally sent unsigned in order to delay actual payment. Envelopes are intentionally addressed to the wrong creditor in order to evidence the mistake and have a good excuse for delayed payment. Checks are intentionally drawn out to the wrong amount with the hope that they will be returned for correction. Checks are drawn with insufficient funds. The creditor is phoned to demand proof of delivery to the purchasing firm, who falsely states that it has no invoice or record of delivery, thereby requiring a month's delay until the trucking firm digs out a copy of the delivery slip. The vendor is told that the check is in the mail when in fact it has not even been drawn. Upon receiving a visit from the creditor's sales person, you request your secretary to state that you are tied up in an all-afternoon meeting. The creditor is falsely told that other vendors in the industry are offering more lenient payment terms and that he or she should follow suit. Upon receiving a call from the creditor, you tell your secretary to state that you are out of the office. When the creditor's sales person finally gets to see the purchaser's purchasing agent or controller, the controller cheerfully says how delightful it is to see the sales person again, which is a lie because the controller dreads seeing the person who has been expecting payment on the overdue account. In fact, before indicating delight, the controller said "Good afternoon," which in itself is a lie because the controller is actually irritated with the sales person who has been pestering the controller with phone calls. When the sales person asks the controller, "How are you?" the controller automatically says, "Fine, thank you," even though the controller actually had a headache since early morning. After the sales person leaves and the controller's headache has worsened, the secretary comes in and asks if it is all right to leave early for some trivial reason. The controller answers "Yes," even though this is the third time in the past two weeks that the secretary left early and the controller is actually seething inside.

The above examples illustrate the full range of lies, from those that are unconsciously made to be courteous and friendly to those that are planned or intentionally made in order to further the person's negotiating goals. Which of these lies are unethical, are illegal or should be disclosed upon being discovered by someone else in the liar's company?

The basic trade-offs in lying are the negatives on one hand and the positives on the other. Is a criminal act being committed; is a fraud being perpetrated; will the lie be discovered and therefore credibility and trust destroyed? These are the negatives. On the other hand, the positive consequences of lying can be quite an incentive: gaining more favorable terms, closing the deal, avoiding a lawsuit, saving the other person from embarrassment, reducing tax liability and so on. For any particular negotiating circumstance, each negotiator must allow his or her own conscience and ethical principles to play a factor in evaluating the trade-offs.

It is obvious that many business executives, especially the Machiavellians discussed in Chapter 10, will bluff and lie when it is expedient and the consequences are not risky. History and any daily newspaper show that some executives still believe in crime. For instance, dozens of industry leaders broke the law with contributions to Nixon's reelection campaign to assure good treatment from the White House. At the same time, there are many executives who believe in the power of the understatement, discussed in Chapter 5, and will not stoop to exaggeration, bluffing and outright lies.

Some people are strong self-monitors of their body language. They're sensitive to gestures and messages sent out to others, and they can lie rather successfully. Certainly, regardless of your ethics, you do not want to lie if you do not hide it well. The following six statements are a modified excerpt of a lie detector test and will give you an indication of whether you are a strong or weak self-monitor. Rate yourself from 0 to 5, with 0 being *no* and 5 being *yes*. Put down your true feelings, not what you think the ratings should be, because there are no correct answers. An interpretation of your responses follows.

1. I only argue for ideas I believe in.
2. I do not put on airs to impress or entertain people.
3. I do not need advice from friends to choose movies, books or music.
4. I am the person people think I am.
5. At a party, I keep the jokes and stories going.
6. I am not friendly toward people I am with when I dislike them.

If the sum of your ratings is less than five you are probably a skilled liar in body language.

If the sum of your ratings exceeds fifteen, you are in danger of losing credibility and cooperation when you lie because your body language sends out signals the moment you do not believe what you say.

DETECTING DECEIT

Whatever ethical category you fall into, you must always recognize the possibility and perhaps probability that a stranger who is negotiating with you may be lying, bluffing or exaggerating. How do you detect dishonesty, omissions and puffery?

A lie can be detected by observing and evaluating many factors, such as how people speak, the substance of what they are saying, their body language, what they wear, where they stand or sit, and their handwriting. However, as with lie detector tests you must first establish what a person's normal manner of speech, content of conversation, body language, proxemics and handwriting are for questions and issues that you know he or she is telling the truth about. Then, you can calibrate how that person deviates from previous conversation and actions by asking a few loaded questions that you already know the answer to and that are designed to cause anxiety on his or her part and provide the opportunity for bluffing and lying.

When people lie, there are definite changes in the way they talk. Studies show that their speech will generally have a higher fundamental pitch and will sound less fluent because of nervousness. Stuttering, repetition of phrases, the insertion of nonsubstantive phrases, broken phrases and hesitations between phrases are all elements detracting from fluency, whose sudden appearance or increase in intensity indicates the holding back of something or the utterance of a false statement.

The reason fluency declines is that the person's ego must inhibit the truthful or revealing communication while simultaneously maintaining a smooth flow of conversation, pretending that nothing is being concealed or edited. Quite often, the concealment will involve the substitution of the truthful or undesirable message with one or more false and/or innocuous messages. There are actually three reasons why a person's voice pitch and fluency change. First, the most obvious, as already mentioned above, is that a person's ego finds it difficult to monitor voice and fluency while simultaneously trying to fill in the conversational gaps left by omitted information that is being substituted by false, misleading and incidental statements. Second, the person may actually wish to be caught or not succeed in the decpetion because of his or her conscience. Third, the person does not want to be caught, but guilt, shame and/or anxiety about lying or being discovered compound problems of concealment and substitution.

Other voice characteristics of lying are a change in the person's voice volume, the length of his or her answer, the time it takes to respond to your last question and the rate at which the person is talking. If there is a sudden change in any of these characteristics, be suspicious. Studies show that people who are preoccupied with lying generally speak less and say things more slowly, in addition to pausing longer for concealment and substitution before answering a question.

Although we cannot detect microtremors, indicative of stress due to lying, with the human ear, a sophisticated electronic instrument called the voice stress analyzer does just that with accuracy that rivals polygraph instruments. See Chapter 9 for a more detailed discussion.

Clearly, the substance of what the liar says to you should be compared with prior answers for consistency and your common-sense expectations as to what his or her answer will truthfully be. The content of what the person says should also have a certain degree of specificity and detail to take the communication out of the realm of fiction.

There are certain nonsubstantive statements that are defensively made just prior to a concealment or lie for the express purpose of throwing the other party off track and reassuring the party of the liar's honesty. Be suspicious of any person who starts off a response or proposal with any of the following or similar phrases: "Believe me," "I'm not kidding," "I have to tell you," "I wouldn't lie to you," "Incidentally," "Before I forget," "Honestly," "Sincerely," "Frankly," "To tell you the truth," "You are not going to believe this," "I'll try" and "We'll make every effort." Studies show that communications leading off with these reassurances are very likely to be dishonest or misleading in some manner because of the person's defensive need to do everything possible to hide the lie or concealment.

A person's ego will show discomfort, anxiety, difficulty in lying convincingly and/or subconscious desire to be caught or unsuccessful by means of various body changes and movements, some of which can be controlled and others that cannot. For instance, accomplished liars may be able to fully control their facial gestures and voice, but there is little they can do to prevent perspiration and dilation and contraction of their pupils unless they wear tinted glasses and gloves or keep their hands in their pockets or behind the desk—or are far enough away to avoid detection.

In Chapter 6, the various facial and body indicators of great anxiety and probable deceit are discussed, as well as the fact that because the head and face can be more easily controlled nonverbal leakage of lying more often occurs in other body movements, especially the hands. A brief summary of key facial indicators of lying are the various ways of avoiding eye contact, increased blinking, sudden pupil contraction, coughing, nose blowing, a deliberate blank look, keeping the head rigid, smiling more than usual and any other exaggerated gesture are some of the important facial characteristics of deceit. Remember, true feelings register most clearly on the left side of a person's face.

Other body language indicating deceit, as discussed in Chapter 6, includes: assuming a rigid posture that lacks relaxed movement; stroking the nose with a finger; putting a hand across one's mouth; touching the face or back of one's neck with the palm of the hand facing the other person; running the hand through one's hair; scratching, smoothing, stroking or clutching a part of one's body with one's fingers; clenching one's hands; finger tapping; rubbing one's thumbs together; picking at one's cuticles; wringing one's hands; tightly squeezing a pen, cigarette, cigar, or arm rest; foot tucking; foot tapping; engaging in abortive flight movements with one's legs; and ankle crossing.

As pointed out in Chapter 6, one's signature or key statement serves as a clear indicator of deceit if it varies in aspects such as slant, indentation, size and configuration from most of the letter. Deceit is also indicated by reversals of letter direction and gaps in some of the vowels.

What should you do when you detect one or more signs of possible deceit? Do you bow out of the deal, raise your demands to make the risk worthwhile or fight it with your own deceit? One effective tactic is to simply ask; "Are you sure?" or, "Do you really mean that?" The person who is lying or concealing something quite often will become very defensive, in which case you will know that this person doubts what he or she is saying, lacks confidence in his or her beliefs or has lied outright. Sometimes the person will be relieved to confirm your own apprehension with a face-saving remark like, "Now that you mention it, I guess I'm really not sure," or, "Maybe you are right about questioning this."

BIBLIOGRAPHY

CHAPTER 1

ANDREE, R.G. *The Art of Negotiation*. Lexington, Massachusetts: Heath Lexington Books, 1971.

CARNEGIE, D. *Public Speaking and Influencing Men in Business*. New York: Association Press, 1959.

DRUCKMAN, D. (Ed.) *Negotiations: Social-Psychological Perspectives*. Beverly Hills, California: Sage, 1977.

GIBLIN, L. *How to Have Confidence and Power in Dealing With People*. Englewood Cliffs, New Jersey: Prentice-Hall, 1956.

ILICH, J. *The Art and Skill of Successful Negotiation*. Englewood Cliffs, New Jersey: Prentice-Hall, 1973.

LINKLETTER, A.G. *How to Be A . . . Super Salesman*. Englewood Cliffs, New Jersey: Prentice-Hall, 1974.

———. *Yes, You Can*. New York: Simon & Schuster, 1979.

MURIEL, J.A. *Born to Win*. Reading, Massachusetts: Addison-Wesley, 1971.

NIERENBERG, G.I. *The Art of Negotiation*. New York: Hawthorn Books, 1968.

PENNEY, J.C. *What an Executive Should Know About Himself*. Chicago: Dartnell Press, 1971.

RAPAPORT, A. *Two Person Game Theory*. University of Michigan Press, 1966.

RUBIN, J.Z. and BROWN, B.R. *The Social Psychology of Bargaining and Negotiating*. New York: Academic Press, 1975.

SPERBER, P. *Negotiating in Day-to-Day Business*. New York: American Negotiating Institute, 1976.

SPERBER, P. *The Science of Business Negotiation*. New York: Pilot Books, 1979.

ZARTMAN, I.W. (Ed.). *The Negotiation Process: Theories and Applications*. Beverly Hills, California: Sage, 1978.

CHAPTER 2

ANDREE, R. G. *The Art of Negotiation*. Lexington, Massachusetts: Heath Lexington Books, 1971.

BEARDSLEY, M. C. *Thinking Straight*. Englewood Cliffs, New Jersey: Prentice-Hall, 1966

COOPER, J.D. *The Art of Decision-Making*. Garden City, New York: Doubleday, 1961.

DRUCKER, P.F. *Management*. New York: Harper and Row, 1974.

DUBRIN, A.J. *Survival in the Office*. New York: Mason/Charter, 1977.

HODNETT, E. *The Art of Problem Solving*. New York: Harper & Row, 1955.

KARRASS, C.L. *Give and Take*. New York: Thomas Y. Crowell, 1974.

LINKLETTER, A.G. *Yes, You Can!* New York: Simon and Schuster, 1979.

MACCOBY, M. *The Games-Man*. New York: Simon and Schuster, 1976.

NIERENBERG, G.I. *The Art of Negotiation*. New York: Hawthorn Books, 1968.

PENNEY, J.C. *What an Executive Should Know About Himself*. Chicago: Dartnell Press, 1971.

RUBIN, J.Z. and BROWN, B.R. *The Social Psychology of Bargaining and Negotiation*. New York: Academic Press, 1975.

SPERBER, P. *Intellectual Property Management: Law-Business-Strategy*. New York: Clark Boardman, 1974.

————. *Negotiating in Day-to-Day Business*. New York: American Negotiating Institute, 1976.

————. "Liability-Proofing Your Client's Products" in Poust, J.G., and Ross, K. (Eds.), *Products Liability of Manufacturers: Prevention and Defense*. New York: Practicing Law Institute, 1977.

————. *The Science of Business Negotiation*. New York: Pilot Books, 1979.

————. *Corporation Law Department Manual*. Chicago: American Bar Association, 1980.

CHAPTER 3

ANDREE, R.G. *The Art of Negotiation*. Lexington, Massachusetts: Heath Lexington Books, 1971. ·

BARTEL, P.C. *Biorhythm*. New York: Franklin Watts, 1978.

HENLEY, N.M. *Body Politics: Power, Sex, and Nonverbal Communication*. Englewood Cliffs, Prentice-Hall, 1977.

ILICH, J. *The Art and Skill of Successful Negotiation*. Englewood Cliffs, New Jersey: Prentice-Hall, 1973.

KARRASS, C.L. *Give and Take*. New York: Thomas Y. Crowell, 1974.

————. *The Negotiating Game*. New York: World, 1970.

KISSINGER, H.A. *White House Years*. Boston: Little, Brown, 1979.

KORDA, M. *Power! How to Get It, How to Use It*. New York: Random House, 1975.

KOSMOS INTERNATIONAL, INC. *Biorhythm Computer Owner's Manual*. Fort Worth, Texas: Radio Shack, 1979.

LEVIN, E. *Levin's Laws*. New York: World, 1970.

LINKLETTER, A.G. *Yes, You Can*. New York: Simon and Schuster, 1979.

NIERENBERG, G.I. *The Art of Negotiation*. New York: Hawthorn Books, 1968.

PROSHANSKY, H.M. et al, (Ed.) *Environmental Psychology: Man and His Physical Setting*. New York: Holt, 1970.

SHOOK, R.L. *Winning Images*. New York: MacMillan, 1977.

SPERBER, P. (Ed.) *Corporate Law Department Manual*. Chicago: American Bar Association, 1977.

————. *Intellectual Property Management: Law-Business-Strategy*. New York: Clark Boardman, 1974.

————. *Negotiating in Day-to-Day Business*. New York: American Negotiating Institute, 1976.

————. *The Science of Business Negotiation*. New York: Pilot Books, 1979.

CHAPTER 4

ANDREE, R.G. *The Art of Negotiation*. Lexington, Massachusetts: Heath Lexington Books, 1971.

BELL, R.I. *Having It Your Way*. New York: Norton, 1977.

BERD, R.E. *A Guide to Personal Risk Taking*. New York: AMACOM, 1974.

DRUCKMAN, D. *Negotiation, Social-Psychological Prospective*. Beverly Hills, California: Sage, 1977.

FAST, J. *Creative Coping*. New York: William Morrow, 1976.

GREENBURGER, F. *How to Ask for More and Get It*. New York: Doubleday, 1978.

GOFFMAN, E. *The Presentation of Self in Everyday Life*. New York: Doubleday, 1959.

ILLICH, J. *The Art and Skill of Successful Negotiation*. Englewood Cliffs, New Jersey: Prentice-Hall, 1973.

KARRASS, C.L. *The Negotiating Game*. New York: World, 1970.

————. *Give and Take*. New York: Thomas Y. Crowell, 1974.

KENT, G. *The Effects of Threats*. Columbus, Ohio: Ohio State University Press, 1967.

KISSINGER, H.A. *The Necessity for Choice*. New York: Harper & Brothers, 1961.

————. *White House Years*. Boston: Little, Brown, 1979.

KOEHLER, J.W. *The Corporation Game*. New York: MacMillan Publishing, 1976.

KOGAN, N. *Risk Taking: A Study in Cognition and Personality*. New York: Holt, 1964.

LECKER, S. *The Money Personality*. New York: Simon and Schuster, 1979.

LEVIN, E. *Levin's Laws*. New York: M. Evans, 1980.

LINKLETTER, A.G. *Yes, You Can!* New York: Simon and Schuster, 1979.

————. *How To Be A Super Salesman*. Englewood Cliffs, New Jersey: Prentice-Hall, 1974.

MACCOBY, M. *The Games-Man*. New York: Simon and Schuster, 1976.

MURIEL, J.A. *Born to Win*. Reading, Massachusetts: Addison-Wesley, 1971.

NIERENBERG, G.I. *Creative Business Negotiating*. New York: Hawthorn Books, 1971.

————. *The Art of Negotiation*. New York: Hawthorn Books, 1968.

PEALE, N.V. *The Power of Positive Thinking*. New York: Prentice-Hall, 1952.

RINGER, R.J. *Winning Through Intimidation*. New York: Funk & Wagnalls, 1974.

RUBIN, J.Z. and BROWN, B.R. *The Social Psychology of Bargaining and Negotiation.* New York: Academic Press, 1975.

SPERBER, P. (Ed.) *Corporate Law Department Manual.* Chicago: American Bar Association, 1977.

———. *Intellectual Property Management: Law-Business-Strategy.* New York: Clark Boardman, 1974.

———. *Negotiating in Day-to-Day Business.* New York: American Negotiating Institute, 1976.

———. *The Science of Business Negotiation.* New York: Pilot Books, 1979.

TOFFLER, A. *The Eco-Spasm Report.* New York: Bantam Books, 1975.

———. *Future Shock.* New York: Random House, 1970.

———. *The Third Wave.* New York: William Morrow, 1980.

CHAPTER 5

ALBANO, C. *Transactional Analysis on the Job.* New York: AMACOM, 1974.

AMERICAN ENTREPRENEURS' ASSOCIATION. *Negotiating Techniques.* Los Angeles, California: Chase Revel, 1978.

ANDREE, R.G. *The Art of Negotiation.* Lexington, Massachusetts: Heath Lexington Books, 1971.

BLUMENTHAL, H. *Promoting Your Cause.* New York: Funk & Wagnalls, 1974.

BOWER, S.A. and BOWER, G.H. *Asserting Yourself.* Reading, Massachusetts: Addison Wesley, 1976.

CARNEGIE, D. *How to Win Friends and Influence People.* New York: Pocket Books, 1963.

———. *Public Speaking and Influencing Men in Business.* New York: Associate Press, 1959.

CHESKIN, L. *Secrets of Marketing Success.* New York: Wiley, 1967.

———. *Why People Buy: Motivation Research and Its Successful Application.* New York: Liveright, 1959.

COLE, R.W. *Current Issues in Linguistic Theory.* Bloomington, Indiana: Indiana University Press, 1977.

DUNLOP, J.T. and CHAMBERLAIN, N.W. (Ed.) *Frontiers of Collective Bargaining.* New York: Harper and Row, 1967.

DRUCKMAN, D. (Ed.) *Negotiations: Social-Psychologican Perspectives.* Beverly Hills, California: Sage, 1977.

FAST, J. and FAST, B. *Talking Between the Lines.* New York: Viking Press, 1979.

FAST, J. *Weather Language.* New York: Wyden Books, 1979.

GALBRAITH, J.K. *The Affluent Society.* Boston: Houghton Mifflin, 1969.

GIBLIN, L. *How to Have Confidence and Power in Dealing with People.* Englewood Cliffs, New Jersey: Prentice-Hall, 1956.

HALBERSTRAM, D. *The Best and the Brightest.* New York: Random House, 1972.

HALL, E.T. *The Hidden Dimension.* New York: Doubleday, 1966.

IKLE, F.C. *How Nations Negotiate.* New York: Harper & Row, 1964.

ILLICH, J. *The Art and Skill of Successful Negotiation.* Englewood Cliffs, New Jersey: Prentice-Hall, 1973.

KARRASS, C.L. *Give & Take*. New York: Thomas Y. Crowell, 1974.

KORDA, M. *Power! How to Get It, How to Use It*. New York: Random House, 1975.

LINKLETTER, A.G. *Yes, You Can!* New York: Simon and Schuster, 1979.

———. *How To Be A Super Salesman*. Englewood Cliffs, New Jersey: Prentice-Hall, 1974.

———. *Public Speaking For Private People*. Indianapolis, Indiana: Bobbs-Merrill, 1980.

NIERENBERG, G.I. and CALERO, H.H. *Meta-Talk*. New York: Trident Press, 1976.

———. *The Art of Negotiation*. New York: Hawthorn Books, 1968.

PACKARD, V. *The Hidden Persuaders*. New York: Pocketbooks, 1963.

PENNEY, J.C. *What an Executive Should Know About Himself*. Chicago: Dartnell Press, 1971.

RUBIN, J.Z. and BROWN, B.R. *The Social Psychology of Bargaining and Negotiation*. New York: Academic Press, 1975.

RYCKMAN, W.G. *What Do You Mean By That?* New York: Dow Jones-Irwin, 1980.

SHOOK, R.L. *Winning Images*. New York: MacMillan, 1977.

SMALTZ, P.R. *Salesmanship*. Paterson, New Jersey: Littlefield, Adams & Co., 1960.

SPERBER, P. *Intellectual Property Management: Law-Business-Strategy*. New York: Clark Boardman, 1974.

———. *Negotiating in Day-to-Day Business*. New York: American Negotiating Institute, 1976.

———. *The Science of Business Negotiation*. New York: Pilot Books, 1979.

STARR, D.P. *How to Handle Speechwriting Assignments*. New York: Pilot Books, 1978.

TAYLOR, V.L. *The Art of Argument*. Metuchen, New Jersey: Scarecrow Press, 1971.

VAN DERSAL, W.R. *The Successful Supervisor*. New York: Harper & Row, 1974.

VAN FLEET, J.K. *Power With People*. West Nyack, New York: Parker Publishing, 1972.

WHEELER, E. *How to Sell Yourself to Others*. New York: Dell, 1962.

ZARTMAN, I.W. (Ed.) *The Negotiation Process: Theories and Applications*. Beverly Hills, California: Sage, 1978.

CHAPTER 6

BALLOU, R.O. (Ed.) *The World Bible*. New York: Viking Press, 1964.

BERRY, L.B. (Ed.) *Biblical Quotations*. Garden City, New York: Doubleday & Co., 1968.

BIRDWHISTLE, R.L. *Kinesics & Context*. Philadelphia: University of Pennsylvania Press, 1970.

BLOOMENTHAL, H. *Promoting Your Cause*. New York: Funk & Wagnalls, 1974.

BOWER, S.A. and BOWER, G.H. *Asserting Yourself*. Reading, Massachusetts: Addison-Wesley, 1976.

CARNEGIE, D. *Public Speaking and Influencing Men in Business*. New York: Association Press, 1959.

———. *How to Win Friends and Influence People*. New York: Pocket Books, 1963.

CERF, B. *The Laugh's on Me*. Garden City, New York: Doubleday & Co., 1959.

CHESKIN, L. *Secrets of Marketing Success*. New York: Wiley, 1967.

———. *Why People Buy: Motivation Research and its Succesful Application.* New York: Liveright, 1959.

———. *Color Guide for Marketing Media.* New York: MacMillan, 1954.

———. *Business Without Gambling.* Chicago: Quadrangle Books, 1963.

DANNER, J. *People-Empathy.* West Nyack, New York: Parker Publishing, 1976.

EISENBERG, H. and EISENBERG, L. *The Public Speaker's Handbook of Humor.* New York: Association Press, 1967.

DAVIS, F. *Inside Intuition.* New York: McGraw-Hill, 1973.

FAST, J. *Body Language.* New York: M. Evans & Co., 1970.

———. *The Body Language of Sex, Power and Aggression.* New York: M. Evans & Co., 1977.

GOFFMAN, E. *The Presentation of Self in Everyday Life.* Garden City, New York: Doubleday Anchor, 1959.

HALL, E.T. *The Hidden Dimension.* New York: Doubleday, 1966.

———. *The Silent Language.* Garden City, New York: Doubleday, 1959.

HANAN, M. et al. *Sales Negotiation Strategies.* New York: AMACOM, 1977.

HENLEY, N.M. *Body Politics.* Englewood Cliffs, New Jersey: Prentice-Hall, 1977.

HENRY, L.C. *Five Thousand Quotations for All Occasions.* Garden City, New York: Doubleday, 1945.

HINDE, R.A. (Ed.) *Nonverbal Communication.* Cambridge, Massachusetts: Cambridge University Press, 1972.

HOMANS, G.C. *Social Behavior: Its Elementary Forms.* New York: Harcourt Brace Jovanovich, 1974.

KARRASS, C.L. *Give & Take.* New York: Thomas Y. Crowell, 1974.

KORDA, M. *Power! How to Get It, How to Use It.* New York: Random House, 1975.

LAIRD, D.A. and LAIRD, E.C. *Practical Sales Psychology.* New York: McGraw-Hill, 1952.

LINKLETTER, A.G. *Yes, You Can!.* New York: Simon and Schuster, 1979.

———. *How To Be A Super Salesman.* Englewood Cliffs, New Jersey: Prentice-Hall, 1974.

———. *Public Speaking For Private People.* Indianapolis, Indiana: Bobbs-Merrill, 1980.

LOWEN, A. *The Betrayal of the Body.* London: Collier Books, 1967.

MARTIN, D. *The Executive's Guide to Handling a Press Interview.* New York: Pilot Books, 1977.

MOLLOY, J.T. *Dress For Success.* New York: Wyden, 1975.

NIERENBERG, G.I. and CALERO, H.H. *How to Read a Person Like a Book.* New York: Pocket Books, 1975.

PENNEY, J.C. *What an Executive Should Know About Himself.* Chicago: Dartnell Press, 1971.

POLING, D.A. (Ed.) *Courage and Confidence From the Bible.* New York: Signet, 1951.

PACKARD, V. *The Hidden Persuaders.* New York: Pocket Books, 1963.

RICHARDSON, E.L. *The Creative Balance.* New York: Holt, Rinehart and Winston, 1976.

SCHUTZ, W. C. *Joy.* New York: Grove Press, 1967.

SEIGMAN, A. and POPE, B. (Eds.) *Studies in Dyadic Interaction: A Research Conference.* New York: Pergamon, 1970.

SMALTZ, P.R. *Salesmanship.* Paterson, New Jersey: Littlefield, Adams, 1960.

SOLOMON, S. *How to Really Know Yourself Through Your Handwriting.* New York: Taplinger, 1973.

SPERBER, P. *Intellectual Property Management: Law-Business-Strategy.* New York: Clark Boardman, 1974.

———. *Negotiating in Day-to-Day Business.* New York: American Negotiating Institute, 1976.

———. *The Science of Business Negotiation.* New York: Pilot Books, 1979.

TRIPP, R.T. (Ed.) *The International Thesaurus of Quotations.* New York: Thomas Y. Crowell, 1970.

VANDERBILT, A. *The Amy Vanderbilt Complete Book of Etiquette.* New York: Doubleday & Co., 1978.

VAN DERSAL, W.R. *The Successful Supervisor.* New York: Harper & Row, 1974.

WEITZ, S. *Nonverbal Communication.* New York: Oxford University Press, 1974.

WHEELER, E. *How to Sell Yourself to Others.* New York: Dell, 1962.

WHITE, R.M. *The Entrepreneur's Manual.* Radnor, Pennsylvania: Chilton, 1977.

CHAPTER 7

ALBANO, C. *Transactional Analysis on the Job.* New York: AMACOM, 1974.

ANDREE, R.G. *The Art of Negotiation.* Lexington, Massachusetts: Heath Lexington Books, 1971.

BERNE, E. *Games People Play.* New York: Grove Press, 1964.

———. *Beyond Games and Scripts.* New York: Grove Press, 1976.

BOWER, S.A. *Asserting Yourself.* Reading, Massachusetts: Addison Wesley, 1976.

BURID, R.E. *A Guide to Personal Risk Taking.* New York: AMACOM, 1974.

CARNEGIE, D. *How to Win Friends and Influence People.* New York: Pocket Books, 1963.

CHESKIN, L. *Secrets of Marketing Success.* New York: Wiley, 1967.

———. *Why People Buy: Motivation Research and Its Successful Application.* New York: Liverright, 1959.

DANNER, J. *People–Empathy: Key to Painless Supervision.* West Nyack, New York: Parker, 1976.

GALBRAITH, J.K. *The Age of Uncertainty.* Boston: Houghton Mifflin, 1977.

———. *The Affluent Society.* Boston: Houghton Mifflin, 1969.

———. *Economics, Peace and Laughter.* Boston: Houghton Mifflin, 1971.

———. *The New Industrial State.* Boston: Houghton Mifflin, 1977.

GIBLIN, L. *How to Have Confidence and Power in Dealing With People.* Englewood Cliffs: Prentice-Hall, 1973.

HEIDER, F. *The Psychology of Interpersonal Relations.* New York: Wiley, 1958.

ILICH, J. *The Art and Skill of Successful Negotiation.* Englewood Cliffs, New Jersey: Prentice-Hall, 1973.

JAMES, M. *The OK Boss.* Reading, Massachusetts: Addison Wesley, 1975.

JUNG, C.G. *The Undiscovered Self.* New York: Mentor, 1958.

KARRASS, C.L. *Give & Take.* New York, Thomas Y. Crowell, 1974.

KISSINGER, H.A. *White House Years.* Boston: Little, Brown, 1979.

LAIRD, D.A. and LAIRD, E.C. *Practical Sales Psychology.* New York: McGraw-Hill, 1952.

LINKLETTER, A.G. *How to Be A Super Salesman.* Englewood Cliffs, New Jersey: Prentice-Hall, 1974.

————. *Public Speaking For Private People.* Indianapolis, Indiana: Bobbs-Merrill, 1980.

————. *Yes, You Can!* New York: Simon and Schuster, 1972.

MAMIS, J.G. and CLARK, S.I. *Man and Society.* New York: Macmillan, 1963.

MEININGER, J. *Success Through Transactional Analysis.* New York: Grosset & Dunlap, 1973.

NIERENBERG, G.I. *Creative Business Negotiating.* New York: Hawthorne Books, 1971.

NIERENBERG, G.I. *The Art of Negotiating.* New York: Hawthorne Books, 1968.

PACKARD, V. *The Hidden Persuaders.* New York: Pocketbooks, 1963.

REVEL, C. *Negotiating Techniques.* Los Angeles, California: International Entrepreneurs Association, 1978.

RINGER, R.J. *Winning Through Intimidation.* New York: Funk & Wagnalls, 1974.

RUBIN, J.Z. and BROWN, B.R. *The Social Psychology of Bargaining and Negotiation.* New York: Academic Press, 1975.

SHOOK, R.L. *Winning Images.* New York: Macmillan, 1977.

SMALTZ, P.R. *Salesmanship.* Paterson, New Jersey: Littlefield, Adams & Co., 1960.

SPERBER, P. (Ed.) *Corporate Law Department Manual.* Chicago: American Bar Association, 1977.

————. *Negotiating in Day-to Day Business.* New York: American Negotiating Institute, 1976.

————. *The Science of Business Negotiation.* New York: Pilot Books, 1979.

————. *Intellectual Property Management: Law-Business-Strategy.* New York: Clark Boardman, 1974.

STARR, D.P. *How to Handle Speechwriting Assignments.* New York: Pilot Books, 1978.

STEINER, C. *Scripts People Live.* New York: Grove Press, 1974.

STODDARD, E. *How to Remember Names and Faces.* New York: Doubleday, 1958.

STRAUSS, G. and SAYLES, L.R. *Personnel.* Cambridge, Massachusetts: Houghton Mifflin, 1959.

VAN FLEET, J.K. *Power With People.* West Nyack, New York: Parker Publishing, 1972.

WHEELER, E. *How to Sell Yourself to Others.* New York: Dell, 1962.

ZUMIN, L. *Contact: The First Four Minutes.* New York: Ballantine, 1973.

CHAPTER 8

ANDREE, R.G. *The Art of Negotiation.* Lexington, Massachusetts: Heath Lexington Books 1971.

BELL, R.I. *Having It Your Way.* New York: Norton, 1977.

BOWER, S.A. and BOWER, G.H. *Asserting Yourself.* Reading, Mass: Addison-Wesley, 1976.

BLOOMENTHAL, H. *Promoting Your Cause.* New York: Funk & Wagnalls, 1974.

COFFIN, R.A. *The Negotiator.* New York: AMACOM, 1973.

COHEN, H. *You Can Negotiate Anything*. Secaucus, New Jersey: Lyle Stuart, Inc., 1980.

DRUCKMAN, D. *Negotiations: Social-Psychological Perspectives*. Beverly Hills, California: Sage, 1977.

GREENBERGER, F. *How to Ask for More and Get It*. New York: Doubleday, 1978.

ILICH, J. *The Art and Skill of Successful Negotiation*. Englewood Cliffs, New Jersey: Prentice-Hall, Inc., 1973.

KARRASS, C.L. *The Negotiating Game*. New York: World, 1970.

———. *Give & Take*. New York: Thomas Y. Crowell, 1974.

KISSINGER, H.A. *White House Years*. Boston: Little, Brown, 1979.

KORDA, M. *Power! How to Get It, How to Use It*. New York: Random House, 1975.

LEVIN, E. *Levin's Laws*. New York: M. Evans, 1980.

LINKLETTER, A.G. *How To Be A Super Salesman*. Englewood Cliffs, New Jersey: Prentice-Hall, 1974.

NIERENBERG, G.I. *The Art of Negotiation*. New York: Hawthorne Books, 1968.

———. *Creative Business Negotiating*. New York: Hawthorn Books, 1971.

REVEL, C. *Negotiating Techniques*. Los Angeles, California: American Entrepreneurs' Association, 1978.

RUBIN, J.Z. and BROWN, B.R. *The Social Psychology of Bargaining and Negotiation*. New York: Academic Press, 1975.

SPERBER, P. *Intellectual Property Management: Law-Business-Strategy*. New York: Clark Boardman, 1974.

———. *Negotiating in Day-to-Day Business*. New York: American Negotiating Institute, 1976.

———. *Science of Business Negotiation*. New York: Pilot Books, 1979.

———. (Ed.) *Corporate Law Department Manual*. Chicago: American Bar Association, 1980.

WHITE, R.M. *The Entrepreneur's Manual*. Radnor, Pennsylvania: Chilton Book Co., 1977.

ZARTMAN, I.W. (Ed.) *The Negotiation Process: Theories and Applications*. Beverly Hills, California: Sage, 1978.

CHAPTER 9

ALBANO, C. *Transactional Analysis on the Job*. New York: AMACOM, 1974.

BLAKE, R.R. and MOUTON, J.S. *The Managerial Grid*. Houston, Texas: Gulf Publishing, 1974.

BROTHERS, J. *How to Get What You Want Out of Life*. New York: Simon & Schuster, 1978.

CARNEGIE, D. *Managing Through People*. New York: Simon & Schuster, 1978.

DRUCKER, P.F. *Management*. New York: Harper & Row, 1974.

———. *The Practice of Management*. New York: Harper & Row, 1954.

———. *The Effective Executive*. New York: Harper & Row, 1967.

———. *The Age of Discontinuity*. New York: Harper & Row, 1969.

DUBRIN, A.J. *Survival in the Office*. New York: Mason/Charter, 1977.

FURST, C. *The Strategy of Change for Business Success*. New York: Potter Crown, 1969.

GALBRAITH, J.K. *The New Industrial State*. Boston: Houghton Mifflin, 1977.

HALDANE, B. *How to Make a Habit of Success*. Washington, D.C.: Acropolis Books, 1968.

HERZBERG, F. et al. *The Motivation to Work*. New York: Wiley, 1959.

JAMES, M. *The OK Boss*. Reading, Massachusetts: Addison-Wesley, 1975.

LECKER, S. *The Money Personality*. New York: Simon & Schuster, 1979.

McGREGOR, D. *The Human Side of Enterprise*. New York: McGraw-Hill, 1960.

MACHIAVELLI, N. *The Prince*. Italy (16th Century).

MEININGER, J. *Success Through Transactional Analysis*. New York: Grossett & Dunlap, 1973.

NICKERSON, W. *How I Turned $1,000 Into a Million*. New York: Pocket Books, 1962.

PEARSE, R.F. *Manager to Manager*. New York: AMACOM, 1974.

PICKLE, H.B. *Personality and Success: Business Managers*. Washington, D.C.: Small Business Administration, 1964.

QUICK, T.L. *Person to Person Managing*. New York: St. Martin's Press, 1977.

RICHARDSON, E.L. *The Creative Balance*. New York: Holt, Rinehart and Winston, 1976.

SCHAFER, R.C. *How Millionaires Made Their Fortunes*. New York: Pyramid Books, 1970.

SMALL BUSINESS ADMINISTRATION. *Personality and Success*. Washington, D.C.: Government Printing Office, 1964.

SPERBER, P. (Ed.) *Corporate Law Department Manual*. Chicago: American Bar Association, 1980.

————. *Intellectual Property Management: Law-Business-Strategy*. New York: Clark Boardman, 1974.

————. *Negotiating in Day to Day Business*. New York: American Negotiating Institute, 1976.

————. *The Science of Business Negotiation*. New York: Pilot Books, 1979.

STRAUSS, G. and SAYLES, L.R. *Personnel*. Cambridge, Massachusetts: Houghton Mifflin, 1959.

VAN DERSAL, W.R. *The Successful Supervisor*. New York: Harper & Row, 1974.

WEISSELBERG, R.C. and COWLEY, J.M. *The Executive Strategist*. New York: McGraw-Hill, 1969.

WEXLEY, K.N. and YUKL, G.A. *Organizational Behavior and Industrial Psychology*. New York: Oxford University Press, 1975.

CHAPTER 10

ALBANO, C. *Transactional Analysis on the Job*. New York: AMACOM, 1974.

BOWER, S.A. and BOWER, G.H. *Asserting Yourself*. Reading, Massachusetts: Addison-Wesley, 1976.

BRESLIN, J. *How the Good Guys Finally Won*. New York: Viking Press, 1975.

BURGER, C. *Survival in the Executive Jungle*. New York: MacMillan, 1964.

BYRD, R.E. *A Guide to Personal Risk Taking*. New York: AMACOM, 1974.

DuBRIN, A.J. *Winning at Office Politics*. New York: Van Nostrand Reinhold, 1978.

GETTY, J. P. *How to be a Successful Executive*. Chicago: Playboy Press, 1971.

HALDANE, B. *Career Dynamics*. New York: Bernard Haldane Associates, 1976.

————. *How to Make a Habit of Success*. Washington, D.C.: Acropolis Books, 1964.

JAMERSON, R. *The Professional Job Changing System*. Verona, New Jersey: Performance Dynamics, 1976.

JAMES, M. *The OK Boss*. Reading, Massachusetts: Addison Wesley, 1975.

KOEHLER, J.W. *The Corporation Game*. New York: MacMillan Publishing, 1977.

LINKLETTER, A.G. *How to be a Super Salesman*. Englewood Cliffs, New Jersey: Prentice-Hall, 1974.

————. *Yes, You Can!* New York: Simon and Schuster, 1979.

MACCOBY, M. *The Games-Man*. New York: Simon and Schuster, 1976.

MEININGER, J. *Success Through Transactional Analysis*. New York: Grosset & Dunlap, 1973.

QUICK, T.L. *Person to Person Managing*. New York: St. Martin's Press, 1977.

RICHARDSON, E.L. *The Creative Balance*. New York: Holt, Rinehart and Winston, 1976.

RICHMAN, E. and BRARA, A. *Practical Guide to Managing People*. West Nyack, New York: Parker Publishing, 1975.

ROBERTSON, J. *How to Win in Job Interviews*. Englewood Cliffs, New Jersey: Prentice-Hall, 1978.

SPERBER, P. *The Science of Business Negotiation*. New York: Pilot Books, 1979.

STEINER, C. *Scripts People Live*. New York: Grove Press, 1974.

TARRANT, J. J. *How to Negotiate a Raise*. New York: Van Nostrand Reinhold, 1976.

WEISSELBERG, R. C. and COWLEY, J.M. *The Executive Strategist*. New York: McGraw-Hill, 1969.

CHAPTER 11

DuBRIN, A.J. *Survival in the Office*. New York: Mason/Charter, 1977.

FAST, J. *The Body Language of Sex, Power and Aggression*. New York: M. Evans & Co., 1977.

HENLEY, N.M. *Body Politics*. Englewood Cliffs: Prentice-Hall, 1977.

JOSEFOWITZ, N. *Paths to Power*. Reading, Massachusetts: Addison-Wesley, 1980.

KORDA, M. *Power! How to Get It, How to Use It*. New York: Random House, 1975.

MOLLOY, J.T. *The Woman's Dress for Success Book*. New York: Random House, 1975.

NIERENBERG, G.I. and CALERO, H.H. *How to Read a Person Like a Book*. New York: Pocket Books, 1975.

TOFFLER, A. *The Eco-Spasm Report*. New York: Bantam Books, 1975.

CHAPTER 12

BIDERMAN, A. D. and ZIMMER, H. (Eds.) *The Manipulation of Human Behavior*. New York: Wiley, 1961.

BOK, S. *Lying*. New York: Pantheon, 1978.

BRESLIN, J. *How the Good Guys Finally Won*. New York: Viking Press, 1975.

CALIFANO, A. *A Presidential Nation*. New York: W. W. Norton, 1975.

FAST, J. *The Body Language of Sex, Power & Aggression*. New York: M. Evans & Co., 1977.

GALBRAITH, J. K. *The Age of Uncertainty*. Boston: Houghton Mifflin, 1977.

GOFFMAN, E. *The Presentation of Self in Everyday Life*. Garden City, New York: Doubleday Anchor, 1959.

GOLDMAN-EISLER, F. *Psycholinguistics: Experiments in Spontaneous Speech*. New York: Academic Press, 1968.

JONES, E.E. and NISBETT, R.E. *The Actor and the Observer: Divergent Perceptions of the Causes of Behavior*. Morristown, New Jersey: General Learning Press, 1971.

JONES, E.E. *Ingratiation*. New York: Appleton-Century-Crofts, 1964.

JONES, E.E. and WORTMAN, C. *Ingratiation: An Attributional Approach*. Morristown, New Jersey: General Learning Press, 1973.

KARRASS, C.L. *Give & Take*. New York: Thomas Y. Crowell, 1974.

KISSINGER, H.A. *White House Years*. Boston: Little, Brown, 1972.

MACCOBY, M. *The Games-Man*. New York: Simon & Schuster, 1976.

NIERENBERG, G.I. and CALERO, H.H. *Meta-talk*. New York: Trident Press, 1976.

———. *How to Read a Person Like a Book*. New York: Pocket Books, 1975.

REID, J.E. and INBAU, F.E. *Truth and Deception*. Baltimore, Maryland: Williams & Wilkins, 1966.

RICHARDSON, E.L. *The Creative Balance*. New York: Holt, Rinehart and Winston, 1976.

SOLOMON, S. *How to Really Know Yourself Through Your Handwriting*. New York: Taplinger Publishing Co., 1973.

SPERBER, P. *Negotiating in Day-to-Day Business*. New York: American Negotiating Institute, 1976.

———. *The Science of Business Negotiation*. New York: Pilot Books, 1979.

WEITZ, S. *Nonverbal Communication*. New York: Oxford University Press, 1974.